CW00552490

THE GOD OF THE GULAG
VOLUME TWO

THE GOD OF THE GULAG

VOLUME TWO

MARTYRS IN AN AGE OF SECULARISM

JONATHAN LUXMOORE

GRACEWING

First published in England in 2016
by
Gracewing
2 Southern Avenue
Leominster
Herefordshire HR6 0QF
United Kingdom
www.gracewing.co.uk

ISBN 978 085244 584 6

Typeset by Gracewing

Cover design by Bernardita Peña Hurtado

Soul of my Saviour sanctify my breast,
Body of Christ, be thou my saving guest,
Blood of my Saviour, bathe me in thy tide,
wash me with waters gushing from thy side.

Strength and protection may thy passion be,
O blessèd Jesus, hear and answer me;
deep in thy wounds, Lord, hide and shelter me,
so shall I never, never part from thee.

Guard and defend me from the foe malign,
in death's dread moments make me only thine;
call me and bid me come to thee on high
where I may praise thee with thy saints for ay.

[*Anima Christi*, attributed to Pope John XXII, 1244–1334]

CONTENTS

FOREWORD

BY THE END of the 1950s, more than four decades had passed since Lenin and his Bolshevik militants had first seized power in Russia. The aim of communism was still very much alive—to create an egalitarian society ruled by the working class under the direction of the Party avant-garde. Intimidation and coercion were still indispensable tools for pursuing that aim; and so were the arbitrary pressures deployed by the secret police with their agents and informers. But the open brutality and terror of the early years had given way to administrative forms of repression and control. They might still return; but for now at least, they were unnecessary.

The extension of communist power to post-War Eastern Europe had brought a new wave of arrests, trials and purges, as the Party identified its enemies and took steps to neutralise and eliminate them. Here too, however, the emphasis was on surveillance and harassment, rather than physical force and violence.

Lenin's state had functioned through mechanisms and structures which deflated and destroyed individual identity. Yet personal choice and responsibility had survived. In the Roman Empire, the ruling system had also required the suppression of those who resisted—in the Roman case, by refusing to sacrifice. Its despotic rulers had claimed proprietory rights over their subjects and slaughtered those who offended them. They had also eliminated opponents pre-emptively—just as King Herod had killed John the Baptist, according to Josephus, 'to forestall any revolutionary movement.' Yet local officials had made their own judgements and applied their own sanctions, depending on local conditions. For all the dreadful brutalities, the tide of persecution had ebbed and flowed, enabling St Paul, as a Roman citizen, to believe he could still use the Empire's institutions to spread the faith.

What had made communism distinctive was its state ideology, whose architects had sought to impose their own exclusive truth on society. The Roman state had claimed a religious sanction and fought the 'atheism' of Christians. By contrast, the communist state had espoused atheism and fought the religiousness of Christians. It saw the Christian faith as a rival ideology with its own contrasting view of the world and humanity, which upheld a sovereign realm of spiritual freedom beyond everyday reality, and which believed in the 'inner man' when programmed efforts were being made to eradicate him. Churches and religions were tools of capitalism, allies of the class enemy, instruments of a reactionary world order. Eliminating them was an essential step towards building an equal and just communist society.

In this way, the state had taken the initiative against its own citizens, persecuting them not for what they had done, but for what they were and what they might do. It had identified its enemies not as individuals, but as whole groups and classes; and it had condemned them *a priori*, giving them no chance to correct their faults. Christ's exhortation to his followers, 'Render unto Caesar the things that are Caesar's, and unto God the things that are God's' (Mt 22: 21), may have worked under Roman rule. But it was hardly possible under a system which expected the absolute, indivisible subservience of hearts and minds.

Whereas Rome had taken the offensive to defend existing society and repress those who challenged its values, communism had gone to war to destroy that society and root out those who upheld its values. It had punished traditional virtues and rewarded anti-virtues, and heaped praise on those who helped eliminate the old and elevate the new. Christian victims could lament with Isaiah: 'Woe to those who call evil good and good evil, who put darkness for light and light for darkness' (Is 5: 20). But they were victims of a revolution which had swept all before it. Like Susanna in the Book of Daniel, they were offered impossible choices: 'I am hemmed in on every side. For if I do this thing, it is death for me; and if I do not, I shall not escape your hands'

(Da 13: 2–23). Like Rome before it, Moscow had become the figurative Babylon. Its rulers had corrupted 'laws and statutes, morality and philosophy,' and 'planned to fortify earth against heaven.' Whereas the persecutions of Diocletian had been stopped by war, however, there had been no Constantine to overthrow Stalin.

Things were different now—at least to outward appearances. Yet hostility to the Church and contempt for the faith still remained fundamental to the communist programme. So did the dream of a 'new man' and new world order, nurtured first by the French Revolution and later taken up with enthusiasm by popular anti-clerical movements in the Nineteenth Century—in which all thoughts and actions became rational and objective, and were motivated by an unquestioning loyalty to the new society with its sacrosanct principles of liberty, equality and fraternity.

Against this background, the paradigms of persecution and testimony created in the Early Church were still very much in evidence. The motives and methods of the rulers remained, in the end, much the same. So did the dilemmas and choices facing their victims, whose forms of witness looked and sounded much as they had done in centuries past.

Yet the age of revolution was also giving way to an age of secularism, in which efforts would be made to impose scientific atheism and rid the world finally and forever of religious superstition and obscurantism. Any respite in this struggle would be temporary, any concessions and accommodations purely tactical. There would still be persecutors and oppressors—and there would still, inevitably, be martyrs.

1 A SEARCH FOR NEW BEGINNINGS

> *Now who is there to harm you if you are zealous for what is right? But even if you do suffer for righteousness' sake, you will be blessed. Have no fear of them nor be troubled, but in your hearts reverence Christ as Lord. Always be prepared to make a defence to anyone who calls you to account for the hope that is in you, yet do it with gentleness and reverence; and keep your conscience clear, so that, when you are abused, those who revile your good behaviour in Christ may be put to shame. For it is better to suffer for doing right, if that should be God's will, than for doing wrong.*
>
> 1 P 3:13–17

SOON AFTER HIS election, Pope John XXIII had announced plans for a major Church council, to which all Catholic bishops would be summoned to help discern the 'signs of the times.' In the Soviet Union, where Khrushchev's gestures of openness had not softened the anti-religious campaign, it was assumed the Council would strengthen the Catholic Church's anti-communist stance. Stalin's old church fixer, Georgy Karpov, had handed over in February 1960 to Vladimir Kuroedov, from the Party's Propaganda and Agitation Department. Whereas Karpov had favoured stable relations with the Catholic Church, to avoid fuelling hostility and anti-Soviet propaganda, Kuroedov and his Central Committee allies were confident a more combative line could still drive 'clerical reactionaries' into submission.[1]

The first Party analysis in 1959 concluded that, for all John XXIII's conciliatory signals, the planned Council would attack communist ideology, and establish a common front between the

Vatican and Orthodox Ecumenical Patriarchate of Constantinople against both the Soviet state and Russian Orthodox church. Patriarch Aleksi was against any Orthodox participation in 'a council led by Catholics.' Sending observers, he pointed out, would wrongly imply recognition of the Pope's primacy. But Kuroedov wanted the Moscow Patriarchate to be proactive against the Pope's 'reactionary initiative'. Meanwhile, the Patriarchate's new director of external relations, Bishop Nikodim Rotov, saw possible advantages for his church as well. It could gain prestige and contacts abroad by being more assertive, Nikodim argued. Certainly, the price would be even greater subservience to Moscow's directives. But this might in time prove manageable and yield greater benefits.[2]

Nikodim concluded that the Russian church should take part in the Council, not least to prevent the Ecumenical Patriarchate from dominating the Orthodox participation. 'Our absence will help our enemies strengthen, unite and organise behind our back into a united front against us,' he noted in a report. 'There is a need for the Vatican and the West as a whole to see our "goodwill" regarding rapprochement among all Christians.'[3] As time went on, Khrushchev began to concur. Change appeared to be underway in the Vatican, it was argued, as a struggle took place between the reactionary church hierarchies of Ireland, Spain and Latin America, and the more progressive, reforming bishops of France, Germany and Britain. This could be producing a more flexible attitude to communism.

Such deductions were encouraged by a visit to Moscow by Mgr Jan Willebrands, Dutch secretary of the Vatican's new Secretariat for Christian Unity, who went out of his way to stress the Pope's pastoral and ecumenical concerns 'from a shepherd's heart.' Anatolij Krassikov, a *TASS* correspondent, who would be personally introduced to the Pope when the Council started, recalled long debates in Moscow over the position of the Vatican, which had been labelled in the *Grand Soviet Encyclopaedia* just a few years earlier as 'an oppressor of free human thought, a messenger of obscurantism, a tool of Anglo-American imperialism and an active instigator of a new imperialist world war.' While Party hardliners pressed for a tougher stance, *Komsomolskaya Pravda* had excoriated the Vatican as a 'living corpse,' which would not be revived 'whatever vestments the corpse is dressed up in and whatever spells are recited over it.'[4] By the time the Council opened in October 1962, Moscow's position, outwardly at least, had changed.

There was another reason why it had changed, which had more to do with geopolitics than ideology. During the same month, the Soviet installation of nuclear missiles in Cuba had brought an ultimatum from the US Kennedy Administration. The world appeared to stand on the brink of war, and John XXIII appealed to both sides via their embassies in Rome. His text, published in *Pravda*, noted how a return to negotiations would 'stand as evidence before history.'[5] Two days later, Khrushchev agreed to pull the missiles out.

Interviewed by an American journalist that December, the Soviet leader insisted the Pope's face-saving appeal had been 'the only gleam of hope.' He now saw that the Church's aim was 'to serve all humanity,' not just Catholics; and he now wished to 'extend contacts.' He himself had come from a religious background, Khrushchev added; and he had never been against 'religion as such.' Soviet anti-religious repression had been the fault of the Orthodox church, whose priests 'weren't men of God, but the Tsar's gendarmes.' But he and the Pope were both would-be reformers of their respective worlds. A new-look Soviet Union was making common cause with a new-look Vatican. 'We have no more trouble with the Church,' Khrushchev insisted. 'We can even protect it if keeps out of politics.'

The Pope reciprocated, sending an envoy to Patriarch Aleksi's eightieth birthday celebrations a few months later. There were now 'unmistakeable signs of deep understanding,' John XXIII noted in his Christmas Message—'new prospects for fraternal trust and the first glimmers of a calm future.'[6]

Most East Europeans were unaware of the complexities of the Cuban Missile Crisis, and were informed only of Khrushchev's valiant role in averting war. Although the Soviet leader's overture to the Church caused surprise, other regimes followed suit and agreed to allow church representatives to participate in the Council, reasoning that their presence would counter the talk of persecution and elicit a positive reaction from progressive Catholics in Europe and Latin America. Yugoslavia sent 24 of its 27 bishops. Czechoslovakia gave passports to four, accompanied by minders from the pro-regime MHKD priests' association. Even Bulgaria, where the Pope had been the Vatican's apostolic visitor in 1925–34, allowed a bishop to attend.

The Polish government, in particular, made efforts to influence its church contingent. Several prelates were refused passports, including the much-harassed Bishop Kaczmarek and Archbishop Kominek, while a single Polish lay adviser, Stefan Świeżawski, was allowed to travel to Rome only in late 1964. Wyszyński instructed the refused bishops' auxiliaries to stay at home; so only 25 of Poland's 33 approved church leaders made it for the opening session. The regime later relented and allowed more bishops to go; but it made clear it would expect a 'constructive attitude' in return.[7]

The Soviet government, for its part, carefully choreographed its gestures for propaganda purposes. Five of Lithuania's approved priest-administrators were permitted to go as observers, accompanied by KGB agents, in what was seen as a bid to push the Vatican into approving them. But the exiled Bishops Steponavičius and Sladkevičius were, predictably, barred from leaving, as was another bishop, Petras Maželis of Telšiai. Even then, the regime was nervous. A month before the Council opened, the old and fragile Bishop Matulionis died after a rigorous search of his apartment by KGB agents.

There was speculation in the West about the precise tactics being played out, as well as scepticism about what the Pope was calling his *aggiornamento*, or opening up. Although the Russian Orthodox church sent two clergy observers, Vitaly Borovoi and

Vladimir Kotliarov, both were said to be secret Party officials, and their presence was bitterly contested by exiled Ukrainian Greek Catholics, whose only surviving leader, Metropolitan Slipyi, was still languishing in a Siberian camp. A protest was duly signed by exiled Ukrainian bishops, and a plea for Slipyi's release passed to the Moscow Patriarchate. In December 1962, having denied any knowledge of Slipyi's case, Khrushchev agreed to release him, on condition that 'no political case' was made of it. 'One more enemy in freedom doesn't scare me,' the Soviet boss reputedly retorted. But Slipyi's 'crimes against the Soviet people' were not being forgiven. This was not a pardon.[8]

Slipyi, not surprisingly, was reluctant to accept Khrushchev's 'act of goodwill,' and insisted he would only return if reinstated immediately in his Lviv archdiocese. In the end, the 71-year-old was persuaded to leave the country by Mgr Willebrands. He arrived in Rome, via Vienna, on 9 February 1963, having seen the last of his Lviv patrimony through the windows of a speeding train, limping into the Grottaferrata abbey because of frostbite on his right foot. Slipyi's hand had been broken by guards and he had expected to be shot on many occasions. His years of trial could be compared to the harsh personal odyssey described by St Paul (2 Co 11:23–28). Like Cardinal Mindszenty, who was just two weeks younger, he would become a potent symbol of resistance for the martyr Church.

Slipyi had been offered his freedom two years earlier when he was brought back from Siberia to Kiev to negotiate with the regime. But his precondition, lifting the ban on his Church, had been rejected. In two letters to Nikolai Podgorny, the Ukrainian Party First Secretary, he had again repudiated the 1946 Lviv Synod, insisting its decisions were taken uncanonically without Greek Catholic participation. Communist officials appeared incapable of seeing his Church in anything other than political categories, Slipyi pointed out. But no 'real communists' would recognise its forced merger with Orthodoxy as legally valid. Greek Catholics were growing stronger abroad and in the catacombs;

so they would not die out. It was ironic that an atheist state, which had persecuted the Orthodox church as a Tsarist bastion, had now taken sides with the same church in a struggle against them.[9]

In Rome, Slipyi was nevertheless asked by the Vatican to maintain a 'prudent silence' about conditions in the Soviet Union, so as not to 'transform the Slipyi affair into a political question.' Most of the documents on his denunciation and trial, including 30 volumes of prosecution protocols, were discreetly 'lost.' Although his departure was billed in the West as a major Soviet concession, Slipyi felt humiliated. 'What is this freedom to me, if my Church is still suffering?' the Ukrainian metropolitan had asked in his Mordovia labour camp. He had promised never to leave Ukraine 'unless under forced escort.' 'But the voice of Pope John XXIII summoned me to the Vatican Council,' Slipyi later recalled. 'His call was an order—in it I saw the incomprehensible intention of God's wisdom.'[10]

What were long-harassed Christians to make of these new developments? The freeing of Slipyi suggested a conflict was being played out between the twin priorities of diplomacy and testimony. These were complex issues. Testimony was always a duty for Christians, whatever the conditions and circumstances; and while diplomacy might occasionally rescue a church leader, it could not rescue whole church communities. The apparent tension did, however, set the scene for Khrushchev's next 'concession' a month later, when, on 7 March, the Soviet leader's son-in-law, Alexei Adzhubei, editor of the Soviet Communist Party's *Izvestiya* daily, arrived at the Vatican for a Papal audience with newspaper directors. When the audience ended, Adzhubei and his wife, Rada, were led to the Pope's library for a private meeting. They had come as Khrushchev's envoys, prompting fresh talk of 'new openings.' But the conciliatory episode provoked hostile comment. Vatican Radio ended its news bulletin with material on Soviet anti-religious persecutions, re-quoting a message from John XXIII after his election about the 'slavery of individuals and masses' under communism. 'Communist tactics have truly changed, changed so much as to succeed sometimes in lodging doubt,' the broadcast continued. 'Unfortunately, the reality is different than the propaganda. Communism remains what it was: atheistic and materialistic, both theoretically and in practice.'[11]

As the first ever by a communist official, Adzhubei's visit was widely considered to have overcome a psychological barrier. Although carefully choreographed, however, it achieved nothing of substance. The Pope himself was said to have deflected an attempt by Adzhubei to discuss diplomatic ties between Moscow and Rome. 'The Apostolic See is ready to establish relations with any state,' his chief of protocol later explained. 'But they have to be founded on a reliable guarantee by the other party to assure freedom for the Church.'[12]

To buttress the morale of anxious East Europeans, the Pope sent an apostolic letter, *Magnifici eventus,* to all Slavic bishops two months later, released in Slipyi's presence, praising the centuries-old loyalty of Greek Catholics.

There would be one more spectacular release during the Council—this time of the Czech Archbishop Beran, who was freed from exile at Radvanova 'as a beggar' in October 1963 with four other interned bishops. In February 1965, Beran packed some clothes and books in a bag and, accompanied by Casaroli, left for Rome, where he was made a cardinal the same month and lingered on for four more years before succumbing to cancer at the age of 80.

His freeing was hardly a major gesture. But John XXIII had already reciprocated with a new encyclical, conceived during the Cuban crisis, which appeared to lend philosophical and theological justification to a new attitude to communists. Peace of earth could never be guaranteed, the Pope acknowledged in *Pacem in Terris* (11 April 1963), without the 'diligent observance of the divinely established order.' The Church's teaching was 'perfectly consistent with any system of genuine democracy,' since it recognised that people had a right to choose their rulers. Political authority was 'never absolute.' It was a postulate of the moral order; and it derived from God. 'Consequently, laws and decrees passed in contravention of the moral order, and hence of the divine will, can have no binding force in conscience,' the Pope warned. 'Any government which refused to recognise human rights or acted in violation of them, would not only fail in its duty; its decrees would be wholly lacking in binding force.'[13]

The encyclical's championship of the right of resistance recalled principles set out centuries before by St Thomas Aquinas. But it broke new ground by condemning states which exercised 'an unjust oppression of other countries or an unwarranted interference in their affairs.' After his experiences the previous autumn, John XXIII had strong words about the East-West military confrontation, appealing for an end to the arms race and a ban on nuclear weapons. *Pacem in Terris* listed the human rights which all people were entitled to, including religious liberty—'which the martyrs in vast numbers consecrated by their blood.' It flirted with the idea of world government and praised the 1948 Universal Declaration of Human Rights as a 'step in the right direction.' But the time had also come, the encyclical said, for Catholics to co-operate in good causes with non-Christians who retained a 'natural moral integrity.' Even those who had 'fallen into error,' after all, still had the capacity to 'regain the path of truth.'

> We must make a clear distinction between false philosophical theories about the nature, origin and purpose of the universe and of man, and the practical measures that have been put into operation as a result of these theories, in social and economic life, in cultural matters and in the management of the state. For whereas theories, once formulated, remain unalterably fixed and frozen in the words that express them, the measures to which they give rise are constantly subject to alteration as circumstances change. Besides, who will deny that good and praiseworthy elements can be found in such measures in so far as they

> conform to the rules of right reason and reflect the lawful aspirations of men?[14]

The encyclical's distinctions—between theory and practice, 'the error and the person who is its victim'—were carefully nuanced. But the upbeat tone was a clear departure from the Vatican's 1949 declaration, condemning co-operation with communists. It also appeared to condone controversial moves such as the Church-state accords in Poland and Hungary. False doctrines should be left to fade away, the encyclical implied, rather than hardened by condemnations. Far from shunning a hostile world, Catholics were called to 'win admission to the institutions' and 'influence them effectively from within.'[15]

Pacem in Terris was well received by those who had sought a place for the Church in Eastern Europe. It was the first encyclical addressed not just to Catholics, but to 'all people of goodwill'; and it contradicted communist ideology's view of the Vatican as defender of an outmoded *status quo*. To Catholics longing for the Church to shake off its past associations, this was something of a dream come true. When the Pope died on 3 June, *Izvestiya* lauded him for taking up the challenge of 'establishing on earth a lasting and fruitful peace, which is of interest today to people of various religious, political and social convictions.'[16]

Would the Vatican now be less outspoken in its support for harassed Christians? Although John XXIII's conciliatory stance set the tone for the rest of Vatican II, their plight was not neglected. In November 1964, a new 'Dogmatic Constitution,' *Lumen Gentium*, predicted that Christians would still face persecution and be called to lay down their lives for their brethren, as St John's Gospel had declared. For the Church, martyrdom remained 'the highest gift and supreme test of love,' the constitution noted. 'And while it is given to few, all however must be prepared to confess Christ before men and to follow him along the way of the cross amidst the persecutions which the

Church never lacks.'[17] A message of solidarity was sent to all bishops who, for political reasons, had been unable to attend the Council. Three months later, Paul VI made the exiled Slipyi a cardinal and 'major archbishop,' as well as an adviser to the Vatican's Congregation for Eastern Churches.

Later that year, a Declaration on Religious Freedom called for the rights of faith to be 'recognised and respected by all,' and deplored the use of force 'to wipe out or repress religion.' There were forms of government, the declaration regretted, where, 'despite constitutional recognition of the freedom of religious worship,' the authorities 'strive to deter the citizens from professing their religion and make life particularly difficult and dangerous for religious bodies.' Finally, a new 'Pastoral Constitution,' *Gaudium et Spes*, warned of a new age of moral extremes, in which the world would be 'disposed to freedom and slavery, progress and decline, brotherhood and hatred.' People were repudiating political systems which hindered liberty, and which victimised citizens for the benefit of 'political parties or governing classes.' The Church, for its part, was fostering the rights of man worldwide, including the rights of conscience, which embodied 'man's most secret core, and his sanctuary.'[18]

Even then, many bishops wanted a clear condemnation of communism, and of the atheism associated with it. Others disagreed. The youthful Archbishop Alfred Bengsch of Berlin had been appointed a week after his city was divided by the wall in August 1961. His Church would be described by Casaroli as 'living in a kind of ghetto, able to breathe but not to be free.' If communism was condemned, the German nevertheless argued, the Church would also have to condemn 'every materialist ideology,' including those of the West. Bengsch was also against using 'media terms' such as 'free nations' and 'Church of Silence,' believing they would 'surely occasion new repression.' The Church had a right and duty to condemn atheistic communism, he conceded. But to do so heavy-handedly would give communists 'an easy and very welcome opportunity to prove to the inexperienced that the Church is engaging in political actions.'[19]

Such thinking was strongly contested. Bishop Pavol Hnilica, the Slovak Jesuit who had fled to Rome after being secretly consecrated, warned of communist ambitions to 'spread atheism to the entire world.' He was not motivated by hatred of communism, Hnilica insisted, only by 'concern for the persecuted.' The Jesuit had consulted the newly exiled Cardinal Beran, who broadly supported him. He was bitterly attacked in Czechoslovakia by the pro-regime Fr Plojhar. It was 'provocative and unjustified,' Plojhar told a broadcast meeting of the clergy peace movement, for *emigrés* like Hnilica to 'presume to speak in the name of the Czech and Slovak people they had betrayed,' and to help their country's enemies by conspiring against the conciliatory stance of John XXIII.[20]

Other Council participants warned against fashionable illusions about 'peaceful coexistence.' They included an exiled Chinese archbishop, Mgr Paul Yu Pin, who signed a statement with over 300 others demanding a more forceful attitude to communism. Yet the conciliatory lobby won the day. It was argued that communism had a 'multiplicity of meanings,' and comprised political and economic views not properly under discussion. Cardinal Koenig of Vienna believed Marxism's atheistic character had much to do with 'distorted expressions of religion.' The Croatian Cardinal Franjo Šeper believed the 'egoism of Christians' was largely to blame for communism and atheism by 'falsely invoking the name of God' to defend the established social order.[21]

Both cardinals sat alongside Hnilica on the committee which drafted *Gaudium et Spes*, the Council's last major document. This made no direct reference to communism or Marxism. Instead, it contained three sections on atheism, acknowledging that it often derived from 'a violent protest against the evil of the world' and reflected a 'critical reaction against the Christian religion.' 'Believers can thus have more than a little to do with the rise of atheism,' the Pastoral Constitution added. 'To the extent that they are careless about their instruction in the faith, or present its teaching falsely, or even fail in their religious, moral or social life, they must be said to conceal rather than reveal the true nature of God and religion.'

As a concession to objectors like Bishop Hnilica, a footnote was added listing previous Papal statements on communism, including Pius XI's *Divini Redemptoris* of 1937 and John XXIII's *Mater et Magistra*. But it avoided mention of the Vatican's 1949 declaration condemning co-operation.[22]

For all the conciliatory gestures, Hnilica and his supporters could point out, there had been no significant improvement in the conditions facing Christians under communist rule. In some respects at least, they could be said to have worsened. In October 1964, the Soviet Communist Party had finally ousted Khrushchev, complaining of his immodest, erratic style, and appointed Leonid Brezhnev as First Secretary in his place. There were hopes of change; but just a month later, a Soviet Communist Party resolution demanded an intensification of 'atheist upbringing.' By 1980, the document vowed, human consciousness would be 'finally liberated from religious superstitions.'

A Soviet report, put together with material from church informers and KGB agents in Rome, noted that there had been 'no united view' at Vatican II on key international issues. Instead, differences had intensified, strengthening the 'progressive tendency' which favoured peaceful coexistence after the 'malicious attacks on communism' under Pius XII. This had been a disappointment to 'aggressive, imperialistic circles,' who had counted on 'an all-out crusade against communism.' Although Greek Catholics had highlighted persecution, their efforts had been contested, as the Church strove 'to adapt to contemporary conditions and find new ways of preserving and strengthening itself.'[23]

The Vatican Council had brought signs of a thaw in inter-church relations. The Orthodox Ecumenical Patriarch, Athenagoras I, had been barred from attending the Council by fellow-bishops from Greece. But Pope Paul VI had sent him a hand-written letter in 1963, the first direct communication since the Sixteenth Century; and in January 1964, the two finally met on Jerusalem's Mount of Olives. The following November, the Vatican Council issued a Decree on Ecumenism, calling for reconciliation with the Eastern Churches and acknowledging the rich heritage of those who had born witness 'even to the shedding of their blood.' There would be no more pejorative talk of 'schismatics.'

The conciliatory tone was reaffirmed in December 1965, when Pope and Patriarch agreed to 'erase from memory' the mutual excommunications imposed at the 1054 Great Schism. Their declaration, regretting 'the offensive words, the reproaches without foundation and the reprehensible gestures' of the past was followed up with separate instructions on the recognition of baptisms, mixed Catholic-Orthodox marriages and ecumenical co-operation. In 1967, the two again met in Rome.[24]

The Moscow Patriarchate's own contacts with the Vatican had been observed closely in Eastern Europe. They were, indeed, something new; and Catholics were unsure about the implications. Archpriest Borovoi, one of the two Russian observers, had studied in Warsaw in the 1930s and spoke Polish well. Although he met Wyszyński only briefly, it was enough for the Polish cardinal to be impressed by Borovoi's view that all Christians were part of God's plan, and to conclude that that he was far from being the Party apparatchik or 'false priest' some had supposed. There were doubts, however, as to how representative Borovoi could be of Orthodox Christians, when his own participation had needed such careful arranging with the Soviet rulers. The Russian church's subservience to the regime had provoked a conservative, traditionalist reaction in some parts of the Orthodox world, while many young people had defected to the Baptists, Adventists and other groups who promised a more intense, non-conformist spirituality.

Vatican II had been much debated at the KIK, or Catholic Intelligentsia Club, in Warsaw, founded as one of Gomułka's concessions in the late 1950s. *Gaudium et Spes* was believed to signal a major shift in the Church's position, distancing it from the reactionary forces of the past and confirming the much-admired Personalist vision. As such, it opened the way to a broader dialogue with non-Catholics, including Marxists. Religiousness, it was argued, could no longer be identified as something internal and subjective without wider consequences. Nor could it be 'linked unavoidably and fatalistically with a socially passive and politically conservative stance.' The Council had summoned Christians to be active in defence of ethical values. This would have consequences for the communist system.[25]

The repentant Marxist, Leszek Kołakowski, had discussed Vatican II at length during his discreet meeting with Cardinal Wyszyński in 1963. He believed it amounted to a 'new Counter-Reformation,' aligning the Church for the first time with social justice. Yet there were voices of discord. Some Catholics distrusted talk of 'opening the Church to the modern world' and were suspicious that the Council had failed to tackle communism. Words such as ecumenism and collegiality had different associations under communist rule. Many believed the Council's diagnosis of current challenges had been determined by a Western outlook. John XXIII's celebrated peace encyclical, *Pacem in Terris*, had deplored colonialism in the Third World but said nothing about colonialism in the heart of Europe. It had rejoiced that 'soon no nation will rule over another, and none be subject to an alien power,' and that class rivalry was 'rapidly becoming a thing of the past'; but it had made no mention of Eastern Europe, where Soviet dominance and class hatred were institutionalised.[26]

Poland's Catholic bishops took exception to media talk of 'progressives' and 'reactionaries' in the Church. Wyszyński had been angered by a document titled 'Opinion of Catholic Circles in Poland,' apparently drafted by liberal Catholics at *Tygodnik Powszechny* and the KIKs, which had been sent to the Vatican's

Secretariat of State and read over the US-funded Radio Free Europe. This criticised Gomułka's failure to honour the promises of 1956. But it also criticised Wyszyński's combative view of Poland as a 'Christian bulwark' and called for a Church-state agreement. The cardinal was outraged that it had been circulated behind his back and ended up in the hands of the regime. It claimed to be motivated by concern for the Church; but it was 'really an attack on the Primate'—written in poor Italian and full of 'hazy, exaggerated, mendacious argumentation.' Wyszyński claimed to have 'easily recognised' the document's authors. But the KIKs denied involvement, and the blame eventually settled on Stanisław Stomma, the Znak deputy, further exacerbating Wyszyński's doubts about the group's attitude and position.[27]

There were other worries about Vatican II. Some Catholics objected to the conciliatory, self-critical treatment of atheism in *Gaudium et Spes*. A decree on Catholic Eastern Churches had recalled the 'special duty' of Greek Catholics to foster Christian unity with non-Catholic churches, but made no mention of their persecution. A decree on bishops had called for an 'active fraternal interest' towards those in difficulty, but offered no guidance to bishops forced out of their sees and languishing in prison. A decree on religious life, *Perfectae caritatis*, had made no mention of monks and nuns driven from their orders and forced to live in secrecy.[28]

The misgivings intensified in March 1967, when Paul VI released a new encyclical, *Populorum Progressio*, calling for a 'new humanism.' Christians would not accept any system based on 'atheist or materialist philosophy,' the Pope warned. They also knew revolutionary uprisings, other than in response to 'manifest, long-standing tyranny,' merely brought new disasters. But the growing imbalance between rich and poor nations was fuelling inequalities and unrest. Political freedom was not enough—proper social and economic structures were needed too. The Pope claimed to have drawn on his observations during Third World visits before his election. Against a background of Soviet expansion and Western left-wing agitation, however, *Populorum Progressio* sounded inflammatory. The *New York Times* branded the encyclical 'strongly leftist, even Marxist in tone.'[29]

Sure enough, Paul VI's appeals attracted communist interest. A Politburo member of the French Communist Party, Roger Garaudy, had written a book in response to John XXIII's *Pacem in Terris,* agreeing that the 'general forward trend' was inducing Christians 'to discuss and plan for the future with Marxists.' The Catholic Church was giving up its role as part of the 'mere ideological superstructure' of capitalist society, Garaudy argued, and opting for a 'productive and militant eschatology.' The book made no mention of Soviet repression and insisted Christians were subject to 'bureaucratic vexation,' rather than persecution. Like the church in pre-revolutionary France, Garaudy noted, the Russian church had been linked to a feudal regime of 'exploitation and oppression.' But the mistreatment of believers contradicted Soviet principles and was 'frequently denounced and censured by higher authority.' Through dialogue with Christians, Marxists could 'rediscover beneath the myths the aspirations which brought them forth,' while Christians could transform their faith into a vehicle for social and political commitment. The book was endorsed with an introduction by the revered German Jesuit, Fr Karl Rahner, and with an epilogue by another theologian, Fr Johan Metz.[30]

In Italy, the Communist Party leader, Palmiro Togliatti, had also responded positively to *Pacem in Terris.* Communism was still certain of victory, Togliatti insisted. There could, in the end, by no philosophical rapprochement with Christians; but there could a 'reciprocal understanding and search for common goals.' There had been dialogue between Marxists and Catholics in Italy's wartime resistance, while the idea of an 'outstretched hand' had surfaced in the 1950s. The encyclical's apparent distinction between practical political experience and spiritual and metaphysical enquiry was something of a tradition in Italian philosophy, associated with the work of the liberal idealist, Benedetto Croce (1866–1952). Since most industrial workers were also

Catholics, this was understandable. Even then, both the Vatican's *L'Osservatore Romano* and the Jesuit *La Civiltà Cattolica* warned Catholics to be 'vigilant' towards Togliatti's overtures.[31]

Even if dialogue were possible, there would be problems finding genuine partners who enjoyed acceptance by the Church and the Party. Two Jesuit theologians, Edward Huber and Gustav Wetter, had studied Soviet philosophy and visited Moscow; and in 1965–7, a large group of mostly German-speaking philosophers and theologians held a series of meetings under the auspices of the Munich-based St Paul's Society (*Paulusgesellschaft*) to explore how Christians and Marxists could come closer. But the participants were not typical, and the best interlocutors from Eastern Europe were barred from attending.[32]

In Eastern Europe itself, a Berlin Conference of European Christians, founded in 1964, was bringing 'progressive Catholics' together for occasional debates in East Germany. A Prague-based Christian Peace Conference, convened in 1958 by the Czech Josef Hromádka, was also attracting prominent left-wing Christians such as the German Lutherans, Martin Niemöller and Helmut Gollwitzer, with a pledge to promote the Christian vision alongside socialist values. The Czechoslovak regime had followed Vatican II carefully and endorsed the calls for co-operation. But it was also concerned the Council would make the Church 'more attractive' and 'better prepared for activities in society.'[33]

On the diplomatic front, the Vatican's September 1964 agreement with Hungary had set something of a precedent. For all the conciliatory talk, there had been expectations that Rome's line could harden under Paul VI, as Catholic *emigrés* highlighted the continuing persecution. But Casaroli's forays into Eastern Europe suggested it was possible to look beyond the distrust and hostility even to future talks with Moscow itself. By the time Vatican II ended, US troops were massing in Vietnam to resist communist expansionism, and the Pope was warning of a 'new and terrible war.' But Paul VI had supported the Council's decision not to condemn communism directly. His first encyclical had acknowledged the realities of Eastern Europe—'an oppressed and degraded society, deprived by its rulers of every spiritual right.' Given the 'absence of sufficient freedom of thought and action' and 'the calculated misuse of words in debate,' dialogue was 'very difficult, not to say impossible.' In many cases, it would be nothing more than 'a voice crying in the wilderness,' and the Church's only possible witness would be one of 'silence, suffering, patience and unfailing love.' But 'for the lover of truth,' the Pope insisted, 'discussion is always possible.' Some communists were 'men of great breadth of mind,' who sincerely believed they were 'serving a demanding and noble cause.' They used concepts from the Gospel—'brotherhood of man, mutual aid, human compassion'—which suggested their impulses were similar to those of Christians and might even 'bring them back to God.'[34]

On the ground, the suffering nevertheless continued. Visiting the Roman Catacombs in September 1965, two months before Vatican II ended, Paul VI recalled that part of the Church was still 'staying alive with difficulty.' If the Vatican avoided 'raising its voice too often and vehemently in justified protest and pain,' this was 'not because of a lack of knowledge or underestimation of the true face of things, but out of regard for Christian patience and so as not to provoke even greater evil.'[35]

Casaroli, for his part, was clearly aware of these complex contradictions. For all the diplomatic hopes, he conceded, communism had a 'clear and undiscussible strategic plan' against the Church and faith—and no tactical understandings would change this. It was also strongly entrenched; and it appeared to have time on its side.

> The very fact that the Vatican recognised the communist regimes as interlocutors and sought contacts with them confirmed not only their strength and stability, but also their trustworthiness. In such discussions, these regimes would seek to use all possible means to obtain benefits at

> the Church's expense, offering it little or nothing, making commitments and giving assurances which they would then not keep. The only criterion of morality for them was usefulness for the cause... So talks would signify the abandonment, if not the repudiation, of that part of the persecuted Church which had remained the most faithful, to the point of heroism. Bishops, priests, monks, nuns, laity, generously engaged in the struggle with communist violence, could form the impression they were now viewed as a barrier in the search for an understanding, unlike their more compliant and amicable brethren and fellow-believers... Was it not better, therefore, to hold the banner high, fight on for the rights of the Church and religious freedom, continue resisting without concessions or deals made in illusory hope, in scraps without dignity. If the Church was to disappear as an institution in some country, deprived of its bishops, clergy and temples, was it not better to die on its feet, placing trust in the One who raises the dead?[36]

That had long been the view of leaders like the Hungarian Cardinal Mindszenty. But Casaroli was sure, even so, that the contacts were worthwhile. In June 1966, six months after the end of Vatican II, Tito's Yugoslavia became the second communist state to sign an understanding. As with Hungary, local bishops were not involved in the two years of formal talks, and Casaroli was said to have countermanded Archbishop Šeper of Zagreb when he raised objections. Official photographs now showed the Vatican official drinking champagne with his communist hosts.

In Poland, the latest deal was criticised by Bishop Choromański as bringing few if any benefits. How could the Church's future in countries like Yugoslavia be decided by a Vatican diplomat? There must full participation by local church leaders and clear conditions, notably an end to repression. But Casaroli defended his thinking in talks with Wyszyński. Although 'great difficulties' remained in Hungary and Czechoslovakia, Yugoslavia's bishops had reported an 'easing of tension.' The situation was different in each country, so the solutions had to be different too.[37]

Gomułka's regime had kept a close eye on Rome's negotiations with other communist governments, as well as on reactions to Slipyi's release, Adzhubei's Vatican visit and Casaroli's missions. A Central Committee member, Zenon Kliszko, had been sent to Rome in 1963, officially to attend the Italian Communist Party congress, but also to spread a favourable account of his regime's religious policy. Kliszko had attacked the Polish Church's 'reactionary stance' in a lecture at the Gramsci Institute, provoking a riposte from *L'Osservatore Romano*. But the Vatican's agreements with Hungary and Yugoslavia had highlighted the case for a similar accord with Poland, the Gomułka regime argued. It would calm Catholic opinion inside the country and counter claims of persecution—something which worried Western communist parties. It would also help undermine Wyszyński and neutralise German influences on the Vatican's thinking, especially over Poland's Western Territories. Certainly, the Vatican would demand more for the Church in Poland than it had in Hungary and Yugoslavia, where the Catholic clergy's 'damaging political activities' had long since been reined in. This could compromise state sovereignty and cause 'disorientation' among Party activists. Yet the benefits of diplomatic contacts were usually 'more favourable for governments,' the regime concluded. They also allowed the Church 'to be crammed more effectively into a specified framework.'[38]

It was possible that Moscow was thinking in the same direction. The Pope met the Soviet Foreign Minister, Andrei Gromyko, at the United Nations in the autumn of 1965, and again in April 1966 when Gromyko stopped off at the Vatican. The two encounters were a prelude to something more significant on 30 January 1967, when Nikolai Podgorny, now chairman of the Supreme Soviet assembly, became the first communist head of state to be given a private Papal audience. Little information was given about their discussion. But Casaroli was sufficiently encouraged to follow it up with a note to the Soviet Embassy in Rome, proposing the nomination of a Vatican representative to the Soviet Union in return for the appointment of bishops for Ukraine and Belarus.

Kuroedov, the Council for Religious Affairs chairman, rejected the 'Vatican pretensions,' insisting Catholic needs were already 'served in full.' As Vatican II had demonstrated, Rome was being 'forced to reform itself under pressure from the mass of believers.' But it was still 'the enemy of communism,' Kuroedov persisted. With the apparent failure of Khrushchev's latest anti-church campaign, however, it was becoming ever clearer that religion could not be eradicated. Was it not better, some Soviet officials now asked, to allow the Church some institutional protection as a price for loyalty?[39]

In January 1965, a Soviet Party resolution had condemned 'violations of socialist principles directed against believers' and allowed some priests to return home after having their prison and camp sentences reviewed. No objection had been raised the previous November when the apostolic administrator of Latvia's Riga archdiocese, Fr Julijans Vaivods, was appointed a full bishop. Vaivods was subservient; but he also wielded personal authority in his Church, something that could not be said of Fr Juozapas Stankevičius, administrator of the Kaunas archdiocese in neighbouring Lithuania. Rome had refused to make Stankevičius a bishop. So the Soviet regime settled instead, when he retired, for Fr Juozas Matulaitis-Labukas, who was consecrated in December 1965. It was a convenient choice. Matulaitis-Labukas, a prison veteran, was believed to have agreed to collaborate with the KGB.

Moscow dropped hints via its embassy that other concessions could be expected if the Vatican closed down Lithuania's embassy-in-exile and restricted Vatican Radio's contacts with anti-Soviet groups. Yet these were just scraps from the Soviet table. Although the Vatican's charm offensive had its supporters, it also highlighted the contrast between diplomatic niceties and hard realities. Khrushchev's deposition in 1964 appeared to have put talk of 'new openings' in doubt, while Vatican II had highlighted the isolation of the Soviet Union's far-flung Catholic communities, many of which still relied, as in the Middle Ages, on hand-written prayer-books and conducted their religious activities in total secret. The communist regimes hoped to keep local churches as backward as possible. They were reluctant to publish the Vatican II documents, fearing they might help modernise religious life.

Meanwhile, the repression continued under the new Soviet boss, Brezhnev. There were fewer clergy arrests now in Lithuania and other republics, while anti-religious measures were becoming more administrative than physical. But restrictions were soon tightened under a new Penal Code in 1966; and that February, the tentative thaw came to an abrupt end when two dissident writers, Andrei Sinyavsky and Yuri Daniel, were given labour camp sentences after a public trial for anti-Soviet activity.

Something had nevertheless changed in the atmosphere. Sinyavsky, the son of a much-jailed socialist revolutionary from the early Soviet years, had become known abroad for his satirical short stories. He was also a friend and pupil of the much-persecuted Boris Pasternak, who had been forced to refuse the Nobel Prize for his epic *Doctor Zhivago*. Pasternak's village funeral in May 1960, after a secret Orthodox liturgy, or *panikhida*, had attracted thousands of admirers from nearby Moscow, suggesting a new self-confidence among Russia's small community of dissenting intellectuals. When Sinyavsky was arrested in December 1965, his supporters held a symbolic demonstration in Pushkin Square, during which, instead of denouncing the regime's illegality, they adopted a new tactic of demanding respect for the Soviet Union's constitution and international commitments. The new dissidents were open about their actions and became well-known, at least in Moscow. They also attracted international media coverage, forcing the KGB to show restraint.

One of the new breed was Aleksander Solzhenitsyn, whose *One Day in the Life of Ivan Denisovich* had been approved for publication in 1962 by Khrushchev himself and even studied for a time in Soviet schools. Solzhenitsyn had fallen foul of the Party and been expelled from the Soviet Writers Union after a scathing 1966 letter against censorship. His works were confiscated, including his allegorical *The First Circle,* which carried echoes of Dante's *Divine Comedy* and Milton's *Paradise Lost* in its depiction of sinners punished in the Siberian cold. Although his manuscripts were later returned, Solzhenitsyn was now barred from publishing them.

There were rumblings of discontent in other republics. In Ukraine, where it had taken till the end of the 1950s to eliminate the last anti-Soviet guerrilla fighters, a well-known literary critic, Ivan Dzyubat, had demanded equal rights for all nations and peoples during a September 1966 visit with other intellectuals to the wartime pogrom site of Babi-Yar, near Kiev. 'We must judge each society not by its superficial technical achievements,' Dzyubat had declared, 'but by what the individual means to it, how it values human dignity and human conscience.' Religious dissent was still strong in Ukraine, and Catholic communities were less easily intimidated. One local official complained of how 'parish activists' in Vinnitsya had taken to bombarding his office with 'streams of appeals, letters, complaints and requests for a permanent priest.'[40]

Religious dissidents were showing greater boldness in Russia too. In 1965, much-harassed Baptist communities set up their own independent council of churches. That December, two Orthodox priests, Fr Gleb Yakunin and Fr Nikolai Eshliman, deplored the tragic state of their church in a letter to Patriarch Aleksi I and Podgorny. The letter was copied to Russia's bishops; and one of them, Archbishop Yermogen of Kaluga-Borovsk, outraged the authorities by declaring support for it. Yermogen had already been removed from a diocese in Uzbekistan for defying Soviet restrictions, and had been accused of 'slanderous fabrications on the alleged lack of rights of the church and believers.' He was now dismissed again and banished to a monastery. But the incident proved that not all Orthodox hierarchs were subservient.[41]

The Council for Russian Orthodox Church Affairs calculated that, out of a total Moscow population of six million, only 180,000 attended Christmas services. But there were complaints about religious influences among Soviet Party and state officials. In one report, the KGB produced a list of academics and teachers who sang in church choirs and visited monasteries.[42]

Soviet officials were particularly wary of high-profile personalities who might show religious sympathies. The cosmonaut, Yuri Gagarin, had been proclaimed a hero in April 1961 for becoming the first human being in space aboard his Vostok 3KA-2 spacecraft. Gagarin was said to have showcased his atheism while exiting the earth's orbit, proclaiming 'I don't see any god up here.' The remark did not appear, however, in verbatim transcripts of his flight; and it was later shown to have been made, not by the cosmonaut, but by Khrushchev during a Party plenum on anti-religious propaganda. In reality, Gagarin was a baptised Christian, as a friend discovered while visiting Moscow's St Sergius Laura monastery and Church Archaeology Museum with the cosmonaut on his thirtieth birthday in 1964. The Museum included a model of the Christ the Saviour basilica, blown up by Stalin in 1936. 'Yuri peered inside it and said to me, "Valentin, look what a lovely thing they've destroyed!" He kept looking at it for a long time,' recalled Colonel Valentin Petrov, an Air Force Academy professor. 'Some time after our trip, speaking at a Central Committee plenary session on youth education, Gagarin openly suggested the Christ the Saviour church should be rebuilt as a monument of military glory and outstanding Orthodox work.'

The cosmonaut, who received at least one petition from Christians as his sympathy for the faith became known, returned to the Soviet space programme after a brief spell as a Supreme Soviet deputy, but was killed when his MIG-15 crashed near Kirzhach in March 1968. Petrov himself was accused of 'drawing Gagarin into religion' after their 1964 church visit. He nevertheless continued to take Air Force training crews regularly to the St Sergius and St Daniel monasteries.[43]

Did such tentative, ephemeral acts of resistance have some wider significance? There had been signs of defiance in the rest of Eastern Europe. In Czechoslovakia, none of the bishops freed with Archbishop Beran in 1963 had been allowed to resume their episcopal functions. The Slovak Bishop Vojtaššák, crippled by his 24-year prison sentence, survived until August 1965, dismissing ironically regime claims that he had now become a free citizen. When he died in hospital, aged 87, the StB restricted access to his funeral. But 110 priests and 3500 lay Catholics made it to Vojtaššák's home-village of Zákamenné near the Polish border.

In May 1964, the Greek Catholic Bishop Hopko was also released on three years' probation after Vatican intervention. Orthodox control over Greek Catholic parishes and properties was being 'further consolidated' in Slovakia, according to the regime. Yet references continued to 'illegal practices by a religious sect.' In April 1965, the head of the State Secretariat for Religious Affairs, Karel Hrůza, visited Moscow to discuss the lingering Greek Catholic problem.

Hopko had described his prison experiences alongside the wheelchair-bound Bishop Gojdič in Leopoldov as a 'higher education in humility.' He had shared cells with 'criminals, spies and insane people,' and been reduced to 'a shadow of a man' by the time he was freed after treatment for depression. The bishop was sent to a former Cistercian monastery of Osek in Bohemia, where he lived alongside 160 elderly nuns. He was allowed to visit his sister in the US and celebrate the twentieth anniversary of his consecration; and he was relieved he could now 'lead a truly spiritual life.' But Hopko was shocked when he visited his home-village:

> There is only an Orthodox priest there and the people are forced to attend the Orthodox church, even my own

> relatives. They explained to me that they wanted to pray and hear God's word. In case some of the villagers attended services in the Roman Catholic church three villages away, the Orthodox broke all their windows... I told my cousins they should always remember they are Catholics and they attend the Orthodox church only out of necessity. In case of a death in the family, they should tell the Orthodox priest the dying person is a Catholic and that they called him only because there was no Catholic priest in the village.[44]

By early 1965, when Beran left for Rome, 36 Roman or Latin Catholic priests and 29 religious were still behind bars in Slovakia, of whom a dozen were now in their second prison decade and 27 judged too 'strongly hostile' to be released. Many Catholics were shocked when, that February, Bishop František Tomášek was named to succeed Beran as administrator of the Prague archdiocese. Tomášek had spent three years in the Zeliv labour camp after being secretly consecrated by Archbishop Matocha in October 1949 in the Vatican's Prague nunciature. He was widely believed to have been recruited as a collaborator by the secret police.

The StB continued to seize religious books from abroad, many sent via Poland, while Catholic clergy remained vulnerable to violence. The Franciscan rector of Bratislava's St Jura parish, Fr Emanuel Cubínek, reported receiving death threats; and in December 1965, just after Christmas, he was killed at home, clad in his habit, with a single revolver shot. Over 200 priests joined Trnava's apostolic administrator, Bishop Ambróz Lazík, for the Franciscan's funeral; but his killer, widely thought to be a professional hit-man, was never identified.

Fr Antonín Zbarbík, vice-provincial of the Czech Jesuits, died of pneumonia in prison after being misdiagnosed and treated too late for influenza. Meanwhile, the StB took action repeatedly to 'destroy the authority' of Bishop Pobožny of Rožňava, the only diocesan still at large in Slovakia, monitoring his talks with Mgr Casaroli when the Vatican trouble-shooter visited in June 1967, and noting with amusement how he had played a transistor radio to muffle the conversation from its listening devices.[45]

There had been much interest among church leaders and communist officials everywhere in Hungary's September 1964 agreement with the Vatican. In practice, however, the accord had made little difference. Four of Hungary's five Catholic bishops were 'Patriot Priests' and rumoured communist agents, while the Bishops Conference president, Archbishop Béla Hamvas, had defended the communist programme at Vatican II as 'worthy of recognition by Christians.' As the Council ended, the Hungarian Embassy had even laid on a reception for the bishops at Rome's Academia Ungarica, where a Polish observer described Hamvas as 'exhausted and internally broken.' Cardinal Wyszyński had pointedly turned down a similar Rome reception when it was offered by the Polish regime.[46]

In neighbouring Romania, the veteran communist First Secretary, Gheorghe Gheorghiu-Dej, died suddenly in March 1965, prompting rumours that he had been dosed with cancer-causing radiation while visiting Moscow. A surprise successor, Nicolai Ceauşescu, was elected by the Central Committee and set about consolidating his power. In July, the Romanian Workers Party was renamed Romanian Communist Party, adopting a five-year economic plan to continue the Stalinist era's heavy industrial production; and in August, 'freedom of conscience' was guaranteed by a new constitution.

Yet Christians from various denominations were still dying in Romania. The veteran Lutheran pastor, Richard Wurmbrand, was freed from a fresh 25-year sentence under a 1964 amnesty and allowed to emigrate after being ransomed for $ 10,000 by Christian friends in Norway. Wurmbrand described to a US Senate subcommittee how he had watched a young Christian being beaten and taunted while tied to a cross at the experimental Piteşti prison, and a 'half-mad' Catholic priest being forced to say Mass with human excrement. On the Danube Canal, where Wurmbrand's wife had been a forced labourer, an Orthodox clergyman had defiantly told his guards he had been ordained knowing that thousands of Christians had been killed for their faith, and was now more certain than ever that 'prison is no argument against religion.' 'I have been in prison among the weak ones and the little ones,' Wurmbrand told his influential audience. 'But I speak for a suffering country and suffering church, and for the heroes and saints of the Twentieth Century. We have had such saints in our prisons to whom I did not dare to lift my eyes.'[47]

Ceauşescu's regime had allowed Catholic bishops to attend the Vatican Council's final session. In November 1967, Austria's Cardinal Koenig visited Romania, in the first high-level direct contact with the new regime, agreeing as a precondition that he would have no dealings with Greek Catholics. A Latin letter from the Pope to Bishop Hossu, published on the front page of the Vatican's *L'Osservatore Romano*, nevertheless urged Catholics to remember St Paul's exhortation: 'We rejoice in our sufferings, knowing that suffering produces endurance, and endurance produces character, and character produces hope' (Rm 5:3–4). In October 1968, Ceauşescu's premier, Ion Gheorghe Maurer, visited the Vatican with his Foreign Minister, and an adviser to Casaroli's department, Bishop Giovanni Cheli, paid a return visit to Romania. Cheli was allowed to travel around the country, meeting government officials, but was told Greek Catholics were off-limits. The same applied when he returned in 1969 and 1970. The head of a German-based Catholic charity, Kirche in Not, Fr Werenfried van Straaten, was given short shrift by the Department of Cults when he proposed sending humanitarian aid to Greek Catholic clergy.[48]

The Catholic position still seemed close to hopeless in Romania. Church life was still governed by the 1948 Law on Cults, which prohibited submission to a foreign ecclesiastical power—a restriction which also applied to the small Gregorian-rite Armenian church, which had its headquarters in Echmiadzin. Whereas the Orthodox church had been given its own statute back in 1949, and was viewed by the communist regime as a useful tool of national identity, the Catholic Church was still denied such recognition.

Romanian Catholics could be thankful, even so, that they were not living in Albania, where Enver Hoxha had been inspired by violent events in China to proclaim his own cultural revolution. In a speech to the Central Committee on 6 February 1967, the Party leader declared that Albania had become the world's first state 'fully cleansed of religion.' A nationwide campaign was duly launched by Hoxha's youthful Red Guards, with police backing, to close all remaining places of worship and make prayers and services illegal in compliance with the 'will of the people.' 'The youth and other masses of the people in villages and cities rose to their feet, demanding that the churches and mosques, temples and monasteries, all the "holy places" be closed down,' the Albanian Party decreed, 'and that the clergy give up their parasitic life and become working people living like everyone else by their own work and sweat.'[49]

As with previous waves of anti-religious savagery, drastic measures were taken against clergy who resisted. A 32-year-old, Fr Mikel Beltoja, ordained five years before at Shkodra cathedral, continued ministering secretly after his church at Dajç was closed, despite warnings from his family that he could be killed. Beltoja was the youngest of several brothers. He was eventually chained to the door of his church, now a culture centre, where locals were made to spit on him in scenes reminiscent of the officially incited anti-Christian frenzy described by Eusebius in the Early Church. The priest was then given a seven-year jail term; but this was replaced by the death sentence when he spoke out in court against the regime.

Another young priest, Fr Marin Shkurti, ordained at the same time, also continued his ministry in villages around his Stajkë parish. On a stormy night in early 1968, judging the atmosphere too dangerous, Shkurti fled with family members by boat to neighbouring Montenegro. They reported to the Yugoslav police, who detained them and then sent them back to Albania, where

Shkurti was taken to Shkodra and shot as an example in April 1969. The man who had ordained them, Archbishop Ernest Çoba, secretly consecrated in 1952, was dragged by Red Guards into Shkodra's main square, where he was beaten and left for dead after refusing to renounce his faith. Cared for by his sister, Çoba found work as a gardener, but was later murdered by his guards for celebrating an Easter Mass in prison.

Shkodra's Franciscan church and friary were set alight in spring 1967 and four surviving monks killed, while the city's cathedral had its historic facade removed and was turned into a museum. Other priests were publicly beaten and told to beg forgiveness for 'misleading the people,' while younger clergy were forced to take jobs in factories or on collective farms. In November 1967, the official *Nëntori* daily proclaimed that all 2169 of Albania's mosques and churches had now been destroyed or converted into cinemas, dance halls or housing blocks. They included 372 Catholic places of worship. Professing any religion had become a serious offence, much as Christianity had become under the reign of Diocletian. Citizens were duly notified by pamphlets that they were now living in a 'fully atheist state.'

A People's Assembly decree the same month annulled all previous regulations, including a 1949 decree providing state subsidies for Albania's three principal faiths in compensation for the seizure of their properties. Although all religious activities were now outlawed, Hoxha recognised that his Party still faced a challenge. The aim, he told the Central Committee, was to raise a new generation imbued with scientific knowledge in place of 'old concepts such as religion.' But it was a mistake to suppose religion merely consisted of churches and mosques, priests and imams. It was a lot more complex and deeply rooted. Hoxha was to remain obsessed with the need to eradicate all vestiges of religion, insisting it had been imported by invading powers as an instrument of power and domination. The real religion of Albanians had to be 'Albanianism.'[50]

Was it all destined to be so bleak? There were areas of relative calm in Eastern Europe. Besides allowing most of Yugoslavia's Catholic bishops to attend Vatican II, Tito's regime had permitted two young priests to begin publishing an information bulletin, *Glas Koncila* (Voice of the Council) for the country's beleaguered Catholics. Launched in October 1962, this had become a weekly newspaper, achieving a circulation of 170,000. The June 1966 protocol, establishing diplomatic relations with the Vatican, formally accepted Rome's jurisdiction in religious and ecclesiastical affairs and the free exercise of Christian rites. It obliged the Vatican in return to 'condemn every act of political terrorism or similar criminal forms of violence' and ensure Catholic clergy would not 'abuse their functions for political ends.'[51] Yugoslavia's bishops, left out of the talks, were outraged by the implication that such a pledge was needed by the Church. But the protocol signalled a partial easing of control over religious communities. Having been deliberately kept at odds by the regime, in line with its tactic of divide and rule, Catholic and Orthodox theologians exchanged visits; and in 1967, two decades after a Catholic archbishop had taken up residence in Belgrade, less than a mile from the Serbian Orthodox patriarchate, Cardinal Šeper of Zagreb finally met Patriarch German.

Raw persecution was still occurring even in the relative calm of Poland. Fr Władysław Findysz had been ordained in 1932 after studying in Przemysł with the Blessed Jan Balicki (1869–1948). He had survived the Nazi occupation of southeastern Poland, as well as a savage 1944 Soviet counter-offensive which left much of his parish at Nowy Żmigród in ruins. With the War over, the priest had attracted communist hostility by helping members of Poland's Greek Catholic minority deported during *Akcja Wisła*. His movements were restricted and he was barred from teaching the catechism. In 1955, the local UB noted that he had nevertheless 'used the pulpit to spread hostile propaganda,' such as by urging Catholics not to contract civil marriages.[52]

Findysz was finally arrested in November 1963 for 'inciting hatred between believers and non-believers' after he sent a letter to parishioners warning those living outside sacramental marriages that they risked losing their rights as Catholics. The priest's lawyer defended his action, citing freedom of conscience provisions in Poland's constitution and questioning the objectivity of the prosecution witnesses. But Findysz refused to apologise and was transferred to Kraków's notorious Montelupich Street prison, where he was denied proper treatment for thyroid problems and developed a tumour. Even then, the court rejected a church request to have him released temporarily on compassionate grounds, citing the seriousness of his crime. A visiting priest testified to the personal hostility of prison officials, recording how he was cut off by the guards when he tried to hear Fr Findysz's Christmas confession.

An appeal by Bishop Franciszek Barda was finally accepted by the Supreme Court in Warsaw after the atheist journal, *Fakty i Myśli,* had bitterly accused Findysz of 'doing what he can to become a martyr for the faith by colliding with the law.'[53] But the tumour was found to be inoperable when the priest was at last referred to a specialist unit, and he died that August at his Nowy Żmigród presbytery. After his funeral, attended by Bishop Barda and 130 priests, Findysz was widely recognised as a martyr. His parish cemetery grave became a place of prayer and pilgrimage.

The Catholic Church was relatively independent and self-confident in Poland, and its leaders could deliver tough statements. Gomułka, the Party boss, had blamed Wyszyński for blocking attempts to improve his regime's international image at the time of Vatican II. Although his Party envoy, Zenon Kliszko, had hinted at a possible concordat, using his 1963 Gramsci Institute address as a trial balloon, the priorities were clearly quite different. Whereas Gomułka required Vatican recognition of Poland's 'Recovered Territories' and a weakening of Wyszyński's domination, the cardinal wanted an end to harassment and persecution. Wyszyński did little to impede the regime's contacts with Rome; but he refused to get involved and made clear Church-state ties should improve at home before there was any serious talk of an accord. Manoeuvering around these preconditions would drag on for years.

Meeting Gomułka in April 1963, Wyszyński had listed some of his grievances: administrative controls by the Confessions Office, interference with religious teaching and the refusal of passports and church-building permits. The Party was 'losing society's confidence,' he warned Gomułka, as well as its 'authority among the workers.'

> Wyszyński: This is a total state, not a democratic one. A democratic state need not know everything and be everywhere.
>
> Gomułka: It is indeed a democratic state—our ideas of democracy are different.
>
> Wyszyński: There are different democracies, but there's no such democracy which simply wishes to control the person in his every action and deed... You shouldn't laugh, sir, for if you laugh, it's the best proof you don't know what is happening in Poland...
>
> Gomułka: Father cardinal, you may know your priests better, but I know my officers and policemen better, and I know better what's going on. And my opinion, my discernment, are better than yours. You are trying to make a generalised issue out of specific incidents.
>
> Wyszyński: Oh no, my brother, there are too many such incidents, too many throughout Poland. And they aren't occurring as some local violation, but on a mass scale—this is what all the distress is about. My dear sir, if only you had a cap or shirt of invisibility, shielding you from human eyes, so you could move a little among people.
>
> Gomułka: But I know the people well.

> Wyszyński: You see the people only through their representatives.
>
> Gomułka: That's not true... You don't like our system, father.
>
> Wyszyński: No, I don't.[54]

Despite their heated exchanges, the two had agreed to revive a joint Church-state commission. Within months, however, the incipient openness had evaporated. 'This lawlessness restricts elementary human rights to full development of the personality—it belongs in the same rank as those crimes for which Nazi felons still stand before the courts today,' the Bishops Conference told priests in a combative letter. The hint of that communist malefactors might one day be in the dock was a sign of the bishops' self-confidence.

> It's true that thousands, even tens of thousands of functionaries in Poland do nothing but invigilate and seek out new spiteful opportunities for oppressing church life in our country... But we have truth and justice on our side, as well as the wishes of the working masses.[55]

The real showdown was still to come. The bishops had assured Gomułka they would oppose 'anti-Polish revisionist statements' by the German Church during Vatican II. The War had ended just two decades before, and emotions were still brittle. In the summer of 1965, however, defying warnings of public anger, Lutheran churches in both countries had drawn up a programme for reconciliation. There were calls for a similar Catholic gesture; and that November, an appeal for trust and friendship was duly despatched by the 34 Polish bishops and archbishops in Rome to their German counterparts. The German-language text condemned Nazi wartime crimes. But it also acknowledged the post-War sufferings of German civilians and invited the German bishops to attend Poland's upcoming Christian Millennium celebrations 'with a calm conscience.' It concluded with a controversial sentence: 'In this most Christian and human spirit, we extend our hands to you, pledging forgiveness and asking for it.'

Wyszyński was no friend of the German bishops. But he had seen the gesture, by his own account, as a means of rebuilding Polish-German relations. He also believed better ties were a precondition for Vatican recognition of the 'Recovered Territories,' and that it had fallen to the Church to show the way when communist propagandists were intent on merely sustaining and stoking anti-German feeling. He had not, however, notified the regime or counted on such vigorous condemnation. Now even the Catholic Znak deputies were criticising the bishops' initiative and justifying the 'bitter reactions.' 'This text is political and has nothing to do with religion,' the Party Central Committee hit back in an irate resolution. 'This time, the bishops have gone too far, in openly declaring against the policy of People's Poland on issues fundamental to our nation's future.'[56]

A short German reply three weeks later welcomed the Appeal as 'valuable fruit of our common Council work,' but appeared to deepen the crisis by calling for a 'settlement satisfactory and just to all sides,' a demand depicted as revisionist by Poland's communist media. Wyszyński felt badly let down. The German bishops' 'reserved response' had fallen well short of their Lutheran confreres' a few months before. They had clearly failed to grasp the importance of his Church's gesture. Forgiveness could only be granted, Archbishop Kominek, the Appeal's main author, cautioned West German TV, to those 'who are ready for penance and genuinely feel a sense of guilt.'[57]

The exchange touched off the most acerbic communist propaganda campaign for a decade, attacking the 'anti-national and anti-socialist' Polish Church for falsifying history and fuelling German territorial claims. Factory workers in Gdańsk and Wrocław demanded that Wyszyński and Kominek be barred from returning from Rome, and there were threats that both could face arrest. The Bishops Conference defended the Appeal that December, insisting it had been a 'peaceful and ecumenical expression' with no political purpose. Wyszyński would concede, however, that he had been too busy in Rome to prepare Polish Catholics for the initiative.[58]

Although the cardinal was refused a passport to return to Rome in January, it was felt that further direct action might prove counterproductive by encouraging the 'internal consolidation of the clergy.' Gomułka nevertheless used the dispute as a pretext for the next Church-state feud—this time over Poland's 1966 Christian Millennium. The Bishops Conference had sent invitations to the Pope and foreign church leaders, and Christian commemorations were launched at Gniezno in April at the end of Wyszyński's nine-year novena of prayer. Determined to turn the anniversary into a state occasion, the regime set out to disrupt the church events, which included a Mass for 30,000 at Jasna Góra in May. Thousands of priests were called in for intimidatory warning talks, and police, activists and collaborators were deployed with cameras and microphones. When the sacred Black Madonna icon was sent on a tour of the country, the truck was stopped by police on several occasions, while crowds were broken up with batons and teargas in Kraków, Lublin and Gdańsk when they chanted anti-communist slogans. Eventually, the icon was seized and taken back to Jasna Góra. A police unit was posted at the gates for the next six years to ensure it stayed put.

The Polish bishops protested and were accused of inciting riots. Privately, however, the regime admitted the Church's links with society had been little diminished by the previous year's furore over the bishops' Appeal. There were again disagreements within the Party over the merits of physical repression and ideological persuasion. 'The fact is that the Millennium slogans, especially on ethnic and social issues, struck quite an important note in the believing part of Polish society,' the Central Committee conceded in a report. 'The Millennium celebrations have shown with total certainty how any attempt to restrict the Church administratively misfires, and rather provides an impulse for stronger religiousness.'[59] Regime hardliners hit back, announcing plans to close six more Catholic seminaries and sack their rectors. The bishops responded with a pastoral letter, warning of 'great dangers to the Church,' and the closure plans were dropped. Although some figures saw advantages in a continuing Church-state confrontation, local officials complained of a general tiredness with the anti-church campaign.

Gomułka had one final point to make. The bishops had asked the Pope himself to close the Millennium year by celebrating the main *Wigilia*, or Christmas Eve, Mass at Jasna Góra in person that December. Gomułka, again not consulted, had made his views clear. The Polish bishops' 1965 Appeal, he told workers in Poznań, had 'absolved Hitlerite criminals in the name of reactionary political aims.' It would be 'a sign of acceptance of this harmful policy' if the Polish government now agreed to a Papal visit.

Gomułka attacked Wyszyński's idea of Poland as a 'bulwark of Christianity.' It was, he told workers, 'an offence to the Polish-Soviet alliance.' There had been a faint hope that the regime might just see propaganda benefits in allowing the visit. A Central Committee ideologue, Andrzej Werblan, travelled to Rome for talks; and when Casaroli visited the Central Committee in November, he was told the regime was not against the visit in principle. It could not allow it, however, 'in an atmosphere of tension in Church-state relations, caused by the stance of the hierarchy, and especially Wyszyński.'[60]

It was claimed that Casaroli had agreed not to inform Wyszyński about his contacts with Party officials. The Polish Primate still believed the Vatican's June accord with Yugoslavia had been unfavourable to Church-state relations in Poland. He remained wary of Casaroli's manoeuvrings. When the Vatican diplomat returned for more Central Committee dealings in February 1967, he assured the Polish bishops he would do nothing without their agreement. But he also caused offence by meeting the Pax leader, Bolesław Piasecki, whom Wyszyński had avoided since 1953. Casaroli used his regime contacts to press for concessions in areas like church-building; but his Party interlocutors insisted these were impossible because of Wyszyński's attitude and demanded that the Vatican punish rebellious clergy with canonical sanctions. In the event, the diplomacy stalled. No further forays were made until the 1970s.

In 1967, Paul VI finally named apostolic administrators for Poland's Western Territories. Despite the move, Cardinal Wyszyński was again refused a passport to attend a Synod of Bishops in Rome; so other bishops refused to go as well. With both sides exhausted by disputes over the Appeal and Millennium, the tensions appeared to ease. But conflicts continued below the surface. The regime persisted with efforts to restrict religious teaching; and when parish rectors were ordered to submit inventories of church possessions, the Bishops Conference instructed them to ignore the order. This was branded illegal by the Confessions Office. But no action was taken, and most clergy disregarded the regime directive.

The regime continued to refuse permits for new churches, claiming religious needs were already being met. Although 198 new parishes were created in 1967–70, only a dozen churches and chapels were approved out of 406 building requests. One prelate who managed to circumvent the building ban was Bishop Ignacy Tokarczuk, the fiery Bishop of Przemyśl, who had been one of the clergy evacuated from Lviv with Archbishop Baziak back in 1944. Tokarczuk's 'hostility to communism' was well known, and the regime had barred him from obtaining a parish rectorship. But there had been a mix-up over candidates for the southeastern Przemyśl see, and the regime had failed to notice Tokarczuk's name until it was too late. In his inaugural sermon in February 1966, the new bishop denounced communism for its 'abnormal, miscellaneous attacks on religion, God and the truths of faith.' Warnings were delivered by the local authorities, while the Confessions Office in Warsaw voiced shock that a 'decided opponent of communism—Cardinal Wyszyński's man' had gained the Przemyśl post.[61]

Years of conflict lay ahead. Tokarczuk was denied a passport to travel; and when Wyszyński appointed him to the new Church-state commission a year later, the government protested. The Primate refused to back down and the commission was shelved before it had started work.

Tokarczuk found an answer to the shortage of churches in his diocese by taking over Greek Catholic places of worship left derelict during *Akcja Wisła*. He then continued to build others, defying planning rules by registering them as temporary structures. His every move was shadowed. By the end of his first year in office, the SB had eight secret collaborators in the Przemyśl curia and seminary, providing details on everything from Tokarczuk's family background to the font on his typewriter. It also boasted a key agent, 'Zefir,' who filed information on the bishop's domestic life. Tokarczuk was undeterred. 'I sincerely love my homeland and nation,' he told local Catholics in June 1967.

> I foster respect for the state power and teach this respect to others, and I'm pleased with progress in economic, social and other areas, expressing this at every step. But I cannot stay silent when, in particular instances, the rights of citizens are violated. I speak out in the conviction that, by demanding justice, law and order, I am better serving the Church and Poland's state interests.[62]

The regime claimed to have monitored 132 of Tokarczuk's sermons in a single year, concluding that most were anti-state. It did everything to discredit him, depicting him as a Ukrainian, rather than a Pole, who enjoyed special favour with the exiled Cardinal Slipyi, and inciting his priests against him. It considered arresting him outright, or allowing him to go abroad and then barring him from returning. But it knew from the earlier case of Bishop Kaczmarek that such measures never worked—only the Pope could dismiss a serving bishop. So it did its best instead to persuade the Vatican that Tokarczuk was a liability who would impede a Church-state accord.

Efforts continued to infiltrate the Church more widely. Priests, especially capable clergy destined for promotion, were routinely approached by SB agents seeking an 'exchange of views,' and then often registered without their knowledge as operational contacts. So were prominent lay Catholics. Janusz Zabłocki, the *Więź* editor, was invited to Warsaw's Nowy Świat cafe by a certain 'Colonel W' and asked what he thought about religious teaching in schools and other issues. He used the opportunity to complain about restrictions on his journal's print-run. 'I know there are expectations from their side,' Zabłocki noted in his diary, 'that this odd contact will shape itself over time into some more institutionalised co-operation. From my side, I'm giving them no basis at all for any such hope; but I can't prevent them thinking this way.' When Zabłocki was in Rome during Vatican II, 'Colonel W' unexpectedly turned up and asked his advice about getting around the city.[63]

It was not surprising that one of the charges against Bishop Tokarczuk should be 'Zionism.' In March 1968, Gomułka's regime decided to close a Warsaw Grand Theatre production of *Dziady* (Forefathers) by the national poet, Adam Mickiewicz. The patriotic drama about Poland's 1830 November Uprising captured with Romantic-era pathos the pain and despair of the Partitions. It had an obvious contemporary resonance; and its sudden end sparked angry protests at the nearby university. These were brutally dispersed by the MO, Poland's Civic Militia. But calls for cultural and intellectual freedom spread to Kraków, Gdańsk and Poznań. In the crackdowns which followed, 2700 protesters were arrested and dozens jailed or drafted into the army.

Gomułka used the March events to purge his Party opponents, blaming 'liberals' for inflaming discontent and 'Jews, Zionists and revisionists' for exploiting it. The anti-intellectual campaign had anti-semitic overtones, and up to 20,000 surviving Polish Jews were forced to leave the country. It strengthened the hand of the

SB as a tool of political repression. But it also dealt another blow to the Party's ideological pretensions.

Poland's bishops condemned the repression, calling for the release of arrested students and an end to 'drastic methods of punishment and interrogation.' 'The rubber truncheon is never an argument for a free society,' the premier, Józef Cyrankiewicz, was warned in a March letter. Following the row over their 1965 Appeal, however, the bishops were wary. The dispute was widely seen as pitting rival communist and intellectual elites against each other; and they felt it unwise to intervene. Gomułka believed the Church had played a restraining role and rewarded Wyszyński with a permit to visit Rome.[64]

The Bishops Conference again chose not to protest directly when another major controversy erupted, this time involving the deployment of Polish Army units to neighbouring Czechoslovakia. When the reformist Alexander Dubček had been appointed Communist Party leader here in January, appealing for social renewal, Czechoslovakia's beleaguered Christians had detected signs of change. Prominent Catholics had joined the Church's surviving bishops in a petition demanding the release of political prisoners, rehabilitation of sentenced clergy and revival of religious orders. By March, the Central Committee was talking about a new church policy.

In Prague, Bishop Tomášek thanked Catholics in a pastoral letter for upholding the faith and called on them to take responsibility in the 'great work' now awaiting them. Besides being a suspected StB collaborator, Tomášek was said to belong to the pro-regime MHKD priests' association, which had tellingly welcomed his appointment. He came from a traditional Moravian farming family, was viewed as dull and submissive, and had been treated coldly by Cardinal Beran, whom he had replaced three years before. At the Vatican Council, Tomášek had been watched constantly by StB minders in his rooms at Rome's Nepomucen Institute.

Something had changed, however. Visiting Rome that April, Tomášek was advised to avoid formal contacts with the new

Dubček regime. Pope Paul VI spoke sympathetically of what was already being dubbed the 'Prague Spring'; but the Vatican was clearly anxious about associating the Church with 'reform communism.' In a letter home, however, Tomášek quoted the prophecy of Isaiah about peoples rising from darkness, illuminated by God's glory: 'And nations shall come to your light, and kings to the brightness of your rising' (Is 60:1–4). He compared his own dilemma with that of St Peter, the simple, unlettered fisherman called to serve as the rock of the Church. The Church was not seeking privileges, he now assured priests in a tough message, only its rights 'in a democratic society needing its evangelical service.' The wave of repression had affected everyone; and the time had come to stand up for all those 'ridiculed, insulted, refused, intimidated, rejected from social life, persecuted, interned, imprisoned.'[65] In his residence, Tomášek began receiving clergy and order members who had fallen victim to communist misrule. He offered to take part in negotiations.

The momentum quickened. Priests and lay Catholics were freed from prison, and there were rumours that Cardinal Beran could return. In March, sensing the tide had finally turned against him, the notorious Fr Plojhar resigned from the government. So did other MHKD officials, such as Fr Ján Dechet, capitular vicar of Slovakia's Banská Bystrica diocese and a co-organiser of the Christian-Marxist *Paulusgesellschaft* dialogues. A new clergy committee, untainted by collaboration, was appointed to help run the Prague archdiocese. Meanwhile, a Movement for Conciliar Renewal, the DKO, was set up at the initiative two lay Catholics, Václav Frei and Jiří Neměc, to promote the Vatican II reforms and press for religious freedom.

Some clergy resisted. 'The so-called DKO has demanded I be dismissed from my functions, claiming I "betrayed the Catholic Church" and have for long not been a priest, but a collaborator with communists,' the vicar-general of Rožňava diocese, Fr Zoltan Belák, an StB informer tasked with reining in Bishop Pobožny, complained to the Interior Ministry. 'They put up placards against me, with my photograph and the words, "Traitor Judas, we'll turn him into gulash." They also organised demonstrations against me and broke my windows, landing me in hospital.'[66]

Yet the reform movement gathered strength. In May, Bishop Tomášek travelled to the sanctuary of Velehrad to chair the DKO's first assembly. A total of 16 bishops turned up—some secretly ordained, such as the Slovak Jesuit, Bishop Ján Korec, who had been freed from Valdice in February. So did former Catholic political prisoners such as František Křelina and Václav Rence, and banned theologians like Josef Zvěřina, Oto Mádr, Antonin Mandl and Bonaventura Bouše. Calls were made for church access to education and the media, the appointment of new bishops and better contacts with Rome. Meanwhile, a letter was sent to Dubček, listing Greek Catholic sufferings and demanding an end to activities by 'people making no secret of their unfriendly attitude to the Church.'[67]

A petition to Czechoslovakia's Culture Ministry, urging the re-legalisation of religious orders and freeing of Christian prisoners, was signed the same month by over 8000 secretly active monks and nuns from around the country. Although no full answers were given, there were some concessions. Catholic writers and poets, long removed from libraries and bookshops, were republished, while four times as many candidates were admitted during 1968 to the country's two surviving Catholic seminaries. In eastern Slovakia alone, 83 new churches and 47 parishes were dedicated. The *Katolícke Noviny* Catholic weekly had its print-run increased from 42,000 to 60,000.

Slovakia's Evangelical Lutheran church had already suffered severely, with a tenth of its pastors jailed or 'in work,' and half threatened with losing their licences. In April, the church's general council warned that Protestants were being 'brought into direct opposition' by a 'vulgarly applied anti-religious and anti-church struggle,' which had resulted in the 'clear violation of their civil rights.'[68]

In a gesture of solidarity with Greek Catholics, the Latin Catholic curia in Košice summoned a meeting of priests, many of whom had survived thanks to help from Latin Catholic clergy. Over 130 turned up and called for the 1950 Prešov council, which had formally merged their church with Orthodoxy, to be revoked. 'Orthodox clergy have received letters urging them to return to the Greek Catholic church with their believers,' a Culture Ministry official reported.

> The Orthodox church has been accused of usurping the Greek Catholic church's property (churches, parish houses) and doing nothing to help injured Greek Catholic clergy and laity. In some places, Orthodox priests are charged with being Bolshevik agents, sent among the people to destroy their church.[69]

The regime had received intermittent petitions earlier, demanding the Greek Catholic Church's re-legalisation; and in June, it finally gave in and decreed that the Church could resume its activities. Attempts to arrange talks between Greek Catholic and Orthodox bishops broke down, and local communities took matters into their own hands. By the summer, 206 of Slovakia's 241 Greek Catholic parishes had declared themselves reunited with the Church again, mostly via local plebiscites. Five were dissolved and 20 were taken over by Slovakia's Latin Catholic Church. Fewer than a dozen chose to stay Orthodox.

The Greek Catholic revival was resisted. In October, the remains of the tragic Bishop Gojdič were exhumed from the Leopoldov prison cemetery by his brother, Fr Stefan Gojdič, and a close friend, Fr Marián Potáš, and reinterred with regime consent in Prešov's St John the Baptist cathedral. The cathedral was now back in Greek Catholic hands, although the bishop's residence was still occupied by the Orthodox. Meanwhile, Bishop Hopko was allowed to leave his home-village of Osek, but complained that other Slovak clergy were blocking his reappointment as bishop because he was an ethnic Ruthenian. Hopko took his case to the Vatican, but was told the Slovak government had also rejected his nomination because of his Ruthenian background. Rome appointed another priest, Mgr Ján Hirka, instead, naming Hopko as his auxiliary. The prison veteran was unimpressed by Vatican assurances that this was only a temporary solution. Rome had treated him 'like a child,' Hopko lamented, to appease the communist regime.[70]

Such disputes had already been overshadowed by much more drastic events. On 21 August, alarmed by Dubček's reformist line, Moscow had ordered an invasion to preserve communist rule in Czechoslovakia. The show of strength—27 divisions with 400,000 troops and 6300 tanks, supplemented by fraternal forces from Bulgaria, East Germany, Hungary and Poland—was intended to stifle any thought of resistance. Even then, 90 Czechs were killed, mostly in Prague, and hundreds injured protesting in the streets.

The Warsaw Pact operation took place just two days after Tomášek and his fellow-bishops had been received by President Ludvík Svoboda and a requiem Mass in Prague's St Vitus cathedral had commemorated victims of the Stalinist 'cult of personality.' Tomášek himself remained defiant, appealing for peace and replacing collaborationist teachers at his seminary in Litoměřice with Zvěřina, Mádr and Bouše. The Vatican's own reaction was muted. Prague was awash with Soviet troops. But Dubček was still in office; so no one could be sure of what would follow.

In Slovakia, Orthodox clergy were said to have welcomed the Soviet tanks with flowers. But the Greek Catholic Church was left functioning; and in November, when Tomášek visited Rome, the Pope told him he still hoped to see a 'certain improvement' in the Church's situation. By April 1969, Dubček was out. The new Party leader, Gustáv Husák, pledged to maintain the reforms; and in a forlorn last letter to his homeland, Cardinal Beran spoke of his own hopes for a 'new flowering.' It became clear, however, that the Prague Spring 'liberalisation' had been an illusion. Despite the freer atmosphere, the StB had continued to monitor and stifle religious life in the expectation that the reforms would be short-lived. While a reformist, Erika Kadlecová, had taken over the Czech State Office for Religious Affairs, her Stalinist opposite number in Slovakia, Andrej Belanský, had remained at his post. There had been no apology or atonement for past excesses and injustices. Czechoslovakia's Procurator-General would rule later that Dubček's concessions had been of a 'consultative character' only, and had not replaced the repressive laws and regulations adopted after the 1948 communist coup. In November 1969, the Movement for Conciliar Renewal, or DKO, was branded an 'anti-socialist force' by a Central Committee resolution.[71]

Although mass protests against the August invasion soon petered out, there were some dramatic gestures. In January 1969, a 20-year-old Czech student, Jan Palach, doused himself in petrol in Prague's Wenceslas Square and set himself alight in a student suicide pact against Soviet repression. Palach died later in hospital. His mother was refused permission to bury him in his hometown of Všetaty, and he was interred instead at the capital's Olšany cemetery, from where he was later exhumed and cremated when his funeral became the scene of public anger.

The grizzly spectacle, with its echoes of Jan Hus's immolation at Constance 553 years before, was not the first such protest against the invasion. A Polish accountant and father-of-five, Ryszard Siwiec, had burned himself to death in Warsaw's central stadium the previous September in front of 100,000 horrified spectators. Another Czech student, Jan Zajíc, killed himself a month after Palach near the same spot after taking part in a hunger-strike. In April, a toolmaker and Party member, Evžen Plocek, did the same in the main square at Jihlava, leaving a note inscribed with the words of Gramsci, 'Truth is revolutionary.'

Pacifying Czechoslovakia took time. In March, demonstrations broke out when Czechoslovakia beat the Soviet Union in an ice-hockey match, while protests on the invasion's first anniversary in August left five dead and thousands arrested. As the clampdown went on, however, five million people, a third of the population, were screened and 1.5 million sacked from their jobs. Husák, the new Party boss, had himself served nine years of a life sentence for treachery after being branded a 'renegade of the Slovak working class.' He was pressured by Moscow to be ruthless. Half a million Party members were also expelled for backing the Prague Spring reforms, while tens of thousands of Czechs and Slovaks fled the country. For those who stayed, there remained, in the words of one prominent Catholic, Jan Sokol, an all-pervading disappointment.

> It turned out that communism was now finally more stable than ever before, and this meant forever... Step by step, everything was reversed—the humanity, the sacrifice, the solidarity had all been for what? The broken hopes, the deep despair, the subtle, effective pressure, the encouragement of resignation and social apathy—in most Czechs, these aroused the age-old reaction of cynicism.[72]

However short-lived, the Prague Spring had also prompted demands for reform in other communist-ruled countries. With the borders now closed, morale plummeted among those who had counted on change. The East-West balance of power seemed to be shifting in Moscow's favour. The idea of 'peaceful coexistence,' much talked up by Khrushchev, had brought an effective nuclear stalemate, as US power became tied down in Vietnam and communist-backed liberation groups made gains in the Third World.

As power politics ebbed and flowed, new movements were also taking shape inside the Catholic Church. In France, where the crushing of the Prague Spring dealt a death blow to the post-War hopes of leftist idealists, the hardline Communist Party would put the dampers on dialogue in 1970 by expelling its religious bridge-builder, Roger Garaudy, who would go on to announce his conversion to Christianity five years later. Although the journal of progressive Catholics, *L'Esprit,* condemned the Warsaw Pact invasion, it nevertheless welcomed the simultaneous eruption of left-wing student rioting in French cities. 'For the first time in 50 years', Emmanuel Mounier's brainchild enthused, 'the possibility of revolution has appeared outside the communist world.'[73]

In Spain, the PCE's Santiago Carrillo looked to 'progressive Catholics' as potential allies against Franco's dictatorship. By now, most Western Eurocommunists had ceased to view the repudiation of Christianity as an ideological requirement for the Party faithful.

The Vatican remained cautious. In August 1968, the month of the Warsaw Pact invasion, the Secretariat for Unbelievers reiterated John XXIII's conciliatory observation that 'undertakings originating in ideologies hostile to Christianity can arrive at a state which no longer corresponds with their beginnings.' But dialogue should only be undertaken, the Secretariat cautioned, if place and time favoured a 'true dialogue'—it was better not to try at all 'if it is obvious that a faction is using it for its own purposes.'[74]

In some parts of the Church, such warnings were hardly heeded. In Latin America, the 1959 Cuban revolution had been supported by many Catholic clergy for suggesting radical action was possible against social and economic injustices. Proponents of a new 'theology of liberation' gained a symbol in February 1966 when a former Catholic priest, Camilo Torres, died fighting with Colombia's guerrilla National Liberation Army. 'I discovered that revolution was necessary to feed the hungry, to satisfy the thirsty,' Torres had explained when he resigned his priesthood half a year earlier. 'I consider the revolutionary struggle to be a Christian and priestly struggle, since it is only through revolution that we can realise the love men must extend to their neighbours.'[75]

Such thinking appeared to have been encouraged by the encyclical, *Populorum Progressio*. Travelling to Colombia a year later to meet Latin American bishops at Medellín, the Pope warned local *campesinos* not to put their trust in 'violence and revolution.' Documents from the conference distanced the Church from both liberal capitalism and 'the temptation of the Marxist system.' But they also condemned the 'international imperialism of money' and urged the Church to 'lend support to the downtrodden of every social class.' In a declaration, one group of Latin American bishops described 'authentic socialism' as 'Christianity lived to the full, in basic equality and with a fair distribution of goods.'[76]

Language like this caused consternation in Eastern Europe. The stifling of the Prague Spring suggested 'reform communist' ideas would not be tolerated. Moscow reserved the right to send in its armed forces to maintain the Party's dictatorship—this was now dubbed the 'Brezhnev Doctrine.' Some Marxists still hoped socialist ideals could be restored, and believed it was worth staying in the Party to exert an influence from within. Others concluded, however, that the whole communist vision was fraudulent. Any co-operation with its official structures was morally wrong.

Steps were taken to prevent the 'Czechoslovak contagion' from spreading. In Yugoslavia, where the late 1960s had brought a more relaxed climate, Tito had condemned the August invasion. He now cracked down, however, fearing a common front could be in the making in his own country between opponents of communism and moderate Marxists like those from the Praxis Group. In Hungary, Kádár had pre-empted public discontent by instituting a reformist 'new economic mechanism'; but this too was now being rolled back.

In Romania, the new Party boss, Nicolai Ceauşescu, had confirmed his power at an April 1968 Central Committee plenum, eliminating rivals, renaming streets and criticising the transgression of 'socialist laws' under his predecessor, Gheorghiu-Dej. While using anti-Russian feeling to make himself popular at home, he had also pleased the West by becoming the only Warsaw Pact leader refusing to back the invasion. Stalinist abuses, such as the 1954 execution of Lucreţiu Pătrăşcanu, had been condemned, and some cultural freedoms permitted, including books about the post-War repression. Yet the show of reform was an illusion. Ceauşescu won plaudits for his religious tolerance by allowing Romania's Chief Rabbi, Moses Rosen, to reopen a few

Jewish synagogues and by permitting Jews to emigrate. But many were effectively ransomed in exchange for payments from Western supporters, a policy which earned large sums of money for the government. Although the surviving Catholic seminary at Iași was permitted to increase its intake of students from around the country, church life remained as restricted as ever.

In the Soviet Union, a new KGB Fifth Directorate, formed after the Prague Spring, included a department specially concerned with religious groups. The growing practice of petitions had been legalised under an April 1968 statute, which required the authorities to respond within 30 days. Catholics had duly responded, protesting their loyalty while highlighting their grievances, much as Christians had done in the later Roman Empire. But most petitions were rejected. Meanwhile, a violent campaign of searches and beatings was launched in Ukraine against the underground Greek Catholic Church following its re-emergence in Czechoslovakia. One bishop, Mgr Vasyl Velychkovskiy, was arrested and jailed for 'violating the law on cults.'

The Church's leaders abroad made a show of seeking good relations with the Orthodox and called for a 'fruitful dialogue.' But the Soviet regime protested Metropolitan Slipyi's contacts with 'anti-communist *emigrés*'—much as government propaganda in Sixteenth Century England had depicted exiles as traitors and cowards in the pay of foreign powers. Meanwhile, Rome discouraged calls for Slipyi to be raised to the dignity of patriarch. But the metropolitan used his position to highlight his Church's misfortunes, comparing the fate of Ukrainian Catholics to that of the seven martyred brothers in Maccabees.[77]

There were wider stirrings of discontent, especially in western Ukraine, where several nationalist agitators were jailed in the late 1960s. In 1964, an arson attack on the Academy of Sciences Library in Kiev had destroyed 600,000 Ukrainian manuscripts and rare works, provoking popular outrage. Youth groups staged occasional protest readings at a Kiev statue of Taras Shevchenko, the national poet, while the new Party First Secretary, Pyotr

Shelest, made a gesture to national life with a campaign of 'Ukrainianisation' which conflicted with the ideological primacy of Russian language and culture.

The ethnic Tatar population of Ukraine's Crimea peninsula, deported *en masse* by Stalin in 1944, had been campaigning to return to their homeland; and in 1967, after 130,000 Tatars signed a petition, a charge of 'collective treason' was annulled by the Supreme Soviet. The Tatars began trickling back, although any mass resettlement was prevented by Soviet passport laws. The Soviet Supreme Council in neighbouring Belarus passed a resolution on defending cultural monuments around same time, which effectively ended the destruction of the republic's historic churches.

In Lithuania, the Soviet regime had allowed a 'College of Ordinaries,' or prototype Bishops Conference, to be set up in compliance with Vatican II directives, while a new Mass order was printed in 1966 and sent to Lithuanian Catholics abroad, and a church liturgical commission appointed to prepare translations of the Council documents. The commission's creation, intended as a show of religious freedom, was a significant concession, since its meetings were regularly turned into a general discussion of church problems. In November 1966, restrictions were tightened again under new statutes. The setting up of wayside crosses, for example, a Lithuanian speciality, could now be branded a violation of architectural codes. But the statutes also made the law more specific and less arbitrary. In this way, they also made it easier to defend religious rights in court.

Priests and lay Catholics in Lithuania also took advantage of the 1968 decree on petitions, filing at least 20 over the next six years, signed by four-fifths of all clergy. Official statistics suggested just 59 percent of Lithuanian babies were now baptised and only a third of marriages solemnised in churches. But many priests avoided recording the sacraments, so the data were unreliable. Many Party officials, although officially atheist, appeared content to see religion survive, so long as the Catholic Church avoided a 'hostile posture.'[78]

Could something good still come out of the crushing of hopes after the Prague Spring? The Soviet invasion had dealt a mortal blow to the Catholic neo-positivists of Poland, who had still hoped, in the tradition of Emmanuel Mounier, to 'humanise communism.' But it had also highlighted the necessity of building a coalition if any opposition was to be effective. A *Chronicle of Current Events*, launched in 1968, was publicising human rights violations in Russia; and in May 1969, an Initiative Group for Defending Human Rights announced itself, drawing on the example of the Baptist *initsiativniki*, who had attracted praise for their uncompromising demands for religious rights. But Russia's secular dissidents generally avoided religious groups and the *initsiativniki* petitions were ignored. There was little by way of any meeting of minds.

Elsewhere in Eastern Europe, there were signs of some mutual openness at least. The Catholic Church's defence of human rights had been given new force by Vatican II's Pastoral Constitution, *Gaudium et Spes*, as well as by the Decree on Religious Freedom, with its exhortation to Christians to strive, 'even to the shedding of their blood, to spread the light of life with all confidence and apostolic courage.' That message had been spelled out at the Vatican's Synod of Bishops in 1967. Priests must keep away from politics, the Synod cautioned; but they must 'select a definite pattern of action when it is a question of defending fundamental human rights.'[79] It was possible to address the moral dimensions of politics without at the same time being political.

In Poland, local Catholic clergy were showing greater self-confidence. Whereas 90 percent had come from rural origins in 1960, a new generation had now emerged, often from urban intelligentsia origins, who had been educated during the ideological conflicts of the 1950s and had a much sharper grasp of communism's strengths and weaknesses. A report by the government's Confessions Office noted that 'opposition elements' in the

Polish Church had defended the rights of Czechs and Slovaks during the Prague Spring, while Archbishop Kominek of Wrocław had talked of 'hope in a new resurrection' coming from Czechoslovakia. The Office added with satisfaction that the Polish bishops had nevertheless advised against public statements after the August invasion.[80]

Yet the reticence was only tactical. In September 1968, a Bishops Conference pastoral letter for the fiftieth anniversary of national independence stressed the Church's role in freedom struggles. There could be little doubting where the Polish Church's sympathies lay. During the March protests, fugitive Warsaw University students had taken refuge at the nearby Catholic Intelligentsia Club, suggesting some degree of mutual solidarity was possible. Former Marxists and liberal critics of communism, long disdainful of church dogmatism, were beginning to rethink their attitude to an institution which was ready to offer a coherent platform for democratic values.

There was still much wariness. Cardinal Wyszyński's programme for the 1966 Millennium had been unpopular with Catholic intellectuals, who felt its emphasis on popular mass religiousness made little allowance for individual needs. But leading lights from the Intelligentsia Clubs had begun giving lectures with their bishops' approval to parish groups and seminary students. When the Znak MPs had considered resigning their parliamentary seats in protest at the invasion, it was the once-distrustful Wyszyński himself who had insisted they stay on. When Znak's veteran leader, Jerzy Zawieyski, died in June 1969 in suspicious circumstances, fuelling rumours of suicide or an SB operation, some Znak members came closer to Wyszyński.[81]

Popular attitudes to the Church still varied in other countries. In Hungary, its subservience was distrusted by Marxist revisionists, who saw it as a co-opted regime accessory. On the surface, the Church was allowed to function here. But religion was in visible decline, and all independent initiatives were quickly crushed. In August 1970, the Hungarian Bishops Conference inaugurated a

Year of St Stephen with a special ceremonial Mass in Budapest's St Stephen Basilica. Barely three weeks later, five more Catholic priests were arrested for ministering to young people.

Despite the constraints, there were cases of Christian courage in Hungary. Agnès Titmár, the Catholic nun arrested for running an underground convent, had been released under a 1963 amnesty but rearrested in April 1966 for continuing to live the religious life. When freed again five years later, Titmár bought land for her order on the edge of a forest near Kismaros and went on worshipping, encouraged by the assurances of Psalm 37 that God would provide 'refuge in the time of trouble' and one day bring 'the destruction of the wicked.'[82]

Although that prospect still seemed far off, Fr István Tabódy, a former officer in the Hungarian Hussars, had also obeyed his conscience and refused to compromise. In the 1950s, despite AVO surveillance, Tabódy had arranged for clergy officially barred from ministering to help out secretly at Budapest parishes, following Lenin's dictum that 'the true conspiracy is one where legal action is mixed with illegal actions.' An 'underground church' was in the making, and Tabódy had tried to find a bishop to lead it. But he was turned down by Mgr Gellért Bellon, a Pécs auxiliary, one of two bishops consecrated without regime consent, who pointed out that underground bishops in neighbouring Romania and Czechoslovakia had all been 'arrested and neutralised.'

Refusing to give up, Tabódy contacted the Vatican's nuncio to Vienna via the French Embassy, and was told the idea could be considered in Rome. But the priest had trouble approaching other bishops because of regime pressure. In 1961, the AVO had raided his home and seized documents with the names of underground seminarians. Tabódy was interrogated for eight months, and presented as the 'chain figure' in a major plot linking the Vatican with Hungarian anti-state conspirators. He scribbled the words of Psalm 25 on his cell wall: 'Consider how many are my foes, and with what violent hatred they hate me... Let me not be put to shame, for I take refuge in thee' (Ps 25:19–20).

> One of my co-detainees kept telling me: 'You'll be shot and thrown in the Danube waves.' I'd already seen many things, so I also knew I would be accused of espionage and ended up believing these bleeting remarks. The police themselves never stopped reminding me: 'Tabódy, you're already on the scaffold steps—you know that's the fate of spies'... They offered me a contract: I'd agree to collaborate with them, and they'd make me a bishop. In those days, I was still naive and idealistic, so I rejected the idea, repeating to myself: 'But how could they make me a bishop?' Today, I know it was well within their power.[83]

The priest's trial was over in minutes. He spent a dozen years in prison, including several at a former Pauline monastery in Márianosztra, where Cardinal Mindszenty had been incarcerated. He nevertheless remained upbeat, believing his vocation had been 'ripened' by imprisonment, and that his underground work had kept both the regime and official Church under pressure. Tabódy had dismissed his interrogators' talk of 'illegal ordinations':

> I told them it didn't matter if the sacerdotal order was conferred in a cathedral, a room or a wild forest. An ordination by its very essence could not be illegal if it followed church law... They arrested us and dispersed our community; but our sacrifices were not in vain. Inside the 'church of the state,' the very thought that we might effectively become an 'underground church' provoked much fear.[84]

Even in such depressed conditions, there were still seeds of hope. In Czechoslovakia, the StB complained that some priests 'who previously appeared progressive' had now become 'church militants,' inciting others to defy the law. In some regions at least, the regime's anti-faith campaign had made little progress. A survey had suggested more than 70 percent of Slovaks were still religious, with barely 14 percent professing atheism.[85]

In Poland, the promised Church-state joint commission had still not started work, and tensions remained over the 'Recovered

Territories,' where the Pope's appointment of apostolic administrators in 1970 had failed to satisfy either Church or state. Cardinal Wyszyński still had the confidence of his episcopal colleagues, and his popular authority had survived. Meanwhile, Poland's Catholic clergy had expanded by a tenth in a decade, reaching more than 14,000, and efforts to divide and weaken the Church had made little if any headway. In June 1970, the bishops drafted a pastoral letter for the fiftieth anniversary of the 1920 'Miracle on the Vistula.' Wyszyński was warned of 'appropriate consequences' if the 'anti-Soviet text' was read in churches, and the letter was withdrawn. But it was another sign of the Polish Church's growing self-confidence that it had been written at all.[86]

The relative calm was again short-lived. In December 1970, protests erupted in Poland's Baltic ports over pre-Christmas price rises. Gomułka angrily branded it a counter-revolution and despatched army units to Gdynia and Gdańsk, who opened fire with machine-guns, killing 45 (according to the official count). Most were buried secretly to hide the crime, while thousands of others were beaten and arrested as the protests were put down. Yet the Party tyrant's days were numbered. On 17 December, desperate to reassert control, the Central Committee dismissed him and handed power to Edward Gierek, a Party pragmatist from Silesia. In a striking re-enactment of Gomułka's own appeals to Poznań strikers 14 years before, Gierek declared that Polish workers had been 'provoked beyond endurance' and urged them to support his new beginning. Many scorned the offer, believing the Party could never regain public confidence. But others, believing his good intentions, were ready to give his promise of better living standards a chance.

Catholic priests were caught up in the December events. A Jesuit, Fr Herbert Czuma, expelled from Gdańsk for his work with students, was arrested and jailed with his two brothers for links with a new movement, Ruch, which had circulated leaflets urging resistance to the Party's 'totalitarian fascist programme.' Over 100 Ruch members were arrested, and some given heavy sentences for planning to 'overthrow the socialist order by violence.' The Bishops Conference again reacted cautiously, withdrawing another draft pastoral letter criticising the state's policy on abortion and other social ills. The events had 'thrown a completely new light on the internal situation,' Wyszyński told Warsaw clergy. Gomułka had 'failed with his promises and disappointed the nation.' But priests still had to avoid 'political activities.' In Szczecin, where protests had also erupted, the Confessions Office conceded with some surprise that there had been no 'disruptive performances from pulpits'—although some priests had been heckled and 'accused of being communists' when they appealed for 'peace and order.'[87]

Gierek had been identified as Gomułka's likely successor as early as 1963, when he had travelled to Rome during Vatican II and unsuccessfully sought talks in the Vatican. As a former altar server himself, with a deeply devout Catholic mother, he was believed more sympathetic to religious faith. By the end of December, the Polish bishops had duly demanded a 'full normalisation' of Church-state relations, and conditions to ensure freedom of conscience and a 'worthy existence' for the country's inhabitants. Gierek accepted the call and appointed a team of officials to help bring this about.[88]

Were these really signs of a more tolerant attitude? If so, they might well have revived hopes for a secular state, neutral towards worldviews and ideologies, which valued citizens for their readiness to build socialism, rather than for what they believed. In winter 1971, the *Więź* journal marked its fifteenth anniversary by inviting secular dissidents and former communists to a discussion at its offices in Warsaw's Catholic Intelligentsia Club. The former Party theorist, Leszek Kołakowski, now in exile, had long argued that Stalinist repression, far from being an aberration, was the logical consequence of Marxism. The latest search for common ground reflected the universal disillusionment.

In Hungary, the veteran György Lukács had joined in the attacks on Roger Garaudy, Ernst Bloch and other Marxists for their openness to dialogue with Christians, insisting well into the 1960s that the 'absolute crisis of religion' was still to come. By now, however, even Lukács had concurred that communist rule had an 'inescapable tendency' towards Stalinism. Interviewed before his death in 1971, he spoke devastatingly of the 'tremendous evil' underlying the nightmare bureaucracy which had 'suffocated society' in an unreal world with no sense or purpose. Lukács's last work of literary criticism was devoted to Solzhenitsyn, paying tribute to the Russian dissident's role in exposing Stalinist abuses and praising his *Ivan Denisovich* as 'a landmark to the future.' Communism had signally failed, Lukács concluded, to 'connect the decisions of popular political power with personal needs.'[89]

Among Catholics, the feeling was growing that faithfulness to the Church must also mean loyalty to its hierarchy, whose authority had to be preserved when other value-systems were breaking down. This had been the key difference between mere collaborators like Piasecki, who put communist power first, and real Catholics who had worked to find a place for Church and faith in the communist system. There would, of course, be disagreements, as always, over how far Christians could swerve from orthodox teachings in pursuit of practical solutions. Cardinal Wyszyński had objected to talk during Vatican II of 'open Catholicism' and remained distrustful of fashionable slogans such as 'church of the poor.' Far from favouring a modernised 'leftist church,' the communist regimes preferred the Church to be backward and reactionary, so they could more easily and justifiably attack it. In this sense, ideological and philosophical dialogues were ultimately a waste of time. Though resisting some of Wyszyński's views, most Polish Catholics conceded that he was right. 'The Primate is, in reality, quite different than we imagine him,' one diarist conceded.

> He isn't an anachronistic prince of the Church, a traditionalist fixated with the past, or a narrow-minded Polish nationalist incapable of adapting his intellectual mindset to changing times. Nor, even more, is he seized with

worldly ambitions to be an anti-communist political leader, as the Marxists portray him. The cardinal doesn't fit any of these categories and avoids any such created stereotypes... We know now that it's only by maintaining its historical and cultural identity that our nation will live through this period of captivity and prepare itself internally for a time when it can appoint a government with a democratic mandate.[90]

Notes

1 Krassikov, 'The Second Vatican Council,' p. 319; Streikus, *Antykościelna polityka*, pp. 156–9.

2 D. Dunn, *The Catholic Church and Russia: Popes, Patriarchs, Tsars and Commissars* (Aldershot: Ashgate, 2004), p. 161; A. Roccucci, 'Russian Observers at Vatican II,' in Melloni, *Vatican II in Moscow*, p. 54.

3 Roccucci, 'Russian Observers,' p. 59; V. Borovoi, 'Il significatio del Concilio Vaticano II per la Chiesa Ortodossa Russa,' in Melloni, *Vatican II in Moscow*, pp. 73–90.

4 Krassikov, 'The Second Vatican Council,' p. 315; Streikus, *Antykościelna polityka*, p. 162; Przebinda, *Większa Europa*, p. 260.

5 Luxmoore and Babiuch, *The Vatican and the Red Flag*, p. 114; G. Zizola, *The Utopia of Pope John XXIII* (New York: Orbis, 1978), pp. 120–1. It was Pope John's second peace appeal since the Berlin Crisis of 1961. He had also tried to mediate between the French government and resistance fighters in Algeria.

6 Luxmoore and Babiuch, *The Vatican and the Red Flag*, pp. 114–5; Zizola, *The Utopia of Pope John*, p. 137; Casaroli, *Il martirio, p. 39.*

7 Dudek and Gryz, *Komuniści i Kościół*, p. 209.

8 Luxmoore and Babiuch, *The Vatican and the Red Flag*, p. 116; Przebinda, *Większa Europa*, p. 152. The presence of bishops from Lithuania was intended to 'strike a blow against extreme rightist elements in the Catholic Church' and 'restrain reactionary Council participants from making hostile speeches'; Mikłaszewicz, *Polityka Sowiecka wobec Kościoła*, p. 148.

9 Pelikan, *Confessor between East and West*, pp. 63, 149–50.

10 *Ibid.*, pp. 147, 172. Slipyi quoted the words of Dante about the need for firm leadership when the world was divided into God's supporters and opponents; Przebinda, *Większa Europa*, p. 156.

11 Luxmoore and Babiuch, *The Vatican and the Red Flag*, p. 117.

12 Krassikov, 'The Second Vatican Council,' pp. 325–6; Casaroli, *Il martirio*,

p. 42.

13 John XXIII, *Pacem in Terris*, 11 April 1963, nos. 1, 51, 61.

14 *Ibid.*, nos. 14, 113, 158–9.

15 *Ibid.*, nos. 147, 158, 160.

16 *Izvestiya*, 4 June 1963; Zabłocki, *Dzienniki*, p. 481.

17 Vatican Council II, *Lumen Gentium*, 21 November 1964, no. 42.

18 Vatican Council II, *Dignitatis humanae*, 7 December 1965, nos. 6, 15; *Gaudium et Spes*, 7 December 1965, no. 16.

19 According to H. Stehle, *Eastern Politics of the Vatican 1917–1979* (London: Ohio University Press, 1981), pp. 443–4. The author, a German journalist, cites a formal *non placet* allegedly submitted by Bengsch; Casaroli, *Il martirio*, p. 76.

20 Mikloško et al, *Zločiny komunizmu*, pp. 255–6; J. Hnilica and F. Vnuk, *Pavol Hnilica, biskup umlčanej Cirkvi* (Trnava: Dobra Kniha, 1996), pp. 91. 95–7.

21 Luxmoore and Babiuch, *The Vatican and the Red Flag*, pp. 122–3.

22 *Gaudium et Spes*, nos. 19–21; G. Turbanti, 'Il problema del comunismo al Concilio Vaticano II,' in Melloni, *Vatican II in Moscow*, pp. 147–188.

23 'Document 138—secret. The First Session of the Second Vatican Council (Information),' in Corley, *Religion in the Soviet Union*, pp. 229–30; CPSU resolution in Streikus, *Antykościelna polityka*, p. 164.

24 Vatican Council II, *Unitatis redintegratio*, 21 November 1964, no. 4; Common Declaration of Pope Paul VI and Patriarch Athenagoras, 7 December 1965, no. 4, in A. Flannery (ed), *Vatican Council II: The Conciliar and Post-Conciliar Documents* (Newport: Costello, 1988), pp. 471–3. Other Orthodox churches, including those of Russia and Romania, resisted the Ecumenical Patriarch's claim to be leading the way in relations with Catholics; V. Martano, 'Constantinopoli e Mosca negli anni del Vaticano II,' in Melloni, *Vatican II in Moscow*, pp. 269–292.

25 Zabłocki, *Dzienniki*, p. 685.

26 *Pacem in Terris*, nos. 42–3; Luxmoore and Babiuch, *The Vatican and the Red Flag*, pp. 136–6.

27 Raina, *Cele polityki władz PRL*, p. 37; Czaczkowska, *Kardynał Wyszyński*, p. 316; Zabłocki, *Dzienniki*, pp. 495–6.

28 *Gaudium et Spes*, nos. 19–21; Decree on the Catholic Churches of the Eastern Rite, *Orientalium Ecclesiarum*, 21 November 1964, no. 24; Decree concerning the Pastoral Office of Bishops, *Christus Dominus*, 28 October 1965, no. 7; Decree on the Adaptation and Renewal of Religious Life, *Perfectae Caritatis*, 28 October 1965.

29 Paul VI, *Populorum Progressio*, 2 March 1967, nos. 4–6; *New York Times* editorial, 29 March 1967.

30 R. Garaudy, *From Anathema to Dialogue* (London: Collins, 1967), pp. 30, 56, 124.

31 R. Mulazzi-Giammanco, *The Catholic-Communist Dialogue in Italy* (New York: Praeger, 1989), p. 62; *L'Osservatore Romano* and *La Civiltà Cattolica* editorials, 3 October 1964. Both publications were commenting on Togliatti's *Notizie italiane.* Zabłocki, *Dzienniki,* pp. 541–2, 552; R. Burigana, 'Il Partito Comunista Italiano a la Chiesa negli anni del Concilio Vaticano II,' in Melloni, *Vatican II in Moscow,* pp. 189–226.

32 Dunn, *The Catholic Church and Russia,* p. 163; G. Wetter, *Dialectical Materialism: A Historical and Systematic Survey of Philosophy in the Soviet Union* (London: Praeger, 1960). Wetter saw communism as a 'perversion of Christianity and a counter-Church,' whose anti-religious predisposition was a fundamental obstacle to co-operation; but he argued that 'real dialectics' had declined; G. Liechtheim, *Collected Essays* (London: Viking, 1973), pp. 341–2; J. Moltmann, *A Broad Place: An autobiography* (London: SCM, London, 2007), pp. 119–130.

33 P. Fiala and J. Hanuš (eds), *Koncil a Česká Společnost* (Prague: Centrum pro Studium, 2000), pp. 71–93.

34 Paul VI, *Ecclesiam Suam,* 6 August 1964, nos. 101–3.

35 The Pope's speech at the Catacombs, 12 September 1965, in Przebinda, *Większa Europa,* p. 263.

36 Casaroli, *Il martirio,* pp. 74–5.

37 Wyszyński's notes, in Raina, *Cele polityki władz PRL,* pp. 53–7.

38 'Opracowanie wewnętrzne Urzędu do Spraw Wyznań,' in Raina, *Cele polityki władz PRL,* p. 72; Dudek and Gryz, *Komuniści i Kościół,* pp. 210–1.

39 Streikus, *Antykościelna polityka,* pp. 166–7.

40 Szymański, *Kościół katolicki na Podolu,* p. 434; Dzyubat's speech in *Radio Liberty Research,* 9 June 1976.

41 'Document 148. Kaluga Regional Soviet of Workers' Deputies,' in Corley, *Religion in the Soviet Union,* pp. 248–9.

42 'Document 131. Committee of State Security [KGB],' *ibid.,* pp. 210–1.

43 Jonathan Luxmoore, 'Atheist Soviet cosmonaut Gagarin supported church, says colleague,' in *Ecumenical News International,* 20 April 2006; Szymański, *Kościół katolicki na Podolu,* p. 432. Petrov gave the information in an Interfax interview.

44 A. Pekar, *Bishop Basil Hopko STD: Confessor of the Faith* (Pittsburgh: Byzantine Seminary Press, 1979). p. 21; M. Hromník, *Blahoslavený Vasil Hopko* (Trnava: Knižica Posla, 2003), pp. 32–4; J. Pešek and M. Barnovský, *Pod Kuratelou Moci: Cirkvi na Slovensku v rokoch 1953–1970* (Bratislava Veda, 1999), pp. 145–164; P. Šturák, *Dejiny Grékokatolíckej Cirkvi v Československu* (Prešov: Petra, 1999), pp. 212–3.

45 Mikloško et al, *Zločiny komunizmu*, pp. 262–4; Pešek and Barnovský, *Pod Kuratelou Moci*, p. 145; Pavlík, *On the way to Jesus*, p. 40.

46 Zabłocki, *Dzienniki*, pp. 543, 579, 675.

47 Wurmbrand's Senate testimony, in Hefley, *By their Blood*, pp. 208–9.

48 O. Bozgan, *Cronica unui eşec previzibil: România şi Sfântul Scaun în epoca pontificatului lui Paul al VI-lea 1963–1978* (Bucharest: Curtea Veche, 2004), pp. 459–60, 46; Vasile, *Între Vatican şi Kremlin*, p. 262; Prunduş and Plaianu, *Cardinalul Iuliu Hossu*, pp. 232–3.

49 O'Donnell, *A Coming of Age*, p. 142; Keefe, *Area Handbook for Albania*, p. 122.

50 O'Donnell, *A Coming of Age*, pp. 138–9; Keefe, *Area Handbook*, p. 124; Decree 4337, in Courtois, *The Black Book*, p. 409; Pearson, *Albania in the Twentieth Century*, p. 623.

51 Alexander, *Church and State in Yugoslavia*, p. 246.

52 A. Motyka, *Dobry Pasterz: Biografia sługi Bożego Ks. Władysława Findysza* (Rzeszów: Redemptor Hominis, 2003), pp. 93–4.

53 A. Motyka, *Pasterz i Świadek: Droga do chwały ołtarzy ks. Władysława Findysza* (Rzeszów, 2005), pp. 75–9, 84–5; Motyka, *Dobry Pasterz*, pp. 107–8, 111; *Katolicka Agencja Informacyjna* reports, Warsaw, 18 March and 16 June 2005.

54 'Rozmowa Prymasa Polski ks. kard. Stefana Wyszyńskiego z I Sekretarzem KC PZPR Władysławem Gomułką,' in Dudek and Gryz, *Komuniści i Kościół*, pp.211–2.

55 *Ibid.*, p. 214.

56 'Projekt II listu do organizacji Polskiej Zjednoczonej Partii Robotniczej,' in Raina, *Kościół w PRL*, p. 371; 'Orędzie biskupów polskich do ich niemieckich braci w Chrystusowym urzędzie pasterskim,' in *ibid*, 362; 'Pozdrowienie biskupów niemieckich dla polskich braci,' in *ibid*, pp. 362–4.

57 Dudek and Gryz, *Komuniści i Kościół*, pp. 221, 225. Wyszyński believed the Znak deputies had 'believed the Party much more than the Bishops Conference'; Zabłocki, *Dzienniki*, p. 684. For the German perspective, see E. Heller, *Macht, Kirche, Politik: Der Briefwechsel zwischen den polnischen und deutschen Bischöfen im Jahre 1965* (Cologne: Treff-punkt, 1992); T. Urban, *Der Verlust: Die Vertreibung der Deutschen und Polen im 20. Jahrhundert* (Munich: Beck, 2004). The latter makes no mention of the Polish bishops' disappointment.

58 According to his friend, Fr Bronisław Dembowski; Czaczkowska, *Kardynał Wyszyński*, p. 480; P. Madajczyk, *Na drodze do pojednania: Wokół orędzia biskupów polskich do biskupów niemieckich w 1965 roku* (Warsaw: PWN, 1994), p. 133; Raina, *Kardynał Wyszyński*, vol. 6, pp. 33–60; Z. Zieliński, *Kościół w Polsce 1944–2007* (Poznań: Wydawnictwo Poznanskie, 2009), pp. 140–2.

59 Dudek and Gryz, *Komuniści i Kościół*, pp. 240–5.

60 'Notatka Wydziału Administracyjnego KC PZPR o kontaktach polsko-watykańskich w latach 60-tych,' in *Tajne dokumenty Państwo-Kościół 1960–1980* (London: Aneks, 1996), pp. 314–6; Raina, *Cele polityki władz PRL*, p. 47.

61 Dudek and Gryz, *Komuniści i Kościół*, pp. 259–60; P. Chmielowiec, 'Niewygodny ordynariusz,' in *Kościół w godzinie próby*, p. 120–1.

62 *Ibid.*, pp. 127–33; documents on Tokarczuk, in J. Marecki and F. Musiał (eds), *Niezłomni: Nigdy przeciw Bogu—Komunistyczna bezpieka wobec biskupów polskich* (Kraków: WAM, 2007), pp. 433–70.

63 Zabłocki, *Dzienniki*, pp. 487–8; on Polish agents in Rome during Vatican II, S. Cenckiewicz, *Oczami Bezpieki: szkice, materiały z dziejów aparatu bezpieczeństwa PRL* (Łomianki: LTW, 2012), pp. 519–596.

64 Dudek and Gryz, *Komuniści i Kościół*, pp. 266–9; Luxmoore and Babiuch, *The Vatican and the Red Flag*, pp. 140–1; Raina, *Kardynał Wyszyński*, vol. 8, pp. 131–80.

65 B. Svoboda, *Na straně národa: Kardinal František Tomašek v zápase s Komunistickým režimem 1965–1989* (Prague: Vyšehrad, 2006), pp. 16–17, 38–9.

66 Mikloško et al, *Zločiny komunizmu*, pp. 266, 271. Fr Dechet ended life as a crippled alcoholic.

67 Svoboda, *Na straně národa*, pp. 61–3, 69–70.

68 Mikloško et al, *Zločiny komunizmu*, pp. 274, 279–80.

69 *Ibid.*, pp. 277–8; M. Štefanský (ed), *Slovensko v rokoch 1967- 1970: Výber dokumentov* (Bratislava: Komisia vlády SR pre analýzu historických udalostí, 1992), p. 504; V. Judák and S. Danková, *Exodus: Oslavujeme Ťa Bože* (Nitra: Kňazský seminár sv. Gorazda, 1997), p. 106.

70 Pekar, *Bishop Basil Hopko*, pp. 24 6; Pešek and Barnovský, *Pod Kuratelou Moci* , pp. 145–212; J. Caranič, 'Legalisation of the Greek Catholic Church in Czechoslovakia in 1968,' in *E-Theologos Theology Revue*, Berlin, vol. 1/no. 2 (2010), pp. 192–204; Štefanský, *Slovensko v rokoch 1967–1970*, pp. 457–460.

71 Pavlík, *On the way to Jesus*, pp. 45–6, 49; Beran's comment, in *L'Osservatore Romano*, 26 January 1969.

72 Author's interview, Ampleforth, September 1991; J. Sokol, 'Svědectví a izolace' in Fiala and Hanuš, *Koncil a Česká Společnost*, pp. 209–10; Husak's charge-sheet, in J. Mikus, *Slovakia: A Political History* (Milwaukee: Marquette University Press, 1963), pp. 288–92.

73 *L'Esprit* editorial, No. 372, June-July 1968, p. 969; P. Deli, '*Esprit* and the Soviet invasions of Hungary and Czechoslovakia,' in *Contemporary European History*, vol. 9/no. 1 (2000), pp. 39–58.

74 Secretariat for Unbelievers, *Humanae personae dignitatem*, 28 August 1968, nos. III-IV, 2.

75 Quoted in Luxmoore and Babiuch, *The Vatican and the Red Flag*, p. 160.

76 Conference of Latin American Bishops, *Final Document*, 6 September 1968, nos. 9–10, 19; Luxmoore and Babiuch, *The Vatican and the Red Flag*, p. 160.

77 Przebinda, *Większa Europa*, p. 161.

78 Streikus, *Antykościelna polityka*, p. 152.

79 Synod of Bishop, *Ultimis temporibus*, 30 November 1967, no. 2b; *Dignitatis humanae*, no. 14.

80 Raina, *Kościół w PRL*, pp. 527–9.

81 Czaczkowska, *Kardynał Wyszyński*, p. 338. The Primate's troubled contacts were well analysed in A. Friszke, 'Trudny Dialogue,' in *Gazeta Wyborcza*, 28 October 1996.

82 Titmár, 'La confession de foi,' pp. 320–1; J. Wittenberg, *Crucibles of Political Loyalty: Church institutions and electoral continuity in Hungary* (Cambridge University Press, 2006), pp. 183–98.

83 I. Tabódy, 'Vous serez mes témoins,' in Bozsoky and Lukács, *De l'Oppression*, pp. 253–4, 256.

84 *Ibid.*, pp. 258, 261–2.

85 Štefanský, *Slovensko v rokoch 1967- 1970*, pp. 419, 428; Mikloško et al, *Zločiny komunizmu*, p. 265.

86 Dudek and Gryz, *Komuniści i Kościół*, p. 274.

87 *Ibid.*, p. 278; Żaryn, *Kościół w PRL*, p. 149.

88 'Przesłanie Rady Głównej Episkopatu Polski do wszystkich rodaków,' 29 December 1970, in Raina, *Kościół w PRL*, p. 561. Gierek had visited Rome in December 1963; Zabłocki, *Dzienniki*, pp. 505–6.

89 G. Lukács, *Solzhenitsyn* (Cambridge MIT Press, 1971), pp. 7–10. Lukács also repudiated much of his own seminal 1923 work, *History and Class Consciousness*, such as its notions of reification and the historical role of the proletariat.

90 Zabłocki, *Dzienniki*, pp. 617–8.

2 BETWEEN DEFIANCE AND ABANDONMENT

> *Blessed are those who are persecuted for righteousness' sake, for theirs is the kingdom of heaven. Blessed are you when men revile you and persecute you and utter all kinds of evil against you falsely on my account, for so men persecuted the prophets who were before you. You are the salt of the earth; but if salt has lost its taste, how shall its saltness be restored?*
>
> Mt 5:10–13

FOR ALL THE hints of greater tolerance, many Christians still faced harsh conditions at the start of the 1970s. Even when concessions were made, these often compounded the dilemmas. 'It's the martyrdom of caution,' one Lithuanian bishop told Casaroli, the Vatican's roving ambassador.

> I spent so many years in Siberia and I never complained—I could suffer for my faithfulness to the Church and this gave me tranquility. I slept peacefully; and when I woke in the morning, I knew what I had to do. Now, I don't know. Every day I wonder which decisions I should take to serve the Church, priests and faithful entrusted to my care. I hear words of criticism, complaint and rebuke—some consider me too weak and docile towards the government, while others accuse me of lacking circumspection and foresight.[1]

In Czechoslovakia, much thought had been put into a survival strategy for loyal Christians. The much-jailed theologian, Fr Oto Mádr, had returned to prominence during the Prague Spring, assuming the mantle of his one-time mentor, Tomislav Kolakovič, as organiser of the underground church. The ruling communists were least tolerant of Christian theology when it branched into social ethics. But Mádr encouraged those around him to avoid mistakes by anticipating developments. 'None of the civilised rules of politics were valid any more,' he pointed out—'the clenched fist of the Revolution, if need be wearing a glove of lies, aimed only at effecting the will of the Party.'[2]

Two decades earlier, when Beran and his fellow-bishops had been silenced, they had also attempted to leave some practical guidelines for Christians, recalling that 'any age, even an evil age, is God's age.' The initial neutrality of the state had turned to disapproval and discrimination, and then to hostility and repression. Even in the euphoria of the Prague Spring, the anti-religious laws had stayed in force. Yet certain useful lessons had emerged from these experiences, Mádr argued. One was that the dangers from within were greater than those from without. Those who failed the test were most often those whose faith was already flawed, such as priests who had 'gained material opportunities at the price of losing their human dignity.' Another lesson was that no power could be total. The rulers might devise plans; but they could not always carry them out. Nor were their underlings always prepared to connive with injustices. The Communist Party was using direct action against the Church; and its ultimate aim was to destroy the Church internally, through 'spiritual bankruptcy, collapse of structures, dispersal of the flock.' So Christians needed to think carefully and calmly about how to defend themselves—trusting in God's guidance and the 'decisive and surprising impulses' which came from above.

> When the threat comes from without, there is always the danger of that ultimate evil, the collapse of the Church. But at the same time, things which are good and valuable are on offer. When the threat comes from within, however, the situation can be more dangerous, if the Church is not alert to the need for effective defensive measures... Every Christian in the world has to join in the struggle to avert the threat of godless 'horizontalism,' no matter whether

> this springs from Voltaire or from Marx. But the first priority is to declare war on one's own lukewarm idleness: this is what represents the mortal danger. The life and survival of the Church do not greatly depend on external freedom. They depend on inner vitality: on our faith, hope and love; on genuine life with God.[3]

There were elements in Mádr's analysis which recalled the eschatological 'end time' foreseen by Ignatius of Antioch, and the calls for vigilance and unity against the Church's enemies contained in the letters of Polycarp. On the international stage, there was now talk of detente and 'peaceful coexistence,' as recognition dawned that certain geopolitical realities were immutable. Any final hope of redrawing post-War frontiers was dampened by a December 1970 border treaty between Poland and Germany, as well as by a Four Powers Agreement on Berlin in 1971 and 1973 Basic Treaty between the two German states. At the same time, opportunities for co-operation were increasing. East-West trade would expand 25-fold over the decade, while the US President, Richard Nixon, visited Moscow and a US-Soviet SALT 1 agreement was signed on strategic arms limitations.

The Second Vatican Council had challenged the communist regimes over their church policies. They could defuse claims of discrimination and harassment by publishing the Council texts and allowing some liturgical reforms. But the spirit of Vatican II was clearly against any restrictions on church life. It had also prompted clergy and laity to be courageous and assertive. In May 1971, the Lithuanian regime allowed three bishops to make their first formal *ad limina* visit to Rome. Just a few months later, unassuaged, a record 17,000 Catholics were said to have signed a petition to Brezhnev, smuggled abroad and sent via the UN Secretary-General, Kurt Waldheim. Some signatory lists were confiscated by the KGB, so no one knew how many had ultimately supported the protest. But the petition made headlines around the world.[4]

The ecumenical tone of Vatican II had diminished Moscow's capacity to play up tensions between churches. The policy now was to encourage contacts for their propaganda potential, something the Christian Peace Conference and Berlin Conference had already been doing for some years. In 1969, a Moscow conference, called to normalise inter-Party relations after the invasion of Czechoslovakia, had noted how communists were co-operating increasingly with 'broad democratic masses of Catholics' in the belief that they were 'becoming an active force in the struggle against imperialism and for social transformation.'[5] In December 1970, eight months after the death of Patriarch Aleksi I, Catholic and Orthodox theologians met at Bari in Italy, following this up in June 1973 at Zagorsk, where it was agreed that 'socialism contains positive aspects which should be recognised and acknowledged in their values by Christians.'

Even then, the KGB was uneasy. It knew some of the 'new generation' of Orthodox clergy were sympathetic to Catholicism and critical of their own leaders' subservience; and it feared the Vatican would use the new contacts to engage in 'ideological battle' and 'draw the Russian Orthodox church into its orbit.' Rome had refused to grant patriarchate status to Ukraine's outlawed Greek Catholic Church, portraying this as a gesture to Orthodoxy. But it was still supporting the Greek Catholics. During 1972–3 alone, the KGB notified the Central Committee, a total of 380 'catholic figures,' mostly academics, had visited the Soviet Union. Many had been in touch with Orthodox communities during their stay.[6]

From Rome's point of view, the 'small steps' diplomacy ushered in by Casaroli was worth pursuing. Moscow had made a clear distinction between its wish to co-operate for peace internationally and its attitude to Christians internally. This was unlikely to change. But Casaroli believed it offered scope for a trade-off. Official church delegations had already been allowed to visit Lithuania; and when he himself visited Moscow in March 1971, he confidently announced that the Vatican and Soviet Union had 'put an end to monologue and opened a dialogue.'

Both had a 'common interest in peace' and believed they also had a 'common field of action.'

The Soviet record of the talks noted that Casaroli had raised numerous concerns, including the lack of an apostolic administrator in Belarus and the need for equal rights for religious believers under Soviet laws. Rejecting complaints that he was interfering, he had also voiced hopes that things would improve now the situation had 'changed considerably' between Rome and Moscow. Kuroedov, the Council for Religious Affairs chairman, had defended the 'completely normal situation' in his country, insisting it met the needs of religious groups and warning that he could 'give no commitment' when it came to legal or administrative changes.[7]

This called for a complex balancing act. Casaroli was certain he could obtain concessions, provided he gave something in return. He had to keep away from anti-communist militants in the West and avoid an over-rigorous stand on human rights which might merely disrupt the dialogue. But he also had to avoid accusations of a sell-out and distinguish what was necessary and desirable from what was possible and negotiable. 'Was it better to engage in a total struggle—*impavidam ferient ruinae* (let the fearless rest beneath the ruins)—which had once been a source of glory to the Church?' one supporter pondered.

> Or was it better to try to collect a few worthy breadcrumbs for the Church's children as they fell from the table of the tyrannical power?... He believed that even when people remained locked in their own armour-plated prejudices, there was yet always some narrow path for reaching to their hearts, that in a person's conscience there existed a secret light which not even the most relentless institution could extinguish.[8]

Casaroli used words like 'instinct' and 'inclination' to justify his approaches. By his own account, he was up against 'Party functionaries strongly linked to the regime ideology and subject to higher instructions and decisions.' He was accused of pursuing a hopeless cause and fostering illusions. But Paul VI had endorsed

John XXIII's 'intuition'—his 'sense of pastoral responsibility and trust in Providence.' He also believed in diplomacy, and was ready to work with all regimes wherever possible, even the most hostile. The primary aim was to find bishops who were both legitimate and acceptable to the regime, and thus provide religious care for Christians unable and afraid to use the offices of the underground church. In this area, the Vatican could assert demands which the local church could not. For all the talk of communism's immutability, there were also weaknesses and contradictions at work, of the kind which the Prophet Daniel had explained to the ancient Babylonian king, Nebuchadnezzar.

> Communism felt strong and certain of its future, so it was hard and uncompromising. But was it really so strong? And would it really endure for centuries, as its prophets had ordained?... Someone like me, coming from outside the communist world, could quite quickly sense the deepening discrepancy between society, with its labouring classes, and above all its youth—and the regime and its programmes for 'building socialism.' It was like a worm, imperceptibly but relentlessly eating away at the internal organism, which on the surface still appeared full of power.[9]

The Vatican made a major gesture to Poland after ratification of the border treaty in May 1972 by setting up full dioceses in the western 'Recovered Territories': Gorzów, Szczecin-Kamień, Koszalin-Kołobrzeg and Opole. Gierek had wanted a different territorial division and to be consulted about the new bishops. He had been ignored completely. But the aim of a Polish church administration had at least been achieved; and the new regime now made a return gesture by allowing the Church to take over the 4000-plus sacral buildings left behind by the evacuating Germans, together with the lease of hundreds of hectares of former German church land.

It was the first time a communist government had ever agreed to enlarge rather than restrict the Church's assets, and Gierek portrayed it as a major act of largesse. Yet tensions remained. The Polish bishops continued to call for a Church-state joint commission. The regime, for its part, made little secret of its real aims: 'Through direct bilateral negotiations with the Vatican, we can eliminate Wyszyński and deprive the Bishops Conference of its monopoly on contacts with the Secretary of State and Roman curia,' one senior official explained.

> We can also create conditions conducive to an evolution in the Polish bishops' stance and to an acceleration in the process of re-evaluating the political attitude forced on the hierarchy by Wyszyński. Beyond that, the normalisation of relations with the Vatican and presence in Warsaw of a Vatican representative will undoubtedly contribute to bringing the Bishops Conference closer to the state and to the possibility of a personnel regrouping within the Polish Church's hierarchy.[10]

As for the Vatican's openness to contacts, the regime had its own explanations to hand. Several other Vatican officials, including the Jesuit order's Father-General, Fr Pedro Arrupe, had visited Poland to take 'political soundings.' People like this had observed communism's growing worldwide popularity, regime analysts pointed out; and they had concluded that struggling against it 'brought no results and compromised the Church.' The communist regimes were powerful and stable, and it was impossible to return to capitalism. So the Church had to adjust; and the Vatican had to give up its 'anachronistic and ineffective policy of condemnation and frontal attack.' Through 'dialogue and close relations,' it hoped to modify communism while creating a 'solid anti-atheist front' with the Orthodox and gradually rebuilding the Church's position.[11]

The Polish regime was still closely following Rome's dealings with neighbouring states. It believed the 1964 agreement with Hungary, which was still unpublished, had benefited Kádár's regime by requiring clergy to take an oath to the communist constitution and accept a new understanding on the nomination of bishops, and by enabling the regime to 'impose successive new demands.' This was why Poland's own bishops had scorned the Hungarian deal. The 1966 deal with Yugoslavia had been motivated more by 'external facts,' including the need to isolate 'reactionary *emigré* clergy,' and had lent the Pope's spiritual authority to Tito's foreign policy of non-alignment. Attempts were now being made at a '*modus vivendi*' with Czechoslovakia, while in the Soviet Union, the Vatican had agreed to appoint Lithuanian bishops who were 'loyal to the government and system,' and to 'tone down' the Ukrainian Greek Catholic Church's *emigré* hierarchy.

All of this, Poland's rulers concluded, merited 'a positive attitude to Casaroli's initiatives.' The Vatican could be expected to present the same 'catalogue of issues' it had raised in talks with other regimes, including the Church's freedom to teach the faith and conduct its apostolic mission. It saw relations with Poland as a step to closer ties with Moscow and other states; so the regime should present its own catalogue of demands, with diplomatic relations at the forefront. But the ultimate end had to remain the same—'the Church's maximum political neutralisation.'[12]

Would there be any let-up in all this complex brinkmanship? Talks with the new Husák regime in Czechoslovakia had opened in October 1970, despite the suppression of the Prague Spring. Casaroli visited twice over the next two years; and in March 1973, he came back to consecrate four new bishops in Nitra cathedral, assisted by Bishop Tomášek. Czechoslovakia's last resident bishop, Pobožny of Rožňava, had died the previous June, leaving all 13 Catholic sees empty; so this looked like a significant advance. But the new bishops were all members of the pro-regime MKHD, refounded in September 1970 as 'Pacem in Terris,' taking its name from John XXIII's peace encyclical. The capitular vicars who ran the dioceses were all collaborators, while many pro-regime priests who had resigned in 1968–9 had been reinstated, much to the frustration of loyal Catholics.

Casaroli was unwilling to reach a Hungarian-style agreement with Czechoslovakia, since this had plainly demoralised the local church. Other national churches—in Romania, the GDR and elsewhere—had survived without one. Yet there were bitter objections, even so, to his policy of engagement. As Party leader, Husák had launched a harsh clampdown, suppressing the religious orders and other groups which had come back into the open during the Prague Spring. In Slovakia, the Central Committee promised a 'flexible but uncompromising action against the abuse of religious feelings,' and against Christians who had been implicated in an 'ideological and political struggle' against communist power by supporting the 1968 Catholic renewal movement, DKO. A firm Vatican stance against the underground church and 'anti-communist centres abroad'—such as the Czech Sts Cyril and Methodius Institute in Rome—had been a precondition for the new bishops, who had to have 'a good attitude to socialist society.'[13] Yet even after Bishops Július Gabriš, Ján Pásztor, Jozef Feranec and Josef Vrana had been consecrated, Slovakia's most religious eastern districts still had no bishops. Czechoslovakia's Catholic clergy as a whole had dwindled by 60 percent since the 1940s.

Despite the obvious limitations, Casaroli continued his approaches. In August 1970, Yugoslavia became the second communist country after Cuba to exchange an ambassador and pro-nuncio with Rome. The deal implied Tito's final recognition of Rome's jurisdiction over the local church in return for the Pope's final recognition of Yugoslavia's socialist order, and was viewed as a natural corollary to the 1966 protocol on diplomatic relations. The following March, Tito duly became the first Communist Party boss to be received on an official Vatican visit by Paul VI.

The Yugoslav leader clearly viewed the Catholic Church as posing a more complex challenge than the subservient Muslims of Bosnia-Herzegovina or the Orthodox of Serbia. Its identification with Croatia made it naturally wary of the wider Yugoslav state; and it had also come out broadly against communism from the outset. Nationalist feeling had risen in Croatia against Serb hegemony during the late 1960s, in what would become known as the 'Croatian Spring.' Meanwhile, members of the ruling League of Communists (LCY) had joined other intellectuals to urge an end to cultural repression, and the replacement of Serbo-Croat with Croatia's own language. Serbs had responded by demanding equal status for their Cyrillic alphabet, while the Bosnian Muslims had also demanded fuller recognition as a nation and the ethnic Albanians of Kosovo and Macedonia greater regional autonomy. The danger that Yugoslavia might dissolve into inter-ethnic conflict had always preoccupied the regime. It could do little, however, as demands for decentralisation increased.

Dissent centred of Matica Hrvatska, a cultural movement dating from the 1840s which had been revived in the 1960s with a journal, *Kritika*. Catholic priests supported it, providing an additional focus for social and cultural resistance, and warnings from Tito were ignored. In 1972, Matica Hrvatska was duly suppressed in an LCY purge. This left the Catholic Church, once again, as the principal champion of Croatian national rights. Tito might make a show of supporting non-interference and non-alignment internationally; but he was not prepared to tolerate them at home. In 1971, he recognised the Muslims of Bosnia as Yugoslavia's sixth nation and allowed an Albanian-language university in Kosovo and Hungarian-language schools in Vojvodina. But deep dissatisfaction remained.

In Romania, the Greek Catholic Church, though outlawed, continued to reappear, like Banquo's Ghost in *Macbeth*, to haunt its persecutors. Catholic bishops in Austria and Germany had been in touch with Romania's Orthodox church; and in March 1972, an Orthodox delegation visited the Vatican in a gesture of mutual understanding. Travelling to Belgium that May, however, as a guest of Cardinal Leo Suenens, Patriarch Iustinian again insisted no one was imprisoned for their faith in Romania, and that Greek Catholics had consented to their own 'self-dissolution.' The claim, at a press conference, outraged Catholics and the tentative dialogue was quickly suspended.[14]

Despite this, contacts were opening up with Ceaușescu's regime. There was evidence of disagreement over policy towards the Vatican between the hardline Department of Cults and Romania's more moderate Foreign Ministry, which favoured re-establishing the ties broken off in 1950 and perhaps eventually regularising the status of the Greek Catholics. But there were other areas of possible movement too. Romania's smaller Latin Catholic Church had had no legal status since the rejection of its statutes in the 1940s. In February 1972, Ceaușescu's regime allowed Bishop Antal Jakab to succeed the revered Áron Márton, who had been freed in 1967 from 18 years of prison and house arrest. Jakab had himself survived 13 years in jail for attempting to take over the Alba Iulia diocese secretly from Márton when he was arrested in 1949. This seemed the kind of concession Rome could build on.

In May 1973, Paul VI duly shocked the world by receiving Ceaușescu as his 'illustrious visitor' in Rome. Their talks centred on 'international questions,' with the Romanian dictator stressing his much-vaunted independence from Moscow. The Pope raised the issue of Greek Catholics and was assured the 1948 merger with Orthodoxy was irreversible. But Ceaușescu did agree to discuss the Latin Church.[15] That autumn, Casaroli's deputy, Mgr Luigi Poggi, became the first Vatican official to visit Romania.

There were even stirrings in neighbouring Bulgaria. A new Greek Catholic exarch, Metody Stratiev, was deemed sufficiently subservient to be allowed to attend Rome Synods in 1971 and 1974. A year later, in June 1975, Zhivkov became the next Party boss to received by Paul VI, this time in an atmosphere of 'mutual familiarity.' A month after that, the Pope was allowed to appoint two new Bulgarian bishops.

Casaroli explained his thinking to Polish officials in February 1974. The current theory of detente, he pointed out, supposed that East and West, though irrevocably divided, shared certain common interests, and could express these interests in a way which fostered stability and prosperity. The role of the Church in this situation was to assist the process by 'seeking existing convergencies, exploring and fostering them, and creating new convergent planes.' The same line of reasoning was repeated by Paul VI to Rome's College of Cardinals in June 1976. The key criterion for contacts, he explained, was not just their effectiveness but also how they expressed the Church's 'faithfulness of mission.' This was why the Holy See had opened a dialogue—'active and indefatigable, patient and sincere, but also determined in its defence of principles and the proper rights of Church and faithful, and ready for honest and loyal understandings which would conform with these principles.'[16]

The Vatican's new policy still faced a few emotional hurdles. In April 1971, the Pope had discussed Church-state relations in Hungary with its communist Foreign Minister, János Péter. The nomination of lower clergy required notification, rather than approval here; but the Hungarian regime insisted it must consent to the appointment of bishops, who must also take the loyalty oath. This was something the Bishops Conference president, Archbishop József Ijjas of Kalocsa, a man widely believed to have been a communist agent at his appointment in 1964, still hoped pathetically could be reworded with the caveat, *sic decet episcopum* (as is proper to a bishop). It was one of several unresolved issues.

In July 1971, Paul VI had sent a letter to the fugitive Cardinal Mindszenty, now entering his fifteenth year of refuge at the US Embassy in Budapest, where he had been supported with an annual US church donation of $1000. The letter's contents were not disclosed. But two months later, on 28 September, at the Nixon Administration's request, Mindszenty finally left the embassy with an 'amnesty' for his crimes. The fiery Primate was escorted by police cars to the Austrian border and accompanied to Vienna by a trio of Vatican minders. He was greeted by Casaroli, who flew on with him to Rome, where he was met at Fiumicino airport by Cardinal Jean Villot, the Vatican's French Secretary of State. Later that day, Mindszenty concelebrated Mass in the Sistine Chapel with Paul VI, who handed him a ring and pectoral cross, and welcomed the new exile as 'a glorious symbol of the living thousand-year unity between the Hungarian Church and Apostolic See... a symbol of unshakeable strength rooted in faith and selfless devotion to the Church.'[17]

By his own account, Mindszenty had been assured he would remain Hungarian Primate, while handing his 'rights and duties' to an apostolic administrator—much as the imprisoned Cardinal Stepinac of Croatia had delegated his to a coadjutor, Mgr Šeper, in 1954. His own destiny 'would in no way be subordinated to other aims,' Mindszenty was told. But he was also asked not to issue statements, and to keep his recently completed memoirs secret until Rome authorised their release 'at an appropriate time.'[18]

By late October, Mindszenty was back in Vienna, taking up residence at the city's Hungarian Pazmaneum. He had been in Rome for barely three weeks, long enough to encounter a 'general indifference.' But he was again told he must obtain Vatican approval before speaking publicly; and when he sent his memoirs to the Pope, he was cautioned that the Kádár regime would 'punish the entire Church of Hungary' if they were published. Clearly, Mindszenty had been judged an obstacle in the way of better relations; and with the cardinal out of the way, Vatican-Hungarian ties now advanced in leaps and bounds. In a conciliatory gesture that October, the Vatican agreed to lift its 1957 excommunication of the 'peace priests,' Fr Beresztóczy, Fr Horváth and Fr Várkonyi. Six months later, Hungary's Greek Catholic see at Hajdúdorog was reactivated and agreement reached on four new bishops, who were duly ordained in Budapest's St Stephen Basilica by Archbishop Ijjas. In May 1972, a large Hungarian Church delegation, with eight bishops and 60 priests, travelled to Rome to celebrate Pentecost.

The worst was still to come for the exasperated Mindszenty. For on 1 November 1973, despite previous assurances, he was finally asked to resign. The Kádár regime welcomed the move and sent János Péter back to visit Paul VI. However, it was left till the following February, the twenty-fifth anniversary of Mindszenty's trial, to announce that the Esztergom see was now vacant. Mindszenty issued a statement, 'correcting suggestions' that he had retired voluntarily. The decision had been the Holy See's alone.

Looking back later, Casaroli drew a parallel with Pope Pius VII's demand for the resignation of France's recalcitrant bishops to make way for a concordat with Napoleon. He also acknowledged Mindszenty's doubts about the Vatican's stance—from their very first contact, Casaroli recalled, the cardinal had been 'not just scrutinising, but also rather distrustful.'

For his part, Mindszenty had done his best to persuade Paul VI against making 'conciliatory gestures' in expectation of regime concessions. Communist rulers did not react that way—they were far more likely to view such gestures as signs of weakness which they could exploit. Russia's Orthodox church had been persecuted as much in periods of coexistence as of subjugation. Meanwhile, Hungary's communists had made propaganda capital out of their negotiations with the Vatican. But the 'sole result,' Mindszenty insisted, had been the appointment of regime-approved bishops whose actions were 'profoundly detrimental to ecclesiastical discipline.'[19]

The Vatican's policy of engagement might be understandable. But it did, indeed, raise profound questions about balancing diplomacy with testimony. In Poland, there were fears about political pressure exerted on the Pope. The Gierek regime's documents made it abundantly clear that every effort was being made to push the Vatican into accepting the communist system. During Casaroli's visit in February 1974, Wyszyński recalled the kind of values—'faith, love, justice, peace, a spirit of mutual service'—which the Catholic Church was imparting to the nation. 'When a fisherman sails on a calm sea, he can see the bottom and spot every fish,' the Polish Primate told Casaroli and the congregation during a Warsaw cathedral homily. 'But when the sea is disturbed, he sees nothing. To see the issues and tasks facing nation, Church and state, to assess them properly and confront them, needs preliminary calm, balance and patience.' In case the point was missed, the Bishops Conference reiterated its position a month later. The Polish Church supported the Vatican's talks with the regime, it insisted. But there had to be preconditions. The talks had to be 'correct, frank and systematic'; and no decisions should be 'taken without participation by the bishops of Poland.' As Vatican II had established, 'direct responsibility for the Church in Poland' was held by the Bishops Conference.[20]

Having been reprimanded in the 1950s for seeking 'deals with communists,' Wyszyński was now apparently being criticised for impeding them. Yet this was not a time for compromising with communism, he warned a Rome Synod of Bishops the following October. The Vatican's work in Eastern Europe should be imbued with an 'unambiguous Christian courage,' while diplomacy, however commendable, should never be allowed to 'obstruct the spreading of the Gospel.' In Poland at least, the Church was strong through its own resources. If diplomatic deals were needed, they were only 'as tiles on the roof of a building that grows from its own foundations.'[21]

There had been rumours since the 1960s of a plan to move Wyszyński to Rome, like Cardinals Beran and Mindszenty before him. Although these had always been denied, Mindszenty's dismissal was seen by Wyszyński, according to regime informers, as a 'threat and warning' of what might still happen to him if he grew too powerful and impeded the normalisation in relations. Mindszenty had made a mistake in fleeing to the US Embassy, Wyszyński believed. But the Vatican had also been wrong to move him to Rome. A man symbolising the 'unity and suffering' of Hungarians should have remained with his people.[22]

The same anxieties were spreading elsewhere in Eastern Europe. In Romania, Bishop Iuliu Hossu had died in May 1970, robbing the Church of its most forceful defender. Discreetly consecrated in the 1940s by Archbishop O'Hara, the Vatican nuncio, Hossu had been made a cardinal secretly. A year after his death, the Romanian Orthodox synod had adopted a resolution again confirming the annulment of the Greek Catholics' union with Rome. When Ceauşescu had visited Rome in 1973, Romania's five surviving Greek Catholic bishops had demanded that the ban on their Church be lifted, citing their country's constitution and the Universal Declaration on Human Rights.

It was just another forlorn gesture. A new book by Romania's best-known Orthodox theologian, Fr Dumitru Stăniloae, rubbed salt in Greek Catholic wounds by justifying the suppression. The 'voluntary religious reintegration' of Greek Catholics with Orthodoxy had supplied the 'definitive and total renunciation of Uniatism,' Stăniloae calously remarked.[23]

How were these confusing signals to be interpreted? Intense pressure continued against religion in the Soviet Union. In 1970, the writer Solzhenitsyn had been awarded the Nobel Prize for Literature, concluding his acceptance speech with a Russian proverb: 'One word of truth shall outweigh the whole world.' During the same year, however, the dissident *Chronicle of Current Events* had recorded 106 prison sentences for political crimes, including 21 forced incarcerations in psychiatric hospitals. As in Eastern Europe, acts of violent repression were rarer now, and there was less talk of spies and enemy agents. But the police network was growing rather than diminishing. By 1974, Solzhenitsyn himself had been arrested and expelled from the country.[24]

'The struggle with religion was and still remains a progressive task for our Party,' Kuroedov, the Church Affairs director, had reaffirmed shortly before. However unremitting, that struggle had not prevented the spread of clandestine religious activities. In Ukraine, a new Party first secretary, Volodymyr Shcherbytsky, had reversed the 'Ukrainianisation' policies adopted by the Shelest regime the 1960s, as part of an anti-national policy reflected at Brezhnev's behest in other republics as well. In October 1973, the Ukrainian Politburo duly reaffirmed the struggle against 'religious sects'; and in one spectacular act of vandalism, a Polish military cemetery at Orląt in Lviv was flattened by bulldozers.[25] Despite this, hundreds of Greek Catholic clergy were said to be active underground, usually holding civilian jobs, or ministering to Ukrainian communities in Siberia and Kazakhstan. Secret Greek Catholic seminaries had been raided in Ternopil and Kolomiya. So had a secret convent in Lviv, where there were dozens of underground nuns.

Older Greek Catholic clergy, known to the police from previous interrogations, were generally arrested only if their pastoral work went beyond immediate family and friends. Younger, secretly ordained clergy were treated more ruthlessly; but they too remained undeterred. One, Fr Ivan Kryuy, was detained in early 1973 with two state printing house employees for secretly running off Catholic prayerbooks; but not before they had also produced copies of a Catholic missal and hymnbook.

Greek Catholics had survived in other parts of the Soviet Union. In Moscow, two surviving sisters from Anna Abrikosova's pre-War Dominican community, Nora Rubashova and Vera Gorodets, amnestied in 1956, were still holding meetings, doing charity work and making efforts to keep Greek Catholicism alive among students and intellectuals. They were in touch with priests from the Assumptionist-owned St Louis, Moscow's only functioning Catholic church, as well as with the occasional visiting priest from Poland, Germany or France.

Such work still carried grave risks. In August 1969, Bishop Andrei Katkov, who had secretly been given care of Russian Greek Catholics by the Vatican's Congregation for Eastern Churches, had met surviving church members while travelling across Siberia, officially on a visit to family members. Katkov had been invited by a Russian Orthodox metropolitan and had even met Patriarch Aleksi. He fell sick on his return to Italy and was widely thought to have been poisoned. An Orthodox enthusiast for Catholicism, Fr Vladimir Feldmann, secretly ordained into the Latin rite on a tourist trip to Czechoslovakia, set up a clandestine parish for Greek and Latin Catholics in Moscow, but was quickly arrested and deported.[26]

Away from the cities, church life limped on. Polish priests sent occasional reports home to their bishops about ethnic Polish communities in Ukraine, Belarus and Lithuania. Some managed to travel further afield. Fr Roman Dzwonkowski, a Pallotine priest from Lublin, noted how the *kolkhoz* state farms relied on bonded labour, since their employees had no IDs or internal passports and could only leave if assigned elsewhere. With no clergy available and many parents ill-prepared to teach the faith to their children, Dzwonkowski observed, Christian beliefs and practices were largely kept alive by the *babushki*, or old women. Many had received a religious upbringing before the Revolution and hung on to their pre-Soviet prayerbooks and holy pictures.[27]

Dzwonkowski travelled as far as Odessa, which boasted the only open Catholic church in southern Ukraine. He saw places of worship which had been turned onto shops, storage depots or even toilets but still had *Te Deum Laudamus* or similar Christian inscriptions on their facades. Some, built in the Baroque period by noble families, had been artistic and architectural masterpieces. Dzwonkowski was shocked by the crudity of much atheist propaganda. In a Lviv museum, he saw a scaffold said to have been used by Jesuits to hang heretics, and confessional grilles said to have been employed to break the fingers of unrepentant sinners by priests who routinely tipped off the Tsar's police about what they discovered during confessions. The atheist handbook defined prayer as 'a form of magic,' and religion as 'a means for justifying capitalist profit.'[28]

Other small Christian groups—Baptists, Adventists, Mennonites, Old Believers—had shown remarkable resilience, and religious protests were now a significant part of all dissident activities. But the Russian Orthodox church was in a sorry state. Half the 20,000 places of worship still open in 1945 had now been closed, along with half its 67 monasteries and convents. In an open letter to Patriarch Pimen Izvienev, elected in June 1971 to succeed Aleksi I, Solzhenitsyn had rejected the familiar claim that subservience was a necessary price for Orthodoxy's survival. All it had gained, he argued, was a landscape of destroyed churches and poverty-stricken people deprived of hope. Solzhenitsyn drew a contrast with the Catholic Church's defiance in Poland. There was something in his tone which could be compared to the apologias of Tertullian and Justin 17 centuries earlier. 'A church dictatorially ruled by atheists is a sight not seen in two thousand years,' the Nobel laureate commented. 'What sort of reasoning can convince us that the consistent destruction of this church's spirit and body by atheists is the best means for its preservation? Preservation for whom? Certainly not for Christ.'[29]

Solzhenitsyn recalled the letter sent to Patriarch Aleksi in 1965 by Fr Yakunin and Fr Eshliman. Some fellow-dissidents questioned his harshness, objecting that Orthodox leaders were simply doing their best in an impossible situation. But his 'slanderous fabrications' were referred to the Party's Central Committee by Kuroedov, who feared trouble if Russia's best-known contemporary exile linked up with religious protesters inside the country. Agents from the KGB's Fifth Directorate stepped up their infiltration of parishes. Meanwhile, Pimen was pressured to rein in active priests—men like Fr Dmitri Dudko, who had attracted a young congregation at his church of St Nikolai in Moscow, only to be told by the patriarch in May 1974 that his 'open evenings on the faith' had to stop.

Yet other young clergy defied the pressure. Some help was available from Poland, which provided a transit for church contacts, and from *Foyer Oriental* in Brussels, which published Russian-language books. During a Rome audience in January 1973, the Pope himself regretted that Solzhenitsyn had had to publish *August 1914*, his latest work, in Paris because he had not been allowed to print the word 'God' with a capital letter in Russia.[30]

For Catholics, there was still little tolerance. Although single churches remained open for worship in Moscow and Leningrad, there was little by way of a pastoral network. In Belarus, only a quarter of the Church's 400 parishes were functioning, and in western Ukraine, only a dozen parishes out of 493. Priests were allowed occasional two-day visits to pastor-less communities, where they would spend the entire time hearing confessions and dispensing sacraments, sometimes helped discreetly by Greek Catholic clergy. Some, like the much-praised Fr Chomicki of Polonna, were strong personalities, with temperaments forged under the anvils of prison and Siberian exile. The KGB made constant efforts to discredit and intimidate them. Would-be converts, often displaying deep devotion, would come forward for baptism only to be exposed as agents, while stronger clergy would be worn down in 'warning talks.' 'After returning from the Chekists, I had the feeling I had sinned in all my thinking,' remembered one priest, Fr Jan Śnieżyński, in the Georgian capital, Tbilisi. 'I felt anxious and full of dirt—it seemed to me that Satan was helping these people.'[31]

Yet resistance continued. Parishioners gathered to defend their churches and presbyteries from closure; and when Fr Czesław Wilczyński left his parish at Braslav in Belarus to conduct a funeral and lost his *spravka* permit as a result, local Catholics threatened to stop working. The basic catechism continued to be taught in parishes, often by underground nuns facing heavy sentences if caught. Many caused a deep impression with their dedication and self-sacrifice. Despite constant harassment, Fr Chomicki's parish produced six priests and at least eight nuns, while another Pole, Fr Wacław Piątkowski, rector of Niedźwiedzice in Belarus, prepared 11 priests for ordination, sending some on to the seminary at Kaunas for final preparation.[32] While other clergy were sent to Poland for ordination, secret ordinations took place as well, mostly conducted for safety reasons by retired or underground bishops, rather than by legally functioning clergy.

In neighbouring Lithuania, where only seven out of 40 churches were now open in the capital, Vilnius, the petition movement had drawn tens of thousands of Catholics into open criticism of the system and helped break the grip of fear left over from Stalinist times. But it had achieved little in practice; and in March 1972, on St Joseph's Day, a new *samizdat* journal duly began to record the Church's troubles in detail. The *Chronicle of the Catholic Church in Lithuania*, launched at Simnas parish, near Alytus, modelled itself on the *Chronicle of Current Events* in Moscow and testified to the close links now formed between Catholic and secular dissidents.

Not all secular dissidents sympathised with the Catholic Church; but religious rights provided a catalyst for co-operation. The *Chronicle*'s secret compilers studied the situation in other Soviet republics and concluded that the Church's best hopes lay not in accommodation but in resistance. Soviet pledges of dialogue were an illusion, the journal warned: only noisy protests and recriminations could have any impact on Soviet actions. Rome's policy of appointing subservient bishops was a mistake. It would only hasten the Church's destruction from within. 'The future of Catholicism in Lithuania depends not on the number of bishops or administrators, but on pastoral work by dedicated priests,' the *Chronicle* insisted. 'No concessions can be expected from the atheists through bargaining—Lithuania's Catholics will gain just as much freedom as they win for themselves.'[33]

The *Chronicle*'s editor was a young Kaunas Jesuit, Fr Sigitas Tamkevičius, who had interrupted his seminary studies in the late 1950s to do Soviet Army service and been stripped of his licence in 1968 after just four years as a priest. But its central idea—collecting information from trusted people around the country—was attributed to the once-jailed Marian, Fr Pranas Račiūnas. Although the pool of informants was considerable, their identities were known directly to no more than five secret co-operators. Even then, the KGB soon became aware that Tamkevičius was involved, along with Fr Svarinskas, the camp veteran who had helped the post-War Forest Brethren. It obtained copies from its agents and could trace the printing material used to produce them. Within 18 months, it had identified at least a dozen *Chronicle* helpers, including three other priests. But it was still gathering evidence. Meanwhile, the *Chronicle* passed information to Rome and the outside world about arrests and trials, as well as about the demolition of chapels and religious monuments, such as the fabled Hill of Crosses at Šiauliai. 'I was a parish curate with a not very burdensome workload—Holy Mass, a sermon or two on Sundays, visits to the sick,' Tamkevičius later recalled. Both Bishop Sladkevičius and his secret Jesuit provincial, Fr Jonas Danyla, had approved his underground activity. 'There was no religion at school, and everything a priest normally does couldn't be done. So even if I did a bit more than others, I still had plenty of free time... I had only a single room, though, so I lacked good conspiratorial conditions.'[34]

The Lithuanian regime tried to persuade fellow-clergy that the *Chronicle* would merely create new problems. When it failed, it resorted to familiar tactics; and in 1974–5 alone, ten *Chronicle* collaborators were given jail and exile sentences. None of this could stop the journal.

Samizdat titles had appeared throughout the Soviet period. Yet they now had access to new technology, and could print mass editions at different locations. They also had plenty of willing contributors and distributors, particularly from the banned religious orders. A new underground society, Friends of the Eucharist, founded in 1969 by Jadvyga Stanelytė, one of Lithuania's 1500 secret nuns, was organising pilgrimages and helping repair the country's characteristic wayside crosses whenever police destroyed them. Dozens of priests were being trained secretly as well, some after expulsion from the seminary, and sometimes for work in other republics.

Most notable underground activity in Lithuania was supervised by the exiled Bishops Sladkevičius and Steponavičius, who provided advice for the *Chronicle* and checked its content. Here as elsewhere, however, church leaders were adamant that no formal distinction should be drawn between legal and illegal Catholic activities. Wherever communism was in power, they were two sides of a single coin. Virtually everything was done by word of mouth, without any paper chain; and many clergy, working legally, also undertook secret assignments. Some were constantly on the move, deliberately avoiding official registration in order to work more freely. Fr Alojzy Kaszuba, a Capuchin priest from Lviv, worked as a stoker and bookbinder after losing his priest's permit in 1958, and was arrested and given a five-year exile term in 1966. But he disappeared from his work station and went on ministering in Siberia and Kazakhstan until his death in 1977.

The same practices occurred among other religious groups. There were few recognised Muslim mosques in the Soviet Union; so a network of unofficial mosques had spread, often disguised as tea-houses and served by wandering imams. The State Council for Religious Affairs estimated that Muslims had the largest number of 'recalcitrant cult servants,' more even than the defiant Baptists and Pentecostalists.[35]

Underground convents, with hidden chapels, had become common in some Soviet republics, as young women enlisted in banned religious orders, often hiding the fact from their own families. Some helped out quietly in parishes, while others secretly ministered to patients in hospital. Nuns from the Servants of Jesus order travelled regularly to Moscow from Zhytomir in Ukraine to make their confessions before the priest at St Louis's. A Polish priest was said to have arranged a civil wedding with an underground nun in Lithuania to obtain a residence permit, and been deported when the ruse was discovered after they had discreetly separated. In the late Nineteenth Century, a Polish Capuchin, Fr Honorat Koźmiński (1829–1916), had founded 17 separate institutes and congregations for secret non-habited nuns under Russian imperial rule. Some of these, such as the Sister Servants of Mary Immaculate, had now come into their own. The Lithuanian *Chronicle* noted how the official Church received crucial support from this 'Church of the Catacombs,' even as the Vatican was being pressured by the Soviet regime to help suppress it. It only regretted that underground Catholics had no chance of any contact with Rome.[36]

Some even saw a new conception of dissent in the making. In contrast to the professional revolutionaries of the past, the goals this time were limited and peaceful. None of the new generation talked of seizing power, only of questioning the system and its injustices. Direct confrontation would be both unrealistic and morally questionable.

In 1970, buoyed by international media interest, a Moscow Human Rights Committee had set out to monitor the Soviet Union's compliance with its own laws. Its efforts were totally rejected by the regime, which merely relegated it to the criminal fringe. But both the Catholic Lithuanian *Chronicle* and its secular Moscow counterpart concurred on the value of holding the regime to its constitutional pledges of freedom of speech and religion, and agreed that the exposure of human rights abuses could have a restraining effect on government actions. Both knew how to use the Western media, including the radio stations which routinely broadcast their reports of arrests and trials back into the Soviet Union. The growth of underground networks, largely beyond KGB control, was a warning that religious and non-religious citizens could now organise and act when their rights were denied.

Were underground church activities the way of the future? Certainly, they were also spreading in the rest of Eastern Europe, where isolation from the Western world had delayed the Church's modernisation but also kept secularising pressures at bay. In Poland, where the Catholic Church had shown restraint during the Baltic disorders of December 1970, there were still lingering hopes of a more pragmatic, less confrontational line under the latest Party leader, Gierek. Cardinal Wyszyński had been naturally cautious, recalling the disappointed hopes of 1956 when another wave of reforms had been promised. He was right to be. It was becoming apparent that Gierek's regime would be far from liberal in its church policy. Perhaps it had merely talked of a 'new beginning' to appease society and give a good impression internationally.

In the shadows, Poland was home to a well-organised, silent and ruthless security apparatus, whose methods of surveillance, interception and intimidation had been slowly perfected under Party directives. There was more emphasis now on resolving public grievances rather than repressing them. But Gierek himself continued to complain of 'clergy aggressiveness.' The Interior Ministry's church-monitoring 'Department Four,' set up in 1962, had doubled its secret collaborators to over 4000 and had files on every priest and seminarian. It was still working full-time against Wyszyński—to 'undermine his authority in the eyes of public opinion, priests and faithful; inspire the bishops to stand against his despotism; expose and reveal slips in his public statements; hold up to ridicule this figurehead's links with his closest entourage.' In May 1972, the Department launched a new campaign, '*Prorok*' (Prophet), to stop the Primate propagating Catholic social doctrine as an alternative to communism. Meanwhile, a special SB unit, 'Group D,' was formed with local branches to spread 'disinformation and disintegration' in the Church's ranks and physically eliminate inconvenient priests. Efforts continued to fuel tensions between Wyszyński and Poland's other cardinal, Karol Wojtyła of Kraków.[37]

In public, the atmosphere was different. For all the covert hostility, Wyszyński was not now denounced as harshly as under Gomułka. Both the government and Bishops Conference talked of a new era of 'full normalisation,' and there was criticism in regime ranks of the crude, confrontational anti-church propaganda which had characterised the Gomułka period. 'The particular weakness in our activity was the primacy of administrative measures over political, and the lack of elasticity in tackling conflicts,' one Central Committee report conceded in 1971. 'The Bishops Conference has emerged from these public polemics and struggles with a strong hand, even achieving successes. This is why, in state-church altercations, we must avoid drawing believers in on the side of the bishops.'[38]

Yet the Party's basic aim remained the same—to ensure the Church's neutrality, and ultimately its subservience to the communist order. So the basic strategy of intimidation and subversion stayed in place too. The Confessions Office favoured a nuanced approach. The Church had already been allowed to renovate the German Catholic properties abandoned in Poland's Western Territories. The Office now recommended a more moderate approach to processions and pilgrimages. This might be viewed as a sign of weakness, an attempt to buy church support with concessions. It might spur local opposition and fuel further demands. But concessions, skilfully crafted, might also foster greater loyalty and discernment.

The German Dietrich Bonhoeffer's *Letters and Notes from Prison*, published underground in 1970, were widely read among Christians for their contemporary lessons. But Poland's bishops also urged citizens to use the new conditions to table more demands. In Białystok alone, 91 requests were submitted in the first quarter of 1971 for new parishes or sacral buildings. Although only 28 church-building permits were granted nationwide during the year, 73 churches were reported to have been constructed illegally.[39] In February 1972, the Bishops Conference set up a commission to monitor church-building; and within two years, the number of permits had increased to 59. Places of worship for new city areas had long been a church demand. But there were others too, such as access to the media, recognition of the Church's legal status and the right to Sunday rest. Gierek's regime agreed to reduce the taxes imposed on parishes, following a Confessions Office recommendation. But most other demands were left unanswered.

During the same period, a campaign was launched against the Polish Church's pastorate for students, which had been set up after the 1968 disorders. This had 21 centres in Kraków alone, run by the Dominicans, Franciscans, Jesuits and Paulines, with a membership put by the SB at 8000 students. It was seen as a key front in the ideological struggle; and it was heavily infiltrated with agents drawn from student participants. Among the religious orders involved, the Kraków Jesuits were an object of particular attention, because they had contacts with Vatican Radio and 'a special role in defending Catholic doctrine.' At least seven secret collaborators were recruited among them in the 1970s; but this was judged insufficient by the SB. The Dominicans were watched closely as well. One prominent member, Fr Andrzej Kłoczowski, was warned to stop using his monastery for 'collecting petition signatures and conspiratorial games.' 'If similar situations occur in future,' Kłoczowski was bluntly told at the city's police HQ, 'we will be able to find remedial methods in relation to you and your other brethren.'[40] When a Student Solidarity Committee was formed in 1977 after the killing of a Kraków student, Stanisław Pijas, the SB stepped up its efforts.

The northern port city of Gdańsk was also seen as a priority area for disrupting the pastorate, given its links with the outside world and role as a starting-point for parish holidays. In 1971, a special SB operation, codenamed 'Niwa' (Harvest), was launched here to isolate the most active priests and students. The aims were routine: 'internally disintegrating the pastoral milieu; compromising of clerical and lay activists; undermining the trust of young people.' Steps were taken to disrupt parallel church initiatives, such as Sacrosong, a festival of religious songs based in Łódź, which was viewed as a dangerous magnet for evangelisation among the young.[41]

In recruiting clergy informers, the SB looked for well-placed, promising priests who might hold senior church positions in future. Some bluntly resisted its attempts, even for years. Others were abandoned when they failed to provide useful information. 'Neither today nor tomorrow, this month or the next, will I have any time for you,' one priest told his SB minder. 'If you have some issue, please go to the cardinal or file a summons; otherwise, I will not speak with you.' Some former collaborators changed entirely. Fr Józef Gorzelany had been recruited as a 'Peace Priest' in the 1940s, but broke off co-operation with the secret police in the late 1960s when he was assigned to Nowa Huta, Kraków's industrial 'suburb without God.' Gorzelany was spied on by his curates, while the SB spread disinformation in a bid to have him moved. But he survived for another two decades, supervising the building of a massive 'Church of the Ark,' which was dedicated by Cardinal Wojtyła in May 1977 at a ceremony attended in heavy rain by 70,000.[42]

Priests like this could count on inspirational leadership from figures like Ignacy Tokarczuk, the Przemyśl bishop whose surprise appointment had caused such friction in the 1960s. Tokarczuk had not softened. The Confessions Office monitored 656 of his sermons in the first five years of his appointment, concluding that 183 were 'aimed against the foundations of the Polish People's Republic.' In one typical outburst, he was said to have compared regime leaders to 'bandits of old who hid out in the forests' and pounced on weary travellers. The regime continued pressing for Tokarczuk's removal. When this failed to happen, it stepped up the harassment. In February 1975, eight separate microphones were discovered behind radiators in Tokarczuk's curia, all dating from the installation of its central heating system a decade before. Others were found in local church buildings, including the Przemyśl seminary. There could only be one response, Tokarczuk told his parishes in a statement:

> On one side, ardent prayer for these unhappy people who trample on basic human rights, that they may see the evil they do and return to the path of truth; and on the other, ever greater unity between priests, bishops and the Holy Father, and a sensitivity against every attempt to break up the Church.[43]

Regime agents, angered by the defiance, seized cars from Tokarczuk's curia, while the state media stepped up its attacks. Half of all illegally built churches were reported to be situated in the Przemyśl diocese, which had also reopened churches previously used by the deported Greek Catholics. Despite the SB's efforts, some had their walls erected overnight to present a *fait accompli* to local officials, who concluded it was better not to risk a social reaction by bulldozing them. 'Great care is needed,' the Confessions Office conceded with frustration. 'The initiators of illegal buildings, religious gatherings and similar things include our administrative counter-measures in their reckoning, with the aim of exploiting them to the Church's advantage.' Over 130 Przemyśl priests had been fined for illegal activities by the mid-1970s; but parishioners quickly raised the necessary money. At least ten churches were torched by unidentified assailants; but parishioners quickly placed others under guard at Tokarczuk's instruction.[44]

Tokarczuk adamantly denied 'anti-state' accusations; and the regime, for its part, shied away from arresting him. But efforts continued to set the bishop at odds with his clergy and episcopal colleagues. These were not without success. One priest, Fr Franciszek Pustelnik, who had been recruited by the SB during military service, was reported to have hurled a paper-weight in anger through the window of Tokarczuk's office when told he was being suspended.[45]

In Czechoslovakia, trials were still taking place for political offences during the Prague Spring. The sentences—up to five years—were mild in comparison with the Stalinist era. But the chances of legal rehabilitations were also very much reduced: evidence of trumped-up charges and forced confessions was no longer accepted as grounds for an exoneration. Meanwhile, priestly ordinations had been restricted again, cutting Catholic clergy by a tenth, and new measures taken against religious orders, whose members were again barred from teaching and forced to take ordinary jobs. Censorship had been reimposed on church communications, and the proportion of children attending religious lessons cut by half to around 22 percent, thanks to new pressure on parents. Atheist education and publishing had been stepped up, and plans laid to convert a former Franciscan monastery in Bratislava into a new Soviet-style 'museum of free thinking.'

Czechoslovakia's Catholic bishops had been warned not to condemn the new 'Pacem in Terris' priests' association, conceding instead in a pastoral letter that they would evaluate it 'as it contributes to consolidating friendly relations between state and Church.' Given that Czechoslovakia's four new bishops were members, the rest of the hierarchy had little choice. Other clergy felt no such constraints. 'Isn't it proof of a sick conscience on the part of these demoralised priestly personalities that you assure the head of the Church of your loyalty on one side, while showing disobedience to that head on the other?' the much-jailed Jesuit theologian, Fr Josef Zvěřina, wrote to the Pacem in Terris presidium. The bitter reproof, allowing for its contemporary terminology, could have come from the writings of Tertullian or Eusebius.

> You profess loyalty to the Church; yet you also let yourselves be manipulated for political aims, promoting the anti-religious praxis of the regime. What is lacking in your proclamations, and what I vainly seek, is any spirit of the Gospel.

Another prominent Catholic, Václav Vaško, showed how the association routinely cited Biblical passages, the Church Fathers, Papal encyclicals and Vatican II documents out of context to justify its stance. In its hands, Vaško lamented, *Pax Christi* (the peace of Christ) became *Pax Sovietica.*[46]

The new repressive atmosphere had pushed Christians to be more courageous. Some 250 Czech and Slovak priests had been secretly ordained, often in Poland and East Germany, under the 'emergency powers' given to the Church by Pope Pius XII. Many had obtained licences to minister during the Prague Spring, only to see them withdrawn again. One priest was told it was because he had imposed 'reactionary views' on 'progressive-minded citizens' in his sermons, and had also 'gathered and trained a team of servers' in his priest's house.[47]

Vatican II's emphasis on the lay apostolate helped justify the underground church; and here too, it was viewed not as a separate entity, just as a branch of the Church operating outside official procedures and structures. Small groups, or *krúžky,* usually of young, well-educated Christians, had begun to meet regularly after the Warsaw Pact invasion; and by 1975, the network was active in 150 towns and cities. It was helped by the Jesuit Bishop Ján Korec, who had been released from a 12-year sentence under Dubček but not recognised officially as a bishop. Korec had simply gone back to ministering covertly; and over the next two decades, he would personally ordain 120 priests. For security reasons, most were unknown to each other. But some received training at the secret headquarters of the banned Jesuit order above a second-hand bookshop in Moravec. Known to the StB as a 'centre for illegal groups,' this was watched continually, along with other known Jesuit houses in Prague, Ostrava and Brno.[48] But it received books and supplies from Czech Jesuits in Rome and Innsbruck, some of whom had been sent abroad to complete their studies, just as their Sixteenth Century English ancestors had been in the days of the martyred St Edmund Campion.

The Jesuits had been buoyed by a 1968 ruling from the Czech Prosecutor-General that their order still legally existed; and in 1969, the order's Spanish Father-General, Fr Arrupe, had visited the country on a three-day visa as 22 new members took their vows. The ruling was ignored by Husák's regime; and by 1972, most of the surviving Jesuits had been interrogated under their provincial, Fr František Šilhan, who had already survived a 25-year jail sentence. But they continued to print dozens of *samizdat* books—missals, lectionaries, theological translations—using typewriters and carbon paper.

Some underground activities went a bit far. One Czech bishop, Fr Felix Davídek, who had been secretly consecrated in October 1967 after a 14-year prison term, began ordaining married men to help the banned Greek Catholic Church and serve his own underground circles, or *koinótés*. Married clergy were less likely to attract the StB's attention, Davídek argued. But celibacy was unnecessary for priestly vocations anyway, particularly in the extreme conditions of communist rule, which looked set to last forever. In the space of five years, Davídek consecrated nine bishops. He also appointed a female friend, Ludmila Javorová, as his vicar-general; and in December 1970, Javorová became one of five women ordained by him in violation of Catholic teaching as an emergency measure.

The bishop was cautioned by the Vatican; and when he ignored the warning, he received an order banning him from further episcopal work. Davídek took no notice and went on ministering to the *koinótés*, consecrating a further eight bishops, including the Greek Catholic monk, Fr Potaš, who had helped preserve the remains of Bishop Gojdič, and a secret Jesuit, Oskar Formánek. The StB used the phrase *tajná církev*, or 'secret church,' in its files and knew the Church's survival depended more on informal communities like this than on official institutional structures. So it did its best to fuel distrust between the *koinótés* and other underground Catholic groups by tolerating some and suppressing others, and set out to exploit Davídek's rogue ordinations and consecrations to undermine the Church's canonical order.

Something similar had been tried in the Soviet Union, where a false Ukrainian bishop was said to have confused Catholics by announcing his own 'independent church,' arousing suspicions when he repeatedly criticised the Pope in his sermons. In his history of the Early Church, Eusebius had described how the regime of Emperor Hadrian had 'resorted to unscrupulous impostors as instruments of spiritual corruption and ministers of destruction,' using 'impostors and cheats' to turn 'those ignorant of the faith away from the path that leads to the message of salvation.' That would have been a harsh judgment in the conditions of the 1970s; and Czechoslovakia's StB eventually abandoned the ruse in the face of priestly resistance. But many Catholics believed Davídek's own obsession with secrecy and defiance of Rome had risked damaging the Church.[49]

The underground church sent news of religious persecution abroad, where it was chronicled by the veteran Bishop Hnilica in Rome via his bulletin, *Pro Fratribus*. Hnilica helped supply religious literature—some by car from Hungary, some on foot from Poland—and was estimated to have smuggled 100,000 books into Slovakia alone. These were used by underground journals such as *Orientáce*, compiled from 1973 onwards by Catholic clergy in the Spiš diocese, which in turn supplied information to other publications abroad, such as *Studie*, a Czech-language quarterly edited in Rome by Fr Karel Skalský.

How far did such efforts help preserve the faith among ordinary Christians? In Hungary, open religious life had declined drastically by the early 1970s. Religious classes had been scrapped at secondary schools, officially because parents and pupils no longer applied for them, while only seven percent of primary school children were registered for them, compared to 95 percent after the Second World War. Here too, the most dynamic forms of witness were occurring in underground communities.

The Piarist Fr Bulányi had been freed from a life sentence during the 1956 uprising, only to be rearrested at a Budapest tram stop in 1958. Bulányi had lost his post as a chaplain at Debrecen University for refusing to condemn Cardinal Mindszenty, only to see Hungary's bishops cowtowing to the regime; so his frustration was understandable. He had nevertheless resolved to continue his work when released again in 1960. 'My responsibility for others tortured me—I felt this responsibility, and it literally made me ill,' the priest recalled. 'Despite the permanent fear and constraint which hung like a lead weight over the whole country, the small communities tried to live their faith.'[50]

Bulányi responded to regime pressure by preaching a total pacifism. The world's power structures were inherently violent; so there could be no complicity with them, and that included the Church's own hierarchy. There was something in the priest's stance which recalled the vigour of the Donatists in the Early Church, who had rejected the authority of collaborating bishops, and of any clergy ordained by them.

Bulányi was so openly defiant that some Catholics suspected he might be an AVO agent himself. How could he act so provocatively unless he was being protected? Others believed his Bokor youth movement had acquired the features of a sect. But Bokor was only one of many small renewal groups at work in the Hungarian Church. Although they were careful to avoid any open political involvement, all faced continual harassment.

In 1970, three priests from the Regnum Marianum movement were arrested and charged with sedition, in what was to be the last major clergy trial in Hungary. In 1976, however, the State Office handed the Bishops Conference of list of 120 clergy who still had to be 'brought under control' because of their engagement with the 'base communities.' The vigorous pacifism which was Bokor's trademark posed a particular problem, since the communist regime had no clear procedures for dealing with it. Hungary's 15,000 Jehovas Witnesses were not recognised as a faith group, so they had already faced jail for refusing military service.[51]

In neighbouring Romania, even clergy recognised by the state remained vulnerable to sudden restrictions. Article 32 of the 1948 constitution, for example, stipulated that wages could be withdrawn from those who showed 'anti-democratic attitudes.' This was used regularly, particularly against Baptist pastors. There was a carefully choreographed ambiguity about the regime's anti-religious policy. Ceauşescu used Orthodox clergy against anti-communist Romanians abroad, arranging for loyal priests, some already agents of his DIE informer network, to be sent to bring *emigré* parishes under control. Ion Pacepa, a three-star Securitate general who claimed to have been a lifelong 'devout Christian,' recounted how efforts were made to discredit Archbishop Valerian Trifa, head of the 300,000-strong Romanian Orthodox church in North America, a man whom Ceauşescu branded a 'filthy reactionary swine' and ordered his agents to 'crush like a worm.' He also described how Romania's Jewish Chief Rabbi, Moses Rosen, was blackmailed into presenting a positive image of the regime's religious policy abroad after his wife was arrested in London for shoplifting.[52]

In 1972, Romanian state TV showed Ceauşescu attending his own father's village funeral, conducted by an Orthodox bishop with 13 priests. It was a show for public consumption. A year later, in a new show of strength against remnants of the outlawed Greek Catholic Church, a Bucharest lawyer, Maria Angelin, was arrested for assembling 'hostile groups of clergy and laity.' A violent search was made of Angelin's apartment, during which the police found 'objects and tools for illegal Greek Catholic activities,' including communications with the Vatican. The operation was codenamed '*Antidotul*' (Antidote). It was only one of several launched during the decade to cut the underground church's links with the outside world.[53]

In Yugoslavia, where several priests had been arrested for nationalism during the short-lived 'Croatian Spring,' a new constitution in 1974 reaffirmed the separation of Church and state. The Church had nevertheless benefited from a new *modus vivendi* with Tito's regime. Over 3000 students were now enrolled at its 46 seminaries and schools, while the Catholic *Glas Koncila* newspaper, launched during Vatican II, was now appearing fortnightly in 250,000 copies. It was published under the auspices of a regime-controlled theology society, the Christian Present Centre, which had become one of Croatia's largest publishing houses, issuing reviews and books.

There was a measure of free debate in Yugoslavia, even about communist anti-church excesses. Croatia's large Franciscan order had published a pamphlet detailing how, at the end of the War, 30 of its monks had been massacred at western Herzegovina's Široki Brijeg monastery for refusing to remove their habits and renounce their faith. All had been shot by communist soldiers as they knelt on the ground and buried in a nearby cave. The official media complained about the Church's influence among young people, lamenting how local activists persistently underestimated its strength. The Party had reason to be concerned. There had been signs that atheists were going back to the Church as part of a religious revival, and even complaints that Catholics were attempting to infiltrate the League of Communists. Some 200,000 people were now attending the traditional Assumption Day festival each August at Croatia's national shrine of Marija Bistrica.[54]

Even in Albania, the world's first 'fully atheist state,' religious life still survived. Enver Hoxha exulted regularly over his destruction of organised faith. But the struggle against religious customs and worldviews was not over, Hoxha warned: it was linked to the struggle for communism against imperialism, and it would still be 'protracted, complicated and difficult.' 'Was not a crushing blow dealt to religious dogma, that ancient plague, that poisonous black spider, in our country—in the most heroic, daring, wisest, best-considered and most skilful act?' the dictator enthused to his Party Central Committee in 1973, the year he was weakened by a heart attack.

> Was the abolition of the power of religion, along with its apparatus and personnel, an insignificant, conservative act? It was a centuries-old spiritual and material structure; and our Party and people destroyed this structure within a few decades. But the fight to eradicate this cancer from the mentality of the people is still far from ended. A cure for cancer has not yet been discovered, but for religion it has been; and if a struggle is waged in this direction, consistently and with conviction, the cure will no longer take centuries, just a few decades, a few generations.[55]

Foreign travel was not allowed in Albania, and permits were needed for cars, typewriters and refrigerators. Beards were banned as unhygienic—a ruling affecting Orthodox priests and Muslim imams—and in September 1975, a decree was adopted banning 'inappropriate and offensive names' which 'express nostalgia for religion' and requiring citizens to replace them with ancient Ilyrian ones. Placenames were changed at the same time—the village of Shënkoll (St Nicholas), for example, was renamed Ylli i Kuq (Red Star).

At least 20 prisons and camps were still being used for political detaineees here. At the Spaç labour camp in the north, where a rebellion was quickly crushed in 1973, many prisoners were killed in the local mine and their families informed only once their sentences had elapsed. Witnesses recounted how courtrooms were packed with selected audiences when religious believers were dragged in, and how chants of 'to the wall!' or 'hang the traitors!' were relayed over loudspeakers. Guilt was assumed, prosecutors given overwhelming power, and judges made to contend with the orchestrated baying of the mob, much like the procurators of ancient Rome.

Hoxha's anti-religious excesses contradicted the spirit of the age in Eastern Europe. They provoked incredulity, much as those of the Fourth Century Emperor Licinius were said by Eusebius to have done by reversing the tolerant policies espoused by his rival, Constantine.[56]

Even then, there were acts of courage. Lekë Tasi, an Orthodox Christian who had played the cello with Albania's State Radio Orchestra, was exiled to a remote village in 1975 as a suspected 'enemy of the people.' Tasi was also an artist; but the Albanian premier had personally rejected his paintings at his last exhibition in 1966. His father, a former administrator, had died the same year just after being released from a 20-year sentence. One of two uncles had died in prison, while Tasi's brother and sister had also served seven and eight years respectively. The sister was later rearrested. 'She failed to applaud when she was accused of "bad attitudes" at one of the village meetings regularly convened to denounce enemies of the people,' the Christian recalled.

> Locals attacked our house and smashed the windows. And when we failed to turn up for work, the police came and arrested my sister. They had wanted to imprison her anyway. In those days, we were all afraid of seeing cars with 'O1' plates in the village: these were the secret police cars

> which took people away. A new law later made it a civil rather than criminal offence to try to escape. But this was an act of trickery designed to identify disloyal citizens. Many young people were later killed trying to flee the country, and their bodies were dragged through their villages.[57]

Despite decades of 'communist internationalism,' national identities still remained strong. The 1970 Soviet census confirmed that three-quarters of the two million ethnic Germans still living in the country, half of them in Kazakhstan, still considered German their first language—a remarkable statistic for people who had been deported *en masse* by Stalin to compel their assimilation. Many were Lutherans; and in June 1976, the Geneva-based Lutheran World Federation set up a special council to provide Bibles and pastoral care for them via the Lutheran church in Latvia.

Latvia's own Protestants still faced harassment, with some ending up in psychiatric detention. In June 1971, the republic's Baptists founded a Riga publishing house, Khristianin, only to see it closed three years later in a wave of arrests. Yet the Baptists remained active, drafting petitions and highlighting social problems.

In neighbouring Lithuania, many Catholics had a natural oppositional outlook, having faced discrimination from an early age and been barred from studies and careers. Secular dissidents nevertheless complained that Catholics were too preoccupied with religious freedom, while nationalists from Lithuania's folklore groups championed the pre-Christian cult, Romuva, arguing that the best anti-communist symbol should be the dynamic, militant pagan symbol, *Pogon*, rather than the sad, passive Sorrowing Christ of Catholic mythology.

The pagan revival was tolerated by the Soviet authorities, who viewed it as harmless in comparison with the Catholic Church, which still carried by far the greatest patriotic resonance. After the dampening of national impulses in the 1950s and 1960s, most Lithuanians viewed the Church's survival as crucial to that of the nation. Paradigms from the Nineteenth Century were debated in Lithuania, especially events following Russia's suppression of the Polish-Lithuanian uprising in 1863. Similar dilemmas had been faced at the time by personalities like Fr Antanas Mackevičius, who had been executed for his role in the uprising, and Bishop Motiejus Valančius of Samogitia, who had organised the smuggling of books into Lithuania when its language and culture were banned by the Tsars. Parallel moral lessons could be learned from collaborators like Fr Petras Žilinskas, a late Nineteenth Century administrator of the Vilnius diocese, who had become rich after using the Russian language in his churches. Meanwhile, inspiration could also be drawn from the Church's many earlier martyrs who, like their Twentieth Century successors, had felt the pain of persecution for defending what they believed.[58]

When it came to nationalist feeling, Lithuania was to receive a rude awakening. On 14 May 1972, while US President Richard Nixon was visiting Moscow, a 19-year-old student placed his jacket with his name and address on a bench outside the Musical Theatre in central Kaunas, doused his clothes in petrol and set himself alight. Romas Kalanta, the oldest of three brothers, was a Komsomol member and son of a Party activist. He and his friends had apparently drawn lots to decide who should take the desperate action in protest against the suppression of Lithuania's national culture.

The student died in agony in hospital in front of his grieving parents, and Kaunas was quickly sealed off by militia with whips and clubs to deter demonstrations. But news of the spectacular suicide spread by word of mouth, and young people gathered with banned Lithuanian flags outside his family home. The house was ransacked by police, who removed his belongings and detained his parents, forcing his mother to sign a newspaper letter supporting the official version that her son had been mentally unstable and a drug addict. Meanwhile, the city cemetery was blocked off when Kalanta's remains were brought in a police truck and dumped in a remote plot.

There had been demonstrations in Lithuania before, particularly after the violence in Hungary and Poland back in 1956–7, and several Western commentators criticised the suicide and ensuing protests. After the relative calm of the 1960s, however, the incident broke the mould of peaceful dissent and appeared to highlight a still vibrant streak of uncompromising nationalism. Kalanta was said to have considered training as a Catholic priest; but he had no particular connection with the Church, which denied any involvement. Despite this, the regime now took new steps to use the Church hierarchy to tighten its grip on Lithuania's underground faith groups.

A month before the student's death, the bishops had yielded to pressure and condemned the Catholic petition movement, accusing 'irresponsible individuals' of fuelling misunderstandings and drawing 'pessimistic, short-sighted conclusions.' The petitions had shown Catholic unanimity against oppression; so this was classic appeasement. 'Order, unity, consensus, mutual trust, confidence in our supreme pastor, the Pope, and in individual church pastors—these remain the essential characteristics of our Church,' the bishops noted in a pastoral letter.

> But some priests and believers hastily and carelessly appraise diverse facts emerging from the particular moment of history in which the Church lives in our days... Without any legal right to act, such people take inexcusable actions, as if they were not concerned with the Church's future.[59]

The underground *Chronicle* hit back, urging the Vatican to stop appointing bishops who were 'subservient to the atheists' and make no 'diplomatic concessions' based on trust in the regime's 'good faith.' Only a few Catholic priests had read the letter during Mass, its editors pointed out, while some had done so but omitted its 'false passages'. In May 1972, a group of clergy issued their own declaration against the letter. Like the *Chronicle,* they too believed Rome was being misinformed.[60]

New arrests followed. In August 1974, a nun from the Sister Servants of Mary Immaculate, one of Fr Koźmiński's non-habited orders, was detained for helping print the *Chronicle*. Denied a defence lawyer, Nijolė Sadūnaitė was held for nine months and then sentenced to three years' hard labour and three years' internal exile. 'Today is the happiest day of my life,' the nun defiantly told the Soviet court, according to the *Chronicle*.

> For the truth, I'd not only forfeit my freedom, but also gladly sacrifice my life. Nothing evil likes to look at its own image; and that's why you hate everyone who tears off the veil of falsehood and hypocrisy you hide behind.[61]

Sadūnaitė had first become aware of her country's plight in the 1940s, when she had seen the bodies of anti-Soviet partisans dumped naked in the backyard of the police headquarters adjoining her family home at Anykščiai. As in the French Revolution, the KGB had watched closely to see who wept or showed signs of mourning. Sadūnaitė was thrown out of school for refusing to join the Party's Pioneer youth movement but readmitted on technicalities, before joining the Sister Servants in secret. She had taken copies of the *Chronicle* to Moscow, disguised with a wig and makeup, after being shown where to go on an initial trip by Fr Tamkevičius. She had lived with her brother so as not to endanger fellow-nuns, and had sent dozens of letters to other prisoners and exiles, encouraging them to keep their spirits up.

Sadūnaitė held her own against her interrogators, accusing them of violating the Soviet constitution's guarantees of freedom of conscience and being criminals themselves. 'Am I a devil?' one KGB agent asked her. 'No, but you serve the devil—lies and violence are the devil's weapons,' Sadūnaitė replied.

> I began by telling them I loved them like brothers and could give my life for each of them; but if I needed to tell them the truth, then I would tell it, since speaking the truth is the right of one who loves... Then I told them harshly

> that they were worse than murderers, since they killed what was most precious for a person—truth and hope. Lying was their daily bread… 'In comparison with the Lord God, a million people like you are zero, since he is with us everywhere. You think you rule, but in reality you've no power at all. God rules, and it will be as he determines.'[62]

The nun's relatively mild sentence reflected the fact that her case was known about abroad—it had been reported in 32 languages by Vatican Radio alone. But she was assured she would be destroyed by camp life and never return to Lithuania. The railway wagon transporting her and other women to Siberia was labelled 'Prostitutes,' and Sadūnaitė was denied treatment when she suffered a heart attack at Krasnoyarsk.

The Vatican was still being urged to replace Bishops Sladkevičius and Steponavičius, now in internal exile for two decades. The *Chronicle,* mindful of the fate of the Hungarian Cardinal Mindszenty, warned against this. Both bishops were uncompromised and enjoyed public respect, it insisted. For them to be 'pushed aside' would 'psychologically disarm' Lithuania's most devoted priests and deal 'an irreparable blow' to the Church. Both men, routinely shadowed and bugged, had vigorously denied acting or speaking against Soviet power; and Steponavičius wrote to the Lithuanian government in 1972 and 1975, asking to be reinstated. His requests were ignored; so when Sladkevičius was approached about a new church position, he turned this down in solidarity with his colleague.

Worried by the 1972 Kaunas disorders, the regime nevertheless took steps to drive a wedge between religious and nationalist dissent by relaxing some aspects of its anti-religious policy. There was no let-up in school atheism; but some religious teaching was tolerated, and 11,500 copies published of a New Testament, the first since the 1930s. A slight increase was allowed in seminary admissions and a few churches reopened; and in 1976, a group of Lithuanian clergy was allowed to attend a Eucharistic Congress in the US. Recalcitrant priests and parishes were no longer subjected to such heavy fines, and there were no more clergy trials or frontal media attacks on the Church. Religion should not be fought against with 'insults to believers' feelings,' explained the Russian-language *Sovetskaya Litva*. Such 'incorrect methods' merely incited 'religious fanaticism.'[63]

Both the Church's official administrators and the Catholic dissidents claimed credit for the new relaxation, while the *Chronicle* took it as evidence that conciliatory behaviour was self-defeating. 'We saw the "attitude of caution" in avoiding political and national themes didn't work with the Soviet government,' recalled Fr Tamkevičius.

> When our *Chronicle* started appearing, the government had become warier, but it still used repression. So it gradually dawned on us that we should be speaking the truth openly. The Soviet rulers had not altered their policy of persecuting Church and nation—this would only end once Lithuania gained independence.[64]

Whatever the relative merits of appeasement and defiance, the new policy was reflected by personnel changes in the Party. The Commissioner for Religious Affairs, Justas Rugienis, a coarse KGB agent who had addressed bishops dismissively with the over-familiar 'you,' was replaced by a suave historian, Kazimieras Tumėnas. At their first meeting, Tumėnas politely promised to help the bishops resolve the Church's problems. He accompanied them on pastoral trips and attended religious festivals, even appearing with his family at the 1977 Easter Mass in Kaunas cathedral. The change was cosmetic; but it contributed to some softening of the atmosphere.

Although ready to leave religious questions to each republic, Moscow had grown concerned about persistent demands for religious freedom in Lithuania, blaming them, in time-honoured fashion, on 'imperialist propaganda' and the neglect of atheist indoctrination. But it concurred with Tumėnas that traditional forms of repression were not the answer: they merely created martyrs, stiffened disaffection and damaged the Soviet Union's image. It was better to reward good behaviour with minor concessions and keep religious activities in the open, rather than fuelling potentially dangerous underground networks with nationalist links. Given time, this should do more to divide and neutralise the Church than ham-fisted crackdowns.

Arguments like these were gaining acceptance in the Soviet Party. Vladimir Kuroedov, Moscow's Church Affairs director, had concurred that penal sanctions should be reserved for 'exceptional cases' only. It was better 'pragmatically to prepare practically minded cult officials in spiritual schools than have to deal with illiterate fanatics.' The official media still talked routinely of 'religious extremists' and 'agents of imperialism.' But a certain restraint was now evident when it came to open anti-church actions.[65]

The Lithuanian regime was well aware that the diocesan administrators it had manoeuvred into position lacked authority. In one case, three outspoken priests had openly rejected an order from Fr Česlovas Krivaitis, administrator of the Vilnius archdiocese, to move to other parishes, objecting that only Bishop Steponavičius, the rightful ordinary, had the authority to issue such directives. In July 1976, the regime published its first survey of 'the status of religious confessions,' provoking a wave of protests against the restrictions in place. Party notables criticised the atheist propaganda currently on offer. It was 'over-intellectualised,' one official pointed out, and had failed to put forward a 'well-argued critique of Catholic ideological, philosophical, ethical and social conceptions.'[66]

Whereas religious *samizdat* had been stifled after just a few issues in other Soviet republics from Ukraine to Armenia, Lithuania's Catholic *Chronicle* soldiered on, undeterred by KGB efforts. Attempts were made to discredit Fr Tamkevičius and Fr Svarinskas by suggesting their material was distorted and fabricated. But repeated house searches and seizures failed to identify the typewriters used by the *Chronicle*'s editors. 'This publication does great political damage to our country,' Lithuania's KGB chairman resentfully confirmed in 1978.

> After being sent abroad, its material is used widely by our enemy in provocative radio programmes against the republic, in organising anti-Soviet slanderous campaigns against the USSR. Halting the publication and distribution of inimical publications is therefore one of the most important tasks of all security authorities.[67]

The Lithuanian regime had also been unable to prevent contacts with the Church in neighbouring Poland. Catholic clergy regularly managed to cross the border, bringing back whole bags of religious literature and devotional objects; and in 1971 alone, no fewer than 80 priests from Poland defiantly signed the visitors' book at the Aušros Vartai shrine in Vilnius. As the decade wore on, bishops from East Germany and Hungary made visits to Lithuania as well. Total isolation was becoming impossible.

Conditions were not dissimilar in neighbouring Latvia, where the Archdiocese of Riga and diocese of Liepāja were both run by a single apostolic administrator, Bishop Valerijans Zondaks, appointed in 1972 to assist the ageing Bishop Vaivods. Zondaks was also rector of the Riga seminary, which now had around 20 students, while Latvia as a whole was home in the mid-1970s to just 160 Catholic priests and 178 functioning churches. Despite this, human rights petitions were despatched with Catholic signatures to the UN.[68]

In Ukraine, where nationalist agitators were periodically arrested in western districts, Greek Catholics had been urging the Pope since the 1960s to give the exiled Cardinal Slipyi the title of patriarch, with spiritual jurisdiction over church members worldwide. Much to Slipyi's exasperation, Rome still feared the move would enrage Russian Orthodox leaders, and the cardinal was rebuked by Paul VI in 1975 for signing himself as 'patriarch' in correspondence. Moscow claimed to be leading a struggle against imperialism and colonialism, Slipyi had told his Church's exiled synod in November 1971. But the Church should wake up to the grotesque colonialism at work in his own country. He resented the way his priests were continually pressured to adopt Western Latin practices, and the way the Vatican remained silent when the Moscow Patriarchate denounced the Greek Catholics.[69]

Unusually for a religious figure, Slipyi had become something of a figurehead for Soviet dissidents. In December 1974, on his thirtieth anniversary as a metropolitan, he received a letter of congratulations from Solzhenitsyn and editors of the exiled journal *Kontinent*. But he had called the 1971 synod at his own initiative, without Vatican authorisation; and he would speak in his *Testament* of the 'bitter pain' he had experienced in the West, particularly at the lack of support from other Catholic bishops. In 1974, the cardinal recalled how his three decades as metropolitan had consisted 'of writing secret letters, penal servitude, hard labour, constantly moving from one place to another.' He had studied the work of Russian Orthodox bishops exiled after 1917, as well as of Early Church Fathers like Saints Athanasius and John Chrysostom, who had also continued their mission as leaders in exile. But he was perturbed at the 'negative attitude' shown by the Rome curia, at a time when he had done so much since leaving the Soviet Union in 1963 to assert his authority and maintain Greek Catholic unity. The adage *Nihil de nobis sine nobis*—'Nothing about us without us'—should be the guiding principle of Vatican policy; but it was not.[70]

As it celebrated the thirtieth anniversary of Ukrainian Catholicism's suppression, the Russian Orthodox church was in dire straits itself. It now had 18 dioceses in Ukraine, including five annexed from Greek Catholics back in 1946. But it had only one seminary: three others had been closed under Khrushchev. Meanwhile, Kiev's Pecherskaya Lavra monastery, taken over in the 1940s, now had only 43 monks, compared to 150 just 15 years earlier. In December 1974, Russian Orthodox believers sent an appeal to the UN, describing Ukraine as 'a centre of persecution and harassment.' The mood was clearly volatile.

Movements were growing up among Ukraine's ethnic minorities, including its Crimean Tatars, Germans and Jews, the last numbering 150,000 in Odessa alone. The Soviet regime had kept them at loggerheads, in line with its strategy of divide and rule; but they were now seeking a mutual understanding. 'Brezhnev does not speak on behalf of the decorative "Soviet people" or Russian people,' commented one samizdat journal, *Ukrainsky Vestnik.*

> The much-suffering Russian people speak with other lips, the lips of such patriots and humanists as Alexander Solzhenitsyn. Brezhnev speaks for Russian chauvinists... those multinational carrion-crows who croak the Russian chauvinistic song and lean for support on the new exploiting class, whose figurehead, the Party's bureaucratic apparatus, is armed with the predatory teeth of the KGB.[71]

From the vantage-point of East European Christians, perplexing things were happening on the international stage. There was talk of a new Liberation Theology, pioneered by luminaries such as Gustavo Guttiérez and Hugo Assman in Latin America, where the victory of Salvador Allende's socialist Popular Unity government in Chile's 1970 election had fuelled continent-wide demands for radical change. Allende had become the region's first democratically elected leader to establish ties with communist-ruled Cuba. His death in a September 1973 US-backed military coup had severely jolted hopes of a new era. But while Chile's Catholic bishops had sided with Christian Democrat opponents of Allende's revolution, the Church as a whole was divided. When the Vatican opened a nunciature in Cuba in 1974, radicals saw it as a tentative encouragement.

In 1971, the Church's Synod of Bishops had released a visionary report, proclaiming 'good news to the poor, freedom to the oppressed and joy to the afflicted,' and urging the Church to forsake its place 'among the rich and powerful.' The document, drawing on the optimistic language of *Gaudium et Spes,* demanded 'education for justice.' It also called for collaboration with non-Christians who 'in their esteem for human values seek justice sincerely and by honourable means.'

That May, the Pope had sent an apostolic letter to Cardinal Maurice Roy, head of Rome's Justice and Peace Commission, acknowledging the worldwide 'aspirations to equality and participation.' In a sceptical world, it was no longer enough to 'recall principles, state intentions, point to crying injustices, utter prophetic denunciations,' Paul VI said. What was needed was 'effective action.' Christians found themselves in diverse situations; so it was hard for the Church to offer a united message. They had to work out their own 'options and commitments.' The Pope condemned 'bureaucratic socialism, technocratic capitalism and authoritarian democracy'; and he regretted the 'rebirth of utopias,' which had helped create a 'dictatorship over minds—the worst kind of all.' He lamented how some Christians were 'reduced to silence, regarded with suspicion' and 'kept on the fringe of society, enclosed without freedom in a totalitarian system,' while others, 'tempted by radical and violent solutions,' wondered whether Marxism's historical claims 'might not authorise certain concrete rapprochements.'[72]

Cardinal Roy responded with a four-page article in *L'Osservatore Romano* marking the tenth anniversary of *Pacem in Terris*. He spoke of a 'cultural revolution' in the Church—a phrase borrowed from Mao Zedong's recent bloody upheavals in China—and described the doctrine of class warfare as 'the fruit of a lucid dialectic.' He also criticised John XXIII's encyclical for saying too little about justice and liberation.[73]

Many deeply committed Latin American Christians, both clergy and laity, would pay heavily for their defence of the rights the poor at the hands of right-wing death squads. Some of these could claim discreet support from conservative bishops and priests, who believed parts of the Church had become infested with Marxist subversives and needed its own radical purging. For communist-ruled Christians in Eastern Europe, however, the mentality and terminology of Liberation Theology were worrying. Had communist propaganda penetrated Catholic communities in Latin America? There were fears that ideological and political pressures had distorted the Western Church's sense of priorities and instilled a sense of resignation towards the persecution of Christians in the East.

An internal report for Poland's Bishops Conference recalled with frustration that the 1971 Synod had failed to 'show the right proportion' between 'manifestations of injustice in the contemporary world.' Many people in the Third World, lacking practical experience of communism, believed Marxism offered a 'vision of human liberty.' But even in Western societies which enjoyed civil and political freedom, the Polish report noted, Catholic clergy and laity could be heard 'arguing for Marxism.' They failed to see how the Marxist system 'carries within it a new form of human captivity, which goes much deeper than captivity in the capitalist and liberal system since it deprives people of their freedom of spirit.'

This 'conformist attitude to Marxism' had crept into Vatican documents as well, the report lamented; and the 'conspiracy of silence' about communism's crimes against the human conscience would only make communism more aggressive. 'Polish society is deeply sensitive, for historically determined reasons, to the attitude of the Holy See,' the report emphasised. 'What is most painful is that the Catholic Church is silent about its persecuted brethren... This is tantamount to fleeing in fright from a region where crimes are being committed so as not to be a witness to them.'[74]

Some pressures were certainly at work. By the mid-1970s, when a communist coup was attempted in Portugal, communist parties were doing well electorally in Western Europe. In Italy, the PCI won more than a third of votes in 1976, having already held power in half of Italy's regions, including Emilia-Romagna, where its activists had terrorised the Church in the 1940s. The PCI leader, Enrico Berlinguer, disagreed publicly with Moscow on key issues, including the 1968 'tragedy of Prague' and the need for national sovereignty in the communist movement. To the anger of more radical leftists, there was talk of a coalition, or 'historic compromise,' with the Christian Democrats. A home-grown terrorist group, the Red Brigades, sought to block the move in 1978 by kidnapping and murdering the Christian Democrat leader, Aldo Moro. A year earlier, Berlinguer had teamed up with his French and Spanish opposites, Georges Marchais and Santiago Carrillo, to enunciate a new concept—'Eurocommunism.'

Reassured by the latest pledges of benign intent towards the Church, many Catholics had joined the communist parties; and there was a growing literature on the conundrum of how to act alongside Party members while remaining faithful Christians. The French Cardinal Jean Daniélou, who had helped John XXIII compose *Pacem in Terris*, was a luminary in this area; and in December 1975, the Pope responded with an apostolic letter for Vatican II's tenth anniversary. *Evangelii Nuntiandi* recognised the 'profound links' between 'evangelisation and human advancement, development and liberation,' and drew particular attention to poverty, injustice and disease in the Third World. The 'economic and cultural neo-colonialism' which was now rampant could be just as cruel as the 'old political colonialism,' Paul VI pointed out. The Church's primary function was spiritual, and it would not 'substitute for the preaching of the kingdom of God a proclamation of liberation of the merely human order.' But it wanted a system 'more humane, more just, more solicitous for the rights of the individual.'

The letter referred to the 'drama of atheistic humanism,' and distinguished between a secularisation which was 'just and legitimate,' and an ideology of secularism in which God became 'superfluous and an encumbrance.' But it made only two passing references to Eastern Europe, where 'preachers of God's Word are deprived of their rights, persecuted, threatened or eliminated solely for preaching Jesus Christ and his Gospel.'[75]

Even with the Pope's careful qualifications, such texts posed a problem for Christians living under Marxist regimes, by appearing to bypass their objections and undermine their human rights struggle. The oppressed peoples of Eastern Europe and Latin America were like victims of fire and flood. They were aware of each other's plight, and could feel some mutual compassion; but their forms of suffering were so different that neither could experience much real empathy.

There were elements of *Evangelii Nuntiandi* which Christians in Eastern Europe could pick up on, such as its urging of non-violence, inner liberation and independence from political structures. Some contents were potentially applicable, including its summons to more effective preaching and a defence of popular piety. But others were totally irrelevant, such as the letter's call for Christians to use the media.[76] The document's general tone was more likely to bring comfort to collaborating organisations like the Christian Peace Conference in Prague, with its denunciations of Western imperialism, or the Berlin Conference of Catholic Christians, founded in 1964 to develop 'a Catholic doctrine of peace and social justice' in response to *Pacem in Terris.*

Groups like these were finding a sympathetic audience at the Geneva-based World Council of Churches, the main international forum for non-Catholic denominations. During the WCC's fifth assembly at Nairobi in 1975, the Russian Orthodox delegation rejected criticism of the Soviet regime's treatment of religion. Its position was quickly challenged by an appeal from Fr Yakunin and a fellow-dissident, Lev Regelson, which recalled how the Russian church had joined the WCC 'at a time of cruellest persecution of religion,' when Orthodox believers had looked to the Council 'to defend Christianity.' Yet the persecution had continued unabated, Yakunin and Regelson pointed out.

Yakunin's 'personal stance' was rejected by the delegation leader, Metropolitan Yuvenaly of Tulza, who brushed the appeal aside and defended the work of Kuroedov's Council for Religious Affairs. A similar statement was made by the Soviet Union's Council of Evangelical Christians and Baptists, who criticised their own breakaway communities for claiming persecution.[77]

Although several Russian Orthodox representatives later spoke on behalf of religious rights, a draft resolution on the issue was watered down at Orthodox urging, while the Moscow Patriarchate's external relations director, Metropolitan Nikodim, was elected to the WCC's governing body. It was another sign of the abandonment which many Christians now felt.

Notes

1 Casaroli, *Il martirio*, p. 18.

2 O. Mádr, 'The Struggle of the Czech Church: What we can learn from a theological analysis,' unpublished paper for 'A Time for Change,' conference at Ampleforth College, September 1990, p. 5.

3 Mádr, 'The Struggle of the Czech Church,' p. 7–8.

4 Streikus, *Antykościelna polityka*, p. 174.

5 Luxmoore and Babiuch, *The Vatican and the Red Flag*, p. 164.

6 'Document 161. KGB, 25 March 1974,' in Corley, *Religion in the Soviet Union*, pp. 267–9; Przebinda, *Większa Europa*, p. 168.

7 'Document 154. Report of Talks,' in Corley, *Religion in the Soviet Union*, pp. 258–60; *Katholische Nachrichten-Agentur* report, 16 March 1971.

8 Cardinal Achille Silvestrini, in Casaroli, *Il martirio*, pp. 9–10, 17; A. Kardinal Casaroli, *Der Heilige Stuhl under die Völkergemeinschaft: Reden und Aufsätze* (Berlin: Duncker, 1981), pp. 139–148.

9 Casaroli, *Il martirio*, pp. 43, 51–2, 71–2; Streikus, *Antykościelna polityka*, p. 172; P. Rauda, *Nežinomi mums, Viešpatie, tavo keliai* (Vilnius, 2000), p. 408.

10 Raina, *Cele polityki władz PRL*, pp. 65–6.

11 *Ibid.*, pp. 87–8.

12 *Ibid.*, p. 96–7, 101–2. The regime also expected Rome to include the Church's seminaries, religious orders, publishing ventures, properties and tax status as bargaining counters.

13 Miklośko et al, *Zločiny komunizmu*, pp. 284–5, 294.

14 Bozgan, *Cronica unui eşec previzibil*, p. 463.

15 *Ibid.*, pp. 282, 463–6; M. Ştirban and M. Ştirban, *Din Istoria Bisericii Române Unite 1945–1989* (Satu Mare: Muzeului Sătmărean, 2000), pp. 445–6.

16 Casaroli, *Il martirio*, p. 19; Casaroli's Warsaw speech in *Życie Warszawy*, 3 February 1974.

17 Mindszenty, *Memoirs*, p. 237; Archbishop Ijjas's letter to Imre Miklós, in

Havasy, *Martyrs of the Catholic Church*, p. 92. Miklós replied with a curt two-line acknowledgement that he had 'officially noted' the reservation.

18 Mindszenty, *Memoirs*, pp. 237–47. The cardinal bitterly titled this final section 'Complete and total exile'; Luxmoore and Babiuch, *The Vatican and the Red Flag*, p. 167–8.

19 Mindszenty, *Memoirs*, p. 245.

20 'Komunikat konferencji plenarnej,' 29 March 1974 and 'Przemówienie Prymasa Kard. S. Wyszyńskiego,' 7 February 1974, in Raina, *Kościół w PRL*, pp. 649 and 653.

21 Luxmoore and Babiuch, *The Vatican and the Red Flag*, p. 188.

22 Czaczkowska, *Kardynał Wyszyński*, p. 511.

23 D. Stăniloae, *Uniatismul din Transilvania, incercare de dezbinare a poporului roman* (Bucharest: Institutului Biblic si de Misiune al Bisericii Ortodoxe Române, 1973), pp. 207, 403; Bota, *Istoria Bisericii Universale*, pp. 515–6.

24 Courtois, *The Black Book*, p. 260; for Solzhenitsyn's speech, http://www.nobelprize.org/nobel_prizes/literature/laureates/1970/solzhenitsyn-lecture.html.

25 Przebinda, *Większa Europa*, p. 267. In neighbouring Belarus, native-language press and publishing were also cut by half during the 1970s; US Department of State, special report, January 1987, p. 3.

26 M. Mróz, *Z dziejów Rosyjskiego Katolicyzmu: Kościół Greckatolicki w Rosji w latach 1907–2007* (Toruń: Marszałek, 2008), pp. 312–3.

27 Dzwonkowski, *Za wschodnią granicą*, pp. 19–20.

28 *Ibid.*, pp. 200–1.

29 A. Solzhenitsyn, 'An open letter to Pimen Patriarch of all Russia,' in Maclear, *Church and State*, pp. 461–4; M. Scammell, *Solzhenitsyn: A Biography* (London: Paladin, 1986), pp. 764–9.

30 Przebinda, *Większa Europa*, p. 268; 'Document 155. Council for Religious Affairs,' in Corley, *Religion in the Soviet Union*, pp. 261–2.

31 Dzwonkowski, *Za wschodnią granicą*, pp. 177, 201–5.

32 *Ibid.*, pp. 231, 241–2, 257.

33 From *Lietuvos Katalikų Bažnyčios kronika*, no. 10 (1974), in Luxmoore and Babiuch, *The Vatican and the Red Flag*, pp. 189–90.

34 Wołowski and Korzeniewska, *Jak służąc Panu Bogu*, p. 39; V. Spengla, *The Church, the Kronika and the KGB Web* (Vilnius: Katalikų Akademija, 2002), pp. 45–65, 73–108; author's interviews with Tamkevičius, Kaunas, February 1990 and August 1991; J. Luxmoore, 'The Jesuit from the Gulag' in *National Catholic Register*, 14 July 1996.

35 'Document 173. Council for Religious Affairs, Moscow,' in Corley, *Religion in the Soviet Union*, pp. 294–303; J. Boruta and A. Katilius (eds), *Pogrindžio*

kunigų seminarija. XX a. aštuntojo ir devintojo dešimtmečio Lietuvos antisovietinio pogrindžio dokumentai (Vilnius: Katalikų akademija, 2002), pp. 706–7.

36 From *Kronika*, no. 36; *Radio Liberty Research*, 20 June 1979; Dzwonkowski, *Za wschodnią granicą*, pp. 264–5.

37 M. Lasota, *Donosy na Wojtyłę: Karol Wojtyła w teczkach bezpieki* (Kraków: Znak, 2006), p. 233; Isakowicz-Zaleski, *Księża wobec bezpieki*, p. 24; Czaczkowska, *Kardynał Wyszyński*, p. 378; D. Walusiak, 'Kryptonim "Wierni": Krakowskie duszpasterstwa akademickie,' in *Kościół w godzinie próby*, p. 152–3.

38 Dudek and Gryz, *Komuniści i Kościół*, p. 281; A. Friszke, *PRL wobec Kościoła: Akta 1970–1978* (Warsaw: Więź, 2010), pp. 37–41.

39 Dudek and Gryz, *Komuniści i Kościół*, pp. 286, 313.

40 *Kościół w godzinie próby*, p. 161; Isakowicz-Zaleski, *Księża wobec bezpieki*, p. 104; the Pijas story in J. Skórzyński, *Siła Bezsilnych: Historia Komitetu Obrony Robotników* (Warsaw: Świat Książki, 2012), pp. 229–42.

41 J. Wąsowicz, 'Jak gdańska SB inwigilowała duszpasterstwa stanowo-zawodowe,' in *Kościół w godzinie próby*, p. 356.

42 Isakowicz-Zaleski, *Księża wobec bezpieki*, pp. 177–84, 194–5.

43 Marecki and Musiał, *Niezłomni*, p. 530; R. Terlecki, 'Wyborcza fikcja: Wybory do Sejmu PRL w diecezji przemyskiej,' in *Kościół w godzinie próby*, p. 142; P. Raina, *Rozmowy z władzami PRL* (Warsaw: Książka Polska, 1995), vol. 1, pp. 147, 252.

44 P. Chmielowiec, 'Niewygodny ordynariusz: Rzeszowska Służba Bezpieczeństwa wobec ordynariusza przemyskiego Ignacego Tokarczuka,' in *Kościół w godzinie próby*, p. 129; Dudek and Gryz, *Komuniści i Kościół*, p. 316; A. Boniecki, *Budowa kościołów w diecezji przemyskiej* (London: Spotkania, 1980), p. 109.

45 Marecki and Musiał, *Niezłomni*, p. 549. Fr Pustelnik, a curate from Stalowa Wola, was suspended by Tokarczuk in 1975 after operating for the SB under the codename 'Igła.' He later changed his name while studying law but continued to work as an informer in Rzeszów; http://archiwum.dlapolski.pl/informacje/Czytaj-art-2761.html.

46 Svoboda, *Na straně národa*, pp. 88–9; V. Vaško, *Pátá kolona v církvi* (Prague: Pastorační středisko, 1996), pp. 16–17; Mikloško et al, *Zločiny komunizmu*, p. 290.

47 Fr Viktor Trstenský, a parish priest in Stara L'ubovna, in Trstenský, *Nemohol som mlčať*, 380.

48 Pavlík, *On the way to Jesus*, p. 37; Mikloško et al, *Zločiny komunizmu*, p. 302; author's interview with Bishop Korec, Nitra, 15 April 1991.

49 P. Fiala and J. Hanuš, *Skrytá Církev: Felix M. Davídek a společenstvi Koinótés* (Brno: Centrum pro Studium, 1999), pp. 121–3, 303; Eusebius,

The History of the Church, p. 108; F. Mikeš, 'Biskup Felix Maria Davídek, jeho multidisciplinární teologie a řád praxe' (http://www.elabs.com/van/fmd-emau.htm); M. Winter, *Out of the Depths* (New York: Crossroad, 2001); author's interview with Fr Dominik Duka, 10 August 1993.

50 Bozsoky and Lukács, *De l'Oppression*, p. 290; Havasy, *Martyrs of the Catholic Church*, p. 40. Only 117 of the 220,000 primary schoolchildren in greater Budapest were receiving religious education, according to a 1985 inspector's report.

51 Havasy, *Martyrs of the Catholic Church*, p. 73.

52 I. Pacepa, *Red Horizons: Chronicles of a Communist Spy Chief* (Washington: Regnery Gateway, 1987), pp. 282–6, 289. Pacepa, who simultaneously held the rank of advisor to Ceauşescu, acting chief of his foreign intelligence service and state secretary of Romania's Ministry of Interior, claimed to have prayed nightly and meditated until he could 'clearly see the image of Christ crucified on the cross'; *Red Horizons*, 113, 282–5. He defected to the US in July 1978 after President Carter's approval of his request for political asylum.

53 Vasile, *Între Vatican şi Kremlin*, pp. 276–8; Deletant, *Communist Terror in Romania*, p. 212.

54 P. Ramet, 'Catholicism and Politics in Socialist Yugoslavia,' in *Religion in Communist Lands*, vol. 10/no. 3 (1982), p. 263–5. Široki Brijeg, the site of the Franciscan massacre, is now far more famous for its football team.

55 O'Donnell, *A Coming of Age*, pp. 143–4.

56 *Ibid.*, pp. 131–5, 144; Eusebius, *History of the Church*, pp. 328–331. Eusebius's description of Licinius as reverting to persecution was almost certainly one-sided and inaccurate; but Hoxha's outdated repression was undeniably real.

57 Author's interview, Budapest, May 1996; J. Luxmoore, *After the Fall: Church and State rebuild 1990–1996* (Baltimore: Catholic International, 2000), pp. 305–6.

58 M. Sapiets, 'Religion and Nationalism in Lithuania' in *Religion in Communist Lands*, vol 7/ no. 2 (1979), pp. 79–82; C. Nikolajew, 'Zum Zusammenhang zwischen nationaler Identitätsbildung und Katholischer Kirche in Litauen'; PhD thesis, Faculty of Cultural Studies, Eberhard Karls University, Tübingen, 2005, pp. 73–7; Streikus, *Antykościelna polityka*, p. 187. Romuva was destroyed during the northern Christian crusades; A. Terleckas, *Didysis sąmokslas prieš Lietuvą* (Kaunas: Gabija, 1996). p. 49–5.

59 Quoted in S. Vardys, *The Catholic Church, Dissent and Nationality in Soviet Lithuania* (Boulder: East European Quarterly, 1978), p. 148.

60 *Ibid.*, p. 164.

61 *Radio Liberty Research*, 8 May 1987; author's interview, Vilnius, August

1991; J. Luxmoore, 'Restless Survivor,' in *National Catholic Register*, 24 November 1991.

62 Wołowski and Korzeniewska, *Jak służąc Panu Bogu*, pp. 83–4; N. Sadūnaitė, *Geborgen im Schatten Deiner Flügel* (Stein: Christiana, 1989), pp. 73–96.

63 Luxmoore and Babiuch, *The Vatican and the Red Flag*, p. 190.

64 Wołowski and Korzeniewska, *Jak służąc Panu Bogu*, pp. 54–5.

65 Kuroedov's speech to Lithuanian Party leaders, 17 May 1973, in Streikus, *Antykościelna polityka*, p. 189–91.

66 *Ibid.*, p. 194–5.

67 Quote from KGB chairman Juozas Petkevičius, in Spengla, *The Church, the Kronika*, p. 77.

68 *Radio Liberty Research*, 17 October 1978; A. Plakans (ed), *Experiencing Totalitarianism: The Invasion and Occupation of Latvia by the USSR and Nazi Germany 1939–1991* (Bloomington: Author House, 2007), pp. 282–302, 294–5.

69 Przebinda, *Większa Europa*, p. 162–3.

70 Pelikan, *Confessor between East and West*, pp. 173, 218. Slipyi deplored the lack of unity among fellow-bishops, a sin which had 'crept like a thief from the West into our suffering Church in Ukraine.'

71 *Radio Liberty Research*, 6 June 1976 and 6 October 1976.

72 Paul VI, *Octogesima Adveniens*, 14 May 1971, nos. 3, 32, 37.

73 *L'Osservatore Romano*, 11 April 1973; Luxmoore and Babiuch, *The Vatican and the Red Flag*, pp. 161–3.

74 'Pro Memoria Episkopatu Polski o sytuacji Kościoła,' undated 1974, in Raina, *Kościół w PRL*, pp. 682–7.

75 Paul VI, *Evangelii Nuntiandi*, 8 December 1975, nos. 34–9, 50.

76 *Ibid.*, nos. 37–9, 58, 73.

77 *Radio Liberty Research*, 23 February 1976; *Target*, Nairobi, 28 November 1975.

3 FALSE TRAILS AND NEW DIRECTIONS

> *As servants of God, we commend ourselves in every way: through great endurance, in afflictions, hardships, calamities, beatings, imprisonments, tumults, labours, watching, hunger... We are treated as impostors, and yet are true; as unknown and yet well known; as dying, and yet behold we live; as punished, and yet not killed; as sorrowful, yet always rejoicing; as poor, yet making many rich; as having nothing, yet possessing everything*
>
> 2 Co 6:4–5; 8–10

A LEAKED REPORT FROM Kuroedov's Council for Religious Affairs, published in the West, demonstrated that, even by the late 1970s, there had been no real let-up in Soviet efforts to stifle religious practices. The methods of control had outwardly changed. Infiltration and intimidation had taken the place of prison and execution; and it could be claimed that more civilised forms of atheist propaganda were being used in place of primitive Leninist denunciations. In Albania, where repression remained total, communist spokesmen had taken to attacking Moscow for slackening its anti-religious struggle, and were even fantasising about the Soviet regime allying with the Catholic Church to pursue 'hegemonic goals.' But the laws themselves had not changed—only their practical application.[1]

In Poland, Gierek's regime was still relying on disintegration tactics, keeping more effective priests out of major parishes, while backing more pliable clergy who could be blackmailed and compromised. 'At various stages, we can conduct policy more harshly or less harshly, acting sometimes with the force of logic and sometimes with the logic of force,' Stanisław Kania, a Politburo member, boasted to Interior Ministry officials.

> As long as the Church remains a monolith, it will seek a show of strength in its struggle with socialism. We have the possibility to oppose this. Such are the merits of the SB's operational work—its successes are considerable, though hard to formulate statistically.[2]

The Ministry's Department Four had expanded the range of its church monitoring. By 1977, it had 4500 full secret collaborators, with over 2300 clergy, a tenth of the total, in 'permanent contact,' many recruited during military service. In some Polish counties, the SB claimed to have its tentacles on up to a quarter of all Catholic priests. The key prize, as always, remained Poland's bishops, against whom compromising material was continually sought. One bishop was found to have received money from the government's Confessions Office. Another was said to be a paedophile. Meanwhile, the regime tried to regain control over top church appointments. When Cardinal Kominek of Wrocław died in March 1974, it rejected several candidates, including a Vatican-based bishop, Andrzej Deskur, before finally acquiescing in December 1975 to Cardinal Wyszyński's preferred choice, Bishop Henryk Gulbinowicz.

After two decades of conflict with Wyszyński, the regime had come round to the view that he was preferable to other possible church leaders; and in August 1976, when Wyszyński reached the retirement age of 75, it formally asked Rome to extend his primacy. 'At times of greatest weakness for our nation, your stance has revealed the patriotism of a Pole, love of homeland and understanding of our state's vital interest,' the premier, Piotr Jaroszewicz, congratulated the cardinal in a letter. He hoped Wyszyński would go on 'steering the building of the Roman Catholic Church for long years.'[3] It was a remarkable change of tack.

If the praise was something new, however, the regime still continued its efforts, using spies and collaborators, to undermine

Wyszyński's authority and set other bishops against him, while offering to help the strongest episcopal personalities—Karol Wojtyła of Kraków, Jerzy Stroba of Poznań, Jerzy Ablewicz of Tarnów, Herbert Bednorz of Katowice—break free from the Primate's control. Wyszyński and his inner circle of advisers were too adept for such attempts to succeed. The cardinal spoke openly and hid nothing. He also used the SB himself, such as by sending letters he knew would be opened.

The secret police could prove inventive. Several bishops were offered state honours to set them apart from colleagues, but cautiously declined them. Meanwhile, a magazine called *Ancora* appeared, allegedly put together by 'radical priests' aggrieved by their hierarchy's failure to implement Vatican II, only to be exposed as a piece of Department Four disinformation. Although the priority now was to avoid open confrontation, the Church was still denied access to radio and TV, and restricted in its educational work. Catholic teachers were no longer sacked for being religious, but for 'poor work,' while evidence could be planted to discredit the best seminary students by linking them with the SB. The police studied the methods of Catholic milieux such as the Oasis Movement or Kraków's *Tygodnik Powszechny*, noting how they acted to 'transmit Church ideology.' It knew the *Tygodnik* used 'the tactic of writing between the lines' and instructed the censors accordingly.[4]

Polish Catholics could be relieved the SB was relatively restrained. Young East Germans were shot and killed trying to cross the fortified border with the Federal Republic, while a Bulgarian writer, Georgi Markov, was killed in September 1978 while working for the BBC World Service in London, when a micro-engineered pellet containing ricin was fired into his leg from an umbrella. It was just one of several attacks on foreign-based dissidents by Bulgaria's *Darzhavna Sigurnost* and other communist security agencies.

In Czechoslovakia, the Salesian Bishop Štěpán Trochta, a veteran of the Mauthausen and Dachau concentration camps, had survived a 25-year sentence in six separate prisons for 'spying for the Vatican,' before being amnestied in 1960 and sent to work as a manual labourer. Allowed to resume his episcopal office at Litoměřice, Trochta was made a cardinal secretly by Paul VI in 1969, a nomination only made public when Casaroli visited in March 1973. A year later, Trochta died at his see after a savage police interrogation. His death was not reported in any Czech media, and Litoměřice was closed and tightly patrolled on the day of his funeral.

The repression continued. Fr Jaroslav Rusnák, a Bratislava priest who belonged to Pacem in Terris but was known as a good pastor, was beaten to death with a piece of gas piping by unknown attackers in March 1977. The following year, the StB found 80 handwritten manuscripts in the home of the secretly consecrated Jesuit Bishop Formánek, and took 90 witness statements while searching the homes of his friends. Formánek sent a protest letter to the president of Slovakia's National Assembly and was given an 18-month jail sentence for 'hindering supervision of the churches.'[5]

In Romania, Nicolae Ceauşescu's growing personality cult was boosted in 1974, when the Party boss was unanimously elected to the new office of President of the Socialist Republic. Economic problems were growing, as Romania's foreign debt mounted and industrialisation was hampered by a dependency on imported raw materials. But the relative liberalism of the late 1960s had been exposed as an illusion, designed to give Ceauşescu legitimacy. All possible resistance was now being swiftly repressed. Political prisoners were still dumped alongside common criminals in the notorious Jilava prison, where radiation was said to be used to cause cancer among inmates.[6]

In neighbouring Yugoslavia, the Croatian *Glas Koncila* and Slovenian *Družina* Catholic weeklies accused the regime of harassing and intimidating Christians, especially in rural areas. Religious life was still heavily constrained here. New laws, adopted in the wake of a revised federal constitution, tightened curbs on 'public activity by church functionaries off church premises.' Some Yugoslav republics went further. Serbia prohibited the circulation of religious literature other than on church premises, while Slovenia imposed a new ban on Catholic cultural and charitable activities. The Church succeeded in having some of the restrictions modified. In March 1978, the government of Croatia agreed to accept some 25 church-sponsored amendments to a new religious law, after an earlier draft was leaked to *Glas Koncila* and provoked public anger. Even then, Catholic clergy were still barred from ministering in prisons and hospitals, and had difficulty obtaining building and renovation permits. As in Poland, attempts were made to set church leaders against each other—such as the 'reactionary' Archbishop Kuharić of Zagreb and the 'progressive' Archbishop Frane Franić of Split-Makarska, who was an advocate of Christian-Marxist dialogue.

The ruling League of Communists had cracked down on its own internal dissent. The *Praxis* journal, which had tried to promote a 'critical Marxism,' was finally closed down in spring 1975 despite international protests. In a retrospective article, its editors lamented their 'mortal sin' of having 'taken Marxist ideas seriously.' Eight professors from Belgrade University's philosophy faculty were dismissed at the same time, despite protesting their loyalty to Marxism and devotion to the 'revolutionary character of the working class.' They too regretted their 'crime' of 'taking democratic socialism seriously.'[7]

Could such repression endure indefinitely? For all the continuing restrictions, pressures were again mounting on the international stage. The Soviet regime had warned of the dangers posed by the new concept of cybernetics, seeing it as an imperialist plot against progressive social systems. But there was no doubt the range of information and analysis about communism's inner workings had increased exponentially. The Brezhnev Doctrine, adopted after the 1968 invasion of Czechoslovakia, had shown communist power could not be confronted directly. But the gradual economic slowdown was fuelling domestic tension.

Most communist regimes had signed the UN's human rights covenants, highlighting the discrepancy between their public claims and their practical records. The International Covenant on Civil and Political Rights, adopted by the General Assembly in 1966, had added tighter safeguards to the 1948 Universal Declaration, spelling out in Article 18 that everyone had a right to unimpaired 'freedom of thought, conscience and religion' and 'either individually or in community with others, and in public or private, to manifest his religion or belief in worship, observance, practice and teaching.' The right could be limited 'to protect public safety, order, health, or morals or the fundamental rights and freedoms of others.' But the liberty of parents and guardians 'to ensure the religious and moral education of their children in conformity with their own convictions' had to be respected.[8]

In 1973, governments from East and West had endorsed detente by convoking a Conference on Security and Co-operation in Europe. The Vatican was represented; and in August 1975, when the CSCE's 'Final Act' was signed at Helsinki, it helped ensure that 'respect for human rights and fundamental freedoms, including freedom of thought, conscience, religion or belief' was listed as the seventh of ten principles guiding inter-state relations. Although highly detailed, the Final Act was 'politically binding' only; and while a following section, 'Basket Three,' listed 'humanitarian objectives,' this was replete with escape clauses and made no mention of 'rights' as such.

The Act was adopted as the US, humiliated by failure, withdrew from Vietnam; and there were fears it would merely sanction and legitimise Europe's geopolitical division. But concern about human rights had been growing, helped by the arrival of dissidents like Solzhenitsyn and Sinyavsky in the West after their release from labour camps. The detailed exposure of Soviet repression in Solzhenitsyn's three-volume study, *The Gulag Archipelago*, published in the West in 1973, had contributed to the steady abandonment of Marxist idealism and any talk of a 'grand theory' by Western left-wing intellectuals. Addressing the CSCE's opening session during the same year, Casaroli had welcomed the Final Act, predictably, as the 'first sign of European unity.' But other Church leaders were more sceptical. Cardinal Franz Koenig of Vienna, who had devoted a quarter-century to building Church links with Eastern Europe, deplored the 'confessional state of atheism' still reigning after the Act's signature. That October, the Pope himself spoke of Christians 'oppressed by systematic persecution,' even when this was 'disguised by categorical declarations in favour of the rights of the person and life in society.'[9]

Sure enough, the Soviet regime sought to deflate the Final Act's importance, claiming it was a diplomatic initiative only, which had to be 'read properly'—even that Brezhnev had been 'drunk when he signed it.' Yet its references to humanitarian co-operation were seen as a gain for beleaguered East Europeans. A Committee to Defend Believers' Rights was duly formed in December 1976 by the dissident Fr Yakunin, while other independent groups were set up to monitor Soviet compliance.

There was a high attrition rate. The secret police network was expanded in response; and over the next few years, over 40 members of the Ukrainian Helsinki Group alone were arrested. Although most went to prison, at least four died in labour camps. In March 1979, one Ukrainian monitor, Mykhailo Melnyk, committed suicide when the KGB confiscated the only copy of his unfinished doctoral thesis. The village funeral of the dissident, who claimed in a final letter to be trying to protect his wife and young daughters from persecution, took place under KGB surveillance.[10]

There was nevertheless a new sense of self-confidence—and it was being felt most strongly further west. In Poland, where Gierek's promised 'economic miracle' was breaking down through indebtedness to the West, dissidents talked of creating 'democratic spaces,' and looked to the Catholic Church for moral support. Some disillusioned former Marxists had already turned to Christianity, encouraged by sympathetic Catholic milieux such as *Tygodnik Powszechny*. The weekly, founded in 1945, had survived thanks to a judicious combination of courage and discretion. It had adopted—in the words of its veteran editor, Jerzy Turowicz—a 'religious and humanistic ecumenism,' offering a forum for non-Catholic poets and writers who 'felt an affinity between their own vision of the world and Christianity's.'[11]

In 1975, Polish dissidents from various backgrounds came together against a planned constitutional amendment, which would have permanently enshrined the Party's 'leading role,' as well as the 'socialist character of the nation' and Poland's 'permanent and unbreakable alliance with the Soviet Union.' The 59 intellectuals who signed the protest included three priests, Fr Jacek Salij, Fr Stanisław Małkowski and Fr Jan Zieja. All would go on to play opposition roles.

Gierek denounced the signatories as 'furious anti-communists'; but the amendment was toned down, changing 'alliance' to 'friendship' and removing a clause which would have made 'the rights of citizens' conditional on 'fulfilling obligations.' The veteran Catholic Znak deputy, Stanisław Stomma, who had so offended Wyszyński during Vatican II in the 1960s, was excluded from the Sejm when he became the only deputy to abstain on the vote of approval.

In June 1976, price rises triggered strikes in Warsaw and Radom, which were violently suppressed. Gierek again backed down and postponed the rises, suggesting industrial action could achieve results—but not before at least a thousand protesters had been arrested and several killed.

Fr Roman Kotlarz, a parish rector from Radom's Pelagów suburb, had joined the strikers on the street and staged prayers at his church for those sacked and injured. The priest's emotional sermons, denouncing 'lies and injustices,' were tape-recorded by SB agents, and the local bishop's office in Sandomierz warned by Department Four in Warsaw that his activities were 'harmful to the state.' That August, Kotlarz's housekeeper listened in terror as two unidentified visitors beat the priest unconscious at his presbytery. When he died two weeks later, in pain and with shattered nerves, the official post mortem blamed 'natural causes.' But Kotlarz's funeral, though swamped with secret police, was turned into a demonstration by mourners, who held up his open coffin to display his battered body. 'People today want not only money, bread, an apartment, fridge, television or car,' the priest, who came from simple peasant origins and had been moved from previous parishes because of his outspokenness, had told his followers. 'They want truth, justice and freedom. People want respect and are calling for it; and many are finding courage to declare themselves in defence of human dignity.'[12]

A month later, as more strikers were hauled before the courts, a group calling itself the Committee to Defend the Workers introduced itself with an 'Appeal to Society and Government.' This was signed by 14 opposition figures, including the ageing Fr Zieja, a veteran of the 1920 Polish-Soviet war and former chaplain to the wartime AK. The Committee, known by its acronym KOR, united its adherents around a common conviction that Marxist ideology had failed, and that a return to absolute moral values was needed to protect Polish society from decay and collapse.

In a 1971 essay, 'On Hope and Hopelessness,' the exiled ex-Marxist, Leszek Kołakowski, had argued that small, self-organising groups could create the rudiments of a civil society by undermining the state's monopoly on information and bypassing its control. Kołakowski finally rejected and unmasked his old ideology in a monumental study, *Main Currents of Marxism*, published in Paris in 1976–8. By then, he had come close to Christianity in his revised understanding of ethics and human motivation. He was far from alone. Another former communist, Jacek Kuroń, jailed for his critical 1964 'Open Letter to the Party,' had also had talks with Cardinal Wyszyński, describing himself in a *Znak* article as one of Poland's 'Christians without God.' It was just one fragment of a growing web of contacts between the Church and Poland's dissident fraternity.[13]

Two members of Warsaw's Catholic Intelligentsia Club, or KIK, Andrzej Wielowiejski and Stanisława Grabska, had also tried to provide advice and help for striking workers in the capital's Ursus suburb; and some months later, non-Catholic opposition activists were invited to a KIK session on human rights. The activists continued coming, making the KIK, to the regime's consternation, an important forum for opposition exchanges. In May-June 1977, a hunger-strike at Warsaw's St Marcin church in support of jailed KOR members drew together Catholic and Marxist dissidents, with a former Pax member, Tadeusz Mazowiecki, serving as spokesman.

Poland's Catholic bishops were voicing concern about issues well beyond the purely religious. They too had criticised the proposed constitutional amendments; and in June 1976, Cardinal Wyszyński condemned the suppression of the strikes and demanded an amnesty for those arrested. Social peace required 'an appreciation of the situation of hard-working people,' he warned Gierek, as well as 'satisfaction of their rightful demands, greater freedom for expressing their views, more honest information, and especially the restraining of uncontrolled police methods.'[14] Most bishops preferred overtly Catholic opposition groups who identified more closely with the post-War anti-communist struggle, such as a newly formed Confederation of Independent Poland (KPN) and Movement for Defending the Rights of the Person and Society (ROPCIO), which counted several priests among its members when launched in March 1977. But both Wyszyński and Cardinal Wojtyła had contacts with a range of dissidents and did nothing to prevent local parish rectors from providing rooms for their activities.

The regime was furious when the old firebrand Fr Zieja joined the KOR hunger-strike in Warsaw. 'We are dealing with opponents whose action is counted as a provocation—and who are these people?' one Party boss told the Bishops Conference. 'These people who've made themselves comfortable in St Marcin's church have gone there with political aims. Apart from one believing priest, they are either non-believers or Jews.'[15] Some bishops had doubts of their own about the protest. But Wyszyński valued KOR for diverting opposition functions away from the Church, and refused to intervene when other priests—such as Fr Jacek Federowicz, veteran of the post-War Lviv deportations—also offered support. The Primate knew that Kuroń, a former Party enthusiast, had 'once done great harm to the Church.' But now, though not a believer himself, Kuroń saw the Church as a 'great value.' 'It seems conditions of a century ago are returning, when the worker stratum defended itself against the excesses of capitalism,' Wyszyński told another KOR founder and ex-communist, Jan Józef Lipski, when he was sent a copy of the Committee's appeal. 'We need to remind the government strongly today of its obligations under the Labour Code, and build a sense of conscientiousness and respect for the working person.'[16]

Clearly, some common ground at least was emerging between the Church and opposition. In 1971, a young Catholic historian, Bohdan Cywiński, had published a study of Poland's turn-of-the-century intelligentsia, showing how Catholic and secular dissenters under Tsarist rule, far from being at odds, had been linked by a common 'ethical consciousness.' The work, published legally by *Więź*, had obvious contemporary ramifications; and in 1977, another dissident, Adam Michnik, set out an even clearer case for closer co-operation. Michnik, also a former Marxist, had been in Rome during Vatican II, where he had caused an impression with his passionate youthful views and political astuteness. Expelled from Warsaw University and jailed for his role in the 1968 student protests, he had spent 18 months in France at the invitation of the existentialist Jean-Paul Sartre. His book, *Kościół, lewica, dialog* (The Church-Left Dialogue), published in Paris, used the term 'lay Left' to describe Poland's non-communist left-wing tradition, and urged its present-day representatives to build tactical bridges with the Church. Michnik was critical of what he saw as Wyszyński's obsession with the nation's Catholic righteousness. But he concurred that religious rights were essential for democracy.

> I was not so naive as to believe that the Church would embrace isolated intellectuals as real allies. My intention was only to propose a new way of thinking about the Church and its place in the world. I wanted to familiarise a wider audience with the ideas of modern Catholic intellectuals. I wanted to suggest a new approach to religion... I had come to believe that interpretations of religion as 'ideology' or 'false consciousness' were weak and inadequate. The opposition would do well to understand religion as an absolute, as mystery, as *sacrum*... The opposition could survive, I felt, only by grounding itself in the culture at large.[17]

Michnik had written the book at Laski, a Franciscan convent and home for blind children near Warsaw, founded by the saintly Elżbieta Czacka (1876–1961), which had long offered a refuge and place of encounter for people of different ideological backgrounds. It was here, on relatively safe church ground, that Wyszyński had met Kołakowski in the 1960s. But the convent was hosting other curious visitors. The former UB director, Julia Brystigier, 'Bloody Luna,' who had personally tortured priests during the post-War years at Warsaw's Koszykowa Street prison, was one. Brystigier, a Jew by background, knew the Bible well. Although Wyszyński was aware that she had 'many human lives on her conscience,' he had presented her with a New Testament when they met on Good Friday 1949. In later years, Brystigier began visiting Laski, where she was eventually baptised, aged 73, donating money and receiving Communion daily until her death in November 1975.[18]

With its economic worries growing, Gierek's regime could do little to deter the Church from defending human rights, other than with the petty harrassment of police surveillance, property confiscations and passport refusals. It had to hold the Church in check; but it also needed, as one Party official put it, 'fruitful Church-state co-operation in realising important national aims.' These ranged from improved trade ties with the West to a full turnout at elections, which were routinely falsified and could be boycotted *en masse* by parishes and religious orders.[19]

The regime was still trying *ad nauseam* to use the Vatican against the Polish bishops, believing its talks with Rome would help sow divisions. In October 1971, it had sent a delegation to the beatification of the Auschwitz martyr, Fr Maksymilian Kolbe (1894–1941), whom many communists viewed as a Catholic fanatic and anti-semite. Meanwhile, it had again dangled the possibility of a Papal visit in return for improved relations; and it still hoped to get rid of troublesome clerics like Tokarczuk and pressure Church leaders into greater subservience.

The tactic had never worked: while it was obvious that the regime was using its Vatican contacts for propaganda, regime officials also knew the Vatican would 'do nothing to damage the Church in Poland.' Yet the rumour-laden contacts had created differences between the Bishops Conference and Rome. Vatican diplomats like Casaroli were certain Eastern Europe's communist regimes were gaining greater control over their own affairs, and concluded that the local Church should moderate its criticisms accordingly. Good working contacts with Poland, they still hoped, could provide a precedent for better contacts elsewhere. Gierek's regime understood this and did what it could to exploit it.

When Casaroli had visited Warsaw in February 1974, he had been received with full honours, but had still played his cards carefully. It was not yet time, he concurred, for diplomatic relations; and the Vatican's earlier agreements with Hungary and Yugoslavia could not be used as models. Each situation was quite different, and a Church-state compromise was needed first which would identify common interests. Casaroli agreed that Wyszyński's personal temperament posed a problem. But it was the Polish regime which had provoked Wyszyński's rigidity. It should now make concessions.

However sensitive his mission was proving, Casaroli kept the Polish bishops informed; and the result of the talks, in July 1974, was an agreement on 'permanent working contacts.' This had some publicity value for both sides. But it produced little of practical significance. The Vatican appeared to accept Wyszyński's insistence that a Church-state 'normalisation' should first be achieved at home before ties could be truly 'normalised' with the Vatican.[20]

The Primate's links with Rome remained difficult all the same. 'I've never talked to the head of the Church so polemically,' the cardinal noted after an audience with Paul VI in December 1975. He believed that year's much-vaunted Helsinki Final Act would legitimise the East-West division solemnised at Yalta in 1945. He scorned Casaroli's laudatory Conference speech as something which 'could have been said by a Turk or an Arab.' For all his negotiating skill, Wyszyński concluded, Casaroli had failed to understand communism and grasp the experience of local churches. There was still 'too much of the diplomat' in his stance, and 'too little of the follower of Christ.'[21]

There were people in Rome who shared Wyszyński's misgivings. 'Vatican diplomats must be followers of Christ,' agreed Cardinal Villot, the Secretary of State.

> They must speak courageously and not retreat too easily, knowing they have the bishops behind them, as well as a faithful society and often the 'catacombs of Christianity.' They cannot place the Bishops Conference in the background—the Vatican negotiator will leave and the bishops will remain.[22]

In December 1977, Casaroli's diplomatic efforts appeared vindicated when Gierek himself visited the Vatican. But it was little more than a media event. Although the Party boss, fearful of his country's worsening plight, gained some domestic popularity, the basic positions remained unchanged. The new opening to the Church had given 'orthodox Party members' an 'ideological hangover,' one Politburo member warned. It had also left them with a 'sense of being cheated.'[23]

Was Poland to be the perennial exception? Dissidents of different ideological hues, demoralised and silenced after the 1968 invasion, had also found energy to work together in neighbouring Czechoslovakia. On 1 January 1977, copies of a human rights declaration, drawn up to mark Political Prisoners Year, were handed out at an impromptu press conference in Prague. Only 247 people had dared sign 'Charter 77.' But the initiative had many more active sympathisers, ranging from devout Christians to committed Marxists. By the end of that year, despite vigorous arrests and house searches, the movement had issued over a dozen statements.

Charter 77 could place itself in a Czech tradition of small dissenting groups, including those of the Nineteenth Century Romantic era and the wartime resistance, who had sought to preserve national identity under hostile rule. Its philosophical architect, Jan Patočka, insisted its signatories were not questioning state prerogatives or claiming to speak for society. Their protest was founded on a simple conviction—that the state should uphold moral principles and observe its own laws. Patočka had studied with Martin Heidegger and the phenomenologist, Edmund Husserl, and been banned from teaching at Prague University under both Nazi and communist rule. The regime took savage revenge for his latest act of defiance. On 13 March, after a long and savage interrogation, the dissident died of a stroke, aged 69.

In his writings, which were quickly hidden from the StB by a group of youthful followers, Patočka had looked to natural law as a unifying thread between contrasting ideologies. Christian and Marxist dissidents could not wish away their differences. But they could learn to trust and think with each other, now that they were being harassed and persecuted together. 'There is no question that Marxism has failed—communist politicians have discredited it as a value-based orientation,' concurred one former Party member, Zdeněk Mlynář, who had helped pioneer 'reform communism' in the 1960s. 'Everyone now faces three choices: to become emptiness itself; to become a cynic—or to struggle against both by looking for values outside the officially proposed path.'[24]

Charter 77 was signed by a dozen Catholic priests and 15 Protestant pastors, as well as numerous lay Christians—some of whom, like the Catholic historian Jiří Němec, had been active in the 1968 Movement for Conciliar Reform, the DKO. 'Charter 77 does not speak about God or God's kingdom,' one group of clergy explained. 'But it is fighting for freedom in religious matters and in this way serving God's purposes. In this, we glimpse the future universality of Christ's kingdom.'[25]

To their dismay, Czechoslovakia's subservient church leaders reacted differently. Within two weeks of the Charter's appearance, several bishops had been summoned to the Ministry of Culture and a counter-declaration published in the Pacem in Terris weekly, *Katolícke Noviny*, denouncing the Charter's signatories for failing to acknowledge the 'positive achievements' of Czech society in building 'human happiness' and ensuring religious freedom. The bishops insisted they had neither written nor signed the text. But the ageing Prague administrator, Bishop Tomášek, went along with the government ruse. Tomášek had been made a cardinal secretly in April 1976, although the honour would not be announced publicly till later in 1977. It made his cravenness all the more shocking. 'Life in our homeland has been disturbed in recent days by what the daily press has published about a so-called "Charter 77",' the church leader noted in a separate statement. 'We want to make it absolutely clear that we, the bishops of the Czechoslovak Socialist Republic... declare with total insistence that we are not signatories of "Charter 77".'[26]

Despite everything, Tomášek remained the only bishop not seriously compromised by collaboration. He was, therefore, the only hope if the Church's authority was to be brought to bear in defending human rights. It was another 1968 veteran, the Jesuit theologian Fr Zvěřina, who took up the task of pushing him towards greater assertiveness.

Zvěřina, a veteran of Nazi and communist prisons, had spent three decades working out his own theology of persecution and forgiveness. He made short work of Tomášek's half-baked Biblical appeals, upbraiding him for standing on the side of injustice. He referred him instead to St Paul's admonition to 'take the helmet of salvation and the sword of the Spirit which is the word of God' (Ep 6:17). 'I urge you to listen to no one, myself included, but Jesus Christ—resolve to live in truth!' the Jesuit told Tomášek in a letter.

> Your statement was not inspired by the Gospel, but by the needs of shameful propaganda, by a hysterical witch-hunt against those who dared demand that the laws be observed... The Gospel spirit requires that the Church stand up for the despised and rejected, persecuted and defenceless, poor and slandered. So why are we taking sides with the powerful, with those who despise and slander others? How degrading it is that we have to defend religious freedom—irrespective of denomination—not only against the state but even against our own bishops![27]

Zvěřina's stance was mirrored by two Protestant Charter signatories, Ladislav Hejdánek and Božena Komárková, who sent a similar letter to the Evangelical Church of Czech Brethren, reprimanding its leaders for betraying Protestant tradition through their subservience to the state. Dissent was a Christian obligation, the signatories insisted—not 'a bourgeois liberalism which marks a lukewarm faith.'[28]

While highlighting divisions in the churches, Charter 77's moral challenge brought reprisals. In Slovakia, two priests were arrested and stripped of their permits after posting copies to fellow-clergy, none of whom received them. But the Charter also encouraged underground activity.

Fr Tomáš Halík had been elected student leader at Prague University's Philosophy Faculty in 1968, and had considered requesting asylum in Britain when the Soviet tanks rolled in. After a night of prayer, he had returned home, completing his studies and working as an assistant to Patočka, until he was sacked in 1972. With such a background, Halík had no chance of being accepted at either of Czechoslovakia's two official seminaries. So he trained secretly as a priest while working as a factory psychologist, and was eventually ordained on the quiet in Erfurt cathedral during a visit to East Germany. Returning to Prague as a secret university pastor, he helped host discreet seminars by visiting Western theologians such as Johann Metz and Walter Kaspar. He also joined another seminar group, 'Akademia,' in the riverside flat of Radim Palouš, a Catholic philosopher, which was attended up to 1977 by Patočka himself.

There would be many testimonies about Charter 77's impact in mobilising opinion. 'People had lived for decades under a regime which saw all morality as a remnant of bourgeois prejudice,' recalled the writer Josef Škvorecký, who had fled Czechoslovakia in 1968 and made the martyred Fr Toufar famous in a novel, *Mirákl*. 'They now began to appreciate a philosophical and religious worldview which stressed the unchangeable—the objective existence of good and evil, the presence of eternal truth.'[29]

One of the clearest testimonies would be provided by the redoubtable Zvěřina, who had signed Charter 77 as an expression of his Christian convictions. The actual number of Charter signatories was not important, Zvěřina insisted. As the Fifteenth Century Hussites had asserted, 'the numbers matter nought.' What mattered was that Charter 77 had truth on its side, and that most Czechs and Slovaks, whether overtly or covertly, supported it. That it had drawn together people from such different backgrounds—communists and anti-communists, Christians and atheists—also made it a vehicle for rebuilding national unity. This had outraged its opponents; but their crude hostility had merely given the Charter publicity.

Zvěřina was confident he could trust the communists and atheists he was now working alongside. The Biblical concept he used was *agape*, the openness and fellowship which could be shared by a community of the suffering. All opponents of communist injustices—from the Russian Solzhenitsyn to the Romanian Wurmbrand—had deduced much the same. The struggle against hatred and despair could be won—as communism's many martyrs had shown through their 'deeds and blood'—by asserting 'the free unity of truth, the unity of the powerless, of the poor in heart.'[30]

Personal conversions occurred under the influence of articulate Christians like Zvěřina. Eva Kantůrková, a writer and former communist, whose books had been banned when she quit the Party in 1970, signed the Charter a month after its launch. She compared the unofficial, close-knit society it spawned, with its 'sense of mutual solidarity,' to the early Christian communities. Kantůrková met up again through the Charter with lecturers whose seminars she had attended as a student—such as the philosopher Milan Machovec and existentialist Václav Černý. She observed how the harassed Charter dissidents were forced to 'look inside themselves for some stronger form of defence.'

Kantůrková declined to become a practising Christian; but she became a close friend of Zvěřina, and found an outlet for her reflections in an epic biography of the martyred Jan Hus (1369–1415), which she subtitled 'A contribution to national identity.' The Hus legend had contemporary relevance, Kantůrková pointed out, in showing how the voice of conscience could prevail over the voice of compromise and fear. Czechoslovakia's dissidents would not be dragged to the stake; but they would face much the same dilemmas as their tragic precursor five centuries before, or as the Biblical Eleazar, who had refused to make a show of subservience and empty loyalty.

> The burden of the years has marked us with the sign of this ugly event, and our utilitarian, lethargic nature makes us uneasy about Hus's action. Yet the question should not be whether Hus ought or ought not to have gone to the stake, but whether we who live after him could do the same thing too. Those who ask 'should he have gone or not' have

> already answered that he should not. But what Hus asked himself was only whether he would have the *courage* to do so. True moral integrity means making our decision when we do not know where it will end.[31]

There was no direct equivalent of KOR and Charter 77 in other communist-ruled countries. But some religious and secular dissidents now had some points of contact. In Yugoslavia, police detained and interrogated a group of Franciscan priests when they sent a letter to Czechoslovakia's Party boss, Gustáv Husák, protesting the mistreatment of Charter signatories. Mihajlo Mihajlov, a literature specialist at Zagreb University, defended the 'Christian worldview' against its communist detractors, and was compared for his passionate, visionary tone to the early Christian apologists. First jailed in the 1960s for an essay on the Soviet camps, Mihajlov was given another seven years in 1975 for 'disseminating hostile propaganda,' but released early and allowed to emigrate. He had also had to defend Christianity, however, against Marxist dissidents such as the celebrated Milovan Djilas. In Yugoslavia, whatever the moral imperatives of opposition, there was little if any common ground.[32]

In Romania, Ceaușescu had initiated his own cultural revolution after visiting China and North Korea in July 1971, insisting that all cultural life must have a 'militant revolutionary character' to ensure the emergence of the 'new man.' Talk of 'socialist humanism' was mixed with orchestrated shows of adulation for the Party leader. Yet there were occasional gestures of dissent. In 1977, the writer Paul Goma urged citizens to send letters of solidarity to Charter 77, for 'people repressed by the same evil.' The appeal was aired by Western radios, and Goma also wrote to Ceaușescu, denouncing the Securitate. Although he was arrested that April and thrown out of the country, other voices of defiance were raised. 'God preserve me those who want what's best for me,' wrote one young poet, Mircea Dinescu, 'from the nice guys, always ready to inform on me cheerfully—from the priest with the tape-recorder under his vestment...from those angry with their own people.'[33]

Dinescu's reference to spying priests was understandable. But not all Orthodox clergy had knuckled under. The evangelical Lord's Army movement, founded at Sibiu in the 1920s, had been outlawed in 1948, although most of its regional leaders had been freed under the 1964 amnesty. Orthodox priests were warned by their bishops against involvement; but the movement still remained active.

It was, however, Romania's smaller denominations who were proving most assertive in demanding religious freedom. Baptist communities had mushroomed, especially in Transylvania, and numbered some 160,000 by the mid-1970s. They were particularly disliked by the regime, which saw them as a Western fifth column. In 1973, a few concessions were made after Iosif Ton, a teacher at Bucharest's Baptist seminary, led demands for an easing of restrictions. Ton himself was moved from the capital to a small church in Ploieşti, where he was later arrested and severely beaten.

When Ceauşescu visited the US in April 1978, exchanging glowing speeches with his Baptist host, President Jimmy Carter, Baptist signatures were faked on an open letter certifying that Romania assured religious freedom. The ruse had little impact. Community members continued to face harassment—not least under a 1970 decree against hooliganism and delinquency, which prescribed penalties for groups 'expressing through their activities parasitic, anarchistic attitudes contrary to the elementary principles of socialist legality.' But outspoken pastors like Ton encouraged others to speak up. A month after Ceauşescu's US visit, a new Romanian Christian Committee presented an appeal to the Department of Cults, demanding government recognition of Greek Catholics, Seventh-Day Adventists and the Orthodox Lord's Army. Four months later, its members, Ton included, were arrested and jailed for forming an 'illegal group.' But the protest had taken place. It looked set to embolden others.[34]

In the Soviet Union, where Helsinki Groups had been formed to monitor compliance with the 1975 Final Act, the Catholic head of the Lithuanian group, Viktoras Petkus, was given 15 years' hard labour and internal exile in July 1978. But the group, which included an elderly Jesuit, Fr Karolis Garuckas, went on issuing statements. The much-harassed Bishop Steponavičius reported a slight easing of restrictions—although many fellow-clergy still feared links with him.

In Russia itself, dissent was mainly centred around the Moscow-based *Chronicle of Current Events* and prominent figures such as Andrei Sakharov. Brezhnev's new Soviet constitution of 1977 provided another focus for human rights demands; and secular dissidents were now raising religious issues. An Orthodox campaigner, Anatoli Levitin-Krasnov, circulated *samizdat* material on the Ukrainian Greek Catholics and asked Sakharov to speak out in their defence. Meanwhile, representatives of six denominations sent a lengthy appeal to the Supreme Soviet, urging it to change Soviet laws 'before it is too late.'[35]

The growing interest in religious rights was understandable. Lithuania's underground *Chronicle* continued to report all significant arrests and protests, while almost half of all priests signed petitions against the 1977 constitution. This made the Catholic Church a formidable opposition force. 'We need to unite currents of thought which regard Catholicism as the key to national salvation with those prepared to accept a nationalistically inclined atheism,' one non-Catholic *samizdat* duly acknowledged. 'No other force in today's world can help Lithuanians remain Lithuanian as much as religion.'[36] The *Chronicle,* for its part, was careful to acknowledge the contribution of non-Catholics: atheists and agnostics could defend the same values as religious people.

In July 1976, a new Lithuanian religious law had reaffirmed the original Soviet *dvatsatka* rules, barring priests from sitting on their own parish councils. Catholic parishes and dioceses were effectively recognised; but they had no legal right of redress, while meetings and charitable initiatives were forbidden if not directly related to 'performance of the cult.' Priests were still restricted to 'the religious associations which they serve.' They were not permitted to go on visits; and there could be no religious teaching of under-18s—any 'systematic teaching' of minors risked a three-year sentence. It was illegal, meanwhile, to 'lobby in an organised way' for changes in religious legislation.

There was, in short, plenty to protest about; and individual clergy showed little hesitation in doing so. One priest, Fr Virgilijus Jaugelis, ordained secretly in 1975 and quickly jailed, died of cancer after his release, aged just 32, having defiantly urged fellow-Christians in a letter to offer their suffering for 'traitors who have renounced their nation and God.' Another, Fr Antanas Ylius-Vilkas, threatened to burn himself to death, like Romas Kalanta, if the Soviet press continued to accuse him of 'committing atrocities' during the 1940s guerrilla struggle. The priest's former comrades had all been killed, so he had no witnesses against the media libels.[37]

In summer 1977, having avoided involvement with the petition movement, Lithuania's bishops and apostolic administrators pitched in by sending a commentary on the new Soviet constitution to Brezhnev. They asked him to drop the old Article 50 formulation—that freedom of speech was guaranteed 'in conformity with the interests of the working people and for the purpose of strengthening the Soviet system.' The clause gave privileges to certain citizens, they pointed out, while discriminating against the rights of others.[38] This was a significant initiative. It would have been unthinkable a generation before.

As Christian self-confidence increased, complaints also mounted about the Vatican's diplomacy in Eastern Europe. Would Casaroli rethink his strategy? Vatican II's Decree on Bishops had noted that the views of local ordinaries 'should always be especially taken into account' in managing the Church's affairs. The wily Vatican diplomat appeared to have side-stepped this, often offering little more than a terse communiqué that he had discussed 'problems of mutual interest' with regime negotiators. There was scope here for suspicion and frustration.

When Casaroli's deputy, Mgr Poggi, had toured Poland in April-May 1976, the Gierek regime had noted how current disputes over the projected constitutional amendments had fed into a wider political context, including controversy over Berlinguer's 'historic compromise' in Italy and criticisms of the Vatican's 'Eastern policy.' Poggi had accepted that religious freedom was assured in Poland 'in line with normal standards,' the Confessions Office claimed. He had also concurred that the Bishops Conference was attempting to secure 'the position of a political power'; and he had asked that his statements 'be kept secret from the Polish bishops.'

That may have been disinformation. Poggi had indeed shunned any contact with church dissenters and avoided sensitive topics—such as a recent violent police assault on Catholic parishioners in Kampinos forest, north of Warsaw, when they had tried to rebuild a chapel destroyed by the Nazis.[39] But the regime was clearly intent on playing up tensions. Rome now believed the Polish Church's 'hermetic closure to social-political realities' was 'damaging to the interests of the universal Church,' the Confessions Office reported.

> Relations between the Bishops Conference and Apostolic See are characterised by subcutaneous distrust, especially since the opening of permanent Polish-Vatican contacts... The distrust is mutual: the Bishops Conference jealously asserts its independence and exclusivity in shaping ties with the state, whereas the Apostolic See suspiciously observes the bishops' tendency to proceed in their activity without its participation.[40]

The same divisive tactics were still being tried in neighbouring Czechoslovakia, where the Husák regime had sought to use the Vatican to discredit and suppress the underground church. When Mgr Poggi visited in July 1976, the government itself arranged for him to meet three illegally consecrated bishops—the Jesuits Peter Dubovský and Ján Korec, and the controversial Felix Davídek—at Prague's Alcron Hotel. Only Dubovský turned up: Korec claimed to be on holiday and Davídek to be sick. It was enough, however, for Poggi to pass on an order for them to stop ordaining clergy—once again, the Vatican seemed intent on reining in the underground church in the hope of concessions for the legal church. This came as a severe blow; and even when the order was reiterated a month later by another Vatican diplomat, Mgr John Bukovsky, Davídek ignored it, insisting he would follow instructions from the Pope, not the Vatican curia. Korec complied, sending his students across the border instead to be ordained in Poland.[41]

In December 1977, the regime consented when Cardinal Tomášek, the 78-year-old Prague administrator, was named full archbishop and Czech Primate. Already a priest for 55 years, Tomášek had been in touch with Cardinals Wyszyński and Wojtyła in Poland. They had pushed him to be firmer; but he was viewed as a submissive old man. The regime had not allowed Tomášek any auxiliaries, thus ensuring he remained over-worked; and it had had little trouble allowing him to attend bishops' meetings abroad. When he had received his cardinal's hat, government officials had turned up for a celebratory reception in his Hradčany Square residence.

In July 1978, a new Slovak Church province was inaugurated, finally ending Trnava's link with the Esztergom diocese in Hungary. The reorganisation made little practical difference, however, to the lives of Catholics and was mainly used for Party propaganda. The man chosen to head it, Archbishop Július Gábriš, found his appointment blocked because he had made a critical speech at the previous year's Synod of Bishops in Rome. Beneath the polite exteriors, the pressure still continued.

Greek Catholic priests, ordained before communist rule, who had endured savage persecution in the 1950s and 1960s, were gradually dying out in Slovakia. Although the Prešov eparchy was now functioning again, several clergy had lost their priestly permits after 1968, while those still ministering were under tight surveillance. The veteran Bishop Hopko, barred from preaching in his native Ruthenian, had died in July 1976, after spending his final years touring Greek Catholic parishes under the watchful eyes of the StB. There was now no one to ordain new clergy in the eastern rite.

For many Slovak Catholics, the communist state's bitter vendetta dragged on. Robert Manca, a Catholic lawyer, had published a scathing article in the late 1940s, comparing the cases of Socrates and Christ to those of modern-day political prisoners. The regime had pulped the article, 'Two thousand years of political trials,' and ordered Manca's arrest; but Manca, tipped off by a sympathetic prosecutor, had fled from his apartment just in time, crossing a frozen river and making for Prague, where the Czech police had no file on him.

The article had been quoted by the defence during the 1952 show trial of Rudolf Slánský. Despite this, Manca had returned to Slovakia a year later after Stalin's death, marrying and taking a low-profile job. In 1959, however, a local official had come across his records and had him arrested. Although allowed home after a few days in jail, Manca had lost his job, only regaining respectability during the Prague Spring, when he was signed on as a law lecturer at Bratislava University.

His university career was again cut short, this time by the Warsaw Pact invasion, although he was allowed to stay on at Slovakia's Academy of Sciences. In the late 1970s, however, three decades years after his article had first appeared, it was shown by an archivist to the Party's atheism director, who proudly proclaimed the unearthing of a 'subversive Catholic reactionary.' Sacked again, Manca found a low-level job at the Health Ministry, but finally gave up working when a Slovak newspaper republished the article as an 'example of anti-communism.' His saga had parallels with *Žert* (The Joke), a satirical novel by the exiled Czech writer, Milan Kundera.[42]

Hungary's exiled Cardinal Mindszenty had died in May 1975 and been buried at the Marian shrine of Mariazell in Austria, bequeathing a legacy, like the Biblical Eleazar, of self-destructive but unbroken firmness. Four months later, a group of 300 Hungarian priests and laity had been allowed to make a Holy Year pilgrimage to Rome. That November, Hungary's communist premier, György Lázár, had been privately received by Paul VI. By February 1976, Esztergom's apostolic administrator, László Lékai, had been raised to full Archbishop. By April, all 11 dioceses had bishops. By June, Lékai had been named a cardinal in record time.

When János Kádár, the Hungarian Party boss, was himself received by Paul VI in June 1977, the Pope called it the result of a 'slow but uninterrupted' 40-year process which had 'brought the Holy See and Hungarian People's Republic closer.' Hungary's last imprisoned priest, the Piarist Fr Ödön Lénard, was freed a day later. 'Many are following this initiative and its results with a vigilant, often critical eye,' the Pope noted. 'But the last word will belong to history, after the judgement of our conscience.' Religious observances were at their lowest in Hungary—and Church-state ties at their closest.[43]

In Romania, where negotiations with Mgr Poggi had opened in January 1975, the regime's objective remained much as it had always been—to persuade Rome to abandon the outlawed Greek Catholics and recognise their merger with Orthodoxy. It was ready to allow the collaborating vicar-general of Bucharest, Mgr Francisc Augustin, a former political prisoner, to become full bishop. But it was confident it could put off other Vatican demands, such as the reactivation of suppressed dioceses.

Rome agreed to Bishop Augustin's nomination; but it could not agree to abandon the Greek Catholics, who were still, despite years of persecution, showing signs of resilience. In March 1977, four surviving Greek Catholic bishops had written to Ceauşescu, insisting they were not 'seeking privileges or favours,' only the rights promised to citizens under Romania's constitution.[44]

Such gestures of defiance would have been unthinkable in the harsher conditions of Albania. Even here, devotions still survived in private homes, while candles occasionally appeared outside closed churches. But there was real fear. Children were encouraged at school to report on any religious inclinations within their families; so great care had to be exercised in passing on the faith. Back in 1945, there had been six Catholic bishops and 156 priests in Albania. Of these, around 130 had been executed or died of ill-treatment.

Some three dozen Catholic clergy were still at large in Albania, however, including some ordained in the first years of communist rule. The risks were so great that they had to keep their activities secret from each other. Yet the blanket of silence was sometimes pierced. Fr Ndoc Luli was betrayed to police and killed in May 1980 for secretly baptising new-born twins for a relative. The babies were taken away and the mother given eight years' hard labour. A 74-year-old priest, Mgr Shtjefën Kurti, given 20 years for spying in 1945, had found a job in an agricultural warehouse after celebrating his last Mass at Durrës in 1967, only to be arrested again for opposing the demolition of his local church. Kurti was sent to the labour camp at Lushajë, where he was reported for secretly baptising another convict's child in a camp garage. The priest's trial took place in a former church; and in December 1971, he was sentenced to death and shot by firing squad for 'reactionary anti-state activities.' The Pope personally protested when the case was related by an Albanian refugee two years later. The state-run Radio Tirana confirmed Fr Kurti's execution, but insisted he had been killed for 'spying for the Vatican, Great Britain and the United States, anti-state propaganda and economic sabotage.'[45]

Article 53 of Albania's 1976 constitution guaranteed 'freedom of speech, press, organisation, association and assembly.' Article 39 stipulated, however, that 'priority is given to the general interest' and that rights and freedoms 'cannot be exercised in opposition to the socialist order.' Article 25 enshrined the state's right to manage 'the whole of economic and social life through a single and general plan,' while Article 37 reiterated that 'the state recognises no religion whatever and supports atheist propaganda for the purpose of inculcating the scientific materialist world outlook in people.' The country's 1977 Criminal Code, meanwhile, described penal legislation as 'a powerful weapon of the dictatorship of the proletariat' in the struggle against 'socially dangerous acts.' Any action aimed at weakening 'the organisation and direction of state and society' was punishable by 'deprivation of liberty for not less than ten years or by death.'[46]

Albania was an extreme case. Yet other regimes still clung to the view that the attractiveness of communist ideology was certain, sooner or later, to force a rethink by the Church. For all its showy condemnations, one Polish report pointed out, the Vatican had always negotiated and accommodated itself, in the end, to new regimes and social orders. It would do so ultimately with communism—not least since it looked to East European Catholics to buttress its position in the capitalist world, where the faith was steadily declining. Rome's room for manoeuvre was limited by its financial dependency on conservative church leaders in the US and Germany, the report continued. But it had sought to counter communism's anti-capitalist appeal by putting forward its own social reform programmes. These had found expression in *Octogesima Adveniens*, as well as in statements by the French Church, which indicated 'an acceptance of certain not clearly specified forms of socialism.' Meanwhile, its priority was to continue talks with the East European states, rather than with the Soviet Union, where 'tactically inconvenient' figures like the exiled Cardinal Slipyi had reduced the chances of progress. Every concession by an East European regime, by contrast, was 'an argument for concessions elsewhere.'[47]

Certainly, Rome's diplomacy suited the prevailing East-West detente, which gained fresh expression when diplomats gathered at Belgrade in October 1977 to review progress under the Helsinki Final Act. Yet for all Casaroli's hopes for an 'evolution in the system,' conditions on the ground remained repressive. The Belgrade meeting coincided with the fortieth anniversary of Pius XI's pre-War encyclical, *Divini Redemptoris*, which had branded communism 'intrinsically evil.' 'Profound changes' had occurred since the Bolshevik Revolution, the Vatican daily, *L'Osservatore Romano*, acknowledged in a commentary. Yet Pius XI's diagnosis still presented the 'exact criterion.'[48]

The Pope himself was still defending the policy of 'active and tireless, patient and sincere' dialogue. It was intended, he reminded the cardinals, to 'find a way out of a very painful situation and direct it towards justice.' Yet there was exasperation in Rome too. Vatican representatives at Belgrade attacked the mistreatment of Greek Catholics in particular. 'Has the time not ripened, is the historic evolution not sufficiently advanced, to abandon certain harsh practices from the past and hear the voice of millions,' Paul VI told the cardinals again six months later, 'so that everyone—in the same position as other co-citizens and in joint co-operation with all for the public and social good of their countries—may enjoy a proper sphere of freedom for their faith in its personal and communal expressions?'[49]

Certainly, the Church was safer now—other than in Albania. Priests were no longer jailed or shot by administrative order; they were merely harassed and intimidated. If no *modus vivendi* had been conceded, it was at least possible to speak of a *modus non moriendi*. Contacts with the West were no longer so exceptional, and the aggressive denunciations of the 40s and 50s appeared to have moderated. Though attaching high importance to official regime relations, meanwhile, the Vatican had never abandoned the region's unofficial church communities. Vatican Radio continued to broadcast to Ukraine and the Baltic states, while the annual register, *Annuario Pontificio*, still listed the banned Greek Catholic dioceses.

The real problem with the 'small steps' strategy was its very one-sidedness. It raised issues which were vital for the Church but had only a notional significance for the communist regimes, who could make tactical retreats when it suited them, but could just as quickly institute new restrictions. This inevitably curtailed the Vatican's freedom of action. It had to reward regimes which made a show of respecting the Church's rights. But it had little leverage of its own to ensure the deals and bargains were kept.

Lithuanian Catholics had long complained about the Vatican's policy of engagement. Rome sincerely hoped to help the persecuted church, the underground *Chronicle* conceded. But it lacked awareness of local conditions, so would always be outmanoeuvred. Everyone it had any official contact with was under the KGB's control. 'Do not believe the promises of the Soviet government because they will not be fulfilled,' the journal's editors warned.

> Because of the persecution of the faith, pastoral work is already partially in catacomb conditions, and the Soviet government, with good reason, is afraid of the underground because it cannot control it... Government-inspired priests attempt to picture this work as harmful, destructive of Church unity and damaging to normal Church-state relations. However, if the Catholic Church in Lithuania would not adapt itself to underground work conditions, she would be threatened by the fate of the Russian Orthodox church, which has been almost completely smothered.[50]

Efforts were made to influence the Pope via Fr Audrys Bačkis, a prominent Lithuanian in the Vatican's Secretariat of State. But while Casaroli himself never visited the republic, his determination to seek an agreement with its rulers remained undiminished. 'We knew at the time this was a mistake,' the dissident Fr Tamkevičius recalled.

> Casaroli considered it very important that a structure should exist, and every diocese have its own bishop. But we knew the diocesan administrators worked not only for the Church, but also for the KGB. Bishops have always enjoyed

> great authority in Lithuania; so a bishop collaborating with the KGB was worse for the Church than a vacant see.[51]

Was Christian life destined to remain moribund? The new Soviet constitution of 1977 had included a clause on 'the right to conduct religious worship,' but had also preserved 'the right to conduct atheist propaganda.' The imbalance was obvious; and perhaps because of it, dissident religious literature was expanding and finding its way to the West, often recounting mystical experiences close to the desert spirituality of the Early Church. Works from the epoch—Tertullian, Origen, Athanasius—could still be found in some public libraries, while many older citizens still remembered the pre-revolutionary religious atmosphere. Russian intellectuals detailed how their faith, inherited from grandparents, had survived the Bolshevik ravages and been re-nurtured by the metaphysical explorations of great writers such as Tolstoy and Dostoevsky, Berdyaev and Bulgakov. Figures like these, with their profound reflections on good and evil, had much to say to the Soviet generations. So did their modern counterparts—Pasternak, Grossman or Solzhenitsyn.

The regime could enforce its atheism; but it could not eradicate the religious accents and echoes evident in much of Russian literature. When it came to the values of integrity and inner strength, the religious and the secular could reach similar deductions. 'I do not know where I stand on religion,' noted the dissident physicist Sakharov, who had been brought up to attend church by his mother but given up praying at 13.

> I don't believe in any dogma and I dislike official churches, especially those closely tied to the state. And yet I am unable to imagine the universe and human life without some guiding principle, without a source of spiritual 'warmth' which is non-material and not bound by physical laws. Probably this sense of things can be called 'religious.'[52]

Prison and labour camp experiences were still being written about, continuing a tradition born in the days of St Paul and the martyred Perpetua and Ignatius of Antioch. Solzhenitsyn's *The Gulag Archipelago* showed how Christian martyrology had been recreated on a mass scale in the Twentieth Century, as a new mystical narrative emerged from the struggle with fear and uncertainty. It was one of many such works.

Tatiana Goricheva had helped set up a seminar group in 1973, sitting on the floor of a Leningrad basement flat. It had debated thinkers from Husserl to Heidegger, as well as the 'unassailable authority' provided by earlier Christian writers who had faced persecution in their own day. She recalled her own evolution from a 'destructive intellectual' with a taste for the low life, and believed she typefied a new generation which had shaken off the despondency of the past—a past where 'Sisyphus will endlessly roll his stone up the hill and humanity remain enslaved for all time by its corrupt actions, mistakes and follies.'

> The perspective of forgiveness and atonement, unexpected earlier, was suddenly bathed in full light. Christianity freed us from the oppressive karma of the past. Repentance and the confession of sins made possible what was impossible before. The past disappeared; it was no longer there... By the beginning of the 1970s, everyone in our circles was already a believer. Some had come to Christ after very complicated psychological and spiritual quests. Some had come too simply, because not to be a believer was already regarded as provincial and retrogressive. Being a Christian and being cultivated were thought to amount to virtually the same thing.[53]

Once arrested, Goricheva compared her interrogation to the tempting of Christ in the desert. She had taken the advice of Solzhenitsyn to avoid being drawn into talks with the authorities—to 'believe nothing, be afraid of nothing and ask for nothing.' The New Testament had advised persecuted Christians to be 'gentle as doves and wise as serpents.' Once in the KGB's hands, 'a world as cold as a nightmare,' she knew psychological tricks would be used to make her incriminate herself and others by manipulating her fears and weaknesses. The best response, Goricheva realised, was to use prayer to create an 'impenetrable field' around herself. 'When it comes to winning, the devil is always cleverer than we are,' Goricheva concluded. The wisest tactic, when fighting with demons, as the Church Fathers had warned, was to 'take no notice of them.'[54]

Zoia Krakhmalnikova was another who saw the prison experience in religious terms. She recalled how the Byzantine monk, St Simeon the New Theologian (949–1022), had warned against the 'mental demons' of fear and hatred. Fear could have a 'healing power' if it meant a healthy anxiety about the loss of inner freedom and moral identity. But it could stifle and suppress when it meant 'being silent in the face of evil,' losing the capacity for spiritual resistance. This was the fear which had held the Soviet system together—a loss of the notion that human personality had force and value.[55]

Nedezhda Mandelstam, widow of the tragic poet, was more pessimistic. She had agreed long ago with her friend, Anna Akhmatova, that the Soviet Union was witnessing 'the times of early Christianity all over again,' as the 'shadow of the future' hung over a world which no longer felt 'the cold mountain air of Christianity.' Like others, Mandelstam was haunted by the atrocities of the Stalin era, when her husband, Osip Mandelstam, long dead in the camps, had penned poetry about the 'meadowlands of eternity' blotted out by the 'clamour of fevered human strife.' She echoed Solzhenitsyn in deploring the failures of the Russian Orthodox church; and she was contemptuous of Western writers and thinkers—even TS Eliot, with his play on Thomas Becket—who had done little to preserve true values. Elderly people were still defending Stalin after spending years in his camps themselves. Perhaps, as the long-dead Dostoevsky and Soloviev had prophesied, all values would soon be wiped out in a triumph of 'gutless humanism,' which supposed that people, through irrefutable science, could rationalise history and foresee the future.

> This religion—or science, as it was modestly called by its adepts—invests man with a godlike authority and has its own creed and ethic, as we have seen... A good many people drew a parallel with the victory of Christianity, and thought this new religion would also last a thousand years. The more scrupulous developed the analogy further and mentioned the historical crimes of the Church, hastening to point out, however, that the essence of Christianity has not been changed by the Inquisition. All were agreed on the superiority of the new creed which promised heaven on earth instead of other-worldly rewards. The most important thing for them was the end of all doubt and the possibility of absolute faith in the new scientifically obtained truth... They had taken it upon themselves to overthrow the old idols—that is, to destroy the values of the past—and since the tide was flowing in their favour, nobody noticed how primitive their weapons were.[56]

Religious conversions had become common among educated Russians by the late 1970s. Although most new Christians opted for Orthodoxy, some began attending Moscow's surviving Catholic church of St Louis, opposite the Lubyanka. Grigory Lytinsky was baptised in 1978 while studying maths at Moscow State University and became a follower of Fr Aleksander Men, a popular pastor and Jewish convert. Out of the intense religiousness of the underground church, Men had succeeded, by force of personality, in creating an open Christian community of students and intellectuals. Like Soloviev, he was sympathetic to Catholic teaching, and had made it his aim to bring religion and culture, long separated by Soviet policy, back into a harmonious relationship. He was, as one follower put it, 'a lifesaver in a sea without beaches.' When his own mother, a life-long atheist, was on her deathbed, Lytinsky arranged for Fr Men to baptise her.

Another convert from the new generation, Irina Ratushinskaya, also made a significant contribution to the growing Gulag literature. Ratushinskaya, a poet, described elderly women, or *babushki*, from the dissenting True Orthodox church who had been in the camps for decades and still resisted any contact with the Soviet authorities—shunning, like the Christians of the Roman Empire, official documents and even Soviet money. Ratushinskaya was scornful of the International Red Cross and human rights group, Amnesty International, for apparently knowing nothing about these 'gentle, steadfast and humble women,' whose community had refused to recognise the regime-controlled church after the death of Patriarch Tikhon in 1925. 'Nobody but the KGB knows how many True Orthodox Christians perished in the camps,' the poet recalled.

> Even upon release, they would refuse to accept the document attesting to the completion of their sentence. Off they would go, without a single scrap of paper, heading for a new and certain arrest and sentence. From their point of view, this was perfectly normal: were they not suffering for God? In their eyes, it is we who act unnaturally: we submit to Satan and his minions—the Soviet government—in order to escape persecution. And Satan, they know, will never give up of his own accord—he will merely exploit any sign of weakness to his greater gain, penetrate ever deeper into your soul.[57]

Ratushinskaya got to know the Lithuanian nun, Nijolė Sadūnaitė, in the camps, and became accustomed to celebrating both Orthodox and Catholic festivals in various languages. She described how political prisoners were kept in a state of anxiety, in an effort to break them. 'Is it not pathetic that they have designs on our immortal souls?' she remarked contemptuously of her captors.

> But if you allow hatred to take root, it will flourish and spread during your years in the camps, driving out everything else, and ultimately corrode and warp your soul. You shall no longer be yourself, your identity will be destroyed,

> all that will remain will be an hysterical, maddened, bedevilled husk of the human being that once was. This is what shall come before God should such a creature die while still behind bars. And this is just what 'they' want.[58]

The poet detailed how she had found her way to the faith by 'talking to God' while belonging to the Soviet Pioneers youth organisation. There had been problems. She had never held a Bible in her hands, and it was hard to know whom to trust. Many Orthodox clergy were KGB informers; and if she had gone to a church, she and her parents would have been in trouble. Despite this, Ratushinskaya had nourished her religious awareness by reading writers from Pushkin to Mandelstam. Before her arrest, she had been married in a Moscow church by a sympathetic priest.

I remember an abandoned church near Moscow:
The door ajar, and the cupola shattered.
And, screening her child with her hand,
The Virgin Mother quietly mourning...
Must it really happen again and again -
For love, salvation and miracle,
For his open, undaunted gaze -
That here is to be found a Russian Judas,
That the Russian Pilate is reborn?[59]

New Christians like Ratushinskaya were ignored by the Orthodox church, which missed out entirely on the richness and depth offered by the reborn mysticism. Even in the worst conditions, however, the poet never lost hope, believing her own generation would come back to the faith, just as her grandparents' had abandoned it. 'The security which I felt in the labour camp—of knowing that they could only kill my body with torture, nothing more—was something which I'd understood theoretically before,' she recalled. 'But it was another thing to learn that this was actually true. They really *couldn't* do anything. It produced a special kind of strength, like imagining yourself flying, then suddenly finding that you are.[60]

How important were these creative conversions? Back in 1971, Paul VI's *Octogesima Adveniens* had predicted the 'retreat from ideologies' would create an opening to Christianity. In 1975, similarly, *Evangelii Nuntiandi* had acknowledged the yearning of 'intellectuals who feel the need to know Jesus Christ in a light different from the instruction they received as children.' Elsewhere too, there would be many stories of personal conversion against the background of ideological conflict. Former Marxists, who had once placed their faith in communism, were now turning to Christianity, with an understanding deepened by ideological disillusionment, much as the convert St Augustine's had been by Neo-Platonism. 'I had had no previous contact of any kind with religious people,' recalled Zoltán Endreffy, who had been a young leading light of György Lukács's Budapest School in Hungary.

> Priests had been put on trial for 'harming young people' with their 'clerical ideology.' But while reading about the trials in the official press, I'd never given them a second thought. I'd remained entirely under the influence of secular, atheist propaganda, seeing the Catholic Church particularly as obscurantist, retrograde and feudal... I now began to ask myself the question: what made these people believe? At first, I was mystified how intelligent people, in an age of science and modern enlightenment, could actually accept religious dogmas. But I came to realise that faith in dogmas was important. It provided a basic foundation for a believer to become truly selfless, and to gain the strength of conviction and capacity for endurance which made it possible to survive life's hardships.[61]

Endreffy gave up on Marxism and began 'seeking alternative directions,' having seen his system of beliefs shattered by the underground critiques of fellow-intellectuals such János Kis and András Kovács. He abandoned his post as a Marxist lecturer at Budapest's University of Technical Engineering and escaped to work on a farm, much as Tolstoy had once done, where he was converted to Christianity by reading Rousseau, Dostoevsky, Simone Weil and Albert Schweitzer, as well as Hungarian Christian poets such as Mihály Babits and János Pilinszky. Finally, after studying at the capital's Academy of Catholic Theology, to the astonishment of former colleagues, he was formally received into the Catholic Church.

The turning to religion, particularly at this level, posed problems for the communist regimes. They were ready to maintain the churches as museums and tourist attractions, but not as living social and cultural forces; and they responded, predictably, with a mixture of restrictions and carefully calibrated concessions.

Hungary's Catholic Church had a passable infrastructure. Its eight schools and six seminaries were turning out recruits for the priesthood, while its dioceses had resident bishops most of the time. But the documents of Vatican II had been published here only in 1975, while it had taken four years to release a new Bible translation. The Church had clearly become, through its subservient leaders, part of the 'system of compromises,' in a society lulled into quiescence by Hungary's consumerist 'goulash communism.' This is what had so outraged the late Cardinal Mindszenty, who had lambasted the Church as a 'living organism without a head, marked more by mediocrity than by cowardice.'[62]

The Kádár regime felt sufficiently in control to allow Hungary's Catholic bishops to pay an *ad limina* visit to the Vatican in April 1977, and to circulate a pastoral letter against abortion a year later. It permitted the US evangelist, Billy Graham, to visit Protestant communities in the country, and tolerated some discussion of the merits of religion versus atheism. In summer 1978, over 140 students were allowed to enrol in a three-year correspondence course at Budapest's musty Theology Academy, run by the veteran Fr Tamás Nyíri. Yet the government's church affairs director, Imre Miklós, remained firm: while accepting religion as a 'natural phenomenon' in the evolution to a communist society, the regime had 'absolutely not abandoned' its struggle against it.[63]

These were views from the centre. At local level, not everyone was docile. The parish system still functioned in Hungary, though hemmed in with restrictions, while local churches remained open for worship, albeit with shrinking congregations. Beneath the surface of daily life, local clergy often found themselves, as in Poland, locked in a struggle with Party officials to undermine each other's influence. The Party controlled law and administration, education and the media; but some priests fought back in a low-profile resistance from below, playing the system and blocking Party directives.

The Interior Ministry still saw the Church as a danger. Its third department had 421 agents for monitoring clergy, only just below the numbers deployed for youth and culture. Miklós's Office for Church Affairs, the AEH, also had branches in every county to enforce the Party's wishes. It could count on the bishops to transfer or discipline recalcitrant priests, thus avoiding the need to arrest them. If further trouble occurred, it was easy to blame 'reactionary forces abroad' for disturbing the otherwise calm Church-state relationship. 'In the overwhelming majority of cases, the suppression of reactionary forces is being realised by employing political means, with the collaboration of loyal forces and fundamentally as an internal matter for the churches,' one senior official, Szilveszter Harangozó, reported to police chiefs.

> The reactionaries have not been able to create a significant base in clerical or lay circles, or to produce tensions over the question of human rights and freedom of religion such that these would grow into a significant socio-political problem. We have successfully obstructed them in the training of 'standard-bearers,' or leading personalities, capable of uniting their forces.[64]

The reality was not quite so tidy. The frustration was clearly building. In a 1978 memorandum, members of Hungary's Reformed church accused the state of 'turning church leaders into state officials' and training pastors 'to preach political sermons.' The document dismissed the church's election system as a 'comedy' and accused Reformed leaders of 'working against the church's true interests.'[65] Despite secret police pressure, the Greek Catholic church's banned Basilian order was still active in Hungary with over 30 members. Meanwhile, a real sense of religious dynamism was being provided by the 'base communities,' who now claimed some 50,000 members, a statistic rivalling any in Latin America.

Youth pastoral work, forbidden in the 1960s, had been partially tolerated in the 1970s; and Western movements such as Focolare and Charismatic Renewal had reached Hungary, alongside the home-grown Regnum Marianum and Fr Bulányi's Bokor group. Bokor's pacifism was causing problems. Whereas Article 63 of the Hungarian constitution upheld freedom of conscience, Article 70 required military service; so the issue was unclear. The Bishops Conference had ruled it illegitimate to refuse the draft, citing *Gaudium et Spes*. But it had appealed for tolerance towards those who did so.

The hands-on religiousness of the base communities was distinct from the traditional Christianity of the countryside, and the regime was duly concerned. Every Regnum Marianum priest had been jailed at some stage; but many had come to view life on the margins as an opportunity for spiritual development. In 1976, when Miklós's Office had handed the Bishops Conference its list of 120 Catholic clergy who were 'doing harm' through the communities, the reactions had varied. While some bishops had declined to accept the list, others issued warnings and moved their blacklisted clergy to quieter parishes.

Fr Miklós Blanckenstein was one of those who avoided being silenced. As a youth member of Regnum Marianum, founded in the 1890s by the reformist Bishop Prohászka, he had grown up in the humanist tradition of Hungarian Catholicism, which had responded to secularisation by supporting social reform. Stifled during Béla Kun's short-lived revolutionary dictatorship, the movement had revived in the 1930s, before being driven back underground under communist rule. By the time Blanckenstein was ordained, after studying at the Piarist order's Budapest academy, movements like Regnum—which used the name bestowed on Hungary by its founder, St Stephen—had created a dynamic Catholic counter-culture, in contrast to the stuffy compromise politics of the church hierarchy. Blanckenstein's younger brother was a priest as well. 'With materialism taking its toll, encouraged by the state, the Church badly needed new clergy,' he later recalled. 'Since the hierarchy was unable to build a Christian community here, laypeople had to build it themselves, helped by a few dedicated clergy. Such people rarely bothered to oppose the bishops—they just got used to coping on their own.'[66]

Where would such initiatives lead? In East Germany, regime officials promised to lift some religious restrictions during a March 1978 meeting with Evangelical church leaders under their chairman, Albrecht Schönherr. The churches were already relatively free here, at least when it came to social and charitable work, while religious buildings had been restored and religious literature imported from abroad. They had reciprocated by helping develop a distinctive East German identity, which drew on a traditional Protestant respect for governmental authority. The aim had been summed up by Bishop Hartmut Mitzenheim, a long-serving Evangelical leader in Thuringia—'not to be a church against socialism, but a church for the citizens of the GDR who, without violating their consciences, are and wish to remain Christian in a socialist society.'[67]

There had been local problems, however, as clergy protested against militarisation and defended conscientious objection. The smaller Catholic Church, under its now-ailing leader, Cardinal Alfred Bengsch, who had played a leading role at Vatican II, had never formally recognised the GDR. Nor had it adjusted its diocesan boundaries to those of the communist state. Catholics routinely boycotted official institutions, making clergy and laity targets for repression. The absence of Catholic bishops from state ceremonies was admired by foreign diplomats for very publicly de-legitimising the system.

Elsewhere, the plight of Christians still varied. In Bulgaria, the Catholic Church now had only 40 priests, compared to 1237 in the 1940s. In Yugoslavia, a new Croatian law decreed that religious activities should not be 'in contradiction with the state's ideology, constitution and laws.' The previous law of 1953 had required them to be 'in conformity'; so this was an abstract but significant change. A few concessions followed. The Macedonian-Albanian nun, Mother Teresa of Calcutta, was allowed to open a children's home in Zagreb, and there was talk of opening others in her native Skopje and Kosovo. Meanwhile, more Party intellectuals were questioning whether eliminating religion was really a firm communist aim, or just a hypothesis of Marxist theory. If Marxism's real purpose was the transformation to a classless society, then plenty of religious people were co-operating in the task and deserved respect.[68]

Archbishop Kuharić of Zagreb, who had narrowly escaped being murdered by a communist death squad back in the 1940s, had nevertheless assertively defended religious freedom during public discussions of the Croatian law, accusing the now-frail Tito's officials of violating Christian rights. So had his Slovene counterpart, Archbishop Jožef Pogačnik, who had protested when bugging devices were found in his residence. If Marxism was taught at state schools, Pogačnik insisted, religion should be taught as well. 'If religion is a private affair, then so too is atheism,' the Slovene archbishop declared. 'It offends the rights of parents when schoolbooks present a false, "clerical" picture of Christianity.'[69]

Romania had been granted special trade status in 1975 by the US Administration to encourage its show of independence from Moscow. It communist dictator, however, far from modifying his views, had called for an intensified struggle against organised religion. 'Freedom of religious beliefs is one thing,' Ceaușescu told his Party congress. 'The Party's activities in promoting its revolutionary philosophy of nature and society are another.'[70] Party theorists were mobilised. The only valid freedom was 'freedom from God and freedom from transcendence,' one of them reminded activists.

> A man cannot be called free if there lingers in his consciousness the conviction that history is not the result of laws of social development, of class struggle, but of a divine plan, beside which human beings can only be docile performers, mere objects and not subjects.[71]

The population of Bucharest had doubled since 1945; but only a single new Orthodox church had been built in the city under communist rule. Even then, there were complaints that atheist work was not carrying enough weight in schools, and that anti-religious campaigners were often made to feel inferior beside religious pupils. Party members were said to attend church services to avoid trouble with their families and communities, especially in villages where traditional social structures had not been entirely destroyed. Meanwhile, Party experts acknowledged that the 'spiritual dissatisfaction' brought on by industrialisation had tended to encourage 'mystical obscurantist behavior,' while little had been done in Romania to promote non-religious ceremonies as an alternative.[72]

'Spiritual dissatisfaction' had undoubtedly contributed to the spread of smaller religious groups. This was fuelled by provocative incidents, such as when Filip Dinca, an outspoken Baptist pastor from Bucharest, was run down and killed by a Securitate car in May 1977.

Among Catholics, meanwhile, there was talk of a new measure of tolerance. Up to 500 Greek Catholic priests remained active in Romania, and legal associations dealing with history, literature and philology were doing much to keep Greek Catholic culture alive. Masses were sometimes conducted in private houses without police harassment—perhaps in a bid to appease educated

Greek Catholics and attract them into collaborating. A print-run of 10,000 New Testaments, the first since the 1940s, was imported from Paris. Yet underground church life showed little sign of petering out. In March 1978, an underground journal, *Biserica din Catacombe*, began arriving at private addresses. Edited in Cluj by a lay engineer, Mihai Pop, this was the work of a 'Committee to Save the Church United with Rome.'

Although officially tolerated, the Latin Catholic Church still had no legal status, for all Casaroli's diplomacy, and had seen three of its five dioceses abolished for failing to muster the 750,000 members required by the regime. Ironically, Ceauşescu had banned abortion and discouraged divorce, in an autarchic effort to boost Romania's birthrate. But there was no meeting of minds with Catholic leaders. The Church's only recognised bishop, Antal Jakab, an Alba Iulia auxiliary, had suffered brain damage from 13 years of prison beatings. Jakab had been personally consecrated by the Pope in St Peter's Basilica in February 1972, and was allowed occasional visits to Rome. But he could make little impact. His revered Alba Iulia superior, the much-suffering Bishop Áron Márton, was now in his 80s and gravely ill with cancer.

At grassroots level, the atmosphere was different. Orthodox clergy were growing restive, particularly since the death of Patriarch Iustinian in March 1977 after three decades at the helm. Despite decimation, the predominant church still boasted over 9000 priests, spread over 8100 parishes. There were some defiant figures in its ranks. One priest, Fr Alexandru Mazilu, died in October 1978 after spending 34 years in prison. His wife, who had begged constantly for his release, described how their home had been ransacked by police and their family mistreated. Mazilu had been beaten and abused routinely throughout his incarceration.

Another priest, Fr Gheorghe Calciu-Dumitreasa, a former medical student, was dismissed from his teaching post at Bucharest's Orthodox seminary in 1978 for persistently preaching against atheism. Calciu-Dumitreasa was said to have turned informer many years before at the infamous Piteşti 'experimental prison.'

Ordained after his release, he had plainly lost his fear. 'At a social level, freedom means the contest of ideas, whereas in Christ it means liberation from sin and death,' the priest had declared in one of his sermons. 'In our country, atheism rests on the state's authority, whereas faith is in full flight, for it is a fact of life. Authoritarianism enslaves—life liberates.'[73] A year after his dismissal, the priest was arrested and given a 10-year sentence after a closed trial for 'endangering state security' and 'fascist ideology.'

Among his many involvements, Calciu-Dumitreasa had offered spiritual guidance to a 'Free Union of Romanian Working People,' which announced itself after a rare miners' strike in the industrial Jiu valley in August 1977. The strike had lasted a whole week, forcing Ceauşescu to visit the region in person to offer better wages and food supplies. When it was brought to heel, thousands of participants were dispersed to other parts of Romania to head off further resistance, while the 'Free Union' was quickly suppressed with arrests. As the only sustained act of resistance in the 1970s, it had done little to allay the impotence felt by citizens in the face of communist power. But it had indicated a degree of restiveness, which was glaringly at odds with the official veneration of Ceauşescu. At the 1974 Party congress, the communist *conducator* had been compared to Julius Caesar, Alexander the Great and Napoleon, as well as to heroes of Romanian history such as Michael the Brave (1658–1601), scourge of the Ottomans and Hungarians. Religious language and imagery, such as *izbavitor* (saviour) and *slava* (glory), were resurrected from Old Church Slavonic to laud Ceauşescu's greatness. On his sixtieth birthday in January 1978, the dictator was eulogised as 'a demi-god' and 'providential son,' whose birth as saviour of his people could be likened to that of Christ.[74]

Garish personality cults were a Romanian speciality. In the more restrained atmosphere of Poland, they had never assumed comparable proportions. But here too there were signs of growing defiance. Research data in 1978 suggested religiousness was reviving among traditionally secularised social groups, as forms of identity and tradition with a stronger integrative capacity than communist culture were reasserted. After three decades of communism, 92 percent of country-dwellers and 81 percent of town residents still declared themselves believers. Urbanisation and industrialisation had not affected Poland's place as Eastern Europe's most religious society. As in all communist countries, the absence of mediating institutions between state and society had strengthened local group loyalties; and in Poland, these were defined less by age or and class than by ethos and religious belief.

This was where the Polish Church's growing social power lay. Its leaders had become much bolder now in their criticisms, extending them to economic and social injustices, much as Lactantius and other Christian writers had done under the later Roman emperors. The time had come, argued Tadeusz Mazowiecki, co-editor of *Więź*, for all Christians to stand up for legitimate freedoms.

> We cannot forget or fail to criticise the Church's relationship with the forces which generated the formula of human rights in modern times. At certain moments in history, human freedom was asserted against Christianity, making the Church treat liberating tendencies as a sign of rebellion against religion and God... Today, a crucial change seems evident: a shift from the defence of Church and religion to the defence of human rights.[75]

Priestly vocations had mushroomed in Poland from 735 in 1971 to 1174 in 1976, despite the regime's tactical use of the military draft to deter would-be clergy. The Polish bishops protested that aspiring seminarians were subjected to brutal anti-Catholic pressure from communist fellow-recruits. The regime retorted that seminaries were being used by 'shirkers to avoid the army.' Yet it gradually concluded that the tactic was failing and agreed to reduce the draft. Most ordinands were now returning from army service spiritually strengthened and even more defiant than before.

Youth renewal groups had become a major phenomenon in Poland too. The 45,000-strong Oasis, or Light-Life, movement, had worried Poland's bishops by apparently seeking a personal prelature for its much-harassed founder, Fr Franciszek Blachnicki, on the model of the Opus Dei movement. Cardinal Wyszyński was well aware, however, that the SB police were using disinformation to fuel tensions—just it had done against Blachnicki back in the 1960s. He therefore did nothing to constrain the movement. The regime, for its part, tried to restrict Light-Life's activities, claiming its teachers and organisers lacked legal qualifications. But it took no direct action.

By the late 1970s, the Polish Church was running over 200 separate pastoral schemes for colleges and universities, with 40 percent of all students attending their prayers and reflections. The SB deplored the 'disturbing proliferation' and did what it could to rein it in. When thousands of Warsaw students joined the annual foot pilgrimage to the national Jasna Góra shrine in summer 1978, dozens of Department Four agents were sent along as well. They filed a total of 406 reports during the fortnight, and helped disrupt the pilgrimage by damaging cars, sabotaging loudspeakers, setting fire to tents and daubing graffiti.

Church leaders hit back. 'Even dog-keepers can follow their route through the Main Square,' Cardinal Wojtyła complained when the traditional Corpus Christi procession was banned in Kraków. 'This refusal is clearly understood by the whole Catholic society as blatant discrimination against our town's faithful citizens, a direct offence to religious feelings... and a systematic manifestation of how they are second-class citizens.'[76]

In the Soviet Union, the Russian share of the population had now fallen to barely half the total, adding to pressure for other national groups to be better represented in power. This had done little to help religious minorities. Lithuania's underground *Chronicle* was now keeping a record of church life in other republics, from Belarus to Tajikistan, reflecting on the lessons learned. Local conditions varied. Several young priests from the seminary in Riga had been allowed to work in Ukraine, while some were even said to have been permitted to make hospital visits. The Catholic

Church had made great efforts to get priests to the Soviet Union's two million ethnic Germans, half now languishing as deportees in Kazakhstan. The Germans were relatively fortunate in being allowed their own newspaper and radio station, as well as some support from the West German government.

No reliable data existed for overall religious affiliations. Although the official media occasionally gave figures, these varied from the 25–30 percent said by the atheist journal, *Nauka i Religiya*, to be 'still under the influence of religion,' to the 8–10 percent cited by the House of Scientific Atheism in Moscow. Whatever the reality, there had been no official policy changes, and clergy and laypeople still risked harsh sentences for stepping out of line. Schoolteachers still worked with the Komsomol to deter religious practices, while church services were still sometimes disrupted, windows broken and names noted down.

People had, however, become less fearful. Soviet data suggested church marriages had even increased slightly by the late 1970s, after declining sharply over the two previous decades, while as many as 44 percent of children were being baptised. In a striking contradiction of Soviet policy, the young appeared as religious as their elders. Meanwhile, people were reacting more forcefully to police provocations and becoming more brazen with their complaints. Even in distant, impoverished Moldavia, some of the 15,000 surviving Catholics managed to get a letter to the Pope in early 1978, detailing how their churches had all been closed except for a tiny cemetery chapel in the capital, Chişinaŭ. Police and troops had smashed up a church at Rasherevo a year earlier, throwing its sacred objects into a nearby farmshed, while the republic's last priest, Fr Vladislav Zavalnyak, had been stripped of his driving licence and prevented from visiting parishioners.[77]

In Lithuania itself, the *Chronicle* presented snapshots of active, resilient Catholic communities. Students refused admission to the Kaunas seminary, now officially housing just 20–30 ordinands, were routinely studying for the priesthood in secret, often taking manual jobs to remain nearby. Meanwhile, more young people were attending Mass, unconcerned by possible reprisals, as the Church's identification with freedom and patriotism grew stronger in the popular mind. For those in serious trouble, there was a brochure available in Lithuanian and Russian: 'How to behave during interrogation.' It could be used much as the *Acta Martyrorum* had been used in the Early Church—to gain practical advice and guidance. 'The KGB had thought it could scare people, and that the clergy would give up catechising—but the opposite had happened,' recalled the dissident nun, Nijolė Sadūnaitė. Priests were 'growing in spirit as their consciences spoke up.' They were also becoming braver, gaining confidence as those who had been arrested and imprisoned eventually returned and carried on with their work. 'God's grace was at work,' Sadūnaitė concluded, 'since each of the martyrs, of whom there were many, sought grace for those less courageous.'[78]

Petras Plumpa-Pluira, converted to the national cause by a dream many years before, was struck by the new air of self-confidence on his release from prison. First jailed in 1958 for hanging a Lithuanian flag on a Kaunas electricity pylon, Plumpa-Pluira had given up on the Christian faith after reading Voltaire and Rousseau. He had been converted again by de Kempis's *Imitatio Christi* and the Polish mystic, Faustina Kowalska (1905–38), whose diary recounted her Divine Mercy visions as a nun in pre-War Kraków. When he was arrested again in 1974 for obtaining copying machines for the *Chronicle*, the KGB had taken away a picture of the merciful Christ, sent by his wife; and when his three young children had asked Brezhnev to spare him, they were told their petition had been 'considered and rejected.' During his new eight-year sentence, Plumpa-Pluira noticed how more camp inmates had become religious. 'The atheists seemed to have disappeared,' the Lithuanian recalled. 'In the camp for political prisoners, there was practically no one who didn't believe in God. Most came from the intelligentsia, and everyone was to some extent a believer.'[79]

Some reports put practising Catholics at 60 percent of the Lithuanian population. There were no resident bishops left, only apostolic administrators or capitular vicars. Yet petitions and protests were multiplying, and there were rumours that some Soviet officials were discreetly receiving the sacraments themselves. This was clearly troubling to the regime, which had sought to keep all religious expressions public in order to control them. For Catholic dissidents who had kept the cause of church and faith alive, it looked as if the peaceful effort had been vindicated. Underground Christian publishing was no longer confined to the struggle-hardened *Chronicle.* Titles such as *Aušra* (Dawn), *Tiesos Kelias* (Way of Truth) and *Rūpintojėlis* (Sorrowing Christ) had made an appearance, in some cases reviving journals first published under Russian occupation in the Nineteenth Century. The *Chronicle* itself, besides covering other republics, had widened its ambit to include more general cultural and social issues. But the link between Catholicism and national identity remained a constant topic, along with the centrality of religious faith in the Lithuanian struggle.

Some secular journals still criticised the Church's claim to embody the patriotic spirit, and questioned the Catholic view that religious rights were the key to other freedoms. There were also debates on the merits of passive and active resistance. Meanwhile, despite the contacts forged by such figures as Sadūnaitė and Tamkevičius, relations remained uneasy with dissidents in Russia, who were assumed, like most of Lithuania's own Russian minority, to be opposed to Lithuanian national aspirations.

Attitudes were softening. The best-known Russian dissidents were held in awe by their Lithuanian counterparts, while the *Chronicle* acknowledged that their heroic stance had forced Lithuanians to re-examine their traditionally negative view of Russians.[80] Lithuanian *samizdat* had republished articles by Solzhenitsyn and Sakharov, the second of whom had come round to supporting Baltic independence. Meanwhile, Russian dissidents admired the Lithuanians for their courage, humour and sensitivity, and were aware of the potential of religious dissent to mobilise mass opposition—something Russia's own isolated human rights groups could not hope to do.

Yet there was still a sense of distance between religious and secular dissent. Although far from hostile to religious faith, Sakharov himself would show little interest in Christians in his memoirs, beyond noting the 'stiff price' paid by many for choosing 'a life that breeds strength of character.' Sakharov had been moved when attending the trial of Vladimir Shelkov, 83-year-old leader of the Seventh-Day Adventists at Tashkent, noting how Shelkov had already spent 25 years in prisons and camps after being sentenced to death back in 1946. He had also noted the arrest of the Orthodox Fr Yakunin. But he had only realised the 'complex and tragic dimensions of religious persecution' in the early 1970s, Sakharov confessed, when he had observed the trial of Levitin-Krasnov and read accounts of 'anti-religious terror' in the 1920s. He remained critical of Solzhenitsyn for expecting 'too much' from the Orthodox church, and for 'idealising the Russian character and religion.' 'Religious liberty is an important part of the human rights struggle in the totalitarian state,' Sakharov had concluded. But 'for me, religious belief, or lack of it, is a purely private matter.'[81]

Others were closer to Solzhenitsyn, regretting the past failure of Russia's intellectuals to stand up for religion. Dmitri Panin, the writer who had exposed the anti-values spawned by the system, had been the model for a character in Solzhenitsyn's *The First Circle.* He looked back at the assault on the Christian faith which had marked the years after 1917, when 'the Checkist cellars ran red with sacrificial blood' and the young communist state had 'proceeded to mutilate and crush whatever opposed it, secular and sacred, to bury human life under atrocities.' Despite everything that had transpired since those terrible years, Panin was struck by the contrast between the 'tremendous strength of good and the self-destructiveness of evil,' and full of respect for those who had shown devotion to their beliefs rather than resorting to 'compromise and cowardice.' A faith which imposed no obligations would certainly die out, he concluded. The steady march of secularism would ensure it. 'Is it possible for anyone to live honestly under a dictatorship that rejects God and is based on human enslavement?' the writer pondered.

> Atheism denies the existence of God; it denies the divine origin of the commandments passed down from Moses. Consequently, commandments are devised by mere mortals, with only limited validity. Ethical standards designed for an atheistic society, advantageous as they may be for the ruling class, run counter to the vital interests of the rank-and-file citizens enslaved by that class... A man who embodies good must be capable of loving those around him, of sacrificing his well-being or, if necessary, even life itself—his own, not someone else's. And such sacrifices must be made not in the name of putting into effect some grotesque vision of the future, but for the sake of principles which the common man holds dear, which touch on his daily life, which he can understand. [82]

Notes

1 *Religion in Communist Lands*, vol. 6/no 1 (1976), p. 49; *Radio Liberty Research*, 10 June 1980.

2 Dominiczak, *Organy bezpieczeństwa*, pp. 307–8. The regime was still using tax pressure, leaving the troublesome Przemysł diocese with crippling debts of four million zloties; *Kościół w godzinie próby*, p. 138.

3 Dudek and Gryz, *Komuniści i Kościół*, p. 326, 329; J. Widacki, *Czego nie powiedział generał Kiszczak: z Janem Widackim rozmawia Wojciech Wróblewski* (Łódź: BGW, 1992). pp. 64–9.

4 Lasota, *Donos na Wojtyłę*, pp. 248–9; Czaczkowska, *Kardynał Wyszyński*, pp. 376–9, 439; R. Graczyk, *Cena Przetrwania? SB wobec Tygodnika Powszechnego* (Warsaw: Czerwone i Czarne, 2011), pp. 24–73.

5 Mikloško et al, *Zločiny komunizmu*, pp. 304–7.

6 Pacepa, *Red Horizons*, pp. 145–8.

7 Text of appeal in M. Markovic and R. Cohen, *Yugoslavia: The rise and fall of socialist humanism—A history of the Praxis Group* (Nottingham:

Spokesman, 1975, pp. 86–93; O. Gruenwald, *The Yugoslav Search for Man: Marxist Humanism in Contemporary Yugoslavia* (South Hadley: Bergin, 1983); G. Stokes (ed), *From Stalinism to Pluralism: A Documentary History of Eastern Europe since 1945* (Oxford University Press, 1996), pp. 116–121; Ramet, 'Catholicism and Politics,' pp. 263, 269.

8 *International Covenant on Civil and Political Rights*, 16 December 1966, Article 18. The Covenant, legally in force from 23 March 1976, also stipulated, under the same article, that no one would 'be subject to coercion which would impair his freedom to have or to adopt a religion or belief of his choice.' It guaranteed freedom of opinion, expression, assembly and association, and barred, under Article 26, 'discrimination on any ground,' including 'religion, political or other opinion, national or social origin, property, birth or other status.' The Covenant was signed by the Soviet Union and most other communist states (Albania was an exception) in the 1960s and ratified in the 1970s.

9 *L'Osservatore Romano*, 27 June 1975; Luxmoore and Babiuch, *The Vatican and the Red Flag*, pp. 170–2; Casaroli, *Der Heilige Stuhl*, pp. 157–163; H. Liedermann, 'Konferenz über Sicherheit und Zusammenarbeit in Europa,' in H. Schambeck (ed), *Pro Fide et Iustitia: Festchrift für Agostino Kardinal Casaroli zum 70 Geburtstag* (Berlin: Duncker, 1984), pp. 489–514.

10 Dzwonkowski, *Za wschodnią granicą*, p. 273; A. Chojnowski and J. Bruski, *Ukraina* (Warsaw: Trio, 2006), pp. 319, 392; L. Melhorn, *In der Wahrheit Leben: Aus der Geschichte von Widerstand und opposition in dem Diktaturem des 20 Jahrhunderts* (Kreisau: Stiftung für Europäische Verständigung, 2012), pp. 184–193.

11 Author's interview with Turowicz, Krakow, April 1991; on *Tygodnik* in the 1970s, Beneś et al, *Krąg Turowicza*, pp. 341–460; on the weekly's role as an ecumenical forum, A. Mateja, *Co zdążysz zrobić to zostanie: Portret Jerzego Turowicza* (Kraków: Znak, 2012), pp. 213–258.

12 S. Kowalik, 'Ksiadz Roman Kotlarz: Zapomniana ofiara bezpieki' in *Biuletyn IPN*, no. 4 (2011); S. Kowalik and J. Sakowicz, *Ksiądz Roman Kotlarz: Życie i działalność 1928–1976* (Radomskie Towarzystwo Naukowe, 2000), pp. 55–129; S. Kowalik et al, *Byłem z tymi ludźmi. Życie i działalność księdza Romana Kotlarza* (Radom: Katedra Radomska, 2007).

13 Luxmoore and Babiuch, *The Vatican and the Red Flag*, pp. 181, 195–6; J. Kuroń, *Wiara i wina: do i od komunizmu* (Warsaw: Nowa, 1990), pp. 343–5; T. Ceran, *Świat idei Jacka Kuronia* (Warsaw: PWN, 2010), pp. 169–228.

14 Dudek and Gryz, *Komuniści i Kościół*, p. 336; *Gazeta Wyborcza*, 28 October 1996; J. Skorzyński, *Siła Bezsilnych: Historia Komitetu Obrony Robotników* (Warsaw: Świat Książki, 2012), pp. 242–9.

15 Raina, *Rozmowy z władzami*, p. 276; A. Friszke, *Czas Kor-u: Jacek Kuroń a geneza Solidarności* (Znak, 2011), pp. 243–326, 412–419.

16 Czaczkowska, *Kardynał Wyszyński*, pp. 542–3; Skorzyński, *Siła Bezsilnych* , pp. 182–9. Wyszyński quoted several Gospel passages, including the Letter of James, as justification; J. Lipski, *KOR* (Warsaw: IPN, 2006); A. Friszke and A. Paczkowski (eds), *Niepokorni: Rozmowy o Komitecie Obrony Robotników* (Znak, 2008), pp. 381–2.

17 A. Michnik, *The Church and the Left* (University of Chicago Press, 1993), p. xi; Zabłocki, *Dzienniki*, p. 545; B. Cywiński, *Rodowody Niepokornych* (Warsaw: Biblioteka Więzi, 1971).

18 Czaczkowska, *Kardynał Wyszyński*, pp. 116–8; Z. Przetakiewicz, *Od ONR-u do PAX-u: Wspomnienia* (Warsaw: Biblioteka Myśli Polskiej, 1994), p. 83.

19 Dudek and Gryz, *Komuniści i Kościół*, p. 339. Although the regime depended on priests to encourage participation in elections, leading churchmen from Bishop Tokarczuk to Cardinal Wyszyński never voted after the 1950s on principle.

20 *Ibid.*, p. 296–9, 308.

21 From Wyszyński's notes, 'Pro Memoria,' in Raina, *Kardynał Wyszyński*, vol. 14, pp. 65, 187; Casaroli's reflections, in *Der Heilige Stuhl*, pp. 164–190. The diplomat saw his work as reflecting Augustinian theology, and particularly the distinction between two worlds, or cities, in *De Civitate Dei*; M. Merle, 'Droits de l'état, droits de l'homme, droits des peuples, droits des nations,' in Schambeck, *Pro Fide et Iustitia*, pp. 763–782.

22 Czaczkowska, *Kardynał Wyszyński*, p. 515.

23 J. Tejchma, *Kulisy dymisji: Z dzienników ministra kultury 1974–1977* (Kraków: Oficyna Cracovia, 1991), p. 291. Tejchma was Minister of Culture and Art between 1974 and 1980.

24 Z. Mlynář, 'Ekskomunisté a křestane v Chartě 77,' in *Studie* (Rome), vol. 6/no. 60 (1978), pp. 420–1.

25 See 'Our attitude to the statements of Charter 77,' in *Religion in Communist Lands*, vol. 5/ no. 3 (1977), pp. 161–2; Luxmoore and Babiuch, *The Vatican and the Red Flag*, pp. 183, 191.

26 From *Katolicke Noviny*, 23 January 1977; A. Hlinka, *Sila slabých a slabosť silných* (Bratislava: Tatran, 1990), pp. 179–80; Mikloško et al, *Zločiny komunizmu*, p. 309; Tomášek's statement in Svoboda, *Na straně národa*, p. 65.

27 Svoboda, *Na straně národa*, p. 66; full text in *Religion in Communist Lands*, vol. 8/no. 1 (1980), pp. 48–51.

28 Author's interviews with Hejdánek, May 1988, December 1989 and June 1990. Hejdánek, a former pupil of Hromádka, had belonged to the

Protestant *Nová Orientace*, or New Orientation, movement in the 1960s; B. Komárková, J. Šimsa and L. Hejdánek, *Původ a význam lidských práv* (Prague: SPN, 1990); P. Dinuš, *Českobratrská církev evangelická v agenturním rozpracování StB* (Prague: ÚDV, 2004).

29 Author's interviews with Halík and Škvorecký, Prague, August 1990; J. Luxmoore and J. Babiuch, 'Forging the Alliance,' in *Twin Circle*, 9 September 1990; 'A Spiritual Harvest' in *National Catholic Register*, 16 December 1990. On the Akademia seminar, J. Beránek, *Dobrodružství pobytu vezdejšího: Radim Palouš v rozhovoru* (Prague: Karmelitánské nakladatelství, 2006); J. Jandourek and T. Halík, *Ptal jsem se cest: Rozhovory* (Prague: Národní Knihovna, 1997), pp. 99–130.

30 J. Zvěřina, 'On not living in hatred,' in John Keane (ed), *The Power of the Powerless: Citizens against the State in Central-Eastern Europe* (New York: Sharpe, 1985), pp. 207–216.

31 E. Kantůrková, *Jan Hus: Příspěvek k národni identitě* (Prague: Melantrich, 1991), pp. 14–15; author's interviews with Kantůrková, Prague and Warsaw, March/May 1992, December 2000; J. Luxmoore, 'Courage and Truth' in *National Catholic Register*, 25 May 1992.

32 See Vladimir Maximov's introduction to M. Mihajlov, *Underground Notes* (London: Routledge, 1977), p. xii. Mihajlov himself comprehensively debunked Djilas's ideological anti-religious worldview in a review of his 1969 book, *The Unperfect Society*.

33 M. Dinescu, 'Indulgență de iarnă,' in *Democrația naturii* (Bucharest: Cartea Romaneasca, 1981), p. 11; D. Deletante, *Ceaușescu and the Securitate: Coercion and Dissent in Romania 1965–1989* (London: Hurst, 1995), p. 196.

34 Pacepa, *Red Horizons*, pp.219–20. According to Pacepa, Ceaușescu described religion as 'Carter's weakness—where we have to hit him'; Deletante, *Ceausescu and the Securitate*, pp. 226–7.

35 *Radio Liberty Research*, 11 November 1987; author's interviews with Steponavičius, Vilnius, May 1990 and January 1991.

36 *Aušrele*, no. 1 (*samizdat*), 16 February 1978.

37 *Radio Liberty Research*, 23 November 1983; *Lietuvos Katalikų Bažnyčios kronika*, no. 42 (1980); K. Kasparas, *Lietuvos Karas: Antroji Sovietų Sąjungos agresija* (Kaunas: Lietuvos Istorijos Institutas, 1999), pp. 517–9, 554–9; O. Varnagirtė, 'Šventi prisiminimai apie kunigą Virgilijų Jaugelį,' in *XXI Amžius*, no. 12 (2012).

38 'Letter by Lithuania's bishops to the presidium of the Supreme Soviet,' in *Lituanus: Lithuanian Quarterly Journal of Arts and Sciences*, vol. 25/no. 1 (1979).

39 Raina, *Cele polityki władz PRL*, pp. 117–8, 123–6.

40 *Ibid.*, pp. 127–8; Friszke, *PRL wobec Kościoła*, pp. 31–6, 62–8.

41 Fiala and Hanuš, *Skrytá Církev*, p. 132; Korec, *Od Babarskiej Noci*, p. 179; Mikloško et al, *Zločiny komunizmu*, p. 305.

42 Author's interview with Manca, Vienna, August 1993; J. Luxmoore, 'A fugitive at last can rest,' in *National Catholic Register*, 17 July 1994.

43 'Allocution de bienvenue de Paul VI,' in J. Ijjas et al, *Ensemble pour une bonne cause: L'État socialiste et les Églises en Hongrie* (Budapest: Corvina, 1978), pp. 230–2.

44 Text in Bota, *Istoria Bisericii Universale*, pp. 500–1; Bozgan, *Cronica unui eşec previzibil*, pp. 405, 467–8; Ştirban and Ştirban, *Din Istoria Bisericii*, pp. 416–467.

45 Pearson, *Albania in the Twentieth Century*, p. 639; Riccardi, *Il Secolo del martirio*, p. 196–8; E. Jacques, *The Albanians: An Ethnic History* (Jefferson: Macfarland, 1995), p. 509. Albania's clergy were still dying. The Orthodox Archbishop of Tirana, Damnian, jailed during the 1967 'cultural revolution,' had died in November 1973. The Franciscan Bishop Antonin Fishta, who had been ordained capitular vicar of Pult by the ill-fated Bishop Coba in 1957 after lecturing at Shkodra's Franciscan school, died from similar causes in his eightieth year in January 1980.

46 O'Donnell, *A Coming of Age*, pp. 129–31, 143.

47 Raina, *Cele polityki władz PRL*, pp. 131–4.

48 Luxmoore and Babiuch, *The Vatican and the Red Flag*, pp. 163–4.

49 Casaroli, *Il martirio*, pp. 14, 19.

50 Commentary in *Lietuvos Katalikų Bažnyčios kronika*, no. 28 (1977), pp. 264–8; Vardys, *The Catholic Church*, p. 165.

51 Wołowski and Korzeniewska, *Jak służąc Panu Bogu*, pp. 44–5.

52 A. Sakharov, *Memoirs* (London: Hutchinson, 1990), p. 4.

53 T. Goricheva, *Von Gott zu reden ist gefährlich: Meine Erfahrungen im Osten und im Westen* (Freiburg: Herder, 1985), pp. 48–9.

54 Goricheva, *Von Gott zu reden*, pp. 5–9; A. Solzhenitsyn, *The Gulag Archipelago*, vol. 2 (London: Collins, 1975), pp. 614–7.

55 Z. Krakhmalnikova, *Listen, prison! Lefortovo notes, letters from exile* (New York: Nikodemos, 1993), p. 19; N. Mandelstam, *Hope Abandoned* (London: Collins, 1989), pp. 201–3.

56 *Ibid.*, pp. 102, 164–5, 179, 392.

57 Author's interviews with Lytinsky and Alexandr Zorin, Moscow, January 1992; I. Ratushinskaya, *Grey is the Colour of Hope* (New York: Knopf, 1988), pp. 48–9.

58 Ratushinskaya, *Grey is the Colour*, p. 212; I. Ratushinskaya, *Poet against the Lie* (London: Grosvenor, 1991), p. 10.

59 Ratushinskaya, *No, I'm not afraid* (London: Bloodaxe, 1986), p. 133; *In the*

Beginning (London: Hodder, 1990), pp. 70–1, 138. Ratushinskaya, who wrote most of her Gulag poems on soap, was released in October 1986 and allowed to emigrate two months later.

60 Author's interview with Ratushinskaya, London, September 1990.

61 Author's interview with Endreffy, Budapest, May 1992; J. Luxmoore and J. Babiuch, 'The Road to Damascus: Three Eastern European intellectuals of the dilemmas of faith and ideology,' in *Religion, State and Society*, vol. 21/nos. 3–4 (1993), pp. 323–4; Paul VI, *Octogesima adveniens*, no. 52.

62 Quoted in P. Michel, *Politics and Religion in Eastern Europe* (London: Polity Press, 1991), p. 118.

63 Miklós quoted in M. Macqua, *Rome-Moscou: L'Ostpolitik du Vatican* (Louvain: Cabay, 1984), p. 153.

64 K. Ungváry, 'The Kádár regime and the Roman Catholic hierarchy,' in *Hungarian Quarterly*, vol.48/no. 187 (2007). According to data here, the regime had 485 agents to monitor cultural activities and 489 for youth, and only four to keep checks on the 'former ruling classes'; Wittenberg, *Crucibles of Political Loyalty*, pp. 43–5, 178–83.

65 *Ibid.*, p. 182. Brazil's base communities, by comparison, numbered some 40,000 in 1975.

66 Author's interview with Blanckenstein, Budapest, July 1991; J. Luxmoore, 'Future's best hope,' in *National Catholic Register*, 21 July 1991; Havasy, *Martyrs of the Catholic Church*, pp. 141–5.

67 F. Ehlert, 'Suchet der Stadt Bestes! Bischof Mitzenheim Bemühungen um Einvernehmen mit dem Stadt,' in *Kirche in Sozialismus*, no. 14 (1988), p. 97; S. Ramet, *Nihil Obstat: Religion, Politics and Social Change in East-Central Europe and Russia* (London: Duke University Press, 1998), pp. 63–9; Melhorn, *In der Wahrheit Leben*, pp. 227–239.

68 For example, B. Kutin and M. Kerševan; S. Alexander, 'Church-State Relations in Yugoslavia: Recent Developments,' in *Religion in Communist Lands*, vol. 5/no. 4 (1977), pp. 239–40.

69 Interview in *Frankfurter Allgemeine Zeitung*, 29 May 1979; *Vjesnik*, Zagreb, 18 March 1978.

70 *Radio Free Europe Research*, 29 January 1980; *Scînteia*, Bucharest, 7 July 1979.

71 George-Radu Chirovici, in *Contemporanul*, Bucharest, no. 30 (1979); *Radio Free Europe Research*, 29 January 1980.

72 *Ibid.* Deletante, *Ceaușescu and the Securitate*, p. 212.

73 *Ibid.*, pp. 39–40, 221, 230–1; Bota, *Istoria Bisericii Universale*, p. 517; Mazilu's case in Rădulescu and Slătineanu, *Preoți in cătușe*, pp. 139–50; on Protestants, S. Grossu, *Calvarul României Creștine* (Dava: ABC, 1992), pp. 103–208.

74 *Radio Free Europe Research*, 28 January 1988.

75 Article reprinted in T. Mazowiecki, *Druga Twarz Europy* (Biblioteka Więzi, 1990), pp. 79, 88–9.

76 M. Lasota, 'Ulice nie dla Wiernych' in *Kościół w godzinie próby*, p. 85; Walusiak, 'Kryptonim Wierni,' pp. 156–61; Czaczkowska, *Kardynał Wyszyński*, p. 546; Dudek and Gryz, *Komuniści i Kościół*, p. 318; Zieliński, *Kościół w Polsce*, pp. 184–194.

77 *Radio Liberty Research*, 31 March 1981; Associated Press reports, 3 February 1981 and 20 March 1981. The Zurich-based *Glaube in der Zweite Welt* estimated that a third of Soviet citizens still belonged to religious communities at the end of 1970s.

78 Wołowski and Korzeniewska, *Jak służąc Panu Bogu*, pp. 50, 94; Sadūnaitė, *Geborgen im Schatten*, pp. 85–93.

79 Wołowski and Korzeniewska, *Jak służąc Panu Bogu*, pp. 135–6; *Radio Free Europe Research*, 22 July 1980.

80 For example, *Lietuvos Katalikų Bažnyčios kronika*, no. 15, 1976.

81 Sakharov, *Memoirs*, pp. 337, 408–9, 493–4.

82 Panin, *The Notebooks*, pp. 86–7.

4 DIVINE PROVIDENCE INTERVENES

God has exhibited us apostles as last of all, like men sentenced to death; because we have become a spectacle to the world, to angels and to men. We are fools for Christ's sake, but you are wise in Christ. We are weak, but you are strong. You are held in honour, but we in disrepute. To the present hour, we hunger and thirst, we are ill-clad and buffeted and homeless, and we labor, working with our own hands. When reviled, we bless; when persecuted, we endure; when slandered, we try to conciliate.

1 Co 3:9–13

THE SECULARISM AND atheism were here to stay. On 16 October 1978, however, the beleaguered Christians of Eastern Europe were astonished by news from Rome, which seemed to shift in an instant all long-established assumptions. The setting was Rome's imposing St Peter's Square; and the event was the appearance on the Vatican balcony of a newly elected Polish Pope. When Pope Paul VI, exasperated and exhausted, had died on 6 August, few people had imagined that Cardinal Karol Wojtyła of Kraków might be a candidate to succeed him. In barely two months, a few knowledgeable church figures, such as Austria's veteran Cardinal Koenig, aware of Wojtyła's strength of character, had brought his name forward and secured his election.

Although Wojtyła had opposed an outright condemnation of communism at Vatican II, he had helped draft the Polish bishops' hard-hitting statements against communist injustices. Appointed a cardinal in 1967, a year after Poland's fractious Christian Millennium, he had also been in touch with the country's small dissident fraternity, allowing its members to use certain Kraków churches and 'fully accepting' their activities, as one secret police report put it.[1] He had reached out to young people, via assertive movements such as Light-Life; and he was well informed about the rest of Eastern Europe. The idea of a 'living church'—not the version discredited by Russian Orthodox collaborators, but one in which the Church lived and breathed beyond its sacral borders—was close to the new John Paul II's heart.

Those who knew him were aware that Wojtyła had reflected deeply on how the Church might best respond to communist misrule, while building links with key social groups and discouraging the violent resistance which would merely strengthen the regime. He understood communism's strengths and weaknesses, and had found ways to confront and counter its ideological pretensions. In 1969, he had published *Osoba i Czyn* (Person and Act), as a rebuff to Poland's foremost Marxist theorist, Adam Schaff. The book had shown how Marxism's economic and social failures derived from a misunderstanding of human nature. Communists saw activism as a duty, where personal interests were sacrificed for humanity's redemption. But they had also postulated that the 'acting person,' given the correct 'praxis,' could become master of history. For those wishing to surrender themselves to a great cause, this had proved highly attractive.

Wojtyła's task had been to find a counter-proposition to the Marxist vision, and to rediscover a link between transformational activism and Christian ethics. Human actions did indeed shape the world. They could mark the course of history. But good and bad actions were determined by free choice and responsibility—not the moral determinism found in Marxism. Stage by stage, Wojtyła had dissected the Marxist conception of the world. Then, he had reassembled it in a Christian form, reclaiming concepts—alienation, injustice, exploitation—which Marxism had expropriated. He was careful not to speak directly against communism, so the book could be accepted for limited publication. But for a regime whose legitimacy was based increasingly on apathetic acceptance, *Osoba i Czyn* had posed a significant ideological challenge.

The book had offered a concept of participation which Wojtyła called 'solidarity.' It was a form of 'corporate integrity,' he explained, in which civil opposition became a form of social love. The idea had already found expression in a study of Catholic social ethics he had compiled as a young priest and lecturer in the early 1950s. In Wojtyła's hands, the correcting of injustices had become a common social task. Involuntary resignation was no defence. Christians had a duty to be active: the 'person' went with the 'act.'[2]

Wojtyła's nomination as Kraków's archbishop back in 1963 had long been viewed as an error by Poland's communist establishment, just as Bishop Tokarczuk's had been three years later. The regime had dubbed him the 'red cardinal' to mark him off from Wyszyński, the 'black cardinal'; and it saw him as a man out to overthrow the system rather than work within it. Wyszyński spoke in moral categories and had a sense of Poland's state interests; but Wojtyła made political calculations and was seen as wily tactician—a 'cosmopolitan mischief-maker' in contrast to the 'patriot-realist' Primate.[3]

Wojtyła had been concerned at the Western Church's blinkered attitude to communism, supervising the Polish bishops' reports about the infiltration of Marxist influences. But he had also been close to Paul VI. In a series of Holy Week meditations at the Vatican in 1976, he had explained how Christianity had withstood the communist onslaught. Even the Devil, the father of lies, acknowledged God's power, Wojtyła had pointed out, whereas Marxism denied God's very existence and offered a 'full affirmation of man.' In doing so, however, Marxism had helped the modern world rediscover a sense of sin and evil. It had inadvertently strengthened Christianity by making it more aware of what threatened it.[4]

Though differing from Wyszyński temperamentally and intellectually, Wojtyła had also shown unswerving loyalty. Not surprisingly, the SB had kept a close watch on him, as had the Soviet KGB. Material had been kept on him from as early as 1946, while reports via church agents in Kraków, where the Interior Ministry's Section D was especially active, had observed Wojtyła's close contacts with the Vatican and Western Church. It was claimed that Wyszyński had opposed his 1963 nomination and considered his elevation to the cardinalate four years later to be premature. Yet when it came to a confrontation, the SB had confidently predicted, most Polish bishops would be on Wojtyła's side. 'An eventual conflict will depend entirely on internal church forces,' one report explained. 'Sooner or later, the two orientations must descend into conflict with each other, come to blows on various fronts.'[5]

The SB was to be disappointed. Hopes of internal conflict were thwarted by the bishops' faithfulness to Wyszyński's leadership. But agents, with codenames such as 'Delta' and 'Jurek,' were placed in Wojtyła's Kraków household, as well as the nearby seminary and *Tygodnik Powszechny* weekly, to build up a meticulous character profile. Everything from Wojtyła's personal habits to his stance on Church-state issues was charted in minute detail. 'What are Wojtyła's political conceptions—how far are these acceptable to his priests?' Department Four had instructed its informers in 1969. 'Does Wojtyła accept socialism, or is he rather indifferent to the system?... Will he lead a political struggle against the socialist order, or will he abandon this and just do everything to gain the maximum for the Church?'[6]

Questions like this had become increasingly important as Wojtyła's perceived stature grew. The SB kept track of his links with Paul VI, even describing him in March 1970 as 'the Pope's grey eminence.' Four years later, another report outlined his key influence on Papal decisions on Eastern Europe, noting how he had become one of the Pope's 'personal friends with continual access to him at any moment, without diplomatic protocol.' Remarkably, the SB had predicted as early as 1972 that Wojtyła could be a serious candidate for Pope. It knew more than

Wyszyński himself about his international standing. 'About the next pope, two general views are evident: it will not be an Italian, and "reformist cardinals" will not be considered,' a Department Four director noted that December, quoting the retired Archbishop Baraniak.

> If there was a conclave at this moment, the most important candidate would be Karol Wojtyła, who is currently having an excellent run and is very highly regarded in the Roman curia. Baraniak stressed the great tact of Wojtyła, who doesn't speak first when at official events in Rome, only at the end, so he can average out his words and gain authority.[7]

By 1976, a total of 54 close associates had been under full-time surveillance, including his secretary, Fr Stanisław Dziwisz, and friends such as Fr Józef Tischner and Fr Andrzej Bardecki. All possible efforts had been made to damage Wojtyła's authority and create rifts with Wyszyński, such as by fuelling tensions between Wojtyła's Papal Theology Academy in Kraków and Wyszyński's Catholic University of Lublin. By the time Gierek, the Polish Party boss, had visited the Vatican in December 1977, however, the regime had concluded that Wojtyła was now 'a more dangerous opponent' than Wyszyński. 'For many years, he has been building a myth of greatness and infallibility around himself,' the SB seethed.

> It is the myth of a man of providence for the Church in Poland—especially recently, after his meditations for the Roman curia, in which Paul VI participated. This has given Department Four a particularly responsible task: to demythologise the person of the Kraków metropolitan and weaken his position at various levels.[8]

For a time at least, the Department believed it had succeeded. It predicted that Wojtyła's 'lack of political realism, organisational and managerial ability' had eroded his 'popularity and prestige among church dignitaries in the West,' who disliked his 'opposition links and pro-German sympathies,' and his 'excessively outrageous ambition.' Rome had concluded, the agents were sure, that Wojtyła's 'political line' would merely 'cause difficulties in Polish-Vatican relations.'[9]

With John Paul II's election, all such claims and counter-claims became irrelevant. From his very first hours, the new Pope served warning that he would be a formidable opponent, a real-life St Michael leading his heavenly host against the fallen angels of injustice and oppression. 'There is no longer a Church of silence,' he told Wyszyński, recalling Pius XII's famous epithet. 'She now speaks with the voice of the Pope.' Addressing foreign diplomats, he assured them the Church would remain 'open to every country and every regime, according to the proven means of diplomacy and negotiation.' But the Holy See welcomed all representatives—not just those of 'governments, regimes and political structures,' but also 'authentic representatives of peoples and nations.' The Church was not seeking privileges, only appropriate conditions for pursuing its mission. If essential rights were respected, it could coexist without 'inherent contradiction' with any political, social or economic system.[10]

This message was impressed firmly on communist regime officials as they arrived to establish contact. Casaroli, the diplomat-architect of Paul VI's 'small steps,' was raised to Vatican Secretary of State; but changes were clearly afoot. Negotiations would no longer be conducted over the heads of local church leaders. From now on, the Vatican would be acting from a position of strength.

The Papal election had taken place against a background of international tension, leading up to the December 1979 Soviet invasion of Afghanistan—an event which strengthened the hand of Western hardliners such as the newly elected US President Ronald Reagan and Britain's prime minister, Margaret Thatcher. In Poland, it gave a substantial boost to national morale. Just three weeks before, in their strongest statement to date, the Polish bishops had accused the Gierek regime of 'paralysing' national life. The Church was strong and self-confident; and its hardships and concerns had now become a focus of worldwide interest. 'His election brings the problems of nations living in this second world to the centre of attention,' commented the veteran *Więź* editor, Tadeusz Mazowiecki.

> Should diplomacy have primacy over testimony? Or should diplomacy and testimony be inseparable? The Church under John Paul II will not abandon diplomacy. But there has been an awareness from the very outset that progress will not come through armchair politics, but through strengthening the spiritual energy of nations and awakening their life processes.[11]

There would be many accounts of how news of the election was received by Polish Party leaders. Gierek was said to have exclaimed '*O, rany boskie!*' ('By God's wounds!'), when telephoned by a Politburo member, Stanisław Kania—the man who had boasted about the Party's use of 'the logic of force,' and who had described Wojtyła shortly before as a 'bumptious turkey-cock.' The member responsible for Church-state relations, Kazimierz Barcikowski, was given the news while chairing a Party meeting in Kraków on Wojtyła's 'anti-socialist activity.' He was said to have closed the meeting and ordered vodka, muttering vexaciously about how communists would now 'have to kiss the Catholics' arses.'

The latest Confessions Office director, Kazimierz Kąkol, recalled the 'disgust and consternation' expressed at a Central Committee session, which continued through the night, and how Poland's Foreign Minister, Stefan Olszowski, spilled a mug of black coffee over his white trousers. Party officials were partially reassured, according to Kąkol, that it was better to have Wojtyła as Pope than as Primate. This was quickly adopted as the internal Party line. It was even claimed that Party fixers had mounted 'a specified, subtle action' to bring about John Paul II's election.[12]

In reality, the whole anti-church policy had broken down spectacularly. The immediate priority had to be containing the damage and preventing further humiliation. 'The authorities were scared—they sensed Wojtyła would light a bonfire for us,' one SB agent recalled. 'We were all ordered to drop everything and concentrate on finding new contacts against him.'[13]

Publicly, the Gierek regime sent a warm congratulatory telegram, enthusing that such a distinction had been won by a 'son of the Polish nation.' On 22 October, Poland's state TV carried John Paul II's four-hour Rome enthronement live, the first Catholic ceremony broadcast since the 1940s. Meanwhile, the regime probed to see whether the same methods of control could continue. Letters to the Pope were opened for checking but allowed through, while attempts to censor a return letter from John Paul II to Kraków Catholics provoked international protests, suggesting the practice could not be repeated. When Bishop Franciszek Macharski was named as Kraków's new archbishop without obtaining the customary government consent, the regime demurred on condition that future appointments would be consulted. But when Wyszyński's secretary, Fr Józef Glemp, was named Bishop of Warmia in March 1979, the government was ignored again.

The regime sensed a full-blown propaganda assault to discredit the Pope would enrage Polish society. Yet it had plenty of tricks up its sleeve. Macharski, the new archbishop, had spurned attempts to recruit him as a collaborator. But his brother-in-law, Julian Polan-Haraschin, a former Stalinist hanging judge who had served a jail sentence for bribery and forgery, had informed on him regularly. In January 1979, he joined Macharski on a pilgrimage to Rome and gave the SB information about the new Pope's apartments.[14]

Poland's Interior Ministry was under pressure to contain an expected resurgence of Catholic militancy. SB agents were thick on the ground in Rome, alongside Poland's official delegation, by the time of John Paul II's enthronement, attempting to predict 'the main directions and conceptions of Vatican eastern policy' and identify Polish clergy likely to be given posts in its 'main dispositional links.' Efforts were made to recruit informers among those with personal access to John Paul II. There were some notable failures, such as in repeated attempts to ensnare the Vatican-based Bishop Deskur, who had been a candidate to succeed Cardinal Kominek of Wrocław back in 1974. But there were also successes. Fr Juliusz Paetz, a staffer at the Secretariat of State since 1968, informed for the SB regularly during John Paul II's first three years while serving on the Vatican's team for contacts with the Polish government. Paetz's codename was 'Fermo'; and virtually all his material was rated as valuable. The link was discontinued only when the SB suspected the Vatican was using Paetz to plant disinformation of its own.[15]

While the Polish SB's 'residents' and 'illegals' also remained active further afield in other European countries, tracking the Pope's contacts, Rome itself became a veritable hotbed for other communist agents as well. East Germany's Stasi had run a Vatican agent under Paul VI, who had provided 'exact details' of the 1978 conclave. The Stasi had been especially irked by the Polish Church's contacts with Catholic and Evangelical groups in East Germany, to whom Polish Catholics regularly supplied religious literature. The Vatican channel dried up after John Paul's election. But bugs were placed successfully in Casaroli's Vatican apartment by a Slovak relative on behalf of Czechoslovakia's StB, which was said to have recruited two priests from the Secretariat of State and other agents already under Pius XII.[16]

Other communist regimes saw the ideological challenge of John Paul II's election in their own ways. Gierek sought to reassure Moscow that he had the situation under control. He set his Party propagandists to work, highlighting the common aims of communism and Catholicism: peace, humanism and detente. Talk of a reawakened 'Slavic Christian culture,' the Polish Party insisted, could coexist with communist power, not least since the Pope would have to 'take account of the reality he operates in.'[17]

Moscow had its own interpretation of John Paul II's election, however, seeing it as a coup by Church reactionaries, led by

American cardinals. Brezhnev despatched a telegram of congratulations and sent his ambassador to the new Pope's enthronement, alongside a delegation from the Russian Orthodox Moscow Patriarchate. The Patriarchate's youthful foreign relations chief, Metropolitan Nikodim of Leningrad, had collapsed and died of a heart attack in the arms of Wojtyła's ill-fated predecessor, John Paul I, while visiting the Vatican just a month before. Meanwhile, the Soviet media urged the Polish pontiff to continue the line of Paul VI and John XXIII. 'Western commentators are claiming the cardinals specially chose a Pope whose knows what socialism and communism are from his own experience, and can fight against them,' Moscow's *Novoye Vremiya* weekly noted in a show of optimism.

> It seems these commentators are opting for desire over reality, since this interpretation appears far from the truth. As the depressing case of Pius XII shows, anti-communism leads the Church into a blind alley. The very fact of a Polish cardinal's election offers the best refutation of the myth created by Pius XII about a 'Church of silence' in the countries of socialism.[18]

Yet the tensions were evident. The Soviet Foreign Minister, Andrei Gromyko, met the new Pope in January 1979, and was said by Vatican sources to have talked about peace while the Pope demanded assurances about Catholic rights. Gromyko had met John XXIII and paid five visits to Paul VI. By his account, he warned the new Pope against Western 'rumours and misinformation' concerning 'the state of the Church in the Soviet Union.' The Soviet Union had guaranteed freedom of religion 'from the very first day of its existence,' Gromyko insisted. Everything was quite normal. 'Do you consider it normal that more than a million Catholics in Belarus have no bishop and only 20 mostly elderly priests?' John Paul II reportedly hit back. The sounding-out encounter got relations off to a bad start. Three months into the pontificate, the Pope admitted it had been his 'most exhausting meeting' thus far.[19]

At least they had a common language—Russian. Wojtyła had studied great Russian writers such as Fyodor Dostoevsky, Vladimir Soloviev, Nikolai Berdyaev and Sergei Bulgakov, who had prophesied the catastrophe to be visited on their country by Marxism. He had read works by the Great Purge victim, Pavel Florensky, the contemporary historian, Sergei Averintsev, and the symbolist poet-philosopher and Catholic convert, Vyacheslav Ivanov (1866–1949), whose notion of a Europe 'breathing with two lungs,' the eastern and western, would become a favourite idiom. He had also read Solzhenitsyn, with his celebrated predictions that communist rule would collapse once people stopped participating in its collective untruths and rejected its vision of human beings as a 'soulless cogs in a vast machine.' Solzhenitsyn had demonstrated how the struggle against the Christian faith, unleashed during the French Revolution, had created the logical framework for Marx's characterisation of communism as 'naturalised humanism.' It was precisely this 'unbridled humanism,' rejecting Christianity's moral heritage, which had opened the path to materialistic, atheistic communism.[20]

How would be these dramatic new developments be received on the ground? The advent of a Polish Pope, reported by Western radios, sparked enormous interest elsewhere in Eastern Europe. Lithuania's underground *Chronicle* had continued to document the usual round of arrests and interrogations. It now made its position clear.

> We have not been able to understand the Vatican's so-called Ostpolitik, especially in regard to the Soviet Union. We have considered this policy harmful and pernicious to the Church in many respects... It appears that, at the Kremlin's request, the hierarchy of the Russian Orthodox church in Moscow managed to persuade the leadership of the Catholic Church that the best way for Catholics to survive in the Soviet Union was to refrain from any activity

> and simply wait for better times to come. Meanwhile, the government of the Soviet Union has been using all the power and guile it could muster in its relentless efforts to destroy the faith.

The Chronicle also offered the new Pope some advice:

> 1. Atheist governments should not be granted concessions which harm pastoral work.
>
> 2. The affairs of religious believers in Eastern Europe should be entrusted to those in the Vatican best aware of their living conditions.
> 3. Both the official and unofficial Church should receive all possible support, with hierarchies appointed for the 'Church of the Catacombs.'
> 4. No person inclined to make concessions to the government should be appointed bishop.
> 5. Exiled bishops should be consulted about episcopal candidates and greater discipline imposed on clergy.
> 6. More energetic action should be taken to organise global support for persecuted believers.[21]

Having trained secretly for the priesthood himself in Nazi-occupied Kraków, John Paul II could be expected to show sympathy for those now keeping church life alive through the underground networks of the Soviet Union. From Ukraine too, the exiled Cardinal Slipyi hoped he would 'see the necessity of reaching out a helping hand to the oppressed, and not limit himself to words of consolation and exhortations to patience, as his predecessors did.' Ukrainians had suffered historically at the hands of Poles, as well as of Russians and Germans, Slipyi pointed out. Today, facing the same danger, they should be 'united in a common front.' He was sure a Polish Pope would better understand the Ukrainian Church in its 'unequal struggle with atheism.' He also hoped the Pope would remember the Church's forced merger with Russian Orthodoxy and not allow the 'false premises' of a dialogue with the Moscow Patriarchate to prevent him from supporting it—'even if the winds from the Roman curia continue blowing in the opposite direction.'

> Cardinal Wojtyła was a bold fighter in the struggle with this godless doctrine... He knows what it means to fight for the rights of his nation and understands the feelings of the oppressed and downtrodden... The Polish Church and its bishops deserve great recognition for their unity in the struggle with communism, despite the Vatican's unsympathetic Ostpolitik.[22]

Ukraine's impoverished Latin Catholics were full of optimism too. At his new parish in Murafa, the veteran Fr Chomicki received over 300 requests for Masses for the new Pope in the first six months of the pontificate. 'Such joy and happiness fill our hearts we can barely contain it,' enthused one underground nun.

> At one time, when asked my nationality, I replied unhesitatingly that I was a Pole. Later, I had doubts, but now it's all clear. I don't know our nation's history, and I speak and write only with mistakes. But in my veins I have Polish blood; and when I heard a Pole had been elected Pope, I couldn't sleep with emotion.

From Moscow, Fr Yakunin's Christian Committee for the Defence of Believers' Rights sent messages to Slipyi, Wyszyński and Koenig, urging the Catholic Church to 'reach out a helping hand to its brothers in need.'[23]

With Casaroli now the Vatican's Secretary of State—a post said by the Polish SB to combine the functions of premier, Foreign Minister and special tasks plenipotentiary, all rolled into one—the diplomatic networking continued. Yet there signs of a new assertiveness towards Eastern Europe. In December, just two months after his election, John Paul II sent a letter to Hungarian Catholics, praising their Church's achievements. It was published by the Church's much-restricted *Új Ember* weekly; and by April 1979, four new bishops had been appointed, bringing Hungary's Bishops Conference back to full strength.

Vatican Radio began broadcasting regularly in Serbo-Croat to Yugoslavia, and the Pope celebrated a Croatian-language Mass for 10,000 in St Peter's Square. He told Bulgaria's Foreign Minister, Petar Mladenov, the Church expected 'living space' and 'a common, not sterile search for solutions.' By May, two new Catholic bishops had been named for Bulgaria as well. Even in Romania, the only East European country which had not sent representatives to his installation, the Pope appeared ready to make waves. In June 1979, he wrote to Ceauşescu, quoting the Helsinki Final Act and Romanian constitution in defence of the country's outlawed Greek Catholics.[24]

Things were stirring in Czechoslovakia. The Pope had met the timid Bishop Tomášek during Vatican II, and at Cardinal Trochta's funeral in 1974. He now wrote to him, urging his Church to show 'courage and hope.' That was something of a tall order. Repression remained severe and StB surveillance was tight. Eight of Czechoslovakia's 13 Catholic dioceses still had no bishops, and there was only a single priest for every four parishes. Clergy were routinely 'retired' on health grounds by the regime, which paid their salaries, and at least a hundred priests and lay Catholics languished in jail for faith-related offences.

Yet the Husák regime was uneasy. It had failed to snuff out the underground church, which was in closer contact now with secular dissidents from Charter 77. The appointment of Archbishop Gábriš, spokesman for 'extremist clerical forces,' to head the new church province in Slovakia, had clearly been a sign of things to come. 'Greater interest has arisen among Catholic churches here in the orientation of Vatican policy since Cardinal Wojtyła's election,' one Interior Ministry official warned colleagues.

> The ranks of priests and church hierarchs expect the new pope John Paul II to create significantly greater space for religious and social activity by churches in the socialist states... His election was sympathetically received above all by priests with a negative political orientation.[25]

Though worn out and demoralised, Tomášek himself dropped hints that the Pope's message was getting through. Having worried that any resistance would merely endanger the Church further, he now began to meet with Catholic dissidents; and one of them, the veteran Jesuit Fr Zvěřina, who had bitterly criticised Tomášek just two years before, offered to set up an informal committee to help him. 'His initial reply was close to despair,' recalled Fr Halík, the former student leader ordained secretly in East Germany. Tomášek was unaware at the time that Halík was a priest.

> 'Ah, it's all too much,' he sighed. 'I'm all alone with no one to help me.' 'But we'll help you!' I answered. I think that's when he began to change. It was partly in reaction to regime claims that he was just a senile, manipulated old man. But he'd also realised there was no other way. The compromising had failed; government promises were worthless; there'd be no dialogue.[26]

Some communist regimes took the paranoia a bit far. Albania's Party leaders still suspected Soviet and Eurocommunist revisionists of plotting with the Vatican. 'The revolution which brought down all gods and angels from their thrones, emptied all places of worship and chased out the clergy will be defended,' proclaimed a Party newspaper. Only Albania was following the correct Marxist-Leninist policy towards religion—by eradicating it completely.[27]

In March 1979, the new Pope signed off his first encyclical, reaffirming Vatican II's teachings on human rights and social justice. It was said that he had drafted *Redemptor Hominis* just after his election, giving it the air of a personal manifesto. It presented its arguments dynamically, as if in direct response to communist propositions; and it reflected the same self-confidence which had characterised recent Polish Church documents.

Vatican II had highlighted the dangers posed by contemporary atheism, the Pope recalled, 'beginning with the atheism that is programmed, organised and structured as a political system.'

Against this, Christians should be like the 'violent people of God' spoken of in St Matthew's Gospel. The Church approached all cultures and ideologies with an esteem for 'what man has himself worked out in the depths of his spirit concerning the most profound and important problems.' But its task was also to be a guardian of freedom; and this meant distinguishing between authentic and illusory freedoms. The Church was not to be identified with any political system. But it must be aware of man's possibilities, and of what threatened man's dignity—not any abstract man, 'but the real, "concrete," "historical" man.' This Man was 'the primary route the Church must travel in fulfilling her mission.'

Redemptor Hominis highlighted the contradiction between human rights in letter and spirit, a particular problem under communism. Vatican II's Declaration on Religious Freedom had shown how the violation of religious freedom, the most important of all these rights, was indeed a 'radical injustice,' since it offended man's inner nature. 'Even the phenomenon of unbelief, a-religiousness and atheism, as a human phenomenon, is understood only in relation to the phenomenon of religion and faith,' John Paul II continued. 'It is therefore difficult, even from a "purely human" point of view, to accept a position that gives only atheism the right of citizenship.'

This linking of the Gospel with human rights, and human rights with state legitimacy, challenged communist regimes where they were weakest. Instead of denouncing the communist programme, the encyclical showed how the programme had departed from its own ideals and objectives, and forfeited its own legitimacy by violating the principles of power and authority. The Church had made these ideals and objectives its own by reinterpreting them in a Christian way. It was the Church, not the Communist Party, which now stood on the side of humanity. The true 'New Man' had been born not from Lenin's bloody revolution but from Christ's union with mankind through the Incarnation and Redemption.[28]

The Pope's assertive message showed signs of filtering through to Catholic communities in the Soviet Union. The KGB was instructed to 'use all available means' to counter the Vatican's new efforts; and by November 1979, it had come up with a six-point plan, 'Operation Pagoda,' for mobilising Party activists in republics with large Catholic populations and ensuring more regular information exchanges with 'fraternal parties' in Western Europe. The aim was to expose the Church's 'peaceful phraseology' and show how the new Pope posed dangers to his own Church and the wider world.[29]

It was already too late to stifle a wave of Catholic militancy. In Lithuania, a more aggressive Religious Affairs Commissioner, Petras Anilionis, had replaced the smooth-talking Kazimieras Tumėnas, with a brief to restore 1960s-style methods of control. Anilionis considered his options carefully, and came up with a circular 'on the election of Karol Wojtyła as Pope,' outlining how limited concessions might 'deprive extremists of the possibility of profiting from rejection of their demands.' These concessions could include a small increase in seminary admissions and the appointment of a few new bishops. Meanwhile, clergy would be called in for talks, and warned that further advances would depend on whether they used their authority against Catholic dissidents.[30]

The strategy made little headway. Within a month of the Pope's election, five priests had travelled to Moscow for an impromptu press conference, where they announced a new Catholic Committee to Defend Believers' Rights. They included the much-harassed Fr Svarinskas, who had been in prison with the Ukrainian Cardinal Slipyi, and the younger Fr Tamkevičius, editor of the underground *Chronicle*. The new body modelled itself on Yakunin's existing Moscow-based Christian Committee, which had encouraged the Lithuanians to use their potential to attract mass support. It immediately sent the Supreme Soviet and Lithuanian Party bosses a lengthy critique of the religious laws, noting how they contradicted the Soviet constitution and Universal Declaration on Human Rights. Some 20 documents followed over the year, defending not only Catholics but also Orthodox Christians and other denominations.

There were harsh reprisals. By February 1979, the Lithuanian KGB had devised a plan to stifle the Catholic Committee's 'hostile activity.' Efforts against Fr Tamkevičius, who was codenamed 'Tomova,' had become so routine that the KGB and police would sarcastically use the traditional Christian greeting, 'Praised be Jesus Christ!' when they came to search the priest's Kybartai parish house. They still made little headway. But another Committee member, Fr Juozas Zdebskis, suffered scalding when his car was doused in chemicals. Zdebskis, a long-standing KGB target, left the Committee when the communist media claimed the marks were caused by venereal disease.

There were signs that the KGB was resorting to direct action. Its more violent tendencies had been reined in; but intimidation had increased, with a sharp rise in attacks on local churches. Despite this, three-quarters of all Lithuanian clergy put their names to a new wave of petitions to the Soviet rulers during 1979, pointing out the illegitimacy of current laws. One March petition to Brezhnev, demanding the return of Klaipeda's Queen of Peace church, amassed almost 150,000 signatures. The church, built from Catholic donations, had been stripped of its altar and sacred furnishings when it was turned into a concert hall. In August, Catholic clergy appeared among Lithuanian, Latvian and Estonian signatories of a joint declaration, drawn up with Sakharov's backing, together with other Russian dissidents, denouncing the 1939 Molotov-Ribbentrop Pact which had led to their countries' German and Soviet occupation. Such priestly militancy amazed Lithuania's veteran dissidents. It also alarmed Anilionis and his agents.

The *Chronicle*, now in its eighth year, gave news of camp prisoners and published extracts from outspoken sermons. 'I feel I will be forgiven for these words of truth,' one young priest, Fr Ričardas Černiauskas, told his Vilnius congregation after being detained for a week for leading a group of young people to a village meeting:

> If someone kills me, hangs me, slanders me as suffering from venereal disease, stages my suicide, infects me with medical

> means or commits me to a psychiatric hospital, you'll know whose work it is... I became a priest to speak the truth and speak about God—not only in church, as the police have ordered, but wherever I may be: in a barn, in fields, beside a lake, on a lake—or even at the bottom of a lake.[31]

One editorial called the *Chronicle* the 'voice of the fighting church,' and thanked the hundreds of discreet collaborators who had risked their lives collecting information for its pages. Catholics were 'strong and determined in their struggle for God, the Church and human rights,' the *Chronicle* added; they were even more so now that 'the Easter Pope is with us in our struggle and sorrow.'[32]

There were signs that the Church's hierarchy was being encouraged to greater defiance as well. Despite Soviet pressure, Lithuania's bishops had declined to condemn the *Chronicle*, and had said nothing when local priests refused to hand over parish data to the authorities. Superficial Soviet offers—such as the possibility of publishing a Catholic periodical—were rejected as propaganda tricks. It would merely be used as a replica of the *Chronicle* and resemble the periodicals of East Germany, objected the new Bishops Conference chairman, Bishop Liudas Povilonis, who had been arrested for involvement in the Klaipeda church dispute in the early 1960s.

Anilionis's plans to allow new bishops fell through when it became clear that Rome would not bargain. The veteran Bishop Steponavičius had refused to become 'one of the hostages the Holy Father must ransom in consecrating bishops chosen by the Soviet government.' It was rumoured that Steponavičius had been made a cardinal secretly as a mark of his authority. This was untrue. But in 1980, he and his fellow-exile, Bishop Sladkevičius, despatched an invitation to the Pope and received a glowing reply.

Many Catholics would testify to being encouraged and strengthened by solidarity from Rome. In autumn 1979, the Marian Fr Pranas Račiūnas, who had helped set up the *Chronicle*, was debriefed by Anilionis after visiting the Vatican. Like Fr Svarinskas, Račiūnas had also been in prison with the Ukrainian

Slipyi; so he took the opportunity to visit the exiled cardinal while in Rome. He also met the Pope, who asked detailed questions about the Lithuanian Church and predicted a 'general liberalisation' in religious life. The Pope assured Račiūnas that Rome would 'seek accommodations' when it came to selecting new bishops. It would not accept 'compromised priests'; but nor would it accept those 'too much in conflict with the authorities.'

The Vatican knew Račiūnas would have to report back on the conversation; so the encounter was used to make a point. The Vatican's 'so-called eastern policy' remained 'in force,' the Marian priest informed Anilionis. 'But John Paul II intends to implement this policy more actively in future; and if it does not bring tangible results, the present Pope will not hesitate to choose his own line.'[33] Anilionis considered the priest's account important enough to send to Kuroedov in Moscow.

In Slipyi's native Ukraine, there had been fewer signs of Catholic resistance. In December 1978, however, one bold layman, Iosif Terelya, had written to the KGB's head, Yuri Andropov, deploring the use of psychiatric treatment against dissidents. Sentenced to the camps back in 1962, Terelya had twice escaped. After his letter to Andropov, he had been sent to a psychiatric prison, from where he had again escaped, only to be recaptured. The Ukrainian regime had responded to religious restiveness by demanding tougher atheist propaganda. It now attempted to discredit John Paul II by linking him with Cardinal Slipyi's 'fascist past.' At his release in 1963, the regime pointed out, Slipyi had promised to 'devote himself entirely to God.' Instead, he had revived Pius XII's 'crusade against the Soviet Union.' He was now one of the many 'revanchists and enemies of democracy' who looked hopefully to the new Pope.[34]

John Paul II had to tread carefully. If Russian Orthodoxy had been implicated in the suppression of Ukrainian aspirations, so too, at various times, had Polish Catholicism. The Greek Catholic Church was still outlawed and there was no sign of any relaxation. Yet the Pope was ready to do what he could for it. He had met

Slipyi in November 1978, a few days after the cardinal's first emotive statement; and in a long letter to him the following March, John Paul II defended the right of Christians to belong to churches of their choice, citing the Soviet constitution and Universal Declaration. By combining the eastern liturgy with loyalty to Rome, Greek Catholics had created a church in which East and West enjoyed 'full and visible unity.' As such, they could act as a bridge between Catholicism and Orthodoxy.[35]

The Pope called on Ukrainian Catholics to begin preparing for the millennium of the region's conversion in 1988. That was still a decade away. Yet the letter provoked furious reactions in the Soviet Union. Russian Orthodox leaders still viewed the 'Uniates' as a Catholic fifth column, whose very existence seemed to question the validity of Orthodoxy. Patriarch Pimen hit back, accusing the Pope of 'cancelling' the ecumenical openness heralded by Vatican II. A Catholic-Orthodox seminar at Odessa was called off, while Metropolitan Yuvenaly, who had defended Soviet policy at the World Council of Churches, demanded an explanation from Cardinal Willebrands.

While some old Ostpolitik hands in the Vatican appeared wary of the new assertiveness, many Greek Catholics were aggrieved that the Vatican was still in touch with the Moscow Patriarchate at all. There was, indeed, little respite for church members on the ground. Surviving priests still faced harassment for refusing to embrace Russian Orthodoxy, while house searches, confiscations and beatings continued. In May 1980, a Redemptorist monk, Fr Eugenii Vosikevich, was found dead, his mouth stuffed with bread, at the transport base where he worked as a night watchman.[36]

Yet John Paul II persisted. In June 1979, he received Valentyn Moroz, a Ukrainian dissident writer; and in October, during a pilgrimage to the US, he visited the Ukrainian Catholic cathedral in Philadelphia, recalling the 'unnumbered Ukrainian martyrs' who had preferred 'loss of life rather than faith.' The following March, he hosted a synod of 19 Ukrainian bishops at the Vatican, and designated a US-based archbishop, Myroslav Lubachivsky, to succeed the 88-year-old Slipyi. When the bishops met, the 1946 Lviv synod which had outlawed their Church was declared invalid. Patriarch Pimen, enraged again, sent Metropolitan Yuvenaly to remonstrate and threatened to break off relations altogether. But John Paul II stood his ground. Greek Catholics in Poland, whose Ukrainian and Lemki families had been deported under the brutal *Akcja Wisła* back in 1947, had lobbied the Vatican to attend to their 'very urgent matter'; and in December 1981, in recognition of their special needs, the Polish Church was authorised to set up two special vicariates. In Hungary, a similar Greek Catholic vicariate was established in Budapest under the Bishop of Hajdúdorog.

The Soviet government, for its part, stood to gain from any fracturing of Catholic-Orthodox relations. Despite the latest tensions, however, a Vatican delegation under Willebrands paid a visit to Moscow in March 1980, while the Vatican and Moscow Patriarchate were represented in a new Catholic-Orthodox international theological commission, inaugurated at Patmos in May 1980, six months after a visit by John Paul II to the Ecumenical Patriarch, Dimitrios I, in Istanbul. For all the sound and fury, the contacts survived.

Orthodox clergy were still being harassed and intimidated themselves. In March 1981, the Soviet *Trud* daily profiled an atheist club at Pochayev in Ukraine, which had persuaded several monks to abandon their vocations and seek work on the local *kolkhoz.* Such dedicated efforts were bringing about a 'steady decline' in religiosity, *Trud* enthused. The account was heavily one-sided. That August, *samizdat* sources described how the local abbot, Aleksander Yurasev Ambrosii, had fled when police descended on the Pochayev monastery, seizing photocopied prayerbooks and beating the monks, one of whom died after interrogation. Abbot Ambrosii and three others went into hiding, the sources related, and were hunted with helicopters in the Caucasus mountains. There were house searches in Kiev and Odessa in connection with the same case.[37]

Such incidents did little to deter the new interest in human rights, which appeared to be having knock-on effects on other churches as well. In late 1980, the acting General Secretary of the World Council of Churches, Konrad Raiser, a German Lutheran, wrote to Metropolitan Yuvenaly, expressing concern at the latest arrest of Fr Yakunin, who was being held among dangerous criminals at the Lefortovo for 'anti-Soviet agitation.' Raiser mentioned other arrested Orthodox dissidents as well, including Lev Regelson, Aleksander Ogorodnikov and Tatiana Velikanova. Given the efforts invested in bringing the World Council under Soviet influence, this was clearly disappointing.

The arrests had been part of a clampdown after the late 1979 Soviet invasion of Afghanistan, which had also netted the Jewish dissidents Anatoly Scharansky and Aleksander Ginsburg, and the Baptist Georgy Vins. Some would be freed later in prisoner exchanges with the West. But hopes of greater regime moderation had been dashed in January 1980, as Moscow prepared to host the Olympic Games, when the celebrated dissident physicist, Andrei Sakharov, was formally stripped of all state honours.

The clampdown had some effect. The Orthodox priest, Fr Dimitri Dudko, had been sent to the Gulag mines as a seminarian in 1948 and barred from preaching in 1974 by his church superiors. in Moscow. Dudko had been badly injured in a suspicious road accident; but he had continued his ministry, insisting the 'silences and compromises' of Orthodox leaders, far from being a 'legitimate tactic,' should be seen as a betrayal. 'The Church is strong when it is crucified and persecuted,' the diminutive priest had told his young Moscow followers.

> Although the snow still falls sometimes and covers the ground again, and although the freeze continues, the spring will come—this is an act of faith, as well as a reality... I am doing the work of God; and I have placed my hand on the plough to labour in the field of human hearts. I cannot now go back—we know a man who looks behind him doesn't deserve any trust.[38]

Despatched to the Lefortovo, Fr Dudko's heroic resistance quickly crumpled; and in June 1980, barely six months after his arrest, the priest made a sensational recantation, worthy of the darkest days of Christian history. 'I have realised I was arrested not for my faith in God, but for a crime,' he told Soviet TV viewers in a written statement. 'I repudiate what I have done and assess my so-called struggle against godlessness as a struggle against Soviet power… I had great pride and this pride has been lifted. I now see everything in a different light.'[39]

Dudko was reinstated as a paid priest at a suburban Moscow church. His high-profile humiliation as a youth pastor was a useful diversion for the Soviet regime, which still hoped to steer young people towards a committed atheism. Great godless festivals, such as 1 May and the Revolution anniversary, had had their ritual elements steadily developed, while newlyweds still routinely left flowers at monuments to Lenin, the Soviet Union's founder.

The regime felt confident enough to make a few concessions. In November 1980, a tax cut of 15 percent was announced for clergy of all denominations, while sick pay was also made available for the first time from the state. Kuroedov's Religious Affairs Council confirmed that 150 mostly Orthodox religious associations had closed down since 1975 after being 'unable to maintain' their churches and pastors. But it had registered 300 new religious groups at the same time, the Council disclosed, mostly Baptists, Pentecostalists and Adventists, while a thousand churches and mosques had been repaired and renovated.[40] The figures were impossible to verify; but they suggested the Soviet regime was keen to bolster its image.

It had reason to be. By the time Kuroedov's desultory data were released, trouble was stirring in the western reaches of the Soviet empire. The Pope's election had caused ideological confusion in his native Poland. In one survey, over half of all Party members had described themselves as practising Catholics, while a further

22 percent had claimed to be non-practising religious believers. John Paul II's encyclical, *Redemptor Hominis,* linking peace and legitimacy with human rights, had been welcomed by Polish dissidents. It had also spurred Catholics into action.

Within a day of his election, the Pope had notified Poland's State Council chairman, Henryk Jabłoński, that he hoped to visit his homeland as soon as possible. Preparatory talks began in early 1979; and John Paul II's preference was for a May visit to mark 900 years from the martyrdom of St Stanisław, for which he had personally launched a preparatory seven-year prayer cycle. Like the English St Thomas Becket, the Eleventh Century Bishop of Kraków had been murdered while saying Mass by soldiers of King Bolesław the Bold. Communist writers had depicted the saint, who lay buried in Kraków's Wawel Cathedral, as a hostile accomplice of Pope Gregory VII. The Church, by contrast, viewed him as a symbol of civic courage and moral resistance. 'St Stanisław defended his contemporary society from the evil which threatened it,' the Pope told Kraków Catholics in a Christmas message.

> He did not hesitate to confront the ruler when defence of the moral order demanded it. In this way, he became a magnificent example of concern for the people, which we have to compare with our indifference, our negligence, our despondency... Using modern language, we can see in St Stanisław an advocate of the most essential human rights, on which man's dignity, morality and true freedom depend.[41]

The parallels with Poland's post-War Church were obvious; and they irritated the Gierek regime. The regime was nevertheless warned against delaying or blocking the pilgrimage. 'If this leaks out to society, the Primate fears it may arouse unrest and hardship, especially in this uneasy economic situation,' the Bishops Conference secretariat director, Fr Alojzy Orszulik, bluntly notified the Confessions Office. 'If this information reaches the world press in Western countries, it may undermine confidence in Poland, and make it harder to obtain credits and other help.'[42] The message struck home. In February, it was agreed the visit would be postponed till June, but also extended to a full nine days.

Gierek was angered at what he saw as church attempts to exploit Poland's current problems and harness the Pope to 'strengthen its religious and political position in society.' He was answerable to Moscow, and Moscow was growing uneasy. The Polish leader offered reassurances that he had 'taken measures' to deter John Paul II from coming—even though, as a Polish citizen, the Pope could not legally be kept out. 'There has been a certain inconsistency,' Vladimir Kuroedov reported to his Soviet bosses.

> In our view, the measures taken against the Pope's visit to Poland were insufficient... We told our Polish friends that, according to our information, the Pope already has a worked out strategic plan for the Vatican's wide penetration in socialist countries, among which the 'bridgehead' for Catholicism's offensive must be such countries as Poland, Hungary and Czechoslovakia... We tactfully tried to make our friends understand that it is necessary to study more deeply the course of world events connected with the new Pope's activity—not to sit and wait for things to happen, but to take concrete, practical measures.[43]

Brezhnev was said to have urged Gierek right up to the end of May to dissuade the Pope. When it became clear that the visit was going ahead, a huge security operation, '*Lato 79*' (Summer 79) was mounted under Stanisław Stachura, an SB general. Existing clergy agents, such as 'Delta' and 'Jurek,' were primed to get close to the Pope, while 136 additional priest-informers were brought down to Kraków from other dioceses. A total of 360 prison cells were specially prepared, and 'political-operational dialogues' staged with priests and lay Catholics to deter 'attempts to disrupt order and security' by 'people linked with dissident groups or on the social margins,' or by 'fanaticised faithful, the mentally sick and visionaries.'

Like Papal pilgrimages everywhere, John Paul II's homecoming was officially a pastoral occasion. In Poland's case, however, there would be many testimonies of how the atmosphere extended well beyond this. Society stood on the brink of something new and unpredictable. 'At this dramatic moment, we sense the Holy Spirit guiding our common fate,' one 'peasant self-defence community' south of Warsaw noted in a letter to the Pope.[44] The village, Zbrosza Duża, had become famous back in 1969, when local officials had barred Wyszyński from visiting and tried to stop unauthorised Masses in a local chapel. Although the Primate had come eventually, he had been unable to prevent police from arresting the village's priests and turning the chapel into an agriculture shop. Only in 1972, after angry protests, had permission been given for a new chapel.

In the event, John Paul II visited six Polish cities during his pilgrimage, preaching 32 sermons before 13 million people. The Second World War had left Europe divided between rival regimes and ideologies, he pointed out. It now had to rediscover its 'fundamental unity,' by 'opening the frontiers' to the Holy Spirit, and by recalling the rich Christian heritage of 'often forgotten nations and peoples' such as Czechs and Slovaks, Croats and Slovenes, Bulgarians and Lithuanians. 'It is not Christ's will, is it not what the Holy Spirit disposes,' the Pope confidently declared at Gniezno, Poland's oldest Catholic see, 'that this Polish Pope, this Slav Pope, should at this very moment manifest the spiritual unity of Christian Europe?'[45]

The greatest danger to this vision, the Pope made clear, came less from Marxist ideology than from the destructive 'programmed atheism' which was common to all forms of communism. Whereas Gierek had evoked 35 years of communist Poland in his speeches, the Pope appealed to a Polish identity which was infinitely richer and deeper. Peace could only be assured, he cautioned the Party boss, when the nation remained true to its culture and civilisation, its 'social and political subjective reality'—to the 'living tradition' in which, 'through all generations,

Christ's words echo and resound with the witness of the Gospel.' Which 'rational argument,' which system of values, could allow this thousand-year identity be spurned and discarded?

As *Redemptor Hominis* had reiterated, the Church was not seeking 'privileges,' only what was essential for its mission. The Polish bishops had done much, in 'close collaboration' with the Vatican, to establish conditions for normalising Church-state relations; but 'true normalisation' would be possible only when rights and freedoms were fully respected. The bishops were ready for dialogue; but 'authentic dialogue' must respect believers' convictions and ensure conditions for the Church's work. 'We are aware that this dialogue cannot be easy, since it takes place between two concepts of the world which are diametrically opposed,' the Pope conceded. 'But it must be possible and effective if the good of individuals and the nation demands it.'[46] The Church and Vatican, in short, were ready for working relations with the communist regimes. But they would be unbending when it came to the conditions.

Visiting the former Nazi concentration camp of Auschwitz, the 'Golgotha of our times,' the Pope warned against ideologies under which 'the rights of man are submitted to the exigencies of the system, thus rendering them non-existent.' The Church was not afraid of worker movements, he declared in Kraków's industrial Nowa Huta suburb, where the police had battled Catholic protesters over plans for a church 19 years before. It recognised that, in the end, the key issue facing human labour was not one of economics but of dignity. It was also thankful that industrialisation in Poland, far from bringing de-Christianisation, had been matched by the spread of churches and parishes.[47]

John Paul II had returned to Poland from the 'other world' beyond the western border with a language of human rights, and with the full force of a Christian civilisation behind him. He had presented an 'authentic' Poland, a Polish homeland to visualise and work for; and he had also shown that the stultifying structures of communism could be changed—not through violent rebellion, but through a liberation via the free spaces of conscience, morality, culture and identity.

The Gierek regime had long since ruled out fundamental reforms. It had given priority instead to pragmatic economic solutions, a *mała stabilizacja*, or 'small stabilisation' which kept ordinary people preoccupied with daily problems and legitimised the system by generating a web of local interests and loyalties. The Pope's visit had shaken this complacent, fragile edifice to its foundations. He had spoken of a 'moral order,' the order of St Stanisław, and of a 'moral disorder' which came from shallow public subservience. It was right and responsible to demand that this moral disorder be corrected.

Over the previous decade, the Polish Church had spoken up for rights and principles, but had been unable, by itself, to offer clear perspectives for the future. This was what John Paul II seemed to have provided—a sense of the possible. The impulses of rebellion had already been at work among Poles. What they had needed was an authority who could confirm their will for self-determination and show they were no longer dreaming impossible dreams. In the Pope's hands, forgiveness, trust and truthfulness had become political acts, defying the anti-values of the communist system.

There were signs that Gierek's regime had failed to grasp the social and psychological impact of the Papal visit, seeing it only in narrow political categories. Department Four agents travelled to Moscow to discuss its implications with the KGB. But Party hardliners were already accusing the regime of subservience to the Church. One SB official was compelled to deny reports that Interior Ministry staffers and uniformed airport officials had been observed joining the queue to kneel and kiss the Pope's hand.[48] There could be no doubting that the pilgrimage had deepened the polarisation already affecting Eastern Europe, giving a dramatic boost to local Christians and demystifying communist power. The Pope's appeals, steeped in inspirational Christian images, had been relayed beyond Poland. The communist establishments were rattled.

Czechoslovakia's had allowed Cardinal Tomášek to travel to Poland at the last minute, while closing the border to ordinary pilgrims. The Pope's evocation of Europe's spiritual roots was an 'audacious challenge to communism,' its propagandists noted. So were his references to figures like St Stanisław, who symbolised the medieval Papacy's attempt to rule the world. The Vatican was attempting to make up for its past enmity towards the working classes; but a simple glance at Czech history demonstrated that it had always been 'on the side of our enemies.'[49]

Yugoslavia's regime-controlled media gave extensive coverage to the visit, portraying it as proof that 'normal' Church-state relations were possible. For Albania's rulers, it was obvious that the Pope was trying to drive wedges between Eastern Europe and Moscow. This was a natural consequence of Khrushchev's 'bowing his neck' to John XXIII in the 1960s, another sign of the 'ideological degenerateness' sweeping the whole region.

The Soviet government also believed John Paul II was driving wedges. But his strategy went a lot further, Moscow concluded. Party members were puzzled why the Polish government had invited a 'reactionary Pope' in the first place. John Paul II had spoken in Lithuanian during a stopover in the Polish border region of Suwałki, telling enthusiastic ethnic Lithuanians of how 'half his heart' was in their homeland. There were rumours that his own mother had been Lithuanian, and that dramatic developments could now be expected.[50]

The challenge was indeed only beginning. Addressing the UN that October, in the presence of communist ambassadors, the Pope reiterated the damage done to the human spirit by human rights violations, and the 'specific alienation' caused by cutting people off from their 'culture, experiences and aspirations.' Most countries had laws safeguarding freedom of religion and conscience. But some 'structures of social life' condemned the individual for exercising these freedoms. They made him a 'second-class or third-class citizen' and compromised his chances of social advancement, his professional career and 'even the possibility of educating his children freely.' The confrontation between religion and atheism was one of the 'signs of the times'; but it could preserve 'honest and respectful human dimensions' without violating the rights of conscience.[51]

When Hungary's tight-lipped Cardinal Lékai visited Lithuania and other Soviet republics the same month, at Patriarch Pimen's invitation, he assured his hosts that John Paul II would stick to the conciliatory line of John XXIII and Paul VI. Even in Hungary, however, reconstruction was in the air. Research data suggested the decline of religion, having reached rock-bottom in the 1970s, had now gone into reverse, while the centre of gravity in church life was now with youthful city-based renewal movements rather than the traditional religiosity of the countryside. The Kádár regime had made more concessions. Bishops were freer to travel and the Church had opened some Catholic nursing homes, while a new Bible edition had been provided for literature classes in Hungarian schools. At Budapest's half-derelict Catholic Theology Academy, the new correspondence course for laypeople had proved popular. When the Pope dedicated a special Hungarian chapel in the crypt of St Peter's, he reminded parents they still had a right under Hungarian law to request religious teaching at state schools.[52]

Every church leader in Eastern Europe had his local situation to consider; and in most countries, there were signs of restlessness. In a rare show of criticism after Cardinal Bengsch's early death from cancer in December 1979, East Germany's Catholic bishops attacked educational indoctrination in a pastoral letter. Even in Romania, where the veteran Bishop Áron Márton of Alba Iulia would go on protesting the mistreatment of Catholics until his death in September 1980, the *conducator*, Nicolae Ceauşescu, warned Party members that religious beliefs still persisted in their ranks.

In Yugoslavia, where 100,000 Catholics had flocked to Nin, in the biggest ever religious rally, to celebrate the eleventh centenary of Croatian statehood, the Catholic weekly, *Glas Koncila*, talked of a 'Polish example'—an 'awakening and redefinition of modern Catholicism between the Baltic and the Adriatic.' Perhaps sensing the dangers posed by an assertive John Paul II, Tito's regime denied any intention of 'fighting the Church.' Atheism was still an official requirement here for members of the ruling League of Communists. But the regime insisted it was no longer against religion itself. Militant atheism belonged to the Nineteenth Century and would never triumph over religious belief. What mattered was whether citizens supported socialism, not whether they believed in God.[53]

This was a complete turnaround from the late 1940s, when Tito's Partisans had desecrated churches and butchered priests in a campaign to eradicate religious belief. As in Poland, many Party members attended church here; and the official media complained that some appeared torn between their Party loyalty and a desire for religious ceremonies. Religious newspapers—*Glas Koncila* in Croatia, *Pravoslavlje* in Serbia and the Muslim *Preporod* in Bosnia—had demanded that believers be allowed to join the ruling League. There were new claims that the Catholic Church had even encouraged members to join up and gain positions of power. True or false, Cardinal Kuharić was speaking out. At Easter 1980, he returned to the attack, denouncing atheist propaganda in the media and schools. All the propaganda was doing was to undermine morality, especially among the young, leaving 'souls and consciences wounded and destroyed.'[54]

When Tito died in May 1980, just before his eighty-eighth birthday, the Catholic press acknowledged his work for 'brotherhood and unity' between Yugoslavia's peoples, as well as his courage in breaking with Stalin back in 1958 and achievement of a 'new legal framework' for religious rights. Eight months later, when President Cvijetin Mijatović was received by the Pope in Rome, he reaffirmed the line on Church-state relations initiated by the 1966 Protocol and repeated an invitation for John Paul II to visit the country.[55]

Even this did little to appease the Church. Senior Catholic priests, including the Bishops Conference secretary-general, signed a petition to the Federal Assembly, demanding an amnesty for political prisoners. Meanwhile, calls continued for the rehabilitation of Cardinal Stepinac, whose beatification process was now underway. In February 1981, Kuharić defended Stepinac in a cathedral sermon, noting that Catholic priests had also died at the wartime Ustaša's infamous Jasenovac concentration camp, southeast of Zagreb, a place Stepinac had branded a 'mark of Cain' on the independent Croatian state.

The regime hit back. Stepinac had indeed protested to Ante Pavelić, Croatia's Catholic dictator, about Jasenovac, where some 100,000 Serbs, Jews, Gypsies and anti-fascists had been killed. But he had not excommunicated any priests implicated in atrocities by the Ustaša, which had killed at least 300 Serbian Orthodox priests and bishops in a reign of terror, often torching their churches with them. Nor had he taken action against Jasenovac's commander, Fr Miroslav Filipović, a Franciscan military chaplain known as 'Fra Sotona' (Father Devil) for his cruelty, who was hanged at Belgrade in 1946 wearing his friar's robes, after being expelled from his Catholic order.

One of those entering the fray was Croatia's president, Jakov Blažević, who had been a prosecutor at Stepinac's trial back in 1946. He in turn was now accused of 'falsifying history' by Stepinac's former coadjutor, Cardinal Franjo Šeper, who had been kept on by the new Pope as prefect of the Vatican's Congregation for Doctrine of the Faith. Why had the regime only published Stepinac's indictment, Šeper asked, and not his defence documents?[56]

Yugoslavia's official press discerned various tendencies in the Catholic Church, from the 'hostile and nationalistic,' with whom there could be no truck, to the 'loyalists' who were ready to work within the new order. But the reborn debate on Stepinac had tipped things a bit far. 'Stepinac had a historic chance; but he placed himself in anti-history—there can be no more discussion about this,' one official told a national convention. 'Every time Stepinac is dragged out of political mothballs, we shall publicly reply by saying what we think about him and his acts, and about how the Catholic Church behaved under his leadership in the gravest days of the Croatian people's history.'[57]

In the harsher conditions of Czechoslovakia, Christians had also become more assertive. A campaign to discredit the once-docile Cardinal Tomášek, codenamed *Akce Útlum,* had been launched by the StB in early 1979. This envisaged mobilising 'all organised and operative forces' for a 'concentrated blow' against the underground church. It was still possible, insisted the Interior Minister, Jaromír Obzina, to bring Catholics back under the Party's control, by sewing divisions and conflicts and ensuring that, in the event of Church-state conflict, 'the great part of the faithful and the priests will support us, as they did in 1948 and 1949.' Obzina based his strategy on Lenin. 'According to the Leninist thesis, where we have no influence, the influence of our enemies sets in,' the minister explained.

> We will obviously not turn Tomášek into a communist, something we do not foresee; but we will persuade him to abandon his most reactionary ideas… To control a bishop means to control his diocese; and by controlling Tomášek, we will be halfway to controlling the church.[58]

In a throwback to Stalin's quip at Yalta, Tomášek was derided as 'a general without an army.' One Catholic adviser conceded that his Prague Castle residence resembled a scene from novels by the Czech-German satirist, Franz Kafka. A lame, elderly doorkeeper, filmed and monitored by StB agents, would usher visitors into dark, empty rooms, heavily bugged with listening devices.[59] Yet none of this had much impact on underground activities. At least 30 Catholic priests were said to be ministering secretly in Prague alone, while in Slovakia many of the 600 clergy deprived of their *súhlas* licences also remained active. The Church's Oasis movement had spread to Slovakia from Poland after the Prague Spring and unofficially counted 20,000 members.

There was a price to pay. Priests were still being imprisoned or given suspended sentences for ministering without permits and 'hindering supervision of the church' under Article 178 of the Penal Code. A Moravian, Fr Rudolf Smahel, was jailed for four months when the StB seized a religious printing press in Olomouc. Fr Josef Lahuda was jailed for six for unauthorised 'youth encounters,' while the veteran dissident, Fr Josef Zvěřina, was held for six months from September 1979 for 'selling unauthorised religious literature.'

Yet the church revival continued. Christian *samizdat* publishing was increasing and underground pastoral networks spreading. 'Progressive priests' from the pro-regime Pacem in Terris association still vainly sought to defend the legacy of the notorious Fr Plojhar at well-publicised meetings. But Catholics were now receiving clear support from the Pope. In May 1980, John Paul II urged special prayers for Czechs and Slovaks, pointedly invoking the martyred Tenth Century St Wenceslas (Václav), as well as St Jan Nepomucen (c. 1350–1393), the Prague theologian drowned in the Vltava by a jealous King Vaclav IV.

During his Polish pilgrimage, the Pope had spotted a Czech banner in the crowd at Gniezno and read it out aloud: '*Pamatuj, Otče, na své české děti*'—'Father, remember your Czech children.' It was a sign of the bonds of common interest now being forged among Christians throughout the region. Dissidents from the KOR group and Charter 77 had met secretly on the Polish-Czechoslovak border, and a hunger-strike had been staged in a Warsaw church to protest the Husák regime's repression. In July 1979, some 300 prominent Polish Catholics had signed a letter to Tomášek, urging him to intervene on behalf of arrested members of a Charter offshoot, the Committee to Defend the

Unjustly Persecuted (VONS). The committee was acting 'in line with church teaching,' the Polish signatories insisted.[60]

In Poland itself, the Pope's June visit had strengthened opposition self-confidence. 'We have experienced an event whose impact will grow,' KOR had concluded at the time. 'For many in Poland and beyond its borders, listening to the Pope has posed a moral obligation to start and intensify a struggle in defence of rights.'[61] Here too, underground publishing had proliferated, while a 'flying university' was hosting illicit seminars and dissidents using the relative safety of church buildings to meet and talk.

The Gierek regime had made some token concessions, such as lifting restrictions on church processions and abandoning madcap plans for a highway through the Marian shrine at Częstochowa. Yet the distrust was still acute. Even Bolesław Bierut, Poland's ill-fated Stalinist dictator, had done what he said, Cardinal Wyszyński pointed out. By contrast, Gierek, like Gomułka before him, did the opposite and concealed his real intentions.[62] So when, in summer 1980, strikes erupted against new price rises among the 17,000 workers at Gdańsk's Lenin Shipyards, the prospects of a negotiated settlement looked remote. There had been price protests before, most notoriously in 1970, when dozens of Poles had been massacred by trigger-happy police and troops. This time, the strikers showed tactical skill by avoiding a confrontation. Gierek's Politburo, fearing an escalation, also held back on threats of force.

The strike spread fast; and a hurriedly formed co-ordinating organisation, calling itself Solidarity, amassed 9.48 million members in weeks. It called itself a trade union, having discovered a clause in Polish law which still officially allowed workers to form unions. But it was really a social coalition, uniting people of all backgrounds behind a set of common aims.

The sudden emergence of the movement, with its distinctive *Solidarność* logo, owed much to the determined, seemingly quixotic efforts of Poland's 'democratic opposition' over the previous decade. But the dress rehearsal had been the previous year's pilgrimage by the Pope, who had used the word 'solidarity' in his 1969 book, *Osoba i Czyn*. The visit had brought people together in large numbers for the first time, and given the cause of opposition a moral authority which few could question. This was why religious symbols, seemingly neutral but highly charged, were used from the outset to express Solidarity's ideals.

The Polish Church had long demanded better protection of workers' rights, urging that Christian morals be reflected in economic production. 'There is less and less hope of solving the proletarian problem with Marxism,' Wyszyński had concluded in 1977. 'In the final analysis, it is becoming clear that Marxism brings about the rebirth of capitalism by making man an appendage of the productive system and condemning him once more to slavery.' Against this background, the Primate fully understood the latest protests. Output per worker, he pointed out, was barely a quarter of that of the West, while chronic wastage and inefficiency had kept living standards well below what society was capable of achieving. Meanwhile, the Party monopolised economic life, depriving workers of 'freedom of opinion and the means of standing up for their rights.'[63]

Despite this, church leaders reacted cautiously to the Solidarity strikes. The Bishop of Gdańsk, Lech Kaczmarek, sent priests into the shipyards to say Mass and encourage calm. But the Church was uncertain how to respond to an 'independent self-governing trade union.' It was also suspicious of KOR activists like Jacek Kuroń and Bronisław Geremek, who had rushed to the Baltic ports to offer tactical advice. As a mass action, Solidarity seemed poised to gain more in days than the Church had negotiated in years. But the stakes were inordinately high: it could also pay a heavy price.

Stanisław Kania, the Politburo member who had branded the Pope a 'bumptious turkey-cock,' visited Wyszyński on 24 August, requesting talks on how to calm the situation. The Primate warily agreed, and received assurances from Gierek in return that there would be no repetition of the violent crackdown of 1970. Preaching as Jasna Góra two days later, on the feast of the Virgin of

Częstochowa, Wyszyński duly urged Poles to reflect carefully before they burdened the economy with strikes. People would be 'more entitled' to demand their rights, he added, when they had first fulfilled their duties. The homily was broadcast over Polish Radio, which cut out what Wyszyński had also said about 'propagandist atheisation.' Many strikers heard it and concluded that the Primate was supporting the regime.[64]

Controversy over the sermon was quickly overtaken by events. On 31 August, unable to defuse the protests, the regime reluctantly recognised Solidarity as a legal union and accepted its 21 demands. These included shorter housing queues, extended maternity leave and minimum living standards. But the Gdańsk Agreement also listed freedom of speech and association, 'protection of religious feelings' and church access to the media. Less than a week later, Gierek was ousted, just as Gomułka had been a decade earlier, and replaced by Kania as Party boss. Wyszyński had sent his own adviser, Roman Kukołowicz, to counsel the shipyard strikers. He received Solidarity's leader, Lech Wałęsa, for the first time on the day Gierek was dismissed.

Shocked by Solidarity's challenge, the regime had violated a key communist tenet and lost control. It now attempted to neutralise the Church with quick tactical concessions. The Church-state joint commission, stalled since 1967, was restarted on 24 September, while permits were issued for two new Catholic seminaries and a Polish edition of the Vatican's *L'Osservatore Romano*. Work also began on a law, long demanded by Poland's bishops, to legalise the Church's status.

The regime was undecided as to how much more it could concede. The joint commission discussed religious education, building permits and the liquidation of Poland's notorious pro-regime clergy groups. But the SB remained highly active, tracking Church-Solidarity contacts and doing all it could to prevent the Church from extending its influence while the state was weak. Support for the strikers from priests and seminarians was carefully monitored, as were attempts by church leaders to play the role of 'superior arbitrators.'[65]

The Party's Central Committee detected differences between the Pope and Cardinal Wyszyński. John Paul II had sent Wyszyński a letter 'showing solidarity with the strikers,' Kania told his colleagues, whereas the Primate had 'conducted himself seriously' and advised against 'acting against the government.' The Pope had indeed urged the Polish bishops in his letter to 'help the nation in its struggle for daily bread, social justice and the defence of its inviolable rights,' while Wyszyński had advised Solidarity to move slowly and carefully, and follow a 'good strategy.' This did not, however, betoken a lack of enthusiasm. 'There is no doubt about Solidarity: it is what the Church has been struggling for over 30 years,' Wyszyński noted privately. 'Solidarity has broken the back of a monopolistic dictatorship—a monopolistic wrong interpretation of socialism. And socialism is not monopolistic, whatever doctrinal reservations we may have about historical materialism.'[66]

After decades of repression, intimidation and harassment, Polish Christians were facing an extraordinary turn of events. In January 1981, Wałęsa visited the Vatican with an 18-member Solidarity delegation. He assured the Pope his movement's aims were non-political. It was only interested in 'the rights of man, of humanity, to faith and its proclamation,' the Solidarity leader added; and it had learned from John Paul II that 'people must help their neighbours and fellow-men.'

Union rights were essential for human labour, the Pope responded. He hoped Solidarity would go on with its search for justice 'calmly, persistently and fruitfully,' always showing 'the same courage,' as well as 'the same circumspection and moderation.' 'Throughout this difficult period, I have been with you in a special way,' John Paul added—'in the most discreet way, and yet in a manner quite understandable to you and all the world's people.'[67] This was as clear an endorsement as Solidarity could have wished for.

Solidarity's meteoric emergence had fuelled East-West tension. By December, when Warsaw Pact leaders met to discuss the Polish crisis in Moscow, naval movements had been reported in the Baltic, raising fears of a Czechoslovakia-style Soviet invasion. The Pope spoke of 'alarming news' from Poland and appealed for the Virgin Mary's intercession. The Pact's Soviet commander-in-chief, Marshal Viktor Kulikov, was in Warsaw on the day Wałęsa was received in the Vatican; and fears of Soviet intervention were played up by the Polish regime.

In March, when Solidarity threatened a general strike in reaction to police brutality, the Pact announced the 'indefinite extension' of its military manoeuvres, bringing the invasion scare back with a vengeance. Wyszyński was now gravely ill with cancer. He warned the union to tone down its demands, while the Pope sent a message to Brezhnev via the Soviet Embassy in Rome, promising the general strike would be called off if Soviet forces remained in their bases. The Soviet ruler cabled back his agreement; and the Pope notified Wyszyński, who in turn persuaded Wałęsa to cancel the strike call.[68]

When the Church-state commission met that April, government negotiators thanked the Pope and Wyszyński for helping preserve calm. But the atmosphere remained charged. In May, the Polish regime reluctantly recognised another union, Solidarity of Private Farmers, highlighting the common front now existing between industrial and agricultural protesters.

Many Catholics in the Soviet Union could now hear the Mass broadcast from Warsaw and Gdańsk. In neighbouring Lithuania, the hardline Religious Affairs Commissioner, Petras Anilionis, put the number of 'extremist priests' at 150, a quarter of the total. Clergy were all 'well-fed bloodsuckers,' he reminded fellow-officials; and their subversive acts were being backed by the Vatican as a diversion from events in Poland. Extra measures were taken to prevent religious gatherings from being turned into Polish-style rallies. Meanwhile, Lithuania's state radio denounced the 'ardent anti-communists' sitting 'at the microphones of Vatican Radio,' who seemed intent on driving law-abiding Lithuanian Catholics into a confrontation with the Soviet regime.[69]

Anti-religious propaganda was stepped up in Ukraine, especially against Greek Catholics, while in other Soviet republics, extra efforts were made to keep a lid on dissent. They were not wholly successful. In Estonia, some 5000 nationalist students took to the streets of Tallinn, Tartu and Pärnu after the banning of a pop concert and there were 150 arrests. Leaflets calling for strikes were distributed in the capital, while local intellectuals warned of anti-Russian tensions in an open letter to *Pravda*.

Tension was also in the air on the other side of Eastern Europe. In Albania, the veteran Enver Hoxha ordered the execution of several top Party and government officials in a purge, and was said to have shot his own premier, Mehmet Shehu, over the dinner table. The death was described as a suicide. But Shehu was also denounced as 'a dangerous traitor and enemy,' and buried anonymously on wasteland near Tirana. His wife and family were arrested and imprisoned.[70]

Romania had faced its own industrial unrest in August 1977, even under the grip of its narcissistic *conducator*, although nowhere near the scale of Poland's; and in summer 1980, as Solidarity rallied supporters a thousand miles to the north, strikes and demonstrations had broken out at factories in Bucharest, Galați and Târgoviște. A virtual worker uprising erupted a year later in Romania's Motru region, and was swiftly suppressed with arrests, beatings and killings. Yet intermittent protests continued, much to the regime's irritation.

Czechoslovakia had closed its border with Poland, denouncing Solidarity's Catholic links. A government delegation had visited the Vatican for talks in July 1980, as the Polish strikes were erupting. But the talks were inconclusive; and a pre-emptive crackdown had followed to sever any putative church-opposition links. There were reports that special StB units had been formed to disrupt illegal church activities; and when Bratislava seminarians staged a hunger-strike against the pro-regime priests' association, Pacem in Terris, the whole seminary was shut down in retaliation. Atheist propaganda was stepped up and a purge initiated to weed out teachers with religious affiliations, while raids were made on presbyteries and religious houses. In July 1980, two banned Jesuits, Fr František Lízna and Fr Josef Kordík, both Charter 77 signatories, were arrested with four lay Catholics for running an illegal printing press.

Although priests working with young people were cautioned about losing their permits, the regime's religious affairs director, Karel Hrůza, admitted many were returning to religion in search of 'new aims in life.' Meanwhile, steps were taken to block circulation of the Pope's encyclical, *Redemptor Hominis,* and stifle 'legends glorifying the person of Pope K Wojtyla.' In July 1981, however, 30,000 Catholics converged, undeterred, on the Moravian shrine of Velehrad for a summer pilgrimage, the largest since 1945.[71]

Although Yugoslavia enjoyed official relations with the Vatican, its communist rulers were also nervous about John Paul II's ideological challenge. Talk of a Papal visit was quickly torpedoed; and it was hinted that diplomatic ties would suffer if Rome 'behaved provocatively.' In March 1981, Croatia's Socialist Youth Federation was ordered to remove offensive cartoons from its newspaper, which showed Jesus smoking hashish and the Virgin Mary complaining about a lack of contraceptive pills. But the Bishops Conference was outraged by the new media attacks. Religious freedoms were guaranteed under Yugoslavia's laws, the bishops pointed out; but they were still 'noticeably restricted' in practice. In the spirit of Vatican II, the Church wanted a 'sincere and free dialogue' and was ready to co-operate 'on the basis of equality, mutual understanding and respect.' The Catholic Church was conducting its mission 'with the strength of the teaching of Jesus, fully in line with the Holy See,' the Bishops Conference declared that May.

> We love the peoples to whom we belong and are loyal to the legal power, and we decisively reject the reproach that we harbour pretensions of a political nature or any desire for social privileges. However, no bishop can renounce the right to discharge his religious and moral mission unhindered, or the duty to pass moral judgment when this is demanded for the fundamental rights of human beings and the saving of souls.[72]

The regime hit back, highlighting the Church's wide-ranging freedoms and accusing it of offering 'a refuge for renegades, oppositionists and political adventurists seeking room for their murky and dark plots.' Far from 'promoting atheism,' the government now recognised it was 'absurd and stupid to struggle against religious beliefs with administrative measures.' This reflected a proper understanding of Marxism.[73]

Yugoslavia's hard-currency debt was spiralling, while inflation and unemployment had provoked strikes and social disorder. There were demands for full republican status from Serbia's mostly Muslim and ethnic Albanian province of Kosovo, where a summer 1981 arson attack on the Orthodox church's see at Peč sparked an exodus of local clergy. The regime was also concerned, however, about new signs of nationalist militancy among Orthodox clergy. Several priests from the usually submissive Serbian church had been jailed for inciting unrest; and while the Orthodox fortnightly, *Pravoslavlje*, rejected any talk of 'links with anti-communists,' Patriarch German took the unusual step of holding talks with Yugoslavia's federal government president, Veselin Djuranović, to defuse the tension.

There was more to come. In June 1981, a group of Catholic teenagers claimed to have seen the Virgin Mary while herding sheep on a rocky hillside near Medjugorje in Herzegovina. As news of the apparitions spread and thousands converged on the town, regime officials denounced the 'religious hysteria' and accused local priests of using the six teenagers for 'political objectives.' Many clergy expressed scepticism about the visionaries, who claimed the Virgin had warned them against a world 'full of unbelievers and traitors.' Meanwhile, the local bishop, Pavao Žanić of Mostar, reserved judgement and later appointed a commission to investigate the visions.

Action soon followed. In October, a dozen LCY members were expelled for visiting Medjugorje, while its Franciscan parish priest, Fr Jozo Zovko, was accused of helping the youngsters make up the story and given a five-year sentence for 'acts of hostile propaganda' in his sermons. The Franciscans had a tradition of militant autonomy, having vied with the region's bishops since Turkish rule over pastoral care of local parishes. A month later, two more order priests, Fr Ferdo Vlašić and Fr Jozo Križić, who edited a religious newspaper, *Naša ognjišta*, were also given heavy jail sentences for 'enemy activity.' Despite this, the mass influx of pilgrims continued and dozens of miracles were reported.

When tension with the Church was already increasing, the Medjugorje phenomenon put the regime on the defensive. But it also fed a growing assertiveness. The Praxis group, suppressed in 1975, had set up a new journal and pledged to play an 'integrative role' uniting 'progressive intellectuals and critical Marxists,' vowing that 'no amount of repression' would stop it. In an October statement from the sanctuary of Marija Bistrica, the Catholic bishops again condemned anti-religious propaganda and defended the Church's right to speak out.[74]

How was the Polish Pope responding to these events? In September 1980, a month into Poland's Solidarity uprising, Europe's Catholic bishops had met at Subiaco to mark the 1500th anniversary of the birth of the continent's traditional patron, St Benedict, whose monastic movement had marked its history. Their message had ignored the East-West division and addressed Europe as a whole. The Church's task was to be a 'communion surpassing all frontiers,' the bishops pointed out. East-West contacts were making a 'Europe of peoples' possible again, as

Christians made amends for the past by working together, and values 'nourished in the soil of a common past' bound people together over the 'frontiers of religion and ideology.'[75]

This vision of a reunited Europe, 'breathing with both lungs,' was to become a key element of John Paul II's teaching. The post-War division sealed at Yalta had reinforced the ancient East-West rift between Rome and Byzantium; so the restoration of Christian unity had to be a condition for overcoming it. On the last day of 1980, the Pope declared the Ninth Century eastern saints, Cyril and Methodius, co-patrons of Europe with St Benedict. It was a richly symbolic step. Almost two decades had passed since John XXIII had praised the two saints as 'pillars of unity' in an apostolic letter to Slavic bishops, *Magnifici Eventus*. Coming from Thessaloniki, where St Paul had also lived and taught, the two brothers had led a mission to the Slavs of the Danube and Balkans, creating a Slavic alphabet which had made them fathers of Slavic culture and literature, as well as Christian apostles. Whereas Benedict had been a specifically Western figure, embodying the rational outlook of the West, Cyril and Methodius had represented the mystical culture of the East. To proclaim them equal co-patrons of Europe was to pose an ideological challenge. Taken together, the three great saints personified a common spiritual patrimony, 'a union of two currents of the Christian tradition.'[76]

The Soviet media hit back, insisting the Slavic alphabet had predated Sts Cyril and Methodius, while St Benedict's monasteries had been 'seedbeds of obscurantism.' The very idea of a 'Christian Europe' was just a Western ploy to stir up political opposition.

Hostility was mounting and there was drama in the air. On 13 May 1981, a Turkish assassin, Mehmet Ali Ağca, shot John Paul II through the abdomen in the middle of a crowd of 20,000 in St Peter's Square. The 9mm Browning Parabellum bullet narrowly missed killing the Pope instantly by ripping through his central aorta. Even then, surgeons fought for five hours to save his life, leaving him hospitalised for three months.

Western intelligence agencies had warned of previous plots against the Polish Pope, including apparent plans to detonate a bomb during his visit to Jasna Góra in 1979 and to place slow-acting poison in his food. Even with tightened Vatican security, Rome had remained a hotbed of agents and informers. Polish SB operatives were in the square at the time of the shooting and there were claims that Vatican-based Polish clergy had supplied advance information to the Soviet KGB via the SB and East German Stasi. One priest in particular, codenamed 'Prorok' (Prophet), was said to have given the SB 'hundreds of pieces of information' during the assassination plot, as well as on Vatican negotiating tactics and diplomatic contacts with the US and Germany. 'Prorok' had been rated highly. 'Our friends hold a strong operational position in the Vatican, giving them direct access to the pope and the Roman congregations,' the Soviet KGB's Warsaw resident had boasted to Moscow a year earlier.

> Besides experienced agents, to whom John Paul II is well disposed personally and who can obtain an audience at any moment, our friends have also established agent resources among leaders of the Catholic student movement who have permanent contacts with Vatican circles and operational possibilities at Vatican Radio and the papal secretariat.[77]

Publicly, the finger of suspicion pointed at Moscow; and even when Bulgarian agents were found to have been in contact with Ağca, this was widely viewed as a sideshow to camouflage KGB involvement. No firm evidence would ever emerge, however, of official communist complicity. Soviet propagandists, for their part, accused the American CIA and Italian secret services of engineering the outrage to provoke a popular uprising in Poland.[78]

Polish TV interrupted its programmes when news of the shooting broke and brought in a Catholic priest, for the first time ever, as a commentator. The timing was highly sensitive. Solidarity was at its height and Cardinal Wyszyński was now on his deathbed in the final stages of cancer. The regime had prepared itself for the Primate's demise after 33 years at the Church's helm, seeing this as an opportunity to tighten its grip over the Bishops Conference. By the time Wyszyński died on 28 May, however, a fortnight after the Rome shooting, it had concluded that a less dominant Primate would bring new problems by giving greater leeway to radical clergy.

Wyszyński's Warsaw funeral, led by Casaroli, was carried live on TV and attended by a large regime delegation. Behind the scenes, agents were urgently mobilised to steer the nomination of his successor. There were fears that the choice could fall on Bishop Tokarczuk, against whom no amount of SB pressure had ever worked. Department Four duly circulated instructions on how Tokarczuk and other recalcitrant bishops were to be discredited.[79]

The effort proved unnecessary. Less than six weeks later, Wyszyński's own former assistant, Bishop Glemp of Warmia, a canon lawyer, was appointed to follow him as Archbishop of Gniezno and Warsaw. Glemp had been in Rome during Vatican II; but at just 52, he had been a bishop only briefly and had little pastoral experience. Coming from a worker family, he had been a child forced labourer under Nazi rule and had a brother who was a Party member. He had, however, successfully resisted SB attempts to recruit him during his 12 years with Wyszyński. This, with his experience of Church-state negotiations, was widely held to explain why the dying Wyszyński had recommended him—and why the Pope, himself gravely injured, had caused surprise by approving the nomination.

In September 1981, as Solidarity held its first national congress in Gdańsk, the still-convalescing John Paul II released a new encyclical, vigorously backing workers' rights to form trade unions as a 'mouthpiece of the struggle for social justice,' and calling pointedly for 'movements of solidarity' to unite against poverty and exploitation. *Laborem Exercens* did not waste time condemning communism. Instead, it offered a positive affirmation of what the Church had to offer in upholding human dignity. It was possible to speak of justice only when the organisation of life and work allowed the human spirit to develop. By contrast, the 'error of early capitalism' was in danger of being repeated whenever humanity was treated as just an element in the material means of production. The 'great conflict' between labour and capital, which had so marked the course of history, was still finding expression in the conflict between liberalism and Marxism; and it was wrong for Marxism to accentuate this with ideological and political weapons. It was the working person, linked to God by conscience and will, who was history's prime mover, not the external forces of wealth and power.[80]

The encyclical was impeccably timed. The atmosphere had hardened in Poland throughout 1981, and a full-scale confrontation seemed likely. Warsaw Pact manoeuvres were staged in the nearby Baltic to intimidate the Solidarity congress. But the union, undeterred, talked of a 'self-governing republic' and appealed to fellow-workers around Eastern Europe to fight for their own free trade unions. Since Gierek's ouster the year before, the Polish Party had lost a quarter of its membership and become bitterly divided. Power was slipping from its hands, to the alarm of neighbouring communist regimes. Moscow denounced Solidarity's appeal to Eastern Europe as a 'repulsive provocation.'[81]

Western governments, uneasy about the Pope's crusading defiance, were themselves growing nervous about stability in Eastern Europe. So was the Polish Church, whose new, untried leader, Archbishop Glemp, was installed on 25 September. Its leaders believed hotheads from KOR had steered Solidarity in a radical direction; and even when KOR dissolved itself that summer, this was merely taken as proof that the group had successfully infiltrated the union. The Bishops Conference spokesman, Fr Alojzy Orszulik, was given a copy of Jacek Kuroń's 'political programme' by Barcikowski, the Politburo member, that November, and concurred that Wałęsa had lost control to 'radical activists.' Poland's bishops had a 'critical attitude' to Solidarity, Orszulik assured regime negotiators.

Glemp made a last-ditch attempt to broker a compromise on 4 November at tripartite talks with Wałęsa and the Polish Party's new First Secretary, General Wojciech Jaruzelski. 'It is the Gospel and social order which are the Church's politics,' the new Primate declared. 'If we take part in summit talks, we do so to provide that aspect of the truth which concerns the Church—the peace of man's inner order, the peace of kindness.'[82] By then, it was clear that a one-party state could not coexist with an independent union. This was not a time for invoking kindness.

The showdown came in the small hours of 13 December, when Jaruzelski declared a 'state of war,' deploying 1750 tanks, 1400 armoured cars, 70,000 troops and 30,000 police and Interior Ministry agents to impose it. In an early morning broadcast, the general insisted his sole aim was to protect public order within 'the normal mechanisms of socialist democracy.' Poland was 'on the brink of the abyss'; and the restrictions would be lifted once the situation was stable.

Evidence suggested martial law had been under preparation since March. Solidarity had been heavily infiltrated, with 2400 informers in its Warsaw chapter alone, where a quarter of Jaruzelski's forces were concentrated. A list of those to be arrested had been ready in February, and several neighbouring Warsaw Pact armies placed on standby to lend assistance. By all accounts, the union was caught unprepared.[83]

With borders closed, telephones cut, a curfew in force and 10,000 people either behind bars already or facing imminent internment, Solidarity had to decide immediately whether to take to the streets or prepare for underground resistance. A consensus quickly emerged that, while martial law had to be challenged, direct confrontation would merely strengthen the regime's hand.

The Church, caught between the military power of the state and the unrest of a discontented society, faced dilemmas too. Its initial response was quick in coming. Glemp had been notified of the crackdown, with other church leaders, when Barcikowski arrived at his residence at 5.30 am, and had set out for Jasna Góra shortly after. In a hastily prepared address to perturbed young Catholics, he appeared to give Jaruzelski the benefit of the doubt. Echoing the late Wyszyński, he urged Poles to avoid 'mad actions' and recognise that 'the head and reason must rule.' Overcoming evil with good should be the 'programme for Christians,' who should give peaceful consideration to 'a situation aimed at peace, saving life and avoiding the shedding of blood.'

Returning to Warsaw, Glemp appealed for calm again. The regime claimed martial law was 'dictated by higher necessity,' he reminded Catholics at a Jesuit church—'the choice of a lesser rather than greater evil.' If this was correct, then the average citizen should 'subordinate himself to the new situation' and avoid 'a fight of Pole against Pole.' 'It doesn't matter if someone accuses the Church of cowardice, procrastination, deflating the radical moods,' the new Primate added. 'The Church defends every human life; so it will appeal in this state of war, wherever it can, for peace, renunciation of force, an end to fratricidal conflict. There is no greater value than human life.'[84]

Martial law would be far from bloodless. On 16 December, riot police and troops shocked the country by opening fire on striking miners at Silesia's Wujek colliery, killing nine. The new parish priest, Fr Henryk Bolczyk, a moderator with the Light-Life youth movement, had heard confessions at the pitface and stayed with the miners as the tanks rolled in. He now did his best to counsel the grieving families, as other Silesian mines remained on strike. A newly dedicated colliery cross was desecrated overnight in January, but replaced with an even finer one the following day.

Glemp himself remained under intense pressure. 'If the Church keeps up its negative stance,' one regime official warned him after the Wujek massacre, 'it will be responsible for every future drop of blood.' The Primate continued to make statements, lamenting the internments and mass sackings martial law had brought with it. Yet he still counselled patience, fearing more ruthless communist hardliners were lurking in the shadows behind Jaruzelski, perhaps even planning a coup with Moscow's backing. 'No handcuffs, no regulations, no exiles" could destroy Solidarity's ideals', Glemp assured Catholics in early January, again quoting Wyszyński: 'One can, in a heroic gesture, give one's life on the field of battle... But it is sometimes a greater heroism to live and endure.'

With all church sermons closely scrutinised, the caution was hardly surprising. The Pope himself, notified of martial law by Poland's Rome embassy, had also been restrained in his reaction, urging 'a return to the path of renewal' and recalling that the best rulers expressed their 'strength and dignity' through dialogue rather than force. Even after the Wujek colliery massacre, John Paul II had written calmly to Jaruzelski, appealing to 'the consciences of those with whom decisions now rest.[85]

Yet differences soon emerged. The Polish bishops' Main Council drafted a formal protest on 15 December, deploring how the 'moral sense of society' had been outraged by this 'dramatic restriction of civic rights.' At the regime's request, Glemp withdrew the statement. But the text had already been circulated, and several bishops questioned its cancellation. As evidence emerged that martial law had been well planned, most church leaders settled into a judicious defence of the moral high ground, urging an end to restrictions while also appealing for mutual responsibility. 'Social accord makes demands not only on the authorities, but also on the whole of society,' the Bishops Conference declared in February. 'It is society's duty to adhere to a sense of realism in assessing our country's geopolitical situation... This requires us to define our individual and social demands wisely, taking a long-term view of our national future.'[86]

Thousands of Solidarity activists, as well as many prominent Catholics, were still being held at 52 separate internment centres, while illegal strikes were incurring draconian jail sentences of 3–5 years. There was little if any physical violence and torture. But union militants were pressured to leave the country, while their families faced intimidation and blackmail. Party hardliners were said to be demanding full-scale terror to 'teach the people a lesson,' as Lenin had once recommended. Whether or not this was just regime disinformation, all signs of protest were now brutally pacified and thousands sacked in campaign of 'verification.'

Department Four, much expanded since the 1970s, was represented on Jaruzelski's Military Council for National Salvation, known by its acronym as WRON, and had prepared a plan for 'dealing with the Church' under martial law as early as April 1981. This noted that the Church could be relied on to 'tone down and soften the social mood.' But it also set out steps to block church contacts with 'Solidarity extremists and anti-socialist groups,' and ensure militant clergy were denied access to industrial plants.[87]

It would be argued that the regime had exaggerated the Church's capacity to affect conditions. But it took its influence seriously. Department Four filed regular reports to the Central Committee on 'certain aspects of clergy activity,' carefully identifying the different types, from the submissive to the hostile, and discussing what could be done to coax, intimidate and divide them. The regime knew it could appear weak if it relied too obviously on the Church's moderating influence. But there were benefits to be gained from good relations, not least in deterring local parishes from providing sanctuary for the opposition. So it set out to co-opt the Church wherever possible. Church-building permits were freely handed out, reaching 380 in 1980–2, while the Church-state commission re-convened barely a month into martial law.[88]

The commission's minutes illustrated the complex relationship which was now taking shape. At one meeting, Cardinal Macharski, the Pope's successor in Kraków, reminded his regime interlocutors that martial law 'would not have been so easy to impose' without 'the Church's attitude.' 'Martial law's achievements can be accepted to some extent, although we think its very proclamation signifies a failure,' another archbishop concurred. 'We don't deny political methods were used on Solidarity's side and that extremist forces dominated it. This is why we are suffering, although we also see something positive in Solidarity.'[89]

From his vantage-point in Rome, the Pope could take a different line. He had sent Mgr Poggi to Warsaw by train within a week of the clampdown; and he would oppose economic sanctions, a key Western policy. Despite this, Soviet propagandists continued to depict him as the main inspirer of events in Poland. Solidarity had been born, the *TASS* newsagency declared, 'in the bosom of the Catholic Church,' which formed part of a worldwide conspiracy stretching from KOR to the CIA. The Pope was said to be working with President Reagan, who visited the Vatican in June 1982, to channel illicit US funds, and to have even formed a 'holy alliance' for this purpose.

John Paul II was assured by Jaruzelski in a letter that there would be no return to the 'order of relations' which had characterised pre-Solidarity Poland—but also no return to the 'anarchy, rejection of all government actions and economic paralysis' which had come later.[90] There were times, however, when the general's ideological mindset reasserted itself. 'The Church's opinion is that our Party is a gang of thieves,' he told the Central Committee in April 1982. 'We should show the Church itself isn't living at all badly—how it swims in goods and has plenty of corrupt practices in its own past.'[91]

Local bishops continued to protest the repression, speaking out against measures such as a new requirement of loyalty oaths, or *lojalki*. They intervened in humanitarian cases and gave charitable help to internees and their families via groups such as the Primate's Aid Committee, which was run by Catholic Intelligentsia Club members from Warsaw's St Marcin church. Most importantly, they raised no objections to the continued use of church buildings as a secure venue for meetings, lectures and concerts. Clashes frequently occurred outside Catholic places of worship; and shots were fired at four separate churches in Gdańsk, provoking protests from the local bishop. In western Poland, Gorzów cathedral was doused in teargas and had its windows broken. In Gdynia, two priests from the Sacred Heart of Jesus church were arrested for allegedly pelting the police with stones, amid what the bishop denounced as 'malicious and lying accusations.' Meanwhile, tens of thousands attended the Warsaw funeral of a 19-year-old student, Grzegorz Przemyk, when he was detained and beaten to death by police.

Glemp himself had few illusions about Jaruzelski's intentions. He knew, in the general's own words, that 'when the government is weak, it will talk to the Church and make gestures, and when it gets stronger, it will start fighting the Church.'[92] He would, however, be dogged by credibility problems. These merely intensified when, in October 1982, Solidarity was finally banned under a new union law. The Church had urged restraint on the understanding that union rights would be restored. But the Polish regime, gambling that its power was now secure, had reneged on its pledges and assurances. It appeared to have regained the initiative and recouped its battered self-confidence; but it had also forfeited the trust of anyone still hoping for a genuine national accord. This was a pyrrhic victory. The crisis of power and authority would have echoes throughout the communist world.

Notes

1 Lasota, *Donos na Wojtyłę*, p. 262.

2 K. Wojtyła, *Osoba i Czyn oraz inne studia antropologiczne* (Lublin: Wydawnictwo KUL, 1994), pp. 197–9. Schaff's book was *Marksizm a jednostka ludzka* (Warsaw: PWN, 1965). Wojtyła's early two-volume study of political philosophy, published semi-legally in around 200 copies in 1953, was titled *Katolicka Etyka Społeczna* and never republished; see J. Luxmoore and J. Babiuch, 'John Paul's debt to Marxism,' in *The Tablet*, 14 January 2006.

3 Raina, *Rozmowy z władzami*, pp. 223–4.

4 K. Wojtyła, *Znak któremu sprzeciwiać się będą* (Warsaw: Pallotinum, 1976), p. 103. The lectures included references to the former Marxist, Leszek Kołakowski, who had befriended Wyszyński back in the 1960s as part of his efforts to shake off Marxism's 'false philosophy.'

5 Lasota, *Donos na Wojtyłę*, pp. 208, 255; Walusiak, 'Kryptonim 'Wierni,' in *Kościół w godzinie próby*, p. 158.

6 Lasota, *Donos na Wojtyłę*, p. 238; J. Luxmoore, 'Polish institute publishes book showing police tracking of Wojtyła,' in *Catholic News Service*, 20 April 2010. Comprehensive documentation on the SB's surveillance of Cardinal Wojtyła was published by Poland's National Remembrance Institute, in J. Marecki and F. Musiał, *Ku Prawdzie i Wolności: Komunistyczna bezpieka wobec Kard. Karola Wojtyły* (Kraków: IPN, 2009), pp. 37–600).

7 Lasota, *Donos na Wojtyłę*, pp. 251–4.

8 *Ibid.*, p. 259.

9 Activity plan for Interior Ministry Department Four, December 1977, in Dudek and Gryz, *Komuniści i Kościół*, p. 328.

10 Quoted in Luxmoore and Babiuch, *The Vatican and the Red Flag*, p. 204; *L'Osservatore Romano*, 19 October and 15 December 1978.

11 T. Mazowiecki, 'Zadanla inteligencji katolickiej w Polsce wobec wyboru Jana Pawła II,' in Z. Hemmerling and M. Nadolski (eds), *Opozycja demokratyczna w Polsce 1976–1980* (Warsaw: Wydawnictwo Uniwersytetu Warszawskiego, 1994), p. 345.

12 Dominiczak, *Organy bezpieczeństwa*, pp. 311; K. Kąkol, *Spowiedź pogromcy Kościola: Kulisy stosunków Kościól-Panstwo w PRL* (Warsaw: Ethos, 1994), p. 90; Lasota, *Donos na Wojtyłę*, pp. 264–5; A. Michnik, J. Tischner and J. Żakowski, *Między Panem i Plebanem* (Kraków: Znak, 1995), p. 280; 'Zdegustowani towarzysze—reakcje władz PRL na wybór Jana Pawła II,' in *Katolicka Agencja Informacyjna*, 15 October 2012.

13 Luxmoore and Babiuch, *The Vatican and the Red Flag*, p. 206.

14 Isakowicz-Zaleski, *Księża wobec bezpieki*, pp. 112–119.

15 *Ibid.*, p. 186, 272–4. L. Szymowski, *Agenci SB kontra Jan Paweł II: Kto donosił na Papieża* (Warsaw: Penelopa, 2012, pp. 323–4; D. Iwaneczko and J. Tarnawa, 'Ksiądz z nami współpracuje i my ksiedzu pomożemy,' in *Aparat Represji w Polsce Ludowej 1944–1989*, vol. 1/ no. 3 (2006), pp. 282–314.

16 Mikloško et al, *Zločiny komunizmu*, p. 313.

17 Luxmoore and Babiuch, *The Vatican and the Red Flag*, p. 206.

18 *Novoye Vremiya*, 27 November 1978. The newspaper said the election had reflected 'a serious failure by the rightist group of Italian cardinals who've blocked implementation of the Second Vatican Council's resolutions'; Przebinda, *Większa Europa*, p. 267.

19 A. Gromyko, *Memoirs From Stalin to Gorbachev* (London: Arrow, 1989), pp. 271–3; F. Corley, 'Soviet reaction to the election of Pope John Paul II,' in *Religion, State and Society*, vol. 22/no. 1 (1994), p. 56; G. Weigel, *Witness*

to Hope: The Biography of Pope John Paul II (London: Harper Collins, 1999), pp. 298–9.

20 Przebinda, *Większa Europa*, pp. 117, 233–4.

21 Report on the life of Lithuanian Catholics after the election of Pope John Paul II, in *Lietuvos Katalikų Bažynčios kronika*, no. 36 (1979); *Radio Liberty Research*, 20 June 1979.

22 Statement, 3 November 1978; in *Informationen und Berichte: Digest des Ostens*, Koenigstein, no. 1 (1979), pp. 6–8.

23 Dzwonkowski, *Za wschodnią granicą*, pp. 275–6; *Polacy a Kościele katolickim na Wschodzie, 1939–2011* (Toruń: Marszałek, 2011), pp. 89–97; Przebinda, *Większa Europa*, p. 272.

24 Full text of the Pope's letter in Bozgan, *Cronica unui eşec previzibil*, p. 411. On Casaroli, see Szymowski, *Agenci SB*, p. 42.

25 Report of Major-General Vladimir Starek, 12 February 1979, in J. Hartmann, B. Svoboda and V. Vasko, *Kardinál Tomášek: svědectví o dobrém katechetovi, bojácném biskupovi a statečném kardinálovi* (Prague: Zvon, 1994), p. 83; Mikloško et al, *Zločiny*, p. 315.

26 Author's interviews with Halík, August 1990 and November 1999; J. Luxmoore, 'A Spiritual Harvest' and 'A light now extinguished,' in *National Catholic Register*, 23 August 1992; Jandourek and Halík, *Ptal jsem se cest*, pp. 131–150.

27 From *Rruga e partisë*, no. 2; in *Radio Free Europe Background Report*, 14 March 1979.

28 John Paul II, *Redemptor Hominis*, 4 March 1979, nos. 11, 17.

29 Przebinda, *Większa Europa*, p. 115; T. Szulc, *Pope John Paul II: The Biography* (New York: Scribner, 1995), pp. 310–11; Mikloško et al, *Zločiny komunizmu*, p. 314.

30 'Plan for means of realising the resolution of the Central Committee secretariat of the CPSU on opposing the policy of the Vatican,' in Streikus, *Antykościelna polityka*, p. 207.

31 Text in *Lietuvos Katalikų Bažynčios kronika*, no. 49 (1981); *Radio Liberty Research*, 19 January 1982. On Tamkevičius and the KGB, see Spengla, *The Church, the Kronika*, p. 60.

32 Editorial, 'We are not alone!' in *Lietuvos Katalikų Bažynčios kronika*, no. 37 (1979).

33 Luxmoore and Babiuch, *The Vatican and the Red Flag*, p. 208; Wołowski and Korzeniewska, *Jak służąc Panu Bogu*, pp. 48–50; letter of Bishop Steponavičius to Bishop Povilonis, 3 September 1981, in Streikus, *Antykościelna polityka*, p. 208.

34 For example, *TASS*, 9 November 1981; *Radio Liberty Research*, 16 March 1983.

35 *L'Osservatore Romano*, 16 June 1979; Luxmoore and Babiuch, *Rethinking Christendom*, p. 148; Przebinda, *Większa Europa*, pp. 170–2.

36 *Ibid.*, pp. 181–6. On the Vosikevich murder, see *Radio Liberty Research*, 6 November 1980.

37 From *Arkhiv Samizdata* 4567, 13 August 1981.

38 *Le Monde*, Paris, 21 January 1980; *Ecumenical News Service*, 30 October 1982.

39 *Daily Telegraph*, London, 21 June 1980.

40 *The Times*, London, 4 November 1980; Dzwonkowski, *Za wschodnią granicą*, pp. 300–1.

41 *Radio Free Europe Situation Report*, 26 January 1979. The 1979 survey concluded that Party membership now had no 'significant influence' on attitudes to religion; *Kultura i społeczeństwo*, vol. 28/no. 3 (1984), pp. 202–3, 212–3.

42 P. Raina, *Wizyty Apostolskie Jana Pawła II w Polsce: Rozmowy przygotowawcze Watykan-PRL-Episkopat* (Warsaw: Książka Polska, 1997), p. 11.

43 Quoted in Luxmoore and Babiuch, *The Vatican and the Red Flag*, p. 213; Dudek and Gryz, *Komuniści i Kościół*, p. 345.

44 'List KSCh Ziemi Grójeckiej do Jana Pawła II,' 20 May 1979, in Hemmerling and Nadolski, *Opozycja demokratyczna*, pp. 499–502. On agents around the Pope, see Lasota, *Donos na Wojtyłę*, pp. 216, 232–3, 290–5; W. Skalski, *Pierwsza pielgrzymka Ojca Świętego Jana Pawła II do Polski* (Kraków: Wydawnictwo M, 2008), pp. 32–45.

45 Pontifical Mass homily, Gniezno, 3 June 1979, in Luxmoore and Babiuch, *The Vatican and the Red Flag*, pp. 214–5.

46 Address to the 169th plenary session of the Polish Bishops Conference, Częstochowa, 6 June 1979.

47 Pontifical homily, Kraków, 10 June 1979; Luxmoore and Babiuch, *The Vatican and the Red Flag*, pp. 215–6.

48 Lasota, *Donos na Wojtyłę*, p. 309; Skalski, *Pierwsza pielgrzymka Ojca Świętego*, pp. 112–7, 224–238.

49 J. Milota, in *Ateizmus*, no. 3 (1979); Luxmoore and Babiuch, *The Vatican and the Red Flag*, p. 218.

50 Wołowski and Korzeniewska, *Jak służąc Panu Bogu*, p. 47; *Zëri i Popullit*, Tirana, 8 June 1979.

51 Address of His Holiness John Paul II to the 34th General Assembly of the United Nations, New York, 2 October 1979 (Vatican Press Office, 1979), paras. 17–20.

52 Luxmoore and Babiuch, *The Vatican and the Red Flag*, pp. 220–2.

53 *Borba*, Belgrade, 30 January 1984; Bakarić articles in *Vjesnik*, Zagreb, 31 December 1979 and 1–2 January 1980; *Glas Koncila*, 1 January, 23 March,

24 June and 5 August 1979; *Scînteia*, Bucharest, 20 November 1979; *Radio Free Europe Situation Report*, 21 January 1980.

54 *Glas Koncila*, 9 March 1980.

55 *Tanjug*, 19 December 1980, *La Stampa*, 20 December 1980; assessments of Tito, in *Glas Koncila*, 18 May 1980 and *Družina*, Ljubljana, 15 May 1980.

56 Vatican Radio, 25 March 1981; *Večernji list*, 31 January-12 February 1981. Blažević devoted much space in his third volume of memoirs to Stepinac, also quoting from his unpublished diary; *Mač a ne Mir* (Zagreb: Mladost, 1980); *Družina*, 22 March 1981.

57 Branko Puharić, 'Report to the Republican Conference praesidium,' in Tanjug, 5 March 1981; *Vjesnik*, 19 February 1981.

58 Hartmann et al, *Kardinál Tomášek: svědectví*, pp. 83–6.

59 Fr Halík, in Hartmann et al, *Kardinál Tomášek: svědectví*, pp. 115–8; author's interview, September 1990.

60 Luxmoore and Babiuch, *The Vatican and the Red Flag*, p. 221.

61 'Oświadczenie KSS KOR w związku z pielgrzymką Jana Pawła II,' 1 July 1979, in Hemmerling and Nadolski, *Opozycja demokratyczna*, pp. 592–4; A. Micewski, *Kościół-Państwo* (Warsaw: Wydawnictwo Szkolne i Pedagogiczne, 1994), pp. 65–6; on KOR and the Papal election, Friszka, *Czas Kor-u*, pp. 330–6.

62 Czaczkowska, *Kardynał Wyszyński*, p. 146; R. Kukołowicz and P. Bączek, *W cieniu Prymasa Tysiąclecia* (Warsaw: Ad Astra, 2001), pp. 85–7.

63 Speech to September 1980 pastoral conference, in Luxmoore and Babiuch, *The Vatican and the Red Flag*, p. 226; 'Memoriał Episkopatu Polski do Rządu,' 1 April 1980, in Raina, *Kościół w PRL*, pp. 653–4.

64 Wyszyński's homily in Micewski, *Kościół-Państwo*, p. 65; Hemmerling and Nadolski, *Opozycja demokratyczna*, pp. 725–733; Friszke and Paczkowski, *Niepokorni*, pp. 529–531.

65 T. Krawczak and C. Wilanowski (eds), *Kościół w Stanie Wojennym: Wybór dokumentów z Archiwum Akt Nowych* (Warsaw: Pax, 2008), p. 6.

66 'Notatki ze spotkania Prymasa Kard. S. Wyszyńskiego z przedstawicielami NSZZ Solidarność,' 4 January 1981, in Raina, *Kościół w PRL*, p. 197; Kania to the Politburo, in Dudek and Gryz, *Komuniści i Kościół*, p. 353.

67 'Przemówienie Papieża Jana Pawła II,' 15 January 1981, in Raina, *Kościół w PRL*, p. 199. The Solidarity delegation included a top-level informer, codenamed 'Delegat' and later identified as Fr Henryk Jankowski, rector of Gdańsk's St Brygida shipyard church; Szymowski, *Agenci SB kontra Jan Paweł II*, pp. 246–8.

68 Luxmoore and Babiuch, *The Vatican and the Red Flag*, pp. 229, 233. The exchange of messages was documented in East German Stasi archives,

Rzeczpospolita, Warsaw, 6 October 1984; Czaczkowska, *Kardynał Wyszyński*, pp. 595–7. The Pope's exchanges with Brezhnev still awaited publication in 2015.

69 *Lietuvos Katalikų Bažynčios kronika*, no. 50 (1981).

70 O. Pearson, *Albania in the Twentieth Century: A History*, vol. 3 (London: Tauris, 2006), pp. 641–2. In Hoxha's book, *Titoites* (1982), several chapters are dedicated to Shehu's denunciation; J. Halliday, *The Artful Albanian: The Memoirs of Enver Hoxha* (London: Chatto, 1986), pp. 329–330. A fictionalised account of Mehmet Shehu's fall and death was also given in Ismail Kadare's novel *The Successor* (2003); E. Biberaj, *Albania: A Socialist Maverick* (Boulder: Westview, 1990), pp. 36–8.

71 Mikloško et al, *Zločiny komunizmu*, p. 315; V. Vlček: *Kříž jsem hlásal, kříž jsem snášel* (Kostelní Vydří: Karmelitánské nakladatelství, 2006), pp. 190–239.

72 'Statement of the Assembly of the Bishops Conference of Yugoslavia,' in *Glas Koncila*, 17 May 1981; *Borba*, 23 March 1981. *Tanjug*, 27 June 1981.

73 Petar Šegvić, in *Borba*, 28 May 1981.

74 *Glas Koncila*, 25 October 1981, 27 September 1981 and 16 August 1981; *Večernje novosti*, Belgrade, 12 October 1981.

75 'Déclaration des évêques d'Europe,' 28 September 1980, in H. Legrand (ed), *Les Évêques d'Europe et la Nouvelle Évangelisation* (Paris: Cerf, 1991), pp. 93–6.

76 Luxmoore and Babiuch, *Rethinking Christendom*, pp. 147–8; John Paul II, apostolic letter *Egregiae Virtutis*, 31 December 1980, no. 3.

77 Szymowski, *Agenci SB*, pp. 73–89, 96–7, 226–7. 'Prorok' submitted over 600 pages of information and was considered a loyal, high-category collaborator. He was later identified as Archbishop Janusz Bolonek, an employee of the Vatican Secretariat of State's Polish section and later nuncio to Bulgaria and Macedonia; *The Tablet*, London, 26 September 2009; *Polska*, Warsaw, 21 September 2009; *La Stampa*, Milan, 19 September 2009. See also J. Koehler, *Unholy Moles: Communist Espionage Against the Vatican* (Cambridge: Pegasus, 2008. This claims an American Jesuit, Fr Robert Graham (1912–1997), who had helped unmask Nazi agents in the Vatican for Pius XII and continued counter-intelligence functions under later Popes,was tasked by John Paul II after his recovery to dismantle the network, ensuring those implicated were sent home.

78 Lasota, *Donos na Wojtyłę*, p. 319; A. Grajewski (ed), *'Papież musiał zginąć': Wyjaśnienia Ali Ağcy* (Katowice: Gość Niedzielny, 2011), pp. 11–99.

79 Marecki and Musiał, *Niezłomni*, p. 584; Dudek and Gryz, *Komuniści i Kościół*, pp. 369–70; 'Abp Ignacy Tokarczuk: wiedziałem, że mogą mnie zabić,' in *Katolicka Agencja Informacyjna*, 29 December 2012.

80 John Paul II, *Laborem Exercens*, 14 September 1981, nos. 13–14, 20.

81 Luxmoore and Babiuch, *The Vatican and the Red Flag*, p. 241; *Tajne dokumenty Państwo-Kościół 1980–1989* (Warsaw: Aneks, 1993), p. 48; evaluations of the church in *Przed i po 13 Grudnia: Państwa Bloku Wschodniego wobec kryzysu w PRL 1980–82* (Warsaw: IPN, 2006), pp. 419–422. For Soviet dissident views of Solidarity, see T. Kosinowa, *Polski mit: Polska w oczach sowieckich dysydentów* (Warsaw: Biblioteka Nowej Polszy, 2012), pp. 273–326.

82 Homily in Wrocław, in Polish Press Agency, 29 November 1981; *Tajne dokumenty*, p. 168; Friszke and Paczkowski, *Niepokorni*, pp. 529–531.

83 Courtois et al, *The Black Book*, p. 388; A. Paczkowski and M. Byrne (eds), *From Solidarity to Martial Law: The Polish Crisis of 1980–1981* (New York: Central European University Press, 2008); B. Fischer, 'Solidarity, the CIA and Western Technology' in *International Journal of Intelligence and Counter-Intelligence*, vol. 25/no. 3 (2012), pp. 433–4.

84 Dudek and Gryz, *Komuniści i Kościół*, p. 374; M. Kindziuk, *Kardynal Józef Glemp: Ostatni taki Prymas* (Warsaw: Świat Książki, 2010), pp. 185–7.

85 Epiphany homily, 6 January 1981; Vatican Radio broadcast, 16 December 1981; H. Bolczyk, *Krzyż nigdy nie umiera: Refleksje duszpasterza* (Katowice: KWK Wujek, 2009); J. Dziedzina, *Mocowałem się z Bogiem* (Gość Niedzielny, 2009); warning to Glemp from Jerzy Kuberski, Confessions Office director, in J. Żaryn, 'Jan Paweł II i Kościół w pierwszych tygodniach stanu wojennego (dossier),' in *Katolicka Agencja Informacyjna*, 12 December 2013.

86 Quoted in J. Luxmoore, 'The Polish Church under Martial Law,' in *Religion in Communist Lands*, vol. 15/no. 2 (1987), p. 137; Main Council text in Raina, *Kościół w PRL*, p. 251–2; J. Holzer and K. Leski, *Solidarność w podziemiu* (Łódź: Łódzkie, 1990), p. 21; Pope's letter to Jaruzelski in Weigel, *Witness to Hope*, p. 549.

87 Dudek and Gryz, *Komuniści i Kościół*, pp. 368–9.

88 *Ibid.*, p. 381; Krawczak and Wilanowski, *Kościół w Stanie Wojennym*, pp. 16, 49.

89 *Tajne dokumenty*, p. 165; 'Komunikat Rady Głównej Episkopatu w związku z stanem wojennym,' in Raina, *Kościół w PRL*, p. 251.

90 Dudek and Gryz, *Komuniści i Kościół*, p. 384. On the 'holy alliance,' see R. Gates, *From the Shadows* (New York: Schuster, 1996), pp. 236–8, 450–1; P. Schweizer, *Victory: The Reagan Administration's Secret Strategy* (New York: Atlantic Monthly Press, 1994), pp. 85–9, 164–5; G. Weigel, *The End of the Beginning: The victory of freedom, the lost years, the legacy* (New York: Doubleday, 2010), pp. 125–8; Fischer, 'Solidarity, the CIA and Western Technology,' pp. 427–469.

[91] Dudek and Gryz, *Komuniści i Kościół*, p. 381.

[92] Protocol from the PZPR Central Committee secretariat, in *ibid*, p. 387; 'List biskupa Chełmińskiego do diecezjan,' in Raina, *Kościół w PRL*, p. 220; Krawczak and Wilanowski, *Kościół w Stanie Wojennym*, p. 8.

5 A PROMISE OF FREEDOM

If any man would come after me, let him deny himself and take up his cross daily and follow me. For whoever would save his life will lose it; and whoever loses his life for my sake, he will save it. For what does it profit a man if he gains the whole world and loses and forfeits himself? For whoever is ashamed of me and of my words, of him will the Son of man be ashamed when he comes in his glory.

Lk 9:23–26

THE OUTLAWING OF Solidarity destroyed any residual trust which still existed between Church and state in Poland. It also fuelled the spread of illegal underground activity, accompanied by the ubiquitous presence of police agents and informers. Jaruzelski's Military Council was aware that many Catholic parishes were offering a sanctuary for opposition. The old distinctions between 'positive' and 'reactionary' clergy were still in use; and the Party had not given up its age-old hope of 'fully secularising society.' But people of all strata and backgrounds had by now, in Barcikowski's words, 'glued themselves to the Church.' In 1982 alone, five million people defied police and military restrictions to visit Jasna Góra. For now at least, secularisation was unworkable. The regime would have to rely on its old disintegration tactics to rein in the Church.[1]

Petty harassment was the order of the day. Crosses were removed from school classrooms, and efforts made to disrupt the disbursing of food and clothing by parish committees. The supply of Western aid via the Church posed a particular threat to the regime, by extending the Church's patronage. So parish helpers were routinely detained, and rumours spread that church leaders were keeping aid for themselves. SB operatives monitored sermons, and sought evidence that priests were sheltering fugitives. Cardinal Henryk Gulbinowicz of Wrocław, who had survived the Soviet Army's brutal wartime occupation of eastern Poland, would describe how he sheltered regional Solidarity leaders from arrest in his residence and hid a suitcase containing 80 million zloties for the union behind a curtain after its bank account was seized. The SB were tipped off by church informers; but they failed to incriminate the cardinal, who sent his own church observers to 180 separate political trials.[2]

The stance of dignitaries like Gulbinowicz was important for the many priests who felt called to witness with particular vigour and were now being given leeway by their bishops to respond to local needs. In Kraków's showcase industrial suburb of Nowa Huta, where efforts to build a church had been violently disrupted two decades earlier, Fr Kazimierz Jancarz's newly completed church at Mistrzcjowice was linked by tunnels to nearby housing blocks. It hosted Light-Life youth meetings and 'independent culture evenings,' as well as a 'Christian university' offering courses to local workers in history, sociology and economics. Jancarz, a former steelworker, had pledged 'to live and suffer like any average Pole'; and the SB was enraged at how he had brazenly 'created conditions for the gathering of conspiratorial activists.' It took steps to turn neighbouring clergy against him and made several attempts on Jancarz's life. Although not supporting the priest openly, however, Cardinal Macharski took no action. Jancarz, undeterred, went on to set up a 'solidarity vicariate,' using a term from Catholic opposition groups in Chile.[3]

Parishes like this had become a ferment of opposition. In Warsaw, Fr Wojciech Czarnowski's unfinished Divine Mercy church, just around the corner from the Polish Bishops Conference's new headquarters, hosted lectures, poetry readings and art exhibitions, mixing Christian symbols with images of patriotism and suffering. At nearby Podkowa Leśna, Fr Leon Kantorski's church offered an independent forum where non-Catholics and atheists could join in debating 'liberation through truth.'

Already interned after the imposition of martial law, Kantorski paid a heavy price. Windows were broken and statues profaned at his church in overnight attacks, and the initials of the post-War secret police, 'UB,' daubed on its walls. The priest's permit to build an extension was withdrawn 'until the activities cease'; and on one occasion, irate police and SB agents broke into the presbytery and lined up the priest and his helpers, execution-style, against a wall.[4]

Yet the Warsaw diocese ignored regime demands for such priests to be disciplined. Only in one case did the church authorities intervene directly, when another Warsaw priest, Fr Stanisław Małkowski, was banned from preaching after denouncing communism with Biblical rhetoric. Also interned under martial law, Małkowski had resisted pressure to sign the regime's loyalty oath and been released at the Bishops Conference's intervention. It would be inappropriate, he admitted, for church leaders themselves to compare communism to 'satanism and devil worship.' But there was room for a plurality of Catholic stances. Any victim held captive by 'bandits' could and should cry out for help; and in this case, Poland was the victim, and communists the bandits. Dialogue with those monopolising power and coercion might be sought as a moral postulate, Małkowski conceded; but it was useless for achieving real change. The regime had given the Church some degree of freedom as a temporary tactical necessity. But the advances could be quickly reversed; so it was up to courageous priests to stay close to society through a forceful witness. Małkowski's conclusion was clear:

> When you are in prison and you do not know whether you will ever get out, you must work out what to do to remain strong and healthy. You must also be prepared for the two possibilities: remaining imprisoned for a long time or being released. Although it isn't wise or helpful to create false expectations, it's also quite possible that freedom might

> come soon. So the Church's task is to prepare people, both for imprisonment and for freedom.[5]

Małkowski's life was in danger from rogue SB agents; and most fellow-clergy baulked at his provocative, uncompromising testimony. But many shared his view that their hierarchy should speak out more vigorously. In December 1982, Cardinal Glemp made a rare gesture by inviting some 200 local priests to a meeting at his Warsaw curia. For three hours, in a scene recalling confrontations between popular clergy and their aloof superiors during the French Revolution, he sat impassive and stony-faced, as his critics lambasted him for 'acting against the nation' and 'making a deal' with the regime. The Primate's usual contention—that the Church should avoid taking sides and be ready to conduct its mission under any political system—cut little ice. In a surly riposte, he accused the priests of 'behaving like journalists and politicians.'[6]

Whatever epithets were thrown at them, more and more priests were siding with the opposition. Fr Adolf Chojnacki, rector of Zagórz in Poland's southern Bieszczady region, had long been noted for critical sermons, and for allowing his church, an Oasis youth centre, to be used for smuggling religious literature into nearby Slovakia. The SB had tried and failed to recruit Chojnacki in the 1960s when his sister had requested a passport; and from his first arrival at Zagórz, it recorded, his pastoral activity had consisted of a 'campaign of slander against the government.' On every Catholic feast-day, he had 'organised a tendentious and clearly hostile church display'; and at every state festival, he had 'presented the events and facts in a false, one-sided manner.'

In April 1982, the Confessions Office intervened when it heard Chojnacki was being considered for a new parish in Kraków. The priest's behaviour had not changed, it warned the Kraków curia. At Corpus Christi, he had decorated the local procession route with 'politically suggestive props,' such as handcuffs and wreaths of barbed wire. Archbishop Macharski defied the pressure and assigned Chojnacki to the parish. So the SB responded with a slander campaign that the new rector was a paedophile and libertine. A crane was sent to remove Chojnacki's car, while his presbytery windows were smashed and he received threatening telephone calls. None of this had any effect; and in 1985, dozens took part in a hunger-strike under the priest's guidance in support of imprisoned Solidarity members. A year later, as tension continued, Macharski finally backed down and moved Chojnacki to a smaller parish at Juszczyna, south of Kraków. Yet the SB's campaign continued. Chojnacki was sent a letter with a photograph of his alleged daughter, and another picture with his head superimposed on a silhouette of Hitler. The priest, however, went on preaching defiant sermons, 'openly attacking and negating the system in Poland.'

A penitent agent would later divulge how the exasperated SB had finally made plans to kill Chojnacki in a staged road accident. In the event, he survived, later going to work among Polish Catholics in Romania, where he died, aged 69, after 45 years as a priest. At Zagórz, the new priest, Fr Bolesław Wawak, also resisted SB efforts to entrap him into informing on fellow-clergy. When an SB captain made a final attempt, the priest notified parishioners from his pulpit. His name was quickly deleted from the list of 'potential collaborators.'[7]

Some Polish clergy came closer to active resistance. One Warsaw priest, Fr Sylwester Zych, was jailed in September 1982 for hiding a gun used in the killing of a Civic Militia officer on a city tram. Sgt Zdzisław Karos was shot, apparently accidentally, while a group of youths tried to steal his gun. The case was reported in the Soviet media as an example of the 'fascist thugs' and 'armed gangs' now roaming the streets of Poland. While exploiting Zych's sentencing against the Church, however, Jaruzelski's regime dismissed talk of underground resistance. This would be 'completely unrealistic,' the Interior Minister, General Czesław Kiszczak, assured the Polish Sejm. Glemp, for his part, denied that priests were fomenting unrest. The Church wanted peace at every level; and it counted on those pursuing 'other purposes' to respect its places of worship. Yet churches, as meeting places between mankind and God, could not be closed to 'people from outside.' 'The churches are open to all—believers and non-believers,' the Primate insisted. 'We do not want political slogans in our churches; but nor do we want gas canisters thrown into them.'[8]

The jailing of Fr Zych did, nevertheless, raise some important questions. In particular, why was there no widespread violence? There had been plenty of verbal abuse, and much pushing and shoving. But resistance, since the first days of Solidarity, had been peaceful. While some small groups had considered violence, forceful reactions had been avoided, even when protesting friends and relatives were dragged away by brutal riot police. Various explanations would be offered; and the most convincing concerned the nature of the communist system. Solidarity's leaders knew about the passive resistance advocated and perfected by such figures as Mahatma Gandhi. But Poland's military-backed communist regime had little in common with India's polite imperial administrators. More immediate lessons had been learned. 'In Budapest and Prague, we had seen what happens when it is tanks against rocks and bottles,' recalled one union activist, Zbigniew Bujak, who spent several years on the run. 'We had to face the fact that if we chose violence, we would be facing government forces that were better at terror than we were.'[9]

That message was grasped instinctively. But it was also articulated by the Pope. Although no direct link had been apparent at the time, people had begun to see a connection between John Paul II's 1979 Polish pilgrimage and the rise of Solidarity. One moment, in particular, was talked about increasingly, when on the first day of his visit he had invoked the Holy Spirit from Psalm 104 before a congregation of 300,000 at his Mass in Warsaw's Victory Square. 'I call out from the very depth of this millennium; I call out on the eve of Pentecost, I call out with you all,' the Pope had declared, in slow, emphatic cadences: 'Let Your Spirit come down! And renew the face of the earth—this earth!'[10] Knowingly or not, John Paul II had acted as a catalyst for forces already emerging at the time. But he had also helped give them a moral framework, and an understanding of power politics. He knew agreements with communist regimes were worthless unless backed by powerful pressure; and he was aware that Christians, lacking strength to exert this pressure by themselves, had to find common ground with other 'people of goodwill.' Above all, he grasped that the modern world functioned not through governments, but through people—people whose creative, revolutionary energies could be mobilised to break through the barriers of power and ideology. Communism could not be intimidated by confrontation or appeased by diplomacy. But it could be undermined through the power of values, by a moral victory over fear and hatred which ultimately became a political victory.

Christian teaching contained the assurance that justice denied in this world would be compensated for by divine judgment in the next. But the justification of violent resistance also had roots in church tradition. St Thomas Aquinas had defended rebellion against tyrannical powers 'who serve the private interests of rulers rather than the common good,' noting that those who liberated their country by killing an unjust and violent tyrant should be 'praised and rewarded.' In living memory, Pius XI had defended armed resistance as a *malum necessarum*, or 'necessary evil,' against anti-church atrocities in Mexico, and appeared to have justified it again in *Quadragesimo Anno* in 1931. In 1967, Paul VI's *Populorum Progressio* had called for 'solidarity in action,' and accepted 'revolutionary uprisings' where 'there is a manifest, long-standing tyranny which would do great harm to fundamental personal rights and dangerous harm to the common good.'[11]

There were, in short, Christian justifications for resorting to force. Where they became problematic in the case of communism was in St Thomas's emphasis on proportionate means and prospects of success. In 1986, the Vatican would issue a new 'Instruction' in response to Liberation Theology, which acknowledged the 'powerful aspirations' to freedom in the world. The

Instruction was mostly intended for Latin America; but some at least was also relevant to Eastern Europe. The Church accepted the use of armed struggle as a last resort against 'obvious and prolonged tyranny,' the document reiterated; and there were 'situations of grave injustice' in which courage was needed to make reforms and 'suppress unjustifiable privileges.' But passive resistance usually offered a way 'more conformable to moral principles and having no less prospects of success.'[12]

Although elements of that thinking had taken root in Eastern Europe, the preference for passive resistance did nothing to deter Soviet media attacks on the Polish Church's 'reactionary forces' and the Pope's 'subversive activities.' Martial law had dashed US hopes of counter-revolution, Soviet propagandists proclaimed, and dispelled illusions that communism's 'undeniable achievements in overcoming religion' could be rolled back. Yet the resort to military rule in Poland, coming in the wake of Soviet Army brutalities in Afghanistan and mass atrocities by the communist Khmer Rouge in Cambodia, had dealt a death-blow to the communist programme. It had also deepened rifts in the communist movement worldwide.

The Vatican's reprimanding of Liberation Theology brought scornful communist jeers, and was also questioned by conformist Orthodox leaders such as Metropolitan Filaret of Minsk, the Russian church's external relations director, who rejected Rome's 'unfounded, deeply unjust and insulting' criticism of the socialist order. But Western communists had become more sympathetic. The Italian Communist Party had condemned the invasion of Afghanistan and was now criticising General Jaruzelski's 'normalisation' in Poland, as well as the 'false and devious' Soviet claim that Poland's 'counter-revolution' had been provoked by the Catholic Church. The 'progressive force of the October revolution' was now 'exhausted,' the PCI leader, Enrico Berlinguer, had concluded by his death in June 1984. Aiming at a 'secular state' was not the same as imposing atheism.[13]

Were such criticisms having any effect? Soviet officials had kept up their barrage against unofficial faith groups and religious 'opportunists' operating outside the legal framework—'people with a dark past' who concealed 'their anti-social faces behind a religious mask.' Foreign media, including Vatican Radio, reported arrests and house searches, while the Soviet press related confessions by Baptists and Pentecostalists about how they had been used to spread 'bourgeois propaganda' against communism.

Some cases were well known. Georgy Vins, secretary of the Council of Baptist Churches, had been allowed to emigrate with his family in 1979, while Vladimir Shelkov, much-persecuted leader of True and Free Adventists, whose trial had been attended by the celebrated Andrei Sakharov, had died in January 1980, well into his 80s, at a strict-regime labour camp in northern Siberia. Party bosses knew, however, that the spread of alternative faiths was a sign of crisis. Countering it would require a lot more than hamfisted repression.[14]

The Soviet regime's Council for Religious Affairs complained that seven of its annual reports, dating from the 1960s, had been unaccountably 'lost,' while other documents had been leaked to 'anti-Soviet publications.' The Council recognised that the lack of religious literature was embarrassing Orthodox bishops, and recommended printing 100,000 new Bibles. In 1988, the church would be celebrating the millennium of Russia's conversion; so new Bibles would show up 'the bankruptcy of hostile propaganda about oppression.' At the same time, new efforts were made in schools to stress the 'positive values' of atheism, by laying on such novelties as 'atheist discos' and 'young atheist weeks.'

In October 1985, a new Party programme further toned down the hostility to religion, recognising that 'religious prejudices' were best overcome through education, new Soviet rituals and 'heightened labour and social activity.' Every Party member was still obliged to struggle against 'bourgeois ideology and morals' and 'hangovers from the past in people's consciousness.' But it was more important now to 'explain patiently the unsoundness of religious beliefs,' and how they reflected 'people's subordination to social oppression,' without causing unnecessary offence.[15]

The regime was keen to highlight its good relations with the Orthodox hierarchy. Regular contacts were allowed now with Orthodox churches in Romania, Bulgaria, Yugoslavia and Poland; and when Patriarch Dimitrios I of Constantinople travelled to Moscow in August 1987, repaying Patriarch Pimen's Istanbul visit a decade earlier, much was made of the event's historic character as the first such exchange since the Sixteenth Century.

There were complaints that some Party activists had taken the conciliatory message a bit far, and become too reverential towards the Orthodox saints. Meanwhile, no quarter was given to Orthodox dissidents such as Fr Gleb Yakunin and the mystic Zoia Krakhmalnikova, who was jailed again in April 1983 for compiling devotional readings. Reports also continued of severe repression against non-Christian groups. Virtually all Muslim mosques remained closed and the Koran was unobtainable, while only two Buddhist temples had survived, with a handful of monks, since all Buddhist lamas had been wiped out by Stalin in the 1930s. Yet it was possible to glean some information from official publications about less noted religious communities such as the Orthodox Old Believers, who still numbered several hundred thousand, despite savage persecution since the Seventeenth Century.

Elsewhere in the Soviet Union, Moscow's problems were growing. In Lithuania, the underground *Chronicle* had written to Brezhnev, demanding the release of Yakunin and other Orthodox dissidents, thus testifying to the solidarity being forged among human rights campaigners in various republics. The *Chronicle* related how Fr Vladislav Zavalnyuk, the last Catholic priest in Moldavia, had been deported in summer 1980 for ministering outside the capital, Chişinaŭ. It described how a single parish at Pelesa in Belarus had sent 33 petitions to Minsk and Moscow, demanding the reopening of its church, which had been turned into a warehouse in 1962. At another parish near Voronovo, Catholics had reoccupied their church on All Souls Day, hiding the keys and drawing thousands to revived acts of worship.

Such defiance would once have been unthinkable. So would the courtoom statement of Angelė Ramanauskaitė, a Lithuanian teacher from Astravas, when accused of 'dragging children's souls into darkness' by telling them about religion. 'It is not a crime to talk to children about God—the criminals are those who have initiated these proceedings,' the *Chronicle* quoted the teacher as retorting. 'Not only I, but others as well, will go on teaching religion to children, so they will know that religion is not old wives' tales, but the foundation for all human life.' When Ramanauskaitė was fined 50 roubles, well-wishers approached her outside the court and offered donations.[16]

Lithuania's regime was aware that the underground church was expanding and cast about for a new policy. It was proposed that some underground priests could be given legal permits as a way of controlling their activities. At least one, Fr Ignacas Žeberskis, was admitted to the Kaunas seminary for a shortened course after being ordained in secret. In July 1982, however, after negotiations between the Vatican and Kremlin, the regime came up with an even more notable proposition: the long-exiled Bishop Sladkevičius would be allowed back to his see at Kaišiadorys, while a new bishop, Antanas Vaičius, would be named administrator of Telšiai and Klaipeda. Only two other bishops were still at large in Lithuania—Luidas Povilonis of Kaunas and Vilkaviškis, and Romualdas Krikščiūnas of Panevėžys—so this was a significant development when it was agreed with Rome.

Sladkevičius had been partly paralysed by a stroke, and the regime sensed his return would pose few problems. But Vaičius was another matter. Clergy from Telšiai were among the republic's most militant; so the new bishop had to be acceptable to both sides. The regime was confident, even then, that it could quickly neutralise the concession; and in 1983, it duly arrested two of

Lithuania's most renowned priests, Fr Sigitas Tamkevičius and Fr Alfonsas Svarinskas.

Svarinskas, a long-time prison veteran, was the first to be rounded up; and in May 1983, despite mass protests, he received a 10-year labour camp and exile sentence. 'The security organs are eager to get rid of me,' he told his Catholics at his vibrant parish in Viduklė, where the church had suffered several attacks.

> But what can they do? Throw me into prison—but priests are needed there too. Hang me—but I'll be nearer to heaven. What we need most are martyrs! It's those ideas for which people are ready to die which are immortal.[17]

Tamkevičius was arrested in court when he appeared as a witness at Svarinskas's trial, and given a similar sentence. The KGB had interrogated numerous priests to build its charge sheet against him, which ran to 25 volumes. It had also monitored his sermons, such as one in 1981 commemorating fellow-clergy massacred by Soviet soldiers four decades before. 'The worst henchmen are not those who kill the body, but those who murder the human spirit,' the dissident priest had told his congregation. 'Let us resolve to guard our faith like a rock that alone helps us forgive and love even those who do not seem to deserve that love.'[18]

Other arrests followed. Jonas Sadūnas, brother of the underground nun, Nijolė Sadūnaitė, was given an 18-month camp sentence for links with the *Chronicle*, while Fr Jonas Kastytis-Matulionis, who had worked with Tamkevičius at Kybartai after being secretly ordained, received three years after a brutal beating. The new crackdown was intended to disrupt the *Chronicle* and finally break up Lithuania's Catholic Committee. But Tamkevičius's place as editor was quickly taken by a fellow-Jesuit, Fr Jonas Boruta, a physicist who had trained for the priesthood underground. Meanwhile, over 450 priests, three-quarters of the total, signed a Committee petition. 'History will forgive no one who has helped the atheist government destroy the Church,' warned the underground journal, *Aušra*. 'Whatever one's view of religion, everybody who considers himself Lithuanian should realise that contributing to atheist propaganda amounts to a betrayal of Lithuania.'[19]

With Tamkevičius and Svarinskas now packed off to labour camps in Perm and Mordovia, there were fears that their silencing had been a trade-off for the new episcopal appointments. When Lithuania's four bishops were allowed to pay an *ad limina* visit to Rome in April 1983, the first under Soviet rule, their leader, Bishop Povilonis, regretted in his speech that the long-barred Bishop Steponavičius could not be with them. But when Povilonis was raised to archbishop seven months later, after a further Vatican visit, the misgivings grew. Was a crackdown on the underground church the price for improved official relations?

The Pope took steps to reassure worried Catholics. In March 1984, a special Mass for Lithuania was broadcast from his private chapel; and in August, he called on the country's Catholics to be 'joyful in hope and strong in tribulation.' In a telegram, he told Bishop Povilonis he was unable to accept an invitation to visit Lithuania for the sixth centenary of the death of Saint Casimir. The real reason, the Pope made clear, was the Soviet regime's refusal.[20]

John Paul II made another episcopal appointment in 1982, this time in neighbouring Latvia, where Mgr Jānis Cakuls was named auxiliary bishop of Riga with a right to succeed its ageing administrator, Bishop Julijans Vaivods. Conditions were very different here. Catholics made up less than a third of the population and were widely dispersed from their original heartland around Latgale. Vaivods was widely credited, however, with having held the Latvian Church together. Although half of all priests had been imprisoned or deported since 1945, there were still 179 registered Catholic parishes, while 45 students, many destined for other republics, were preparing for ordination at the newly refurbished Riga seminary.

These data were put together during a visit by Bishops Gerhard Schaffran of Dresden and Joachim Meisner of Berlin two months before Cakuls's appointment in November 1982. Just two months later, the Pope surprised the world by naming Vaivods a cardinal. He was 88, so it was an honorary title only. But Vaivods—ordained at Petrograd in 1918 and personally consecrated by Paul VI after three years in a labour camp—would be the Soviet Union's first resident cardinal. It was unclear whether the Soviet regime had been formally notified; but the appointment would clearly be a precedent—perhaps for the naming of a cardinal in Lithuania, where it was wrongly believed that Steponavičius had been already raised to the rank secretly, or *in pectore,* by Pope Paul in the 1970s.

There had been nationalist disturbances in Latvia and the atmosphere was tense. Vaivods arrived in Rome to collect his red hat on the day Fr Svarinskas appeared in court in Lithuania; so the *Chronicle* was suspicious. Did the honouring of Vaivods not signify approval for the 'passive and capitulationist Latvian Church', in preference to the 'bold and independent Church' of Lithuania? Vaivods saw things differently. He was confident he could act as 'a bridge between the Vatican and Moscow.' 'It isn't written down anywhere, but we know how we are to behave—we work quietly and do as much as we are allowed,' the new cardinal told a Western newsagency. 'We still have our faith and our doors are open. Those who want to come can come.'[21]

There were tensions in Ukraine too, where members of the outlawed Greek Catholic Church, estimated at around four million, continued to organise and agitate. Underground clergy had sent an open letter to John Paul II, thanking Divine Providence for a Slavic pope and asking him to remind the Soviet authorities that Greek Catholics would never yield to atheist campaigns. Every betrayal of the Church, the signatories warned, was 'equal to an abandonment of faithfulness to Christ.' The open letter was copied to Brezhnev.[22]

In February 1982, as fellow-bishops gathered to celebrate his ninetieth birthday in Rome, the veteran Cardinal Slipyi sent a pastoral letter to Ukrainian Catholics everywhere, praising their 'courageous resistance to godless coercion.' Slipyi had only two years to live, and some Ukrainians were ready to act more forcefully. In September, as the US Congress adopted a resolution condemning the Church's post-War liquidation, the recently released Iosif Terelya announced an 'Action Group' to campaign for its re-legalisation. Terelya had spent half his 40 years in prisons and psychiatric hospitals. He and his wife had been threatened with death when police searched their apartment the previous June; and his brother, Boris, had been shot dead by the KGB. 'We survived the evil years of Stalinism,' the Greek Catholic told the Ukrainian Party's Central Committee in a protest letter, co-signed with three priests. 'It's strange that a state which declared the principles of freedom, equality and brotherhood as its creed should conduct a campaign of total persecution against its own population, simply for worshipping Christ in its native language.'[23]

There had been occasional hints that the Soviet regime might have been rethinking its attitude to Greek Catholics. But Russian Orthodox leaders remained deeply hostile to Slipyi and implacably opposed to any lifting of the post-War ban. Terelya's aim was to show the Church still existed—and that its members, while resisting 'subordination,' were ready to observe Soviet laws. In June 1983, another group of church members wrote to the Ukrainian government, demanding an end to anti-Catholic propaganda. It was signed by Fr Grigorii Budzinsky, the only surviving member of the ill-fated Greek Catholic delegation, featuring Fr Kostelnyk and Fr Sheptycki, which had visited Moscow in 1944 to discuss the Church's future. Budzinsky had been jailed twice in 1946 and 1957; but he claimed he had Slipyi's authorisation to represent the Church to the outside world. Besides the government letter, he wrote to local newspapers, urging them not to 'print lies' against Greek Catholics.[24]

In September 1984, the revered Slipyi, whose career had begun at Rome's Gregorian University in the 1920s and included four decades of forced labour and exile, succumbed to pneumonia. In his final testimony, he recalled his love for the Church which had always remained 'an integral part of the universal church family.'

It was a love which had marked his thoughts and actions both 'in freedom and in prison.' The Pope had not agreed to Slipyi's request for a patriarchal title. But he knelt to kiss the cardinal's hand as he lay in state, recalling how Slipyi, who had built a cathedral and founded a seminary and spiritual centre during his years in Rome, had 'passed unbroken through tortures and sufferings of the cross similar to those of Christ on Golgotha.'[25]

By now, Terelya's Action Group had begun publishing its own Lithuanian-style church chronicle. The eighth and final issue was hand-written, since the group's two printing presses had been confiscated. It noted that over 80 Greek Catholic priests had been secretly ordained in Ukraine's Transcarpathia region alone since 1981. Of these, around half had been jailed, in one case for merely singing carols. Other priests, now in their 70s, the chronicle noted, had been arrested for a fifth time or more. Regime officials had been active at another level too, the chronicle recorded. In March 1984, they had visited Terelya and Budzinsky, offering to let them create their own autocephalous, or self-governing, church, if they agreed to break with Slipyi.

If true, the offer merely recalled earlier Soviet efforts to entice Greek Catholics away from Rome. When it was rejected, the regime reacted angrily. Vasyl Kobryn, who had taken over the Action Group because of Terelya's ill health, was given three years for 'anti-Soviet slander.' A former militant atheist who had converted during military service back in 1960, Kobryn refused to co-operate in his trial but made a defiant speech at its close. The Lviv edition of *Pravda* noted sarcastically how he had tried to be 'a martyr for the faith, persecuted for his religious beliefs.'

Terelya himself was arrested in February 1985 on a similar charge and given seven more years' hard labour and five years' internal exile. Fr Budzinsky, now 85, was abducted and deposited in a prison hospital for six weeks, while a dozen other Greek Catholics were given final warnings.' Terelya got a message out, denouncing the 'pogrom,' and the arrests were taken up by the

US delegation at the Conference on Security and Co-operation in Europe.[26]

Ukrainian dissidents were still dying. In 1984 alone, four well-known figures, including a distinguished poet, Vasyl Stus, perished in the Perm camp system. Yet Christians remained defiant. In October 1985, Slipyi's successor, Cardinal Lubachivsky, told his Church's Rome synod that 10 Greek Catholic bishops were now active in Ukraine, along with several hundred priests and at least a thousand nuns. Any suggestion that ties with Rome should be downgraded as a price for legalisation was decisively rejected.

The official Council for Religious Affairs in Moscow admitted there was a problem with illegal clergy in Ukraine.[27] But arrests were taking place elsewhere too. In May 1983, Fr Vladimir Nikiforov was arrested in Moscow and accused of conspiring with a US Embassy priest on behalf of the Vatican. In December 1984, a secretly ordained ethnic Pole, Fr Josif Svitnitsky, was arrested for unauthorised services while trying to reach Siberia's scattered Catholics.

Svitnitsky's efforts were understandable. In some remote parts of the Soviet Union, there had been a slight relaxation in official policy. Four Lithuanian priests had been allowed to minister to Catholics in Kazakhstan and Tajikistan, while several new churches had opened, including one at Novosibirsk. Yet there was still a high attrition rate. Many congregations, although officially registered, still had no pastors or places of worship, while legally operating priests often had numerous parishes under their care. Routine church activities, such as pilgrimages and rosary groups, still faced harassment, and many Catholics were fearful about joining in any organised activity.

Little by little, however, the confidence and courage were growing. Although teaching the catechism to children was still banned, large First Communion ceremonies were now routine in the western republics. 'How long will this injustice last?' one group of village Catholics boldly demanded of the new Soviet Party boss, Konstantin Chernenko, after complaining that their requests to register a parish had led to 'persecution and intimidation.' 'We are not afraid to be believers, because Soviet democracy allows this; so we ask you in the name of freedom and free politics, to intervene so that we can stop living in constant fear.'[28]

How had the upheavals in Poland affected the rest of Eastern Europe? The picture, inevitably, remained mixed. In summer 1981, Ceauşescu's regime in Romania had allowed the former prisoner, Mgr Antal Jakab, to succeed the deceased Áron Márton as Latin Catholic bishop of Alba Iulia. In December 1984, a new bishop of Bucharest, Ioan Robu, was consecrated in Rome to succeed the collaborating Francisc Augustin, who had died a year earlier after sitting on Romania's National Assembly.

Having been without a statute since the 1940s, the Latin Church was still unrecognised in Romania, while its other dioceses—Iaşi, Timişoara and Oradea—had been officially abolished. But it was tolerated and said to have 730 priests for its 1.2 million members, which was not a bad ratio. A total of 27 priests had been ordained in Alba Iulia's ancient gothic cathedral just before Bishop Jakab's nomination, and a 160 more were studying at the local seminary, a substantial increase over previous years. When new bishops were named for Timişoara and Oradea in 1983—as apostolic administrators, rather than with full titles—the regime allowed them to function.

Despite this, the Latin Church was critically short of places of worship. It was also identified with Romania's ethnic Hungarians and Germans, and the predominant Orthodox church opposed any concessions to it. Negotiations with the Vatican for the Church's legalisation had been stalled over the regime's refusal to discuss the fate of Greek Catholics. As Origen of Alexandria had remarked sarcastically of the Roman emperors' attempts to erase Christianity, Ceauşescu's regime had simply, 'decreed in its own laws,' against the evidence, that Greek Catholics no longer existed. So what was there to discuss? In his 1979 letter, the Pope had warned Ceauşescu that Greek Catholics would not be forgotten—and they were still making their presence felt. Three secretly consecrated bishops—Alexandru Todea, Ion Dragomir and Ion Ploscaru—had appealed in 1981 to the CSCE, citing Romania's constitution and the 1975 Helsinki Final Act, which Ceauşescu had personally signed:

> One can see everywhere what atheistic indoctrination means: morals grow worse daily, corruption increases, young people become confused and conceited, adults become tired and sceptical, old people become desperate. In a word, the new man, the highly praised 'socialist man,' is a failure. Instead of being loyal, he is a liar and a swindler; instead of being a good worker, he is neglectful; instead of being wise, he is more and more passive, even stupid; instead of being powerful, he is weak.[29]

Some gestures at least were possible. Several Christian political prisoners, including a group of alleged Bible smugglers, were freed under an autumn 1981 amnesty, while the remains of the revered Cardinal Hossu were exhumed and reburied in a proper grave in Bucharest's Bellu cemetery. Meanwhile, tensions were surfacing in the Orthodox church. In April 1981, a group of priests had tabled a 'Testimony of Faith,' criticising the Orthodox hierarchy's servility to the state and demanding greater ecumenical openness and sympathy towards the persecuted Greek Catholics. They urged Patriarch Iustin Moisescu to demand the release of the outspoken Fr Calciu-Dumitreasa, and more rights for the church in religious education, media access, youth work and pilgrimages.

Most of the priests were defrocked or forced to withdraw their signatures, while Iustin's bishops went on praising Ceauşescu's 'peace initiatives.' Yet pressure was mounting. The Pope had also written to the CSCE heads of state, urging greater protection for religious rights; and in January 1982, he again spoke up for Greek Catholics, lauding their role in the 'civic and spiritual education of the Romanian people.' The occasion was the appointment of a Cluj-born archbishop, Traian Crişan, as secretary of the Congregation for Causes of Saints, the most senior Vatican post to be held by a Romanian. John Paul II's 'interference' was protested by Romanian Orthodox leaders, with Patriarch Iustin assuring a French newspaper it was the Orthodox who were 'true martyrs of the faith.'[30]

But the Pope pressed home his point. In June 1983, he created a special exarchate, or bishopric, for Romanian Greek Catholics in the US, naming the Ilinois-born Mgr Vasile Louis Puşcaş as first bishop. That October, in St Peter's Square, he beatified a Sixteenth Century Capuchin friar, Ion Costist, or Jeremiah of Wallachia (1556–1625), giving the Romanian Church its first putative saint. The ceremony was not mentioned in Romania's official media. But the regime marked the occasion by sending a 'special envoy' for talks with Casaroli and allowing the first pilgrimage to Rome.

Ceauşescu went on courting popularity with Western governments with a show of independence from Moscow. He had criticised the Soviet invasion of Afghanistan and refused to send troops to Warsaw Pact manoeuvres; and in 1984, he would defy a Soviet boycott and send Romanian athletes to the Los Angeles Olympics. Yet it was debatable how much this really meant. It may have embarrassed the Soviets; but did nothing to dislodge communist power.

The same was undoubtedly true of Ceauşescu's calculated gestures to religious communities. Bucharest was home to Eastern Europe's only surviving Anglican church, dedicated in 1922, whose one-time parishioners had included the pre-War Queen Marie (1875–1938), a grand-daughter of Britain's Queen Victoria. There had been at least a dozen Anglican churches in Eastern Europe in 1945; and the church of the Resurrection, run by an Australian chaplain, Robert Braun, was used mainly by foreign students and diplomats. Was its existence not just a showcase for buttressing the regime's image?

Gestures aside, international opinion was growing tired of Ceauşescu's double act. Protestant congregations were expanding faster in Romania than anywhere else outside the Soviet Union; and the Party's daily, *Scînteia*, believed these new 'non-atheists' were fostering an 'equivocal and treacherous puritanism' by refusing military service and espousing beliefs 'without any logical foundation.' However, another Party journal, *Era Socialista*, admitted a religious resurgence was underway and rejected 'ossified and dogmatic interpretations' about the inevitable decline of faith.

In the summer of 1982, the Party expelled over 300 members for alleged religious beliefs, while a group of US senators wrote to Ceauşescu, condemning his use of 'prisons, labour camps and psychiatric facilities against religious groups.' The Reagan Administration warned that Romania could face trade sanctions unless it allowed more Jews to emigrate: there were still 120 synagogues in the country, but only three rabbis.[31]

In neighbouring Hungary, a feud was brewing over the Christian base communities, who had been warned by the Bishops Conference in the 1970s to obey the law and avoid 'sectarianism.' New groups were still emerging. Their very dynamism appeared to highlight the official Church's docility and passivity.

In 1979, one group of priests had asked the Bishops Conference to negotiate for Christians to be allowed to refuse military service. Conscientious objection was barred under Article 70 of the Hungarian constitution; and with at least a hundred Hungarians serving related sentences, this had become a focus for Christian unrest. In summer 1981, a church tribunal had ordered a priest from Fr Bulányi's Bokor movement, Fr László Kovács, to be moved from his Budapest parish for encouraging 'pacifist views' among young people. Another, Fr András Gromon, had also been suspended for criticising the move. 'I can understand if an atheist government tries to liquidate our Church or religion—it's their job,' Kovács told a Catholic festival in the southern town of Hajós. 'But I can't agree with leaders of the Church who try to kill our religious community... The apostles didn't seek permits from anyone—they followed Jesus and were ready to give their lives for him.' The priest's silencing was seen as a warning: the bishops would not be supporting conscientious objectors. 'These priests are dreamers who mislead the youth—self-defence and force are justifiable,' Cardinal Lékai insisted in an Esztergom homily. 'This was always the Church's point of view. To avoid war is an ideal solution; but we also need a regulated force.'[32]

Bulányi himself was summoned for talks with Lékai in December 1981. Three months later, a bishops' commission provoked widespread outrage by branding Bokor a 'grave, subversive movement,' which had spread doctrinal deviations and 'mistaken teachings' through 'guileful argumentation.' 'There is an uneasiness among believers who hear uncertain, troubling teachings in certain places,' the Bishops Conference noted. 'Some people, cloaked as inspired innovators, oppose and pay no heed to the church hierarchy… They wish to give a new interpretation to certain Biblical texts and claim special inspirational grace from the Holy Spirit.'[33]

That June, Bulányi was formally barred from ministering. His case had highlighted the Catholic hierarchy's subservience to the communist state; but it had also shown the dangers of dissenting against it. For Christians with energy and initiative, the situation was plainly intolerable, particularly when they were also denied any chance to present their views in the official Catholic media. But Cardinal Lékai defended his position. Hungary's communists had implemented social and ethical principles set out in 1931 by *Quadragesimo Anno*, the Primate brazenly asserted. This was why the Church was not attacking them, and why it favoured negotiating 'small steps' behind the scenes rather than acting 'in theatrical fashion.' The Church was not against the communities in principle. But it could not accept the provocative actions of a minority who appeared to be endangering rather than enhancing Christian life.[34]

Sensing popular pressure, the Bishops Conference asked the Vatican for a ruling; and in May 1983, a letter from Casaroli was duly delivered by Mgr Poggi. This endorsed the bishops' position on base communities which 'evade the authority of their legitimate bishops.' It also 'approved and strengthened' the measures taken 'to preserve the necessary unity of the Hungarian Church.'[35]

Several clergy signed petitions questioning Bulányi's suspension, while the Piarists' superior in Rome, Fr Angelus Ruiz, also added words of support. The Vatican remained firm, however; and when three priests accused Rome of 'standing on the side of the persecutor,' it flatly rejected their open letter. In March 1984, Lékai sacked Béla Hegyi, editor of Hungary's Catholic monthly, *Vigilia*, for publishing criticisms of the Church's stance.

Where would the Pope stand in the dispute? When he had met Hungary's bishops on their *ad limina* visit the previous October, John Paul II had agreed the base communities must accept the hierarchy's direction. But those who did, he made clear, should have full episcopal backing. 'If they are to be called truly ecclesial, these communities must, above all, be in stable unity with their local churches,' the Pope told the bishops. 'I am certain the base communities which observe these guidelines—and I would like to see them all adapt themselves to these norms as soon as possible—will be supported and openly helped by you.'[36] The implication was clear: Bokor and other communities, however dynamic their witness, should submit to episcopal authority; but the bishops should also do more to defend them. For good measure, the Pope urged the bishops to be more active in catechesis and devotions, and in nurturing family life and priestly vocations.

In Hungary itself, the bishops' submissiveness was rewarded, not least by links abroad. In September 1981, Benedictine superiors from around Europe had gathered at the monastery of Pannonhalma for their first meeting in a communist country; and in March 1982, the revered theologian, Karl Rahner, had addressed a conference at the Budapest Academy of Sciences. That October, over 500 Hungarians visited Rome for the Pope's Holy Year; and in November 1984, for the twentieth anniversary of the 1964 Hungary-Vatican agreement, the veteran Imre Miklós attended a private audience with the Pope. It was the first by an official religious affairs director from Eastern Europe.

Conciliatory articles and statements, meanwhile, appeared in the official media, as Miklós listed the Church's 'benefits' under communist rule. Seminarians could keep their Bibles during military service and enjoy leave at Christmas and Easter, he pointed out, while at least 50 charitable institutions had been left in church hands. Meanwhile, clergy salaries were officially subsidised, and almost a third of the state's budget for historic buildings used for the upkeep of churches. No fewer than 17 religious newspapers were in print and 93 religious books had been published in 1984 alone.

If the regime had concluded it could harness church support by allowing greater leeway, this became apparent in summer 1984, when the Lutheran World Federation held its assembly in Budapest. It was the first such gathering in a communist country, attracting 1200 delegates from 98 member-churches, including those of the Soviet Union; and its highlight was the election of Bishop Zoltán Káldy, the assembly host, as LWF president. Káldy's relationship with the Hungarian regime was comparable to that of Cardinal Lékai, who duly praised its 'readiness to compromise.' Religious citizens were 'working for socialism,' Lékai assured his listeners. Although 'certain difficulties' remained, the era of attempts to 'do away with the Church' was now over.[37]

That line of thinking was developed by Bishop József Cserháti of Pécs, secretary-general of the Bishops Conference, who had emerged as a key apologist for Hungary's Church-state model. A full 20 years after the 1964 agreement, Cserháti insisted, ties were 'satisfactory'. It would be 'narrow-minded' for the Church to reject dialogue 'because the other side is atheist.' But the Church, for its part, also deserved a 'show of confidence' from the state—in deeds, not just in rhetoric. The bishop chose his words carefully:

> Co-operation must aim at creating a new humanism that emphasises the community's interests—a broader democracy that stresses the priority of the individual, and the

> promotion of a stronger social bond that could be called socialist democracy, but which is defined primarily as a more human democracy.[38]

Cserháti had a point. But the complex balancing act being performed by bishops like himself continued to repel and alienate those favouring a more robust defence of rights and freedoms. The Hungarian Church had yet to forge the links with liberal dissident groups which were now being consolidated in Poland and Czechoslovakia. Well-known figures such as Miklós Haraszti and János Kis, still Marxist in outlook, were aware of the demoralisation which had bred rampant alcoholism and family breakdown, and the world's highest suicide rate, and which had left young Hungarians with 'no past, no self-consciousness, no conscience of continuity, no values and norms, no political culture and no ideology.' Yet they ignored religion and distrusted the Church. Nor were they interested in the official Christian-Marxist dialogue which had brought luminaries like Rahner to Budapest.

In Czechoslovakia, the frail old Cardinal Tomášek had been fortified by his informal committee of advisers, headed by the redoubtable Fr Zvěřina. Western politicians, such as Germany's Foreign Minister, Hans-Dietrich Genscher, had paid courtesy visits to his residence while in Prague, boosting Tomášek's international standing and forcing the regime to treat him carefully. The cardinal, for his part, was becoming outspoken. It had been a Becket-like transformation.

Catholic *samizdat* publishing had mushroomed in Czechoslovakia, with 700 titles appearing in 1982 alone, including full-scale journals such as *Teologické texty* and *Informace o církvi*, compared to a single hymnbook and church calendar published officially. Meanwhile, underground Christian activities had become ever more self-confident, as more Christian signatures were added to Charter 77. Much to the StB's chagrin, there was evidence that Western pressure was also bringing lighter sentences.

Official talks had continued intermittently with Rome. But there had been little to show for them; and in October 1980, when Catholics had petitioned the Pope to raise their plight at the CSCE, they had also asked him to prevail on Casaroli's team not to negotiate over the head of the local Church. Only three dioceses—Prague, Banská Bystrica and Nitra—had resident Catholic bishops anyway, while one—Bishop Gojdič's Greek Catholic Prešov eparchy—had now been vacant since the 1950s. The regime was still trying to set the bishops against each other. In 1981, when Bishop Gábriš of Trnava had refused to ordain a seminarian with known StB links, he had been ordained instead by Bishop Feranec of Banská Bystrica. Feranec ignored protests by local Catholics, who disrupted the priest's first Mass.

Meanwhile, clergy were still being called up for military service to reduce the presence of young, active clergy; and measures were being taken to ensure only mediocre candidates entered the seminaries. Pressures like these were stepped up in January 1983, when a new head of the government's religious affairs office, Vladimir Janku, replaced the worn-out Karel Hrůza.

Virulent media attacks had continued in the meantime on the Church and Vatican. Slovakia's main *Pravda* daily conceded that an 'underground church' had existed since the 1950s, and was now helping perpetuate 'the action by reactionary forces in 1968.' When martial law had been imposed in Poland, the Husák regime had seen it as a defeat for the line laid down by the Pope in *Redemptor Hominis*. The Church had 'skilfully manipulated' Poland's different social groups, and exploited the Polish Party's pragmatism and lack of respect for 'socialist moral principles.'[39]

The melodramatic denunciations were having little effect now. And in March 1982, the Vatican's Congregation for Clergy responded to Tomášek's growing assertiveness with a show of strength of its own, by effectively banning Czechoslovakia's pro-regime clergy association, Pacem in Terris. The occasion was a decree, *Quidam Episcopi*, barring priests from organisations 'undermining the authority of bishops.' It mentioned two types:

those 'orientated towards trade unions,' and those 'apparently supporting humanist ideals, such as peace and progress, but in reality pursuing political goals.' The decree appeared just before Tomášek was received by the Pope, along with Czechoslovakia's four other surviving bishops. It clearly applied to Pacem in Terris. 'We all know about the activities of this association,' the Congregation's prefect, Cardinal Silvio Oddi, told an Italian newspaper, 'and how brutally it interferes in the religious sphere.'

Younger clergy had refused to join Pacem in Terris, so it was now mostly the preserve of elderly priests. In a Vatican Radio commentary, however, members were given a choice: obey Rome or give up the priesthood. Those who defied the decree would have 'excommunicated themselves.'[40]

Quidam Episcopi was calmly ignored by Cardinal Lékai in Hungary, who insisted his country's collaborationist Catholic movement, Opus Pacis, was controlled by the church hierarchy and could not be used against it. But it provoked angry exchanges in Yugoslavia, where the Bishops Conference used it to warn priests against organisations lacking its approval. In Czechoslovakia, meanwhile, Husák's regime barred the decree's publication. It was no more than a rehash, the press proclaimed, of Pius XII's Holy Office decree of 1949, forbidding Catholics from co-operating with communists. This time too priests would ignore it, thus exposing the weakness of 'political Catholicism.'[41]

This was wishful thinking. When he returned home, Tomášek branded Pacem in Terris guilty of a 'gross infraction of ecclesiastical discipline' and instructed fellow-bishops to make the prohibition known. The decree was read in Czech and Slovak on Vatican Radio; and by August, several dozen clergy had withdrawn from the association. Pacem in Terris contested the Vatican's move in an open letter, reaffirming its loyalty to the Pope and commitment to peace; and there were reports that work was underway to redraft the association's statutes. But when its newspaper, *Katolícke Noviny*, still refused to publish the decree, Tomášek withdrew its entitlement to call itself 'Catholic.'

St Paul had instructed that a Christian who remained 'factious' after one or two warnings should be shunned as 'perverted and sinful...self-condemned' (Tt 3:10); so the cardinal could claim to be upholding Christian teaching. But the regime instructed *Katolícke Noviny*, which had an official print-run of 250,000, to ignore Tomášek's ruling. The weekly continued printing 'with church approval' on its masthead.

When the collaborationist Christian Peace Conference convened in Prague, it claimed that Pacem in Terris had brought benefits to the Catholic Church by helping alleviate the shortage of priests. But Czechoslovakia's *samizdat* journals supported the Vatican. 'As Peter's successor, John Paul II is pastor of the whole Church,' Vatican Radio observed defiantly. 'He does not yield to threats, or succumb to flattery from left or right.'[42]

The acrimony continued. Why, Husák's regime demanded, had there been no parallel ban on 'subversive activity' by priests in Poland? Foreign bishops were refused visas to attend church events in Czechoslovakia, while two elderly Franciscans, Fr Josef Bárta and Fr Ladislav Trojan, were jailed for running an underground seminary in northern Bohemia. Bárta, who had survived a life sentence in the 1950s, died of a heart attack the following December after Western appeals for his release had been ignored.

When the Pope named two new bishops a month later—Dominik Hrušovský for Slovaks abroad, and Jaroslav Škarvada, a former secretary to Cardinal Beran, for Czechs—the regime reacted furiously. Both were men for whom 'hatred of their former homeland has become a profession,' declared *Rudé Právo*. Attacks were made on other exiled prelates as well, including the veteran Bishop Pavol Hnilica in Rome, and Archbishop Josef Tomko, Slovak secretary-general of the Church's Synod of Bishops. Tomko would soon be made prefect of the Vatican's Congregation for the Evangelisation of Peoples and, in May 1985, the first Slovak cardinal. The propaganda became shrill. John Paul II's championship of Christian Europe was just part a 'psychological imperialist war,' conveniently masking the Church's opposition to the Reformation, support for the Austro-Hungarian Empire and adulation for the executed Mgr Tiso.[43]

Even as the months passed, the regime refused to give up on Pacem in Terris. The *Tribuna* daily recalled how the association had grown out of the clergy peace movement of the 1950s, and been refounded in 1969 in response to John XXIII's appeals and the reforms of Vatican II. Its members had worked for peace and engaged in 'civic activity,' the Party newspaper insisted, much as their precursors had done during the Nineteenth Century national awakenings. They had recognised the 'legal and organisational authority' of their bishops; but they had also asserted their right to hold theological views.[44]

Many priests had already left Pacem in Terris, so others were now offered 'loyalty bonuses' for staying. In March 1983, chaired by Fr Antonín Veselý, the association celebrated the thirty-fifth anniversary of the communist coup which had created 'a new and just society.' During the same month, on Palm Sunday, a new wave of arrests landed 250 Catholics in detention, including the Czech Franciscan provincial, Fr František Kubíček, and several elderly nuns. The Franciscans' Superior-General sent a protest from Rome, and leaflets and petitions followed. Most nevertheless remained in custody.

There were warnings that the regime could cripple the Church by retiring all priests over the age of 60—and that Pacem in Terris might relive the ambition of Klement Gottwald, Czechoslovakia's Stalinist ruler, by convoking a Ukraine-style 'reunification synod' and breaking with Rome. Although such rumours were denied, visits were exchanged with Russia's Moscow Patriarchate to discuss the matter.

None of this had any impact on the growing Catholic defiance, however, which had now found a sustained voice in Cardinal Tomášek. In August 1983, the *Kathpress* agency in neighbouring Austria published a letter from the cardinal to the regime's religious affairs secretariat, deploring its wilful concealment of the Church's real hardships. Nothing was being said, Tomášek pointed out, about the 'swoops and house searches,' the vacant bishoprics, the abolished religious orders, the refusal of seminary places and the anti-faith discrimination in schools and workplaces. Czechoslovakia had become, shamefully, 'the last country in the world' with no edition of the Vatican II documents. It was still wasting time and squandering energy on 'old, superfluous conflicts' over religion and science. It was also violating its own constitution.

> How can religious freedom exist here, when the highest public officials say it exists... but repeat that they will persistently wage a struggle against religion by all possible means... Real science is modest today: it does not claim that only its views are true, and it recognises a plurality of views. To treat believers as fools, laden with prejudices from the past, as generally happens in our country, is not only dishonest and untruthful, but also offensive.[45]

Shocked by the old cardinal's words, the regime insisted the letter was a forgery, and took the precaution of denying Tomášek a passport to participate in the Pope's upcoming visit to Austria. But the episode proved embarrassing. Although the name of Fr Zvěřina was bandied around as a possible ghost-writer of the letter, the cardinal did not repudiate it.

Zvěřina himself remained highly active. In March 1984, Vatican Radio broadcast a letter from the theologian, cautioning against using the term, 'underground church.' The idea of an illegal, conspiratorial church was an invention of the communist rulers, Zvěřina insisted. In reality, far from being hostile to the state, secret church activities were a natural response to the unnatural situation created by anti-religious discrimination.

A similar point was made by the Jesuit Bishop Ján Korec, who was still working as a 'third-class citizen' at a Bratislava chemical factory after losing his priestly licence in the 1960s. Korec's letter to Slovakia's *Smena* daily was not published; but the text found its way to the West. He too dismissed the underground church as 'an invention.' Christians were simply seeking, the veteran

Jesuit told the newspaper, 'to make our work, or social relations and our whole life acceptable to God.'

> You must understand that faith for many people today is a matter of life and death—with it stands or falls the meaning of life... Whoever does not understand this does not understand man's soul. We are convinced that all of this arises in our soul, and especially in the souls of the young, by the power of the Holy Spirit, who blows where he will and does not need any permission or official rubber stamp.[46]

Korec's letter expressed the new emerging quality of Christian witness in Eastern Europe, as communist rule faltered and the courage of ordinary people stiffened. In June 1983, the Pope had paid a second visit to Poland, further mobilising popular spirits. Martial law had been suspended, but not formally lifted, and around a thousand Poles were still in prison for 'political offences' such disseminating leaflets. The regime had used the prospect of a new Papal pilgrimage to induce the Church to endorse its 'national reconstruction.' A 'successful visit,' it made clear, would ease martial law's final disappearance.

The Party's Central Committee cautioned that John Paul II's 'messianic ambitions' could reactivate Solidarity and erode stability in neighbouring countries. Even some of the Polish bishops were afraid of his 'unpredictable behaviour,' the Committee noted, while there were worries in the Vatican that his 'one-sided political involvement' was endangering Rome's 'eastern policy.' Church representatives had signed an agreement with the Polish government on the pilgrimage's main themes. But the Pope was not bound by this: he might well ignore it.

The official forecasts were nevertheless upbeat. Church leaders had accepted Solidarity, since it had helped them extend their influence in 'worker and peasant circles'; and they were now co-operating with the state to ensure their gains were not jeopardised. Out of 85 bishops, only a handful ever gave their preaching a 'negative content.' Out of 21,000 priests, only 390 were 'sporadically,' 'frequently' or 'systematically' negative. The priority now must be to cut all church links with the opposition.[47]

The latest Confessions Office director, Adam Łopatka, remained uneasy. 'The Bishops Conference wants us to choose our method of death—by hanging or by shooting,' he told the Conference chairman, Archbishop Dąbrowski, not entirely in jest.

> Foreign speculators are rubbing their hands, saying the Pope's visit will be the final element in blowing up and eliminating the communist government. So the Polish government is caught in a trap: if it consents to the visit, it risks an extremist revolt; and if it doesn't consent, it will have the bishops against it and face popular displeasure.

Łopatka was hopeful for Cardinal Glemp. The Church had its own Central Committee and Politburo, he joked to Party lecturers. Notwithstanding Wyszyński's 1950 agreement and Vatican II, it had always sided with 'reactionary forces'; and in 1980, it had merely renewed its reactionary stance. But martial law had marked a 'political turning point'; and this was thanks to Glemp, who should be helped to strengthen his position.[48]

Church leaders were well informed about the regime's plans. The Bishops Conference was said to have its own informer at Central Committee meetings, prompting a warning from General Jaruzelski that any leaks would be treated as high treason.[49] In the event, regime officials bargained long and hard over the Pope's itinerary, in face of opposition by both hardline communists and Solidarity stalwarts, who feared it would give legitimacy to Jaruzelski's regime. Around a third of Poland's 54 Catholic Intelligentsia Clubs, which had mushroomed since 1980, were closed to prevent gatherings. In Warsaw, the Primate's Aid Committee at St Marcin church was attacked by police, who abducted six volunteers.

On 16 June, however, John Paul II stepped into the Polish cauldron, recalling at the outset the 'bitter taste of deception, humiliation and suffering, of freedom denied and human dignity trampled upon.' Nothing should be allowed to perish, he stressed, 'from the deep foundation it was possible to implant in the souls of the people of God throughout the Polish lands.' The Pope fine-tuned the social teaching he had elaborated in 1979. A nation was genuinely free when it could 'mould itself as a community, determined by a unity of culture, language and history.' A state was truly sovereign when it served the common good, and allowed the nation to 'realise the subjectivity and identity peculiar to it.' The state's sovereignty was thus linked with its capacity to promote the nation's freedom—'to create conditions which enable the nation to express the whole of its historical and cultural identity, to be sovereign *through* the state.'[50]

A special control operation, '*Zorza*' (Daybreak), was launched by the Interior Ministry when the Pope visited Poland's troubled Baltic ports. As a damage limitation exercise, however, the effects were limited. During a 'brutally frank' meeting with Jaruzelski in Warsaw's Belweder Palace, John Paul II insisted his image of Poland was of a 'vast concentration camp,' full of 'hungry, shoeless, ill-clothed people.' Jaruzelski travelled specially to Kraków's Wawel Castle for a second meeting five days later, telling an aide he was worried Party colleagues would see it as an 'act of contrition.'[51] The air of humiliation was worsened by the Pope's insistence on meeting Solidarity's leader, Lech Wałęsa, who was flown to the Tatra Mountains aboard a Polish Army helicopter. It was a symbolic but crucial encounter—an acknowledgement that 'Polish reality' was not solely as the regime defined it.

Even then, some Vatican figures shared the regime's view that the meeting should not have taken place. Unnamed church officials informed Western journalists that the Pope had changed his 'negative view' of General Jaruzelski and now saw him as 'a sensible man' who would 'lead the country out of its crisis.'[52] *L'Osservatore Romano*'s deputy editor, Fr Virgilio Levi, was persuaded to write that the Pope had persuaded Wałęsa to give up Solidarity—in effect, that Church and state had reached a deal on political expediency. It was disinformation; and even when the Vatican disowned the article and forced Levi to resign, not everyone was reassured. But it was clear that the accommodationist stance of some Polish church leaders was not shared by the Pope.

The Pope beatified three Christians during the visit who personified the triumph of human will over human frailty whether in the courage of militant resistance or in the selflessness of aiding the poor. Two had fought in Poland's 1863 January Uprising against Russian rule: Adam Chmielowski (1845–1916), who had later cared for the poor in Kraków; and Rafał Kalinowski (1835–1907), who had worked in John Paul II's Wadowice hometown after surviving exile in Siberia. The third, Urszula Ledóchowska (1863–1922), had worked with the young and homeless in St Petersburg. After a 30-year struggle, the Pope also dedicated Fr Jancarz's church in Kraków's Nowa Huta surburb. Meanwhile, in Warsaw, he again urged Poles to work for a moral victory—a victory which came from 'living in truth, uprightness of conscience, love of neighbour, ability to forgive,' and enabled human dignity and solidarity to triumph over despondency. Poles should not want a homeland 'which costs nothing,' John Paul II added.[53]

A Church-state commission statement, expressing 'mutual satisfaction' with the pilgrimage, was formally accepted by Poland's ruling Politburo two weeks later. But this was for public consumption. Internal Party reports confirmed that the government had protested the Pope's 'call to open rebellion' and programme for 'Poland's total Catholicisation.' John Paul II had given the impression of 'making concessions,' one summary noted, while seven million people had turned out for his open-air Masses, suggesting the Church's 'mobilisation potential' was 'very big but not insuperable.' But the overall tone of the visit had implied a shift from 'temporary political confrontation' to 'ideological-level conflict.'

This was a serious challenge. The Pope's stress on the preconditions for state legitimacy and sovereignty were duly noted. 'The Church is in a triumphalist mood,' the document added. 'We must make the clergy realise the Church obtained this "triumph" not against the state, but thanks to far-reaching co-operation with the state.'[54]

In reality, John Paul II had reaffirmed the struggle for justice and dignity, giving Polish church leaders a chance to start afresh after the hesitancy and indecision. He had given the Solidarity experience a religious, Christ-like dimension, re-endowing its sense of a righteous purpose. The pilgrimage had highlighted the gulf separating the state's structures of power from the moral expectations of society. But the Pope had also reminded his listeners of the necessity of non-violence. True liberation would only be achieved when hatred and revenge were overcome. In a Warsaw University survey, more than four-fifths of Poles declared their trust in the Church, compared to 37 percent who trusted the Party. The regime's attempts to co-opt the Church into supporting 'normalisation' were clearly rebounding against it.[55]

What did neighbouring communist regimes make of the latest Polish spectacle? Although all were following events in Poland closely, Moscow remained acutely concerned. The Vatican was 'mainly interested' in Eastern Europe, one KGB directive observed; but it hoped its new tactics would also spur 'political de-stabilisation' in parts of the Soviet Union. Church leaders in Lithuania and Latvia, refused passports for the Polish visit, were now also barred from travelling to Rome.

In East Germany, the ruling SED insisted the Pope's Polish pilgrimage had resembled a 'crusade against communism, organised by the Reagan Administration.' Yet it took care to collect accurate data on the numbers attending Papal Masses, and concluded that the event had indeed genuinely signalled 'a clear increase in the Catholic Church's influence on all classes and strata.' John Paul II had shown respect for the organs of power and failed to 'back Solidarity directly.' But the report predicted a 'significant escalation' of the Church's 'political offensive,' matched by a 'polarisation of ideological tendencies' within the

Polish Party. Many Polish communists had now 'revealed their true, previously concealed faces as deeply believing Catholics,' the East Germans observed with contempt.[56]

In Czechoslovakia, the Husák regime made a bid to appease the new religious energy by printing 400,000 new hymnbooks, 70,000 catechisms and 200,000 Bibles, as well as dropping hints that more students would be admitted to the country's two seminaries. The realisation was finally dawning that mass religious opposition would pose graver dangers than Czechoslovakia's isolated dissident groups.

In Romania, the Papal pilgrimage was not mentioned by state radio, and only referred to blandly in official newspapers. But a government delegation, the first since the 1940s, had met Casaroli in Rome on the eve of the Pope's Polish visit; and conciliatory articles had appeared in several academic journals. At least one had even accorded a positive historic role to the long-outlawed Greek Catholics in helping maintain Romanian identity. Ceauşescu's regime continued to make use of religion in its peace propaganda, while Orthodox leaders, in contrast to their Catholic counterparts elsewhere, persisted in saying nothing about regime abuses, including the continuing destruction of Romania's historic churches.

Frustration was still growing among lower Orthodox clergy. But tensions were spreading in the Catholic community as well. In September 1984, when Casaroli's roving representative, Mgr Poggi, arrived in Romania to visit local dioceses, the conciliatory exchanges were criticised by those favouring a tougher stance. People like this were looking for leadership to three new Greek Catholic bishops: Octavian Cristian, Justin Paven and Emil Riti. Although all were secretly consecrated by Mgr Ioan Dragomir, auxiliary bishop of Maramureş, there were questions about the validity of the move, which was not authorised by the Vatican. In the case of Bishop Riti, who had spent 14 years in jail, there were also allegations of Securitate collaboration.

For all the hopes and expectations of change, the veteran Eastern Europe-watcher, Cardinal Koenig of Vienna, believed communist aims remained the same. Of course, each government ruled and planned according to local circumstances, Koenig pointed out. But the 'joint line' was still defined in Moscow, which was still 'fighting religion as a matter of principle.' State atheism still asserted a 'total claim' on the human person.[57]

In Poland itself, hopes of a new Church-state accommodation soon vanished, and Party bosses shelved plans to offer the Church legal status as part of a hoped-for deal. Jaruzelski's regime was irritated by 'ridiculous and absurd' claims of religious persecution. But it was still providing justification, through its actions, for them. As relations deteriorated after the Pope's visit, fears again surfaced that the regime was merely biding its time. It would deal once and for all with Solidarity; and then it would deal with the Church.

A campaign was launched to remove the crosses which had been put up in schools, factories and hospitals during the strikes of 1980–1. It faced tough resistance; and the regime accused local priests of using the campaign to whip up ill-feeling, especially among the young. On their side, the bishops branded the campaign a 'provocation' and foresaw an angry social reaction. If the crosses were taken down, they warned, they would merely be put up again, just as after previous campaigns.[58]

Events reached a head at Włoszczowa, near Kielce, when 300 pupils and supporters occupied a school in defence of the crosses. The local government accused the town's priests, Fr Marek Labuda and Fr Andrzej Wilczyński, of orchestrating the action and called on their bishop to discipline them. But the bishop, Mgr Mieczysław Jaworski, condemned the 'intolerant, untruthful and tendentious' media reports about the incident and offered to mediate instead. When both priests were given suspended sentences, Jaworski protested vigorously. Other occupation strikes erupted at schools around Poland; and the campaign against the crosses was discreetly abandoned. But the regime was growing exasperated at the bishops' constant complaints and interventions.

The Church had allowed local priests like Labuda and Wilczyński a degree of independence in responding to local needs. Officially, it distanced itself from openly provocative statements and actions by Catholic clergy. But it still raised no objection when they allowed their churches to become opposition centres. As Vatican II had ruled, the Church did not interfere in temporal governance; and the priests in question were not linked to political factions. But society expected leadership through concrete words and deeds. No one would accept clumsy distinctions between a 'language of politics' and 'language of morality.'

> The Church, always and everywhere, should have true freedom to proclaim the faith and its teachings about society, to fulfil its tasks among people without hindrance, and to make moral judgements even on political issues if fundamental human rights and the saving of souls require it. So a moral evaluation not only of the behaviour of individuals but of all institutions comes within the Church's mission and is of a religious nature. The Church, fulfilling its mission of love, always has the duty to combat evil. It has a particular duty to do this when evil appears in public life.[59]

In its January 1984 report, the Confessions Office had spoken ominously about 'certain priests,' who were delaying normalisation by 'abusing their pulpits' for 'obvious political activity.' The government had hoped the Church would use 'canonical decrees and declarations' to prevent this. Instead, it appeared to be giving them moral support. Łopatka had given Glemp a list of 69 'extremist priests.' It included two bishops: Mgr Tokarczuk of Przemyśl, who was still a thorn in the regime's side, and a Warsaw auxiliary and former seminary rector, Mgr Zbigniew Kraszewski. Some 20 bishops in all, however, were said to be 'causing problems.' This was not a 'blacklist,' the regime insisted. But the sermons and movements of the priests were monitored closely by the SB; and in an internal memorandum, Łopatka's office spoke of 'an illegal nationwide counter-revolutionary organisation of clergy and laity.'[60]

The idea of an organised network was widely viewed as a smokescreen. But it posed a problem for Glemp, who was sensitive to complaints that Catholic Masses were being used politically but could not be seen to be barring clergy from proclaiming the truth. The dilemmas of diplomacy and testimony—conciliating the powerful or standing up for the powerless—were as stark and as pressing as ever.

Martial law had led to a huge increase in Poland's state security apparatus. By 1984, under the direction of General Kiszczak, the SB had over 69,000 operatives, while the Interior Ministry's church-monitoring Department Four boasted a further 18,263 'secret collaborators.' Both the SB and Civic Militia police had been restructured, creating ever greater hazards for local clergy who felt called to a forceful witness. Death threats and beatings had become common again, along with dirty tricks such as sabotaging cars and distributing false leaflets. In one such incident in May 1984, the outspoken Cardinal Gulbinowicz of Wrocław had his car torched while celebrating Mass. Gulbinowicz's movements were monitored by some 40 agents, including a photographer permanently stationed opposite his heavily bugged office.

There were fears that some SB operatives were ready to go further. In December 1982, a Gdańsk auxiliary, Bishop Kazimierz Kluz, who had accompanied Lech Wałęsa on his 1981 Rome visit, died in a suspicious road accident near Trutnowy. Five months later, a well-known Dominican student chaplain, Fr Honoriusz Kowalczyk, who had ministered to strikers and internees, also died in a suspicious collision near Poznań. Even then, Department Four observed an increase in clergy militancy. The Jaruzelski regime's insistence on administrative measures, rather than outright repression, had evidently fuelled SB frustrations.

One priest, Fr Jerzy Popiełuszko, had been sent to Warsaw's Huta Warszawa steelworks in 1980 to minister to striking workers and had since turned his church of St Stanisław Kostka in the nearby Żoliborz district into a centre of resistance. It was, the Confessions Office reported, the 'main base' for subversive priestly activity. 'We're not promising that the SB will stop being interested in such priests, because this wouldn't be true,' Barcikowski bluntly warned his church interlocutors. 'The SB will also be watching the activities of Fr Popiełuszko. He knows this—and his superiors should know it too.'[61]

Born into a poor rural family at Okopy, in northeastern Poland, Popiełuszko had enrolled at Warsaw's Catholic seminary and been ordained by Wyszyński in 1972 after having his health damaged by two years' military service. He had been sent to St Stanisław's after four previous pastoral jobs in the capital, and had celebrated his first of many 'Masses for the Homeland' in February 1982, two months into martial law. The Masses had swiftly been emulated by other priests around Poland.

Fr Popiełuszko's powerful homilies drew on the simple exhortation from St Paul's Letter to the Romans: 'Overcome evil with good.' Most were said to have been approved in advance by his seminary supervisor, Bishop Władysław Miziołek; and when the Pope was shown copies by Fr Tadeusz Boniecki, editor of the new Polish edition of *L'Osservatore Romano*, he sent a personal rosary to the priest in February 1984. If Popiełuszko believed he had John Paul II's blessing, however, he encountered a very different reaction from other church leaders. Under government pressure, Cardinal Glemp admitted giving him 'paternal reprimands.' 'I went to the seminary and met the Primate at the gate,' Popiełuszko recalled of one private encounter.

> We then went into a room, and what I heard here surpassed my worst expectations. It's true the Primate could have been annoyed, because it had cost him a lot to write to Jaruzelski about me. But the accusations against me knocked me off my feet. The SB had respected me more in its interrogations. This isn't an accusation, but a pain which I treat as God's grace to cleanse myself and a stimulus to greater fruit in my work.[62]

For all Glemp's coldness, Popiełuszko had taken his place alongside the charismatic priests of history. Like the youthful Pionius, a contemporary of Polycarp in Smyrna, he was now famous for his 'repeated declarations of belief, his outspokenness, his defences of the faith before the people and the authorities, his public lectures and his friendly aid to those who had yielded to temptation.' Like Pionius and his ancient followers, he too constantly expected arrest. He would become known worldwide for the agonising fate which awaited him.[63]

It was said that Glemp, fearful of being seen to do the regime's bidding by silencing Popiełuszko directly, had attempted to have him study in Rome. The SB was well aware of tensions between the Primate and priests like him; and once the plan fell through, Popiełuszko's fate seemed to acquire a tragic inevitability. His apartment was ransacked, and he was detained and interrogated; and in July 1984, he was formally accused of 'anti-state propaganda' and 'abusing the function of a priest.' The charges were suspended a month later. But on 30 October, Popiełuszko's bound and gagged body was dredged from a reservoir on the Vistula River near Włocławek. He had been abducted 11 days earlier while returning at night from a Mass in Bydgoszcz. He was aged 37, and had been a priest for a dozen years.

There would be different versions of how Fr Popiełuszko had met his end, including claims that he was tortured at a Soviet military base in an effort to recruit him as an informer. Whatever the truth, the shadowy murder bore the hallmarks of a classic Leninist act of terror—killing one to intimidate others.

As such, it backfired disastrously. By the time the priest's body was discovered, the story was all over the international press. Jaruzelski condemned the killing and came up with a quick answer: it had been a 'political provocation' by communist hardliners opposed to his policies of reconciliation. The regime was in the middle, Jaruzelski maintained, surrounded on all sides by forces of confrontation. This would be the court's version too, when four Interior Ministry agents were convicted at Toruń in February 1985. The extremist Popiełuszko had been killed by extremists on the other side; and the Church was largely to blame—it had failed to rein him when it had the chance.

In reality, communist responsibility for the priest's death certainly extended higher—some said to General Kiszczak himself, who drily recorded his 'sincere sympathy and deep pain' in a letter to the Bishops Conference. There was no paper trail to prove it; but there had certainly been incitement. Just a month earlier, Jaruzelski's spokesman, Jerzy Urban, had opted for a more colourful analogy, denouncing Popieluszko as the 'Savonarola of anti-communism' and accusing him of a staging 'black Masses' and 'seances of hatred.'[64]

Cardinal Glemp had been wary of Popiełuszko, perhaps fearing that, as with the youthful Origen of Alexandria, 'his one ambition was to come to grips with danger and charge headlong into the conflict.' He now wrote to Popiełuszko's parents at Okopy, however, covering his own misjudgements by praising the priest as a 'sincere chaplain' who had given his life for Church and nation. On 3 November, over 400,000 people attended Fr Popiełuszko's Warsaw funeral in a massive show of support. The Pope's rosary was placed on his coffin and used as the design for his grave; while in his sermon, Glemp admitted his teachings had been theologically sound. 'It may be that this offering of life was necessary,' the Primate told mourners, 'in order that the hidden mechanisms of evil would reveal themselves, and that the aspirations for good, honesty and trust might be liberated more forcefully.' A month later, the Pope donated a chalice to St Stanisław's church and also praised Popiełuszko as a martyr.[65]

The Popiełuszko case did, indeed, bring communist repression into the spotlight. This was not only humiliating: it was also the first of a series of decisive political blows. 'All the material proves that the supreme administrative organ for religious affairs has really been subordinate to instructions from the secret police,' a distraught Bishops Conference secretary, Archbishop Dąbrowski, told Łopatka after the Toruń trial. 'Church issues aren't dealt with by the administrative organs at all, but by the SB.'[66] The Party's

Central Committee had been due to discuss measures against other radical priests; and some would continue to be threatened and harassed. But violent, arbitrary actions were now made harder. The whole world was watching. In this way, Popiełuszko's death had saved the lives of others in a true act of self-sacrifice. Through his witness, like that of Polycarp and Pionius, he had 'set his seal on the persecution and brought it to an end.'

In a nationwide pastoral letter, the Polish bishops confirmed that Popiełuszko had died a 'heroic priest's death.' Archbishop Stroba, a veteran church negotiator, offered some reassurance to his regime interlocutors. The murdered priest, he told them, was widely seen as a 'saint against the Bishops Conference.' 'But you should calm down your own people,' Stroba warned Łopatka. 'We have a common interest in calming conflicts and emotions.'[67] In reality, Popiełuszko's high-profile death had deepened feelings that a profound moral conflict was being played out in Poland. For a nation attached to its symbols, the contrast between a priest embodying Christian virtue, and his principal murderer, Grzegorz Piotrowski, personifying a godless creed, conveyed powerful images. The psychological barriers separating state and society were now all but insuperable.

The murder of Fr Popiełuszko was reported in other East European countries, where the state media followed the official line that the priest had abused his pulpit for political motives. Newspapers in Hungary highlighted the problems facing atheists in Poland and even complained of 'ideological oppression' by the Church.[68] But Hungarian dissidents sent condolences. The Pope had prayed at Cardinal Mindszenty's tomb at Mariazell during his Austrian visit a year before; and the once-disdainful dissident fraternity was becoming more aware of the importance of Christian opposition.

Popiełuszko's death had unmasked the workings of communist repression, at least in its Polish version, more than any other recent event. Yet it had not been the only such atrocity. Catholic documents submitted to the CSCE detailed at least five clergy killings in Lithuania and Latvia in 1980–1 alone. Fr Bronislovas Laurinavičius had sent a long open letter to Brezhnev in October 1977, accusing the Soviet regime of falsifying history and suppressing Lithuania's language and culture. As a leading member of the Helsinki Group, he had also signed petitions and been attacked by name in *Tiesa*, the national Party daily. In November 1981, according to eyewitnesses, Laurinavičius was attacked outside the Rodina cinema in Vilnius by two men, who then killed him by driving their car over him. The funeral of the much-admired priest was conducted by Bishop Steponavičius.

Fr Leonas Šapoka, who had been arrested in the early Soviet period and now helped edit an underground Catholic journal, *Dievas ir Tėvynė* (God and Country), was beaten to death a year earlier, aged 71, in his presbytery at All Saints parish in Luokė, near Telšiai. Another priest, Fr Leonas Mažeika, aged just 36, was also fatally battered, alongside his housekeeper, in August 1981. Their overnight assailants were arrested for robbery, and at least one death sentence was passed; but little information was divulged in court about either of the attacks, which were widely blamed on rogue KGB hitmen.

In February 1986, it was the turn of Fr Zdebskis, the priest who had been scalded by chemicals after joining Lithuania's dissident Catholic Committee. Zdebskis had been jailed in 1964, a dozen years after his ordination, for teaching the faith to children, and had worked alongside Fr Tamkevičius digging ditches on a land-reclamation project after losing his priestly licence. He was believed by the KGB to have helped edit the underground *Chronicle* after the 1983 arrest of Tamkevičius, and had survived several attacks. Zdebskis was 56 when he was killed with a companion in a collision with a milk truck at Valkininkai, southeast of Vilnius. The deaths were branded accidental and no action was taken.

Other Lithuanian Catholics survived attempts on their lives, including the underground nun, Nijolė Sadūnaitė, who was assaulted and beaten in an attempt to force her to emigrate. 'Aren't you afraid you'll also die under the wheels of a car, like Fr Laurinavičius?' one youthful KGB major demanded of Sadūnaitė during an interrogation. 'I'm not afraid at all,' the nun replied. 'What's the difference between dying in your bed and dying under wheels? What matters is having a clear conscience.'[69]

In neighbouring Latvia, where clergy faced similar pressures, a parish rector, Fr Andrejs Turlajs, was dredged with head injuries from a lake at Latgale in August 1980, while 60-year-old Fr August Zilvinskis was found dead in a forest at Griven in May 1982, six months after disappearing from his parish. Both cases were reported internationally, but given minimal coverage by the Soviet media.

The killing of clergy, both Catholic and Orthodox, was also periodically reported in Ukraine. At Braslav in Belarus, local parishioners recounted how a young Polish Catholic had been bundled into a police car after attending Mass and drowned in a nearby bog. His terrified fiancee had escaped the scene and taken several months to report the incident to a local church committee, who then referred it to prosecutors in Minsk. The man's body had been found and his funeral turned into an anti-Soviet protest.[70]

Clergy killings had featured in Czechoslovakia. A secretly ordained Benedictine, Fr Přemysl Coufal, who was linked to Bishop Davídek's *Koinótés*, had been told by the StB in January 1981 that he must collaborate or be 'dealt with.' The priest was found dead a month later in his Bratislava apartment. The authorities blamed the incident on a gas leak; but his parents and friends, who saw the body, testified that Coufal's head had been badly crushed and his apartment ransacked.

The following October, a 23-year-old lay Catholic activist, Pavel Švanda, was found dead at the foot of a gorge near Brno after travelling to Rome to visit his uncle, the Jesuit Fr Tomáš

Špidlík, a prominent church exile. The death was recorded as suicide, although evidence suggested Švanda had been tortured.

> Do you drink alcohol, and how much? How do you get on with women? Are you for war? Are you for peace?... Do you suffer symptoms of persecution? Do you suffer from depression and fear? What would you do if you were in a cell with two bullies committing acts of violence on you?

These were some of the questions asked of Fr Václav Malý, another unlicensed priest and Charter 77 signatory, when he was interrogated in April 1983.[71] Malý was one of many bearing witness to the continued use, despite pledges to the contrary, of violence and intimidation against Christians.

In Romania, clergy of all denominations still faced harassment by the Securitate. In March 1984, a Catholic priest from Odorheiu Secuiesc in Transylvania, Fr Géza Pálffy, died after being detained for criticising the communist regime's refusal to make Christmas work-free. Fr Gheorghe Calciu-Dumitreasa, the Orthodox priest defrocked by his church and jailed for outspoken sermons, was finally freed under an amnesty in August 1984, weighing just 38 kilogrammes. He had spent a total of 21 years behind bars, latterly in Romania's notorious Aiud and Jilava prisons; and he continued to be watched by armed police and soldiers until allowed to leave the country. No Romanian detainee accused of political crimes had ever been acquitted in court, Calciu pointed out—'no matter how obvious his innocence.'

Among several testimonies smuggled out of Romania, Fr Calciu composed a eulogy to the Polish Fr Popiełuszko, reflecting on the impact of his martyrdom across national and denominational lines. 'You were fated to die,' Calciu wrote, evoking the great martyrdoms of history. It was one of many signs and expressions of the feelings of solidarity now shared by Christians throughout the region, as communist rule faced its final showdown.

> For those who hated you, who hated the light that shone from you, for whom the light within them is darkness, you

> had died long ago—a death without a grave, without a cross and without kneeling... How deliberately and meticulously your murderers worked out their crime, in cold blood and with implacable materialistic logic. But you have risen again in the consciousness of us all, which is the locus of your spiritual resurrection. This is where you have been laid, and this is where you will endure.[72]

Notes

1 Krawczak and Wilanowski, *Kościół w Stanie Wojennym*, p. 8; Dudek and Gryz, *Komuniści i Kościół*, p. 383.

2 J. Luxmoore, 'Polish cardinal says he hid Solidarity members during martial law,' in *Catholic News Service* report, 18 January 2002.

3 Isakowicz-Zaleski, *Księża wobec bezpieki*, pp. 57–60, 62–3; author's interviews with Jancarz in Mistrzejowice, and Jacek Kuroń in Warsaw, November 1986; M. Wyrwich, *Kapelani Solidarności 1980–1989*, vol. 1 (Warsaw: Rytm, 2005), pp. 119–132.

4 Author's interview, Podkowa Leśna, November 1986; Dudek and Gryz, *Komuniści i Kościół*, p. 385.

5 Author's interviews with Małkowski, Warsaw, March and November 1986, February 1993. Jonathan Luxmoore, 'With the fighting priests,' in *The Tablet*, 17 January 1987. Wyrwich, *Kapelani Solidarności*, vol. 3, pp. 198–218.

6 Associated Press, 9 December 1982; Luxmoore, 'The Polish Church under Martial Law,' p. 149; *Tajne dokumenty*, p. 339.

7 Isakowicz-Zaleski, *Księża wobec bezpieki*, pp. 74–5; J. Franczyk, 'Ksiądz Adolf Chojnacki 1932–2001: Boży Buntownik,' in *Kościół w godzinie próby*, pp. 364–37.

8 Vatican Radio, 10 May 1983; *Le Monde*, 24 March 1983; *Literaturnaya Gazeta*, 19 October 1982; Krawczak and Wilanowski, *Kościół w Stanie Wojennym*, p. 7; W. Wysocki (ed), *Kościół i Społeczeństwo wobec Stanu Wojennego* (Rytm, 2004), pp. 8, 90, 289.

9 Quoted in M. Kaufman, *Mad Dreams, Saving Graces: Poland a nation in conspiracy* (New York: Random House, 1989). p. 97.

10 Luxmoore and Babiuch, *The Vatican and the Red Flag*, p. 216. The Victory Square invocation grew in its perceived importance over the next 20 years and was to be immortalised in church paintings and murals.

11 Paul VI, *Populorum Progressio*, 14 May 1971, nos. 4, 29–31, 48; Pius XI, *Nos es muy conocida*, 28 March 1927, nos. 26–7; *Quadragesimo Anno*, 15 May 1931, no. 114; Aquinas's justification in *Summa Theologica*, quest. 42, art. 2,

De Regimine Principum, book 1, ch. 15.

12 Congregation for the Doctrine of the Faith, *Instruction on Christian Freedom and Liberation*, 22 March 1986, nos. 78–9.

13 *L'Unita*, 20 March 1985; W. Veltroni, *La sfida interrotta: Le idee di Enrico Berlinguer* (Milan: Baldini, 1994), p. 204; http://www.treccani.it/enciclopedia/enrico-berlinguer_(Dizionario-Biografico); Luxmoore and Babiuch, *The Vatican and the Red Flag*, p. 246–7.

14 *Radio Liberty Research*, 3 January 1984; 'Document 168. Committee of State Security of the USSR [KGB],' in Corley, *Religion in the Soviet Union*, pp. 284–5.

15 'The new Party programme and atheistic education,' in *Radio Liberty Research*, 14 November 1985; *The Tablet*, 10 November 1984; 'Youth and the crisis of religiosity,' in *Radio Liberty Research*, 21 March 1985.

16 *Lietuvos Katalikų Bažnyčios kronika*, no. 4 (19790; *Radio Liberty Research*, 28 May 1980 and 7 October 1983; *Pravda*, 15 July 1983.

17 *Lietuvos Katalikų Bažnyčios kronika*, no. 57 (1983). Media reports said Svarinskas, first jailed in 1947 for helping the Forest Brethren, had 'used his church as a cover' for anti-state activities; *TASS*, 26 January 1983.

18 *Lietuvos Katalikų Bažnyčios kronika*, no. 66 (1985); J. Luxmoore, 'A Test for Vatican Ostpolitik,' in *The Month*, London, December 1982; *Radio Liberty Research*, 12 August 1983 and 7 October 1985; Spengla, *The Church, the Kronika*, p. 70–5.

19 *Aušra (samizdat)*, no. 28 (1981); author's interviews with Tamkevičius and Svarinskas, Kaunas, February 1990; J. Luxmoore, 'Up from the catacombs,' in *National Catholic Register*, Los Angeles, 20 May 1990.

20 *The Times*, 27 August 1984; Povilonis's speech on Vatican Radio, 25 April 1983.

21 *The Tablet*, 13 November 1982 and 5 February 1983; *Radio Liberty Research*, 13 June 1983.

22 Open letter text in Przebinda, *Większa Europa*, p. 188.

23 Terelya's letter in *Arkhiv Samizdata* 4897; *Radio Liberty Research*, 6 June 1983.

24 *Arkhiv Samizdata* 5091; *Radio Liberty Research*, 13 January 1984; *Neue Zürcher Zeitung*, 16 April 1983.

25 *Insegnamenti di Giovanni Paolo II*, vol. VII/no. 2, Rome (1984), p. 565; Pelikan, *Confessor between East and West*, pp. 147, 230–1.

26 *Arkhiv Samizdata* 5515; *Radio Liberty Research*, 29 August 1985; *Le Monde*, 7–8 July 1985, cited a summer 1984 Ukrainian Party Oblast Committee resolution, ordering the extraction of confessions from 'anti-Soviet clerics' to justify 'administrative measures against the big-mouths.' These were to include the removal of children and compulsory treatment in pyschiatric

hospitals for 'two-thirds of Ukrainian Catholic church activists,' using 'medical staff who have proved their worth.'

27 'Document 181. To the CPSU CC,' in Corley, *Religion in the Soviet Union*, p. 323. This put the number of 'Uniate priests and monks' at 700; *The Tablet*, 12 October 1985; *Radio Liberty Research*, 18 September 1985.

28 Dzwonkowski, *Za wschodnią granicą*, pp. 282–5.

29 *Radio Free Europe Background Report*, 23 September 1981; Church data in *The Tablet*, 28 August 1981, and *Radio Free Europe Background Report*, 27 December 1983; reference to Origen, in P. Kolbet, 'Torture and Origen's hermeneutics of non-violence' in *Journal of the American Academy of Religion*, vol. 76/no. 3 (2008), pp. 548.

30 *Le Figaro*, Paris, 25 January 1982; S. Prunduş and C. Plaianu, *Cardinalul Alexandru Todea* (Cluj: Ordinul Sfântul Vasile, 1992), p. 36; text of the priests' letter in Bozgan, *Cronica unui eşec previzibil*, pp. 441–4.

31 *Le Figaro*, 3 June 1982; *International Herald Tribune*, 4 June 1982; *Scînteia*, 25 May 1982. Romania was home to 200,000 Baptists in 1984, compared to 80,000 in 1960; *Radio Free Europe Background Report*, 15 December 1984.

32 *Új Ember*, Budapest, 20 September 1981; Havasy, *Martyrs of the Catholic Church*, pp. 150–2.

33 *Új Ember*, 21 March 1982.

34 *The Tablet*, 30 October 1982.

35 *Magyar Kurír*, Budapest, 12 May 1983; *Radio Free Europe Background Report*, 21 June 1983.

36 Vatican Radio report, 8 October 1982; *Kathpress*, Vienna, 27 September 1983.

37 *Kathpress*, 6 April 1984; Miklós interview in *Magyar Hírlap*, Budapest,14 January 1984.

38 *Új Ember*, 15 September 1984; *Vigilia*, Budapest, September 1984, pp. 641–650; Havasy, *Martyrs of the Catholic Church*, p. 172.

39 *Pravda*, Bratislava, 5 March 1982; Mikloško et al, *Zločiny*, pp. 304, 317; J. Čarnogurský, *Väznili ich za vieru* (Bratislava: Pramene, 1990), p. 81; J. Šimulčík, *Zápas o nádej: Z kroniky tajných kňazov 1969–1989* (Prešov: Vydavateľstvo Michala Vaska, 2000), pp. 112–141.

40 Vatican Radio, 11 March 1982; *La Repubblica*, Rome, 11 March 1982; Cardinal Oddi confirmed the *de facto* excommunication in a letter to Tomášek, dated 18 March; Hartmann et al, *Kardinál Tomášek: svědectví o dobrém katechetovi*, pp. 97–104.

41 *Frankfurter Allgemeine Zeitung*, 9 February 1983; Havasy, *Martyrs of the Catholic Church*, p. 111; Luxmoore and Babiuch, *The Vatican and the Red Flag*, pp. 263–4.

42 Vatican Radio, 8 May 1982.

43 Karel Hrůza in *Tribuna*, Prague, 30 March 1983; *Rudé Právo*, 21 January 1983. Of the two new bishops, Mgr Škarvada had been a regular broadcaster with Radio Free Europe, Voice of America and Vatican Radio, much to the regime's distaste; J. Škarvada and B. *Svoboda, Svedl jsi mě, Hospodine* (Prague: Karmelitánské nakladatelství, 2002).

44 Vatican Radio, 11 March 1983.

45 *Kathpress*, 24 August 1983; *Katolícke Noviny*, Bratislava, 12 August 1984; *Radio Free Europe Background Report*, 7 September 1984; *Deutsche Presse-Agentur* report, Hamburg, 21 March 1983.

46 *The Tablet*, 18 March 1984; *L'Avvenire*, Rome, 9 March 1984. The regime's reaction, in *Rudé Právo*, 24 September 1984; D. Doellinger, 'Prayers, Pilgrimages and Petitions: The secret church and the growth of civil society in Slovakia,' in *Nationalities Papers*, vol. 30/no. 2 (2002), pp. 215–240.

47 'Notatka Wydziału Administracyjnego KC PZPR,' in *Tajne dokumenty*, pp. 245–7; Courtois et al, *The Black Book*, p. 390.

48 Dudek and Gryz, *Komuniści i Kościół*, p. 396; 'Wystąpienie kierownika Urzędu do Spraw Wyznań,' 15 December 1982, in Raina, *Kościół w PRL*, p. 369.

49 Politburo minutes, in B. Kopka and G. Majchrzak (eds), *Stan wojenny w dokumentach władz PRL 1980–1983* (Warsaw: IPN, 2001), pp. 190–270.

50 Jubilee Mass at Jasna Góra, 19 June 1983, in Luxmoore and Babiuch, *The Vatican and the Red Flag*, pp. 249.

51 Jaruzelski spoke of 'going to Canossa,' a reference to the humiliation of the medieval German emperor Henry IV by Pope Gregory VII; M. Rakowski, *Jak to się stało* (Warsaw: BGW, 1991), p. 56.

52 *Le Figaro* report in *Tajne dokumenty*, pp. 322. *The New York Times*, 29 June 1983 and 3 July 1983.

53 Warsaw stadium Mass, 16 June 1983, in Luxmoore and Babiuch, *The Vatican and the Red Flag*, p. 250.

54 'Ocena wizyty papieża w Polsce,' 24 June 1983, in *Tajne dokumenty*, pp. 289, 330; Raina, *Cele polityki władz PRL*, pp. 136, 148.

55 Luxmoore and Babiuch, *The Vatican and the Red Flag*, p. 255.

56 'Antykomunistyczna krucjata: Kościół polski i Papież w oczach Stasi,' in *Tygodnik Powszechny*, Kraków, 5 June 1994; D. Kneipp: *Im Abseits. Berufliche Diskriminierung und politische Dissidenz in der Honecker-DDR* (Cologne: Böhlau, 2009); E. Kuhrt (ed), *Opposition in der DDR von den 70er Jahren bis zum Zusammenbruch der SED-Herrschaft* (Opladen: Leske, 1999), pp. 573–597.

57 *Herder-Korrespondenz* interview, Freiburg, 18 July 1983; Vasile, *Între Vatican şi Kremlin*, pp. 307–9; M. Birtz, *Episcopul Emil Riti (1926–2006): Tentativa unei recuperări istoriografice—cu documente inedite* (Cluj: Napoca Star, 2006;

J. Paven and M. Rădulescu, *Dumnezeul meu, de ce m-ai părăsit? reeducări, camera 4 spital Pitesti* (Bucharest: Ramida, 1996); R. Birtz (ed), *Fărâme din Prescura prigoanei 1948–1990* (Napoca Star, 2010).

58 J. Wąsowicz, 'My chcemy Boga w książce, w szkole,' in *Kościół w godzinie próby*, p. 279; Dudek and Gryz, *Komuniści i Kościół*, p. 405; Raina, *Cele polityki władz PRL*, pp. 140–6.

59 'Komunikat konferencji plenarnej Episkopatu Polski,' 14 February 1985, in *Kościół w PRL*, p. 458.

60 Luxmoore and Babiuch, *The Vatican and the Red Flag*, pp. 259–260; J. Widacki, *Czego nie powiedział generał Kiszczak: Z Janem Widackim rozmawia Wojciech Wróblewski* (BGW, 1992), pp. 92–3.

61 Dudek and Gryz, *Komuniści i Kościół*, pp. 402–3; Krawczak and Wilanowski, *Kościół w Stanie Wojennym*, p. 290; data for operatives and collaborators, in Walusiak, 'Kryptonim Wierni,' in *Kościół w godzinie próby*, p. 153. On Gulbinowicz, see *Gazeta Wyborcza*, Warsaw, 15 October 2008.

62 G. Bartoszewski (ed), *Zapiski: Listy i wywiady ks. Jerzego Popiełuszki 1967–1984* (Warsaw: Adam, 2009), p. 79.

63 Description of Pionius, who was burned at the stake for refusing to renounce his faith in 250 AD under the reign of Decius, in Eusebius, *The History of the Church*, p. 123.

64 J. Mysiakowska (ed), *Apparat Represji wobec Księdza Jerzego Popiełuszki 1982–1984*, vol. 1 (IPN, 2009), p. 351. On other versions of the priest's death, see Szymowski, *Agenci SB*, pp. 330–4; E. Czaczkowska and T. Wiścicki, *Ksiądz Jerzy Popiełuszko* (Warsaw: Świat Książki, 2004), pp. 267–346; P. Litka, *Ksiądz Jerzy Popiełuszko: Dni, które wstrząsnęły Polską* (Kraków: Św. Stanisław, 2009), pp. 25–65; K. Kąkolewski, *Popiełuszko: Będziesz ukrzyżowany* (Poznań: Zysk, 2010) pp. 174–237. Poland's crime-investigating National Remembrance Institute (IPN) later amassed 90 volumes of evidence on the case from more than 500 witnesses, as well as 66 volumes of police 'operational material' which were not checked at the time.

65 Funeral homily, 3 November 1984, in Luxmoore and Babiuch, *The Vatican and the Red Flag*, pp. 260–1; Glemp's letter, in Mysiakowska (ed), *Apparat Represji*, p. 349; M. Kindziuk, *Świadek Prawdy: Życie i śmierć księdza Jerzego Popiełuszki* (Częstochowa: Święty Paweł, 2004), pp. 263–300; description of Origen in Eusebius, *History of the Church*, p. 180.

66 'Pismo Sekretarza Generalnego Konferencji Episkopatu Polski,' 4 March 1985, in *Tajne dokumenty*, pp. 381–2.

67 'Dokument nr 30' in *Tajne dokumenty*, pp. 398, 401; 'The Martyrdom of Polycarp,' in *Early Christian Writings*, p. 125.

68 *Radio Free Europe Background Report*, 15 February 1985.

69 Wołowski and Korzeniewska, *Jak służąc Panu Bogu*, pp. 64, 90–1. Zdebskis

left a diary recording his harassment by the KGB in the early 1970s when travelling on a mission through Soviet Central Asia; *Gyvenimas mąstymuose: kunigas tarp vagių* (Vilnius: Lituanistika, 1996); Streikus, *Antykościelna polityka*, pp. 210–211; cases of Šapoka and Mažeika in *Lietuvos Katalikų Bažynčios kronika*, no. 51 (1982), pp. 23–26, and no. 52 (1982), pp. 34–7; A. Daniel and Z. Gluza (eds), *Słownik dysydentów: Czołowe postacie ruchów opozycyjnych w krajach komunistycznych w latach 1956–1989* (Warsaw: Karta, 2007), pp. 275–8, 295–7.

70 Dzwonkowski, *Za wschodnią granicą*, p. 293.

71 Vatican Radio report, 23 April 1983; on the Coufal murder, Fiala and Jiří Hanuš, *Skrytá Církev*, p. 117; Hlinka, *Sila slabých*, pp. 229–230.

72 *The Tablet*, 8 September 1984; *Radio Free Europe Background Report*, 30 August 1985; *La Croix*, Paris, 4 May 1984.

6 ALL THINGS MADE NEW

The sufferings of this present time are not worth comparing with the glory that is to be revealed to us... We know that the whole creation has been groaning in travail together till now; and not only the creation, but we ourselves, who have the first fruits of the Spirit, groan inwardly as we wait for adoption as sons, the redemption of our bodies. For in this hope we were saved. Now hope that is seen is not hope. For who hopes for what he sees? But if we hope for what we do not see, we wait for it with patience.

Rm 8:18, 22–25

WHILE THE VERY public killing of Fr Popiełuszko had exposed the tools and mechanisms used against the Polish Church, other communist regimes were also facing pressure over their anti-religious policies. International sympathy for Christians had grown, helped by the tireless efforts of Pope John Paul II. So had a more vigilant interest in religious rights. Yet not everyone was ready to ease up on the repression. Even in Poland, where the Popiełuszko murder had forced the regime to be a lot more cautious, the struggle against the Church continued. The Confessions Office still complained regularly about outspoken clergy and warned of 'appropriate measures.' 'In no other socialist state does the Church have such freedom,' Kiszczak sought to assure the Bishops Conference secretary-general, Archbishop Dąbrowski.

> Its churches are serving as platforms for atheists and impenitent sinners, who are allowed into the pulpits because they spit on the government and the system. I don't believe the Bishops Conference isn't able to bring

> order here. You'll see how the same people will soon spit on the faith and stand against the Church.[1]

Hundreds of Polish priests still belonged to the regime-controlled Caritas association, seized from the Church in the 1950s, while the Church was still heavily infiltrated by SB informers and secret collaborators. There were signs that recruitment had even increased in a final drive to divide it. Virtually all priests, meanwhile, were approached by SB agents, especially those with particular vulnerabilities; and up to 40 percent in some dioceses were believed to have police links.

Some, entrapped earlier, were unable to shake off their SB connections. Fr Wiktor Skworc had been stopped in March 1979 while re-entering Poland from East Germany, where he ministered to Polish Catholics in Dresden, and found to have a large quantity of meat in his car boot. Threatened with jail as a 'speculator,' Skworc, who later became a bishop, agreed to collaborate and continued to meet his SB minders throughout the 1980s. The SB's tentacles could reach a long way. In February 1987, the much-harassed Light-Life founder, Fr Blachnicki, an Auschwitz survivor, died of poisoning at a Polish centre in Germany after being informed on by two Catholic followers.[2]

Jaruzelski himself admitted to a 'carrot and stick principle' with clergy—a 'concrete action of punishing and rewarding.' This was spelled out clearly. 'There's a danger of creating some new Popiełuszko,' the general's Politburo colleague, Barcikowski, bluntly told church negotiators in September 1985. 'There are and will be provocations, and many will be unprovable. As long as a priest meets with Solidarity activists, SB functionaries will go after him.'[3] Yet such threats carried less weight now. Although detentions and fines were still routine, Poland had come a long way from Stalinist terror, as well as from the near-total surveillance which had operated in the 1970s. Society was awash with opposition activists, not all of whom could be tracked and intimidated. Meanwhile, Fr Popiełuszko's death had made clergy less willing to collaborate and compelled the SB to cover its tracks more carefully.

Even in Rome, while SB informers with codenames such as 'Konrado' and 'Ravel' still purportedly supplied information from the Vatican, it was debatable how much of this had real value. There were some serious agents, such as Fr Konrad Hejmo, Dominican director of Rome's Polish pilgrim centre, and Fr Mieczysław Maliński, a friend of the Pope since student days and an informer since the 1950s, who gave information about concrete people, as well as about personal rivalries and animosities at Vatican Radio and other Rome departments. In most cases, however, the regime's much-prized collaborators offered little that could not be pieced together by any observant journalist.

Though given heavy sentences of 14 to 25 years, Popiełuszko's four convicted killers had their terms reduced twice in 1986 and 1987 at the recommendation of General Kiszczak. For the unrepentent ringleader, Piotrowski, who certified that the savagely beaten priest had still been alive when thrown in the Vistula, this meant just 15 years. Feelings ran deep on both sides. Just two years after the priest's death, Jaruzelski himself berated Popiełuszko as 'a martyr not to faith but to the politics of hatred.'[4]

For all the official defiance, Poland was deadlocked. Jaruzelski's regime needed the Church's pacifying influence to hold passions in check. But it resented this influence at the same time, and was still trying to drive wedges. The bishops had been promised $28 million in Western aid for a project to help private farmers, which would have circumvented Western sanctions and attracted even larger foreign donations. But it would have given the Church economic clout; so the Polish government blocked it. In October 1985, when the regime held elections to Poland's Sejm, it offered to allow a 'safe Catholic candidate' to run if the Church made return gestures, such as by condemning 'extremist priests.' No such deal was reached, and only four bishops and a fifth of priests and nuns turned out to vote, in another blow to the regime's legitimacy.

Even after the blocking of the agricultural project, the Church's charity network remained highly active, supported by Western lorry deliveries. Priestly vocations were at their height and hundreds of churches were under construction, while 89 Catholic periodicals were appearing legally with a print-run of 1.5 million. The regime had totally failed to rebuild the Polish Party's ideological structure. It was still talking, with little apparent irony, in old ideological language about 'long-term action to change the ideo-political and worldview positions of society,' while atheist journals, such as *Argumenty i Fakty* (Arguments and Facts) and *Człowiek i Światopogląd* (Person and Worldview), still worked to sway opinion against religion. But talk of 'principled atheism' had become something of a joke. Christianity offered a higher standard of ethics and a more robust and effective worldview. Marxism and communism had been displaced in the eyes of educated, aware citizens, just as the pagan mythologies of ancient Rome had been displaced once their sterile wellsprings were exhausted.

An internal report suggested church attendance among Polish Party members had fallen from half to a third by 1985, while professed belief in God had dropped from 70 to 60 percent. But up to a fifth of Party members admitted obtaining food aid from the Church, while 92 percent favoured allowing religion in schools and believed only the Church could guarantee 'the nation's moral education.' Party hardliners blamed the deposed Gierek. 'We are harvesting the fruits of his policy of ideological capitulation,' the report concluded, 'undergone for the temporary political benefit of gaining limited support from the church hierarchy.'[5]

The dwindling of 'religious' communists had a simple explanation. Most members with genuine ideals had left the Party in protest after martial law, leaving its ranks open to value-free careerists. The regime still persisted in its efforts to divide and rule. In September 1986, it amnestied Poland's 225 remaining political prisoners and announced plans for a civil rights ombudsman and consultative council of public figures. Church leaders had lobbied for the amnesty; but they rejected calls that they should now 'thank the government' by ensuring the released prisoners refrained from 'political activity.' They backed the council idea and agreed to support Catholic candidates. But few respected names agreed to join.

In January 1987, Jaruzelski made a fresh bid for church support by visiting the Vatican to discuss plans for a third Papal homecoming. He had little left to bargain with. John Paul II had consistently demanded a return to the 1980 Gdańsk Agreement. 'The real problem is not between Church and state,' he told Józef Czyrek, Poland's Foreign Minister, in a tense encounter when Czyrek came to propose diplomatic ties again. 'The real problem is between the state and Polish civil society.' Jaruzelski had made some half-hearted attempts to garner Vatican sympathy, sending birthday and Christmas cards to Casaroli with ostentatious pledges of goodwill. When a new roving Vatican ambassador, Archbishop Francesco Colasuonno, was named in May 1986, his regime had voiced hopes that he would bring his diplomatic skills to bear and assert his independence from the Polish bishops.

At a meeting that April, however, Jaruzelski and Glemp had reluctantly conceded that relations would be feasible only when 'essential Church-state problems' had been sorted out.[6] The Polish bishops wanted full recognition of the Church's legal status as a precondition. The regime wanted the Church to sign a declaration first, recognising Poland's 'immutable' socialist order. But how could the Church agree to this, when the regime might then renege on the settlement? The regime wanted the commitments left vague. The Church wanted them precise and clear. This was why there could be no movement.

How was the deadlock in Poland to be viewed elsewhere? Powerful hopes remained focused on the Pope well beyond his homeland. In early 1985, when Czechs prepared to celebrate the eleventh centenary of the death of St Methodius, Husák's regime did its best to play down the event's religious significance and link it to Czech secular statehood instead. The commemoration would coincide closely with the fortieth anniversary of Czechoslovakia's liberation by the Red Army; so Russia's Patriarch Pimen was invited. But Cardinal Tomášek invited the Pope; and there were arrests when 17,000 signatures were collected in support. In a letter to Husák, the cardinal protested the 'unconstitutional measures' being used to impede the Church's celebrations.[7]

The Pope sent his regrets and despatched Casaroli instead; and in July, 150,000 Christians descended on the Moravian shrine of Velehrad to greet him, in the largest religious gathering since 1948. Foreign church dignitaries, such as Cardinal Koenig and England's Cardinal Basil Hume, were refused visas, and there were further arrests and house searches, while two priests who had organised an accompanying youth programme were stripped of their licences for 'hindering supervision.' The Mass, celebrated by Casaroli, was attended by the Czech Culture Minister, Milan Klusák, who was booed and heckled when, in a brief address, he talked about religious freedom. 'Don't worry—everything will come!' Klusák timidly hit back. As a mark of defiance, members of the banned Franciscan order appeared at Velehrad in their habits. They did so again during a pilgrimage to Sastin in Slovakia the following September.[8]

In a letter that April, the Pope had urged Czechoslovakia's clergy to continue evangelising, despite their 'arduous, difficult and often bitter' circumstances. Regime propagandists were still denouncing 'clerical anti-communism, religious obscurantism and extremism.' Meanwhile, with nine Catholic sees still without bishops, the Party continued to claim success in curbing religious beliefs. In practice, however, officials admitted a religious revival had set in. Up to 70 percent of Slovak and 30 percent of Czech children were still being baptised, according to government data, while even civil servants and security officials were known to make discreet appearances at the 117 places of worship still functioning in Prague.[9]

There were reports of a growing disagreement between regime hardliners and those favouring a more conciliatory line. Detentions, interrogations and 'protective supervision' remained routine. Clergy were still liable to be denounced and arrested for offences such as hearing confessions without a *súhlas*; and at least a hundred priests and prominent Catholics were still languishing in jail for faith-related offences. In late 1985, a lay Catholic, Augustin Navrátil, was sent to a psychiatric prison after accusing Husák in a letter of covering up the murder of Fr Coufal. Yet care was being taken not to inflame opinion. As in neighbouring Poland, the order of the day was administrative pressure and petty harassment, rather than public trials and prison sentences.

With Catholic ceremonies and events now seething with opposition feeling, Charter 77 welcomed the new Christian assertiveness. Religious *samizdat* publishing had mushroomed, and mass petitions were in circulation. The frail but transformed Tomášek had clearly positioned the Church on the side of the persecuted, and was stressing the point whenever he could. He told Switzerland's *Neue Zürcher Zeitung* the Church was still 'suffering for Christ and being crucified,' as Christians 'paid with their blood.' He assured *The Times* of London the Church was also 'full of hope and courage.' Like the early Christians in the catacombs, Czechoslovakia's Catholics had had to 'go underground to preserve the faith.'[10]

Although three-quarters of Tomášek's parishes now had no priests, there were plenty of courageous clergy to fill the gap—men like the Jesuit provincial, Fr Jan Pavlík, who had operated cranes in Brno after losing his licence, and his Dominican counterpart, Fr Dominik Duka, who had worked at the Škoda car plant in Plzen since losing his. Like Fr Duka in his time, numerous would-be priests were still being turned down by Czechoslovakia's two seminaries, which now had four applicants for each place. But hundreds of priests were ministering secretly, and more church support was coming for Charter 77. This was thanks in part to the prominent role played by lay Catholics such as the mathematician, Václav Benda, and priests like Fr Malý, who was also active in the Charter offshoot, the Committee to Defend the Unjustly Prosecuted, or VONS. Few clergy had actually signed the Charter and made their endorsement public. But many supported it in their own ways.

Czechoslovakia's traditionally docile Protestant churches were becoming more assertive as well. This reflected pressure from long-standing dissidents like Ladislav Hejdánek and Božena Komárková, and pastors such as Jakub Trojan and Jan Dus, the second of whom, a noted Biblical scholar, was jailed without trial in 1986–7. Reports circulated that the Pope was considering a formal reappraisal of the Bohemian martyr, Jan Hus (1386–1415), a move with major implications for Catholic-Protestant relations, as well as for human rights.

The case of Czechoslovakia highlighted the glaring disparities now evident in Eastern Europe. While a church-building boom was underway in Poland, even small church repairs were impeded in neighbouring Slovakia. Polish Christians had ready access to religious books and periodicals, whereas Slovak and Czech Christians could be arrested for bringing religious literature across the border.

Public Christian defiance could have been expected in the relatively mild conditions of Hungary. But little could be done here without some spark of official church dissent; and Cardinal Lékai had maintained his accommodationist line. The cardinal's stance was challenged by dissident priests working with Hungary's base communities, who had long urged him to be less subservient to the regime's religious affairs director, Imre Miklós. Fr László Kovács, the priest who had been moved in 1981, explained the concerns in one blunt exchange.

> Kovács: There should be a simple chain: the Pope obeys Jesus, the cardinal obeys the Pope, and I obey the cardinal—but things aren't working like that.
>
> Lékai: He says I do what Imre Miklós demands.

Kovács: In my opinion, what Imre Miklós does is consistent with his principles: he's an atheist who wants to kill religion, and I respect his struggle. But I disapprove of the fact that he relies on our own leaders. In my view, the aims of an atheist government have to differ from those of a priest, bishop or cardinal. A cardinal must not serve an atheist government.

Lékai: Thank you.

Kovács: Don't mention it.

Lékai: You don't understand the situation our Church is in.

Kovács: But I know the words of Jesus, and that is enough.[11]

Vatican II's *Gaudium et Spes* constitution had established that the Church was ready to co-operate with any political order, Lékai insisted; and today, as Kádár's regime continued its 'second stage of socialism,' the Church's survival was proof that antithetical value systems could agree on certain points. In June 1985, a year before his death, Lékai allowed three priests, including one of his Esztergom dignitaries, Mgr Imre Bíró, to be elected to Hungary's State Assembly in an apparent flouting of canonical rules.

The Kádár regime had made some gestures. Hungary's four tolerated religious orders had been allowed to open some monastic houses; and in 1985–6, visits were permitted by Mother Teresa of Calcutta, whose order was now active in Hungary, as well as by the Franciscans' Minister-General, Fr John Vaughn, and the Jesuits' Father-General, Fr Hans-Peter Kolvenbach, whose order now had just 90 elderly Hungarian members, compared to more than 400 in 1945. Several new churches were under construction; and in December 1985, a new Catholic hymnal, *Éneklő Egyház*, was published after a decade of work. Meanwhile, seminary admissions were increased, and lay pastors allowed to make up for clergy shortages by conducting baptisms and marriages. Hungary's bishops were permitted to issue pastoral letters on family life; and in October 1986, the latest Christian-Marxist dialogue was organised in Budapest on 'moral values in society.' The veteran Miklós was received by the Pope for a second time in December 1986, and followed to Rome two months later by Hungary's premier, György Lázár.

Serious problems remained. Half of Hungary's eleven Catholic dioceses were in the hands of sick old men, and half of its 2700 priests were past retirement age. Catholic church attendance in Lékai's own Esztergom diocese had dropped to just twelve percent, while three-quarters of Catholics nationwide had completely given up going to Mass.[12] Meanwhile, Christian clergy and laypeople were still being harassed. Members of Fr Bulányi's Bokor movement featured prominently among the 150 Hungarians jailed for refusing military service. Bulányi vehemently denied defying the Pope's authority and accused the bishops of waging a campaign against him: like the prophets of old, he too was being 'persecuted by the high priests of the day.' 'No movement of Jesus can ever be popular,' Bulányi said of Bokor.

> The power of the state constitutes a smaller obstacle than the attitude of the church hierarchy. In politics, real change can often be expected only when those in power have gone, and much the same is true of the Church... I cannot respect Stalin in recognition of all the functions he acquired by killing his opponents. Nor can I respect a body of people who courted state power until it permitted them to become bishops. I respect people who hold to their principles, even at the risk of martyrdom.[13]

Fr Bulányi's case was at least being written about now in Catholic journals like *Új Ember*. That was progress of a kind. Meanwhile, the official media were in a conciliatory mood. When the tenth anniversary of Cardinal Mindszenty's death was commemorated in May 1985, the Party daily, *Népszabadság*, duly compared his 'counter-revolutionary leanings' and 'stubborn anachronisms' to the current harmony in Church-state relations. But it acknowledged that 'mistakes' by Mátyás Rákosi's Stalinist regime had made Mindszenty 'a martyr in many people's eyes.' Calls were heard for the cardinal's rehabilitation.[14]

Conditions were still a lot tougher in neighbouring Romania. Ceauşescu had taken drastic action to stave off economic insolvency. Food and heating were being rationed and those past working age refused medical treatment. Meanwhile, a third of the population was set to be relocated and half the country's 13,000 traditional villages demolished to make way for new mega-communes, or 'agro-industrial centres.' The *conducator*'s paranoid schemes were making communist allies edgy. So were his anti-religious excesses. All published material, from schoolbooks to tourist brochures, studiously avoided any religious terminology; and there were reports that a consignment of 20,000 Bibles, destined for Hungarian Reformed parishes, had been pulped into toilet paper, leaving patches of text clearly visible.[15]

Even more spectacularly, an urban clearance programme, conceived in the 1970s, was now underway in Bucharest, which would see the city's Orthodox monasteries bulldozed and many of its historic churches demolished or re-sited. The madcap plan resembled the harshest actions of China and Albania. Yet there was still no sign of protest from the ageing Patriarch Iustin, who continued, incomprehensibly, to heap glory on Ceausescu as he brought 'happiness and prosperity' to his people.

One in five Romanians had secret police links, so protests were rare anyway. Yet the church clearances were a step too far, and letters of outrage were sent to the government by art historians and architecture specialists. The Mihai Vodă monastery, founded in 1594 by Prince Michael the Brave, was Bucharest's second oldest, the signatories pointed out, 'a symbol of the most precious national aspirations.' The nearby Văcăreşti monastery, built in 1716, held 'outstanding importance for Romanian and southeast European art.' Its loss, to make way for an amusement park, would 'severely amputate' the Romanian past.[16]

Frustrated by Iustin's timidity, more Orthodox priests were also speaking out. The now-exiled Fr Calciu-Dumitreasa, a symbol of

Christian resistance, had condemned the destruction of churches, highlighting the Securitate's lawlessness and branding atheism a 'philosophy of despair.' Inspired by his example, younger clergy were demanding a more forthright response to spiritual needs. At a least a dozen were said to have faced criminal charges.

Fr Alexandru Pop, a priest from Romania's Banat region, was typical of the new assertive breed. In February 1986, Pop sent an open letter to the West, describing the 'grief and revolt' felt by many clergy at Calciu-Dumitreasa's treatment and the undignified silence of Iustin and others. He set out eight demands, including a halt to anti-religious propaganda and the church demolitions, which were leaving Romanians with 'no proper place to marry, baptise their children or mourn their dead.' Other priests were ready, the 39-year-old confidently predicted, to 'carry on the Christian testimony with equal courage and wisdom.'

> I am aware of what is in store for me. It is possible an enquiry or house search will produce evidence, such drugs or foreign currency, to put me on trial and send me to jail. It is possible I will be placed in a psychiatric clinic and declared insane. In our century, all possibilities are open. For the time being, I am alone in signing this message. But there are many who would like to join me.[17]

That March, after two further statements, Fr Pop was duly dimissed by his bishop. Several other Orthodox priests were suspended and defrocked for protesting the hierarchy's subservience and calling on lower clergy to resist. Some had links with the banned Lord's Army renewal movement and friendly ties with Greek and Latin Catholics.

Only one of Romania's five tolerated Latin Catholic dioceses had a bishop and some aspects of church life were close to extinction. There were, nevertheless, cases of defiance. In December 1985, a 29-year-priest, Fr János Csilik, was expelled from his post at Oradea's Catholic cathedral for refusing to surrender the names of parishioners. The outlawed Greek Catholic Church, meanwhile, had gained a vigorous leader in Bishop Todea, who had ordained new priests and celebrated Mass in private homes, despite constant Securitate surveillance.

The rapid growth of Romania's Baptist, Adventist and Pentecostal churches, especially among the young, posed a further ideological challenge to Ceaușescu's regime. Attempts were made to explain away the religious revival. In early 1994, the Party's *Era Socialista* newspaper published a panel discussion, in which it was conceded that the 'spiritual universe' of many Romanians still had a 'mystic-religious background,' despite official predictions that faith must wither in the face of industrialisation.[18]

In September 1985, the regime surprised the world by allowing the US Baptist evangelist, Billy Graham, to make a week-long tour. Graham had visited the Soviet Union twice, in 1982 and 1984; so the authorities had examples to draw on when it came to control and surveillance and extracting propaganda benefits. Although 150,000 Romanians came to hear Graham's sermons in various places of worship, the visit was not mentioned in the media.

Since Christians had become the main source of dissent in Romania, they were now also the regime's key target. In Bucharest, the police intervened brutally when some 200 Adventists occupied a church to prevent its demolition. In Oradea, where the Baptist church, Europe's largest, had survived a demolition attempt in 1984 thanks to US pressure, a leading pastor, Paul Negrut, was warned by his Securitate minders to 'remember what happened to the Polish priest.'[19]

Christian militancy had long been on the rise in Yugoslavia, where the post-Tito regime had admitted mistakes and tried to calm the anti-church campaign. Here too, there were signs of discord within the ruling League of Communists, whose Serb members tended to be more moderate than their Croatian counterparts. Surveys suggested religious beliefs had declined since the 1970s. But they also indicated that attachment to churches was growing stronger, especially in the countryside; so religious affiliations had to be handled carefully. As before, a distinction was made between perceived trouble-makers such as

Cardinal Kuharić of Zagreb and more accommodating figures like Archbishop Alojzij Šuštar, the new Catholic leader in neighbouring Slovenia. Several regime newspapers now had religious affairs correspondents, whose task was to highlight signs of church support for socialism. There was talk of doing more to restore and maintain church premises.

The Party daily, *Borba*, had accused the Pope of violating the old 1966 Yugoslav-Vatican accord by criticising anti-religious policies. The regime was keen, however, to improve relations with Rome. In July 1982, when the veteran Croatian communist, Jakov Blažević, had attacked the Vatican at a Party congress, an unprecedented rebuke had followed in the official *Danas* weekly. In February 1983, when Kuharić headed a Bishops Conference delegation to the Vatican, the Pope paid tribute to the Croatian Church's 'heroic loyalty' and urged it to go on presenting the Christian faith 'without ambiguity' against 'de-sacralisation, materialism, consumerism and hedonism.'[20] The tough wording did not prevent Yugoslavia's Foreign Minister, Lazar Mojses, from attending a Papal audience just one day later.

Christians were still vulnerable, however. Reports surfaced of torture in Yugoslav prisons; and in June 1983, two Franciscan novices, Franjo Vidović and Ivan Turudić, were adopted as prisoners of conscience by Amnesty International after being harshly treated in a bid to deter monastic vocations. Other clergy were given short sentences for insulting the late Tito or 'fomenting tensions,' while a parish priest, Fr Filip Pavić, was jailed for 50 days when he published a prayer in a local religious magazine against the 'theory and practice of materialism.' The lay Catholic editor of *Glas Koncila*, Živko Kustić, was charged with 'false information' after publishing an article about the imprisoned Franciscan novices.

In December 1983, a schoolgirl from Sinj, up the Dalmatian coast from Medjugorje, was jailed for 'irritating the populace' with claims that she too had seen the Virgin Mary. Medjugorje's Franciscan priest, Fr Jozo Zovko, had been released after a publicity campaign abroad, although two other local Franciscans, Fr Vlasić and Fr Krizić, remained behind bars. All three claimed to have suffered 'continuous discrimination' in prison, where they were denied religious literature, like their French Revolution ancestors, and any family or church contacts. Their complaints had 'proved useless,' the three priests testified in a joint letter.

> We know that communists imprisoned in the old Yugoslavia fought for and obtained the status of political prisoners. In prison, they studied Marxist literature, translated Marx's *Das Kapital* and had at their disposal the very books they had been sentenced for. But we live today among criminals, humiliated and deprived of our rights...
>
> Even war criminals convicted after the War at the Nuremberg trials, serving their sentences at Spandau Prison in Berlin, were allowed a priest daily to offer them religious solace, celebrate Mass and give the sacraments. But to us, priests and believers, this is denied even today. We are not demanding any special treatment, only our rights as human beings, prisoners, priests and believers who have dedicated their whole lives to the faith and are ready to live and die for it.[21]

Medjugorje remained an object of controversy within the Church. The local Catholic bishop, Pavao Žanić of Mostar, was vehemently against the new shrine. The apparitions were no more than a 'collective hallucination,' Bishop Žanić had concluded; and the Franciscans were shaming the Church by 'manipulating the sincere longing for the supernatural among the population.' In November 1984, a church commission concurred that there should be no 'organised pilgrimages' to Medjugorje, and no expressions of support from Catholic clergy. The statement, published by the Vatican, was misreported in the Yugoslav media as imposing a ban on visits. This was soon corrected by Cardinal Joseph Ratzinger, prefect of the Vatican's Congregation for the Doctrine of Faith. Patience was needed in evaluating Medjugorje, Ratzinger cautioned. Although Revelation had been completed with Christ, God might still be speaking 'through simple people and extraordinary signs.'[22]

The fate of Cardinal Stepinac remained a major cause for the Church in Croatia; and the official media hit back, partly as a way of attacking Kuharić. Making him a cardinal in January 1983, however, the Pope praised Kuharić for his 'lively and active testimony.' Two dozen bishops and some 300 priests marked the occasion with a Zagreb cathedral Mass, the largest since Stepinac's funeral 23 years before. A month later, Vatican Radio took up Stepinac's case directly, noting how 'sordid and untenable allegations' were making him 'even more attractive and topical for our time.' Stepinac had served 14 years in prison after his 'rigged trial,' the radio recalled. Today, 'like the 14 stations of the cross,' the years were 'taking him via Calvary to the glory of martyrdom and resurrection.'[23]

Since the regime depicted Stepinac as a war criminal, the conflict was certain to intensify. A priest from the northeastern town of Požega, Fr Josip Decić, was give a two-month sentence and heavy fine, despite angry protests, for commemorating Stepinac in a mural at his church—officially because it clashed with the baroque style of the building, which was listed as a cultural monument. Meanwhile, in a February 1984 cathedral sermon, Kuharić compared Stepinac to the English St Thomas More, a man who had chosen to die rather than betray his conscience.

Such claims were furiously attacked by the official media; and the *Vjesnik* daily hit back, quoting the Canon Law maxim used to incriminate More as proof of Stepinac's own guilt—*Quis tacet consentire videtur* ('Who stays silent is seen to consent'). Yet uncertainty had also set in. In February 1985, the hardline Jakov Blažević himself raised doubts about Stepinac's trial. The main 'grievance' against the cardinal had been his refusal to break with Rome, Blažević conceded. If he had been 'a little more flexible,' there might well have been no trial.[24] This clearly called in question the old claim that Stepinac had been condemned for his links with the wartime Ustaša.

For all the regime's efforts, Kuharić himself remained in a strong position. In September 1983, in a significant boost for the Croatian Church, he had hosted the first meeting outside Rome of the Council of Catholic Episcopates of Europe, or CCEE, under its English president, Cardinal Basil Hume. There was talk of a possible Papal visit for 1300th year of Croatian Christianity in September 1984; and although this was shelved, 300,000 Catholics attended a national eucharistic congress at Marija Bistrica when the anniversary came around. A month later, in a further boost, the Pope canonised a Croatian Franciscan and early pioneer of ecumenism, Fr Leopold Mandić (1866–1942), during an assembly of the Synod of Bishops in Rome.

The regime claimed to be concerned about nationalism in Yugoslavia's religious communities. In Serbia's Vojvodina province, ethnic Croatian and Hungarian Catholic priests were reported to be siding with nationalist groups. In Bosnia-Herzegovina, Muslims were said to be using some of their 3000 mosques for general meetings. Bosnia's capital, Sarajevo, hosted Europe's only Islamic theology school; and the regime had allowed some pilgrimages to Mecca to highlight Yugoslavia's non-aligned status. But Bosnian imams, trained in Egypt and Saudi Arabia in the 1960s and 1970, had returned with militant ideas, while some 300 Bosnian students were believed to have attended Islamic universities in the Middle East. In 1983, as the country prepared to host the Winter Olympics in Sarajevo, a dozen alleged fundamentalists, led by Alija Izetbegović, had gone on trial for apparently demanding an Islamic state.

In Croatia, a new Grand Mosque opened at Zagreb in summer 1984, after being delayed by a suspicious fire. There had also been attacks on Orthodox churches in the predominantly Muslim province of Kosovo, provoking a reaction from Serbia's traditionally docile Orthodox church. A petition by priests from Kosovo's Raško-Prizren eparchy was published by the church's *Pravoslavlje* fortnightly, while in a rare interview Patriarch German deplored the government's failure to protect Orthodox sites.

The Serbian church was building links with Orthodox counterparts abroad; and in November 1984, it boosted its prestige by hosting a visit by Russia's Patriarch Pimen. Patriarch German now felt confident enough to widen the complaints. He deplored the continued obstacles to religious education and the 'insurmountable difficulties' in obtaining church-renovation permits. The regime defended its record: 181 Orthodox churches built and 841 restored since 1945, with eight monasteries constructed from scratch and 48 rebuilt. Yet the quoting of dry data, whether accurate or not, could not go far in appeasing the mounting dissatisfaction.[25]

How was Rome responding to the dissatisfaction? Though barred from visiting Lithuania, the Pope had tried to be conciliatory. Approaches were made to the Russian Orthodox church, which routinely endorsed Soviet foreign policy; and in 1982, Vatican delegates were sent to a Soviet-approved peace conference of religious leaders. Vatican Radio glowingly reported a pastoral letter by the US bishops, which appeared to reject President Reagan's nuclear policy; and in September 1983, the Pontifical Academy of Sciences sponsored a declaration on the dangers of nuclear war, signed by scientists from 20 countries, including the Soviet Union. The following February, a Vatican delegation under Jerome Lejeune, a Pontifical Academy professor, attended the funeral of Yuri Andropov, the Soviet Union's latest gerontocratic Party boss.

If Moscow sought propaganda benefits, however, the gestures were quickly counter-balanced. In May 1984, John Paul II responded to long-standing dissident requests by offering prayers for the ailing Andrei Sakharov and receiving his step-daughter. He held private talks with Sakharov's wife, Yelena Bonner, in December the following year when she was granted a brief exit visa for medical treatment.

The Soviet media accused the United States of exerting pressure on Rome, blaming this for the Pope's turbulent tour of Central America in 1983 and for the reining in of Liberation Theology, as well as for John Paul II's constant appeals on behalf of Eastern Europe's Christians. Meanwhile, efforts persisted to undermine the Pope's vision of a reborn Christian Europe.

These had little effect. In a June 1985 encyclical, the Pope lauded the European patrons, Cyril and Methodius, as 'precursors of ecumenism,' who had defended the identity of the Slavs by rooting the Gospel in their language and culture, and creating a 'spiritual bridge' in Europe which remained 'deeper and stronger than any division.' He looked ahead to the 1988 Millennium of the baptism of Prince Volodymyr of Ukraine, whose Christian kingdom had stretched from Ukraine to the Baltic. Like Cyril and Methodius, Volodymyr had maintained ties with both Rome and Constantinople, thus initiating an 'original form of Christianity' centred on Europe's east.

> Europe is Christian in its very roots. The two forms of the great tradition of the Church, the Eastern and the Western, the two forms of culture, complement each other like the two lungs of a single body... In the differing cultures of the nations of Europe, both in the East and in the West, in music, literature, the visual arts and architecture, as also in modes of thought, there runs a common lifeblood drawn from a single source.[26]

The 'two lungs' analogy was not new. The Russian Catholic convert, Vyacheslav Ivanov, had used a similar notion in the 1920s and 1930s to convey the spirit of European unity. So had the Nineteenth Century Russian mystic, Vladimir Soloviev, in his dream of a single universal church. Although the communist regimes poured scorn on John Paul II's Christian vision, some were also keen to gain a share of the Cyril and Methodius legacy. In Yugoslavia, the media debated the saints' Macedonian and Croatian links, while Bulgaria's ruling Party insisted Methodius had used the old Bulgarian language in his teaching missions. The

Party boss, Todor Zhivkov, had unveiled a plaque to the saint in Rome's San Clemente church during his 1975 Vatican visit, and had even awarded himself the title 'Grand Master of the Order of Cyril and Methodius.'

There were some parallels here to the East German regime's harnessing of the Protestant reformer, Martin Luther, whose fifth birth centenary was celebrated in November 1983. Other governments also chimed in with praise for Luther as an early revolutionary and national champion, who had translated the Bible for the ordinary working masses and attacked the reactionary power of Rome.[27]

Moscow, for its part, had not given up on efforts to exploit Christian organisations for its own purposes. When the World Council of Churches had met at Vancouver in summer 1983, with over 300 denominations from a hundred-odd countries, Kuroedov's Religious Affairs Council had complained of pressure from 'anti-Soviet centres.' The regime-controlled Berlin Conference and Christian Peace Conference had lobbied hard in support of Soviet foreign policy at a preparatory planning session in Dresden two years earlier; and when the assembly ended, Moscow was pleased that Soviet 'peace initiatives,' including a condemnation of US nuclear deterrence, were reflected in its final documents. Dissident Soviet Christians had forlornly urged the assembly to debate their plight. But a 'great part' had been played, Kuroedov enthused, by the Russian Orthodox delegation, now under new management following the withdrawal of the Vatican II veteran, Archpriest Borovoi. It would now be 'expedient,' the CRA concluded, to extend the participation of Soviet churches.[28]

The Soviet government had been ready to reward subservience with a tentative relaxation. Unauthorised religious groups were still being broken up, while conflicts still occurred over such tired issues as the composition of *dvatsatka* parish committees. These now generally took the church side, having ceased to be a serious instrument of state control. But teachers remained under pressure to assert their atheist credentials, and parents wishing to pass on the faith to their children were ridiculed in the media for abusing and brainwashing them. Religious books could now be received by post; but Christians who brought them from abroad could still find themselves in labour camps.

Although some churches had been returned, meanwhile, this had generally required years of bureaucratic wrangling, backed up with petitions and occupation protests. Regime officials only responded to protracted mass actions; so Christians had to show they were united and determined. Yet even if renovation permits were secured, the work could still be blocked by administrative subterfuge or violent sabotage. In parts of Ukraine and Belarus, churches were still being destroyed.

There were, however, signs of change. More religious material was being printed and disseminated, while Orthodox pictures and calendars were being sold on the street. The Soviet Party's youth paper, *Komsomolskaya Pravda*, admitted that many members now went to church. The 'absolute majority' were really non-believers, the newspaper quipped; so they were obviously being 'forced' to go by relatives. But other media acknowledged a growing interest in religion, especially among young people, and recorded that the wearing of crosses was now a common sight in cities like Leningrad. Church buildings were already protected under a 1976 law on historical monuments, as well as by decrees barring the theft of icons and other sacral objects. These could often only be protected by elderly parishioners with time on their hands.[29]

The Soviet regime hoped to control any religious revival through public indignation rather than repression. But it knew it had to make certain gestures; and in late 1983, when the Moscow Patriarchate's much-censored journal celebrated its fortieth anniversary, the government made a surprise announcement that it was returning Moscow's confiscated Thirteenth Century Danilov Monastery for use as a new church headquarters. For the first time in nearly three centuries, the Orthodox church's leadership would be based in the capital, rather than at nearby Zagorsk. Up to a hundred monks were to be allowed to live at the Danilov, which would be the fourth monastery operating legally in Russia, alongside a dozen female convents.

The once-unthinkable concession took some explaining. On 11 March 1985, after the short-lived gerontocracy of Chernenko and Andropov, the Soviet Party gained a vigorous new General Secretary, Mikhail Gorbachev. The Pope had received the Soviet Foreign Minister, Gromyko, at a frosty Vatican meeting just a month before; and there was, on the face of it, little reason to expect any transformation. Gorbachev had personally experienced Stalin's terror. Both his grandfathers had been arrested on trumped-up charges, while half the population of his native village near Stavropol, including two aunts and an uncle, had starved to death in the Soviet-engineered famine of 1932–3. But his own background had been exemplary: driving combine harvesters on collective farms and rising rapidly through the Party after joining as a law student in the 1950s.

In November 1979, Gorbachev had co-signed the KGB's six-point 'Operation Pagoda' against the Catholic Church; and at his first congress as Party leader in February-March 1986, he duly declared war on 'reactionary nationalist and religious survivals.' There were warnings that Party members attending religious ceremonies would be expelled, as Lenin had demanded, especially in traditionally Muslim republics like Uzbekistan, where regime functionaries were said to arrive regularly for services at local mosques in official cars.[30]

Yet this was for public consumption only. Behind the scenes, whether officially willed or not, things were changing. Having been far less demanding than smaller religious groups, Orthodox Christians had found strength in numbers and were becoming more assertive. In early 1986, the Patriarchate's journal reported that new instructions had been issued on 'the rights of a person in law,' which appeared to allow religious communities to construct and own their buildings. This clearly contradicted Lenin's 1918 decree on Church-state separation, which had stripped churches of legal personhood and given the state control over all religious properties. The decree had been relaxed in practice; but it was still the formal foundation for all religious legislation. Rumours that it was being scrapped reflected the atmosphere of tentative hope now pervading the Soviet Union.

Several prominent literary figures had revealed their Christian convictions during the centenary of Dostoevsky's death in 1981, while some Soviet intellectuals had criticised the official hostility to Christianity. Since Gorbachev had urged intellectuals to support him, this religious opening was important. But the sympathy for faith extended further. The CRA spoke of an 'outburst' of baptisms at Yaroslavl in Russia's heartland, and instructed its local branches to err on the side of accepting rather than the rejecting new religious groups. Many people were expecting changes in state policy towards religion, the Council noted. But some groups, especially Baptists and Pentecostalists, were still refusing to register themselves, since registration implied compromise with the authorities. Their leaders wielded a 'decisive influence,' the Council warned, and were attempting 'to exploit past errors committed by the state in relation to religion and the church, in particular the practice of administrative meddling on the part of Soviet organs.'[31]

Soviet newspapers published letters from readers on Christianity's usefulness in combating social and moral failings such as alcoholism; and for the first time since 1945, *Pravda* accepted an article by an Orthodox leader, Metropolitan Mikhail of Vologda, attacking contemporary youth culture. Official writers hit back at the implication that atheism had contributed to social and moral decline. They also ridiculed their religious colleagues for—in Lenin's phrase—'flirting with God.' But more liberal titles like *Moskievski Novosti* and *Literaturnaya Gazeta* urged greater tolerance. On the eve of the October Revolution's seventieth anniversary, one journal highlighted the 'many survivals of religious culture' evident in contemporary literature, art and music. Yet in the city of Kirov, there was just a single church for 400,000 local Orthodox Christians, the journal added; and this was so packed on Sundays that 'you can barely raise your hand to make the sign of the cross.' 'The time has come to reject the practice of unfoundedly denouncing religion's heritage,' another writer concurred.

> What happened to us? Who extinguished the light of goodness in our soul? Who blew out the lamp of our conscience, and threw it into the dark, deep pit in which we now grope to find the bottom and some guiding light for the future?... We lived with a light in our soul, acquired long before us by the doers of heroic deeds, and illuminated for us so we would not wander in the darkness, run into trees or into one another, scratch out each other's eyes or break our neighbour's bones.[32]

In November 1987, Gorbachev appeared to endorse the new reformist atmosphere with a book, *Perestroika: New thinking for our country and the world*. This spoke of a 'democratised' communist order, inspired by the twin master-concepts of *glasnost* (openness) and *perestroika* (restructuring). Socialism would still triumph, the new Soviet leader insisted; but it would triumph peacefully, as capitalism was forced to accommodate the righteous demands of the world's downtrodden. As for Moscow's subservient allies in Eastern Europe, each ruling Party had 'sovereign rights'; and some, 'drawing on the Soviet experience,' had failed to 'consider their own specifics.' This 'stereotyped approach' had been given an 'ideological tint' by communist leaders acting as 'sole guardians of truth.'[33]

While most Soviet citizens supported *glasnost*, not all liked the sound of *perestroika*. Coming from a Soviet leader, however, these were extraordinary statements; and religious dissidents and human rights groups took Gorbachev at his word. Petitions landed on his desk for revising or reversing Church-state laws, including those banning private charity which dated from an era when the eradication of all faith was deemed possible and desirable. The very notion of 'scientific atheism' came under attack: neither religion nor atheism could be scientific, the critics observed. Neither, in any case, could be the responsibility of the state.

When dozens of prisoners of conscience were freed under an amnesty in early 1987, most resumed the activities they had been sentenced for, with Fr Gleb Yakunin promptly announcing a new group, 'Church and Perestroika.'

With reforms now part of the daily discourse, Gorbachev's regime was confident it could defend its record abroad. To counter claims of persecution, foreign tourists were encouraged to visit Russia's working churches, while the Soviet Party's Central Committee even proposed sending 50 Orthodox monks back to Mount Athos in Greece to revive Russian church life there. The Russian-owned Panteleimon Monastery, one of 20 in the territory, had hosted 2000 monks before the 1917 revolution, the Central Committee report pointed out. Its revival, after decades of neglect, would have 'state and political importance.'[34]

The veteran Kuroedov had been replaced in 1984 by a new CRA director, Konstantin Kharchev, who informed a conference in the US there were now 49 fully-fledged faith groups in the Soviet Union, together counting 'millions of activists.' Mistakes were still being made, Kharchev noted, by both government and religious leaders. But Gorbachev's reformist regime was 'doing everything' to raise Church-state ties 'to a new level.' In the past, any such claim by a Soviet official would have been dismissed out of hand. Today, with some reservations, Kharchev was widely believed. Sharing the conference platform, the veteran Orthodox troubleshooter, Metropolitan Yuvenaly, quoted from St Paul: 'Night has passed, day has drawn near.' *Glasnost* and *perestroika* embodied a 'new revolutionary process,' Yuvenaly enthused.[35]

The official Moscow Patriarchate now had some tentative links with the Soviet Union's once-shunned Orthodox dissidents. Bishop Feodor of Astrakhan received no reply from Gorbachev when he demanded the reopening of Kiev's Eleventh Century Pecherskaya Lavra monastery; so he sent the letter on to Alexander Ogorodnikov's *samizdat* bulletin. Ogorodnikov, the secretly baptised son of a Party member, had been sent to a psychiatric prison, aged 25, when his religious faith was judged a mental disorder. In early 1987, he was received by Metropolitan Yuvenaly, who voiced scepticism about his ideas but gave him a 'polite, paternal welcome.'[36]

Within a few months, even that unprecedented encounter had begun to look unexceptional. That February, *Literaturnaya Gazeta* caused a minor sensation by publishing an interview with Cardinal Glemp of Poland, the first of its kind in Soviet history. Some months later, the much-harassed Sakharov handed a list of 200 political prisoners to Gorbachev in person when he was invited to the Kremlin for a research seminar. A state commission was reviewing the Soviet Union's religious laws, as the Moscow Patriarchate's journal had reported; and in April 1988, Gorbachev assured Patriarch Pimen the new regulations would respect religious faith by 'restoring Leninist principles.' It was the first top-level Church-state meeting since Stalin's overnight wartime encounter with Russia's surviving Orthodox leaders 45 years before.

Gorbachev believed religious people should be natural supporters of his 'new thinking.' He had reason to be conciliatory. Preparations had long been underway for the 1988 Millennium of the Christianisation of ancient Rus. It was not the first such commemoration. In 1938, Stalin himself had allowed the 950th anniversary to be celebrated as a cultural event. But the regimes of Chernenko and Andropov had been nervous, recalling how Poland's earlier Christian Millennium in 1966 had fuelled Catholic militancy. Well before Gorbachev's emergence, Party ideologists had concurred that efforts should focus on diminishing Christianity's importance in Russian history. Whereas Patriarch Pimen hoped the event would highlight Orthodoxy's patriotic role in a thousand years of Russian statehood, the regime planned to portray it as a stage in the triumph of materialism, and in society's liberation from 'reactionary clericalism.'

The Moscow Patriarchate, undeterred, had broken its silence with a series of conferences and media briefings. As Russian,

Ukrainian and Belarusan historians all claimed a national share in the cultural and religious heritage of Kievan Rus, disputes intensified over proprietorship of the Millennium. Hostile articles appeared the Soviet press, asserting the state's primacy and berating the church for exaggerating its historic role.

From Rome, the head of the still-outlawed Ukrainian Catholic Church, Archbishop Lubachivsky, accused both the Moscow Patriarchate and Soviet government of usurping the Millennium by centering it on Moscow rather than Kiev. The medieval Rus, Lubachivsky pointed out, was not synonymous with Russia. It had included Ukraine, whose ruler, Prince Volodymyr, had made Christianity the faith of his subjects. It was quite wrong, therefore, to present the Millennium as an 'exclusive heritage of the Russian people.'

Greek Catholic services were still banned; and although 35,000 church members risked arrest by signing a petition to the Supreme Soviet, neither this nor an accompanying Moscow hunger-strike had any direct impact. Despite this, Lubachivsky reaffirmed in a special statement that he was now ready 'to extend the hand of forgiveness, reconciliation and love in the spirit of Christ.'[37]

The Pope had looked ahead to the Millennium as a long ago as 1979 in his letter to Cardinal Slipyi, and again in his 1985 encyclical, *Slavorum Apostoli*. He had also received a conciliatory message from Gorbachev during General Jaruzelski's Vatican visit in January 1987. 'The Ukrainian, Russian and Belarusan peoples find in this event not only their Christian identity,' John Paul II now told Lubachivsky in a letter, 'but also their cultural identity and, in consequence, their history.' He recalled the persecution of Greek Catholics under communism, and how their church had given 'so many proofs of her attachment to Rome, not excluding the supreme test of martyrdom.' But the 1596 Union of Brest, which had allowed Ukrainian Christians to keep their eastern liturgy under Roman jurisdiction, had been intended to build a church in which East and West enjoyed 'full and visible unity.' The time for jurisdictional disputes and rival power claims had passed.[38]

For all the conciliatory signals, members of the Ukrainian Church were barred from the Moscow celebrations in June 1988. But a Greek Catholic delegation made it to the city's Sovietskaya Hotel to meet the Pope's envoy, Casaroli, who talked about religious rights in his speech at Moscow's Grand Theatre. John Paul II had sent his Secretary of State, by his own account, to express his 'spiritual participation' in the Millennium. A day after his speech, Casaroli became the first top Vatican official to enter the Kremlin. He presented Gorbachev with a Papal letter, listing the Catholic Church's problems in the Soviet Union, but also pledging readiness 'to throw a bridge over a 70-year divide.'[39]

The Pope despatched similarly upbeat letters to Patriarch Pimen and the Orthodox Holy Synod. He then celebrated the Millennium in his own way, with services in St Peter's Basilica and Slipyi's nearby St Sophia cathedral. That November, he was assured by his old antagonist, Gromyko, now honorary president of the Soviet Union, that the Kremlin would no longer 'stand in the way of the Catholic Church's expansion.' During the same month, Kharchev informed a surprised conference in London that the Soviet Union was no longer an 'atheist state.' Fighting religion, the CRA director insisted, had been a 'distortion of Marxism.' *Moskievski Novosti* carried a long article on the plight of Greek Catholics, prompting an angry riposte from Metropolitan Filaret of Minsk, the Patriarchate's foreign relations director. Filaret had visited the Pope for a private audience two years before. When it came to Greek Catholics, his church was giving less ground than the Soviet state.[40]

Exiles and *emigrés,* heartened by *perestroika* and *glasnost,* were coming back to the Soviet Union, sometimes after decades abroad. Not everyone was convinced. Stalin's only surviving daughter, Svetlana Alliluyeva, who had been received into the Catholic Church at London's Allen Hall seminary chapel in December 1982, returned to the Soviet Union in 1984 but left again two years later, disillusioned, after failing to recognise the country of her birth. Others were also on their way home from the prisons and camps, however, notably after the Supreme Soviet's 1987 amnesty.

In Lubachivsky's Ukraine, confidence in the Soviet government had been dealt a new death-blow when an April 1986 nuclear disaster at Chernobyl sent deadly radioactive dust over neighbouring countries. Pressure from newly formed ecological groups forced the cancellation of a planned nuclear plant in Crimea, whose restless Tartars, deported *en masse* by Stalin, sent Gorbachev a letter from their first congress at Tashkent, demanding the right to return home. Ukraine's last political prisoner, Mykola Horbal, a poet and Helsinki Group member, was freed in 1988 when his third sentence for anti-Soviet agitation was overturned. But public discontent was growing over issues such as the decline of the Ukrainian language. The infamous 1932–3 terror famine, branded an act of genocide by the US Congress, was being discussed openly for the first time.

The Greek Catholic dissident, Iosif Terelya, who had founded a lay Action Group back in 1982, was one of many freed in the amnesty. He promptly called on his Church's clergy to minister openly. More radical figures than himself, Terelya warned, had considered violent resistance after the killing of Fr Popiełuszko in Poland. The Moscow Patriarchate continued to reject any accommodation with Greek Catholics; and in 1988, the Soviet regime outraged Ukrainians by provocatively turning some 700 closed Greek Catholic places of worship over to Orthodox clergy. Yet it was now too late to check the discontent. Dozens of Greek Catholics reacted with petitions to Gorbachev and the Supreme Soviet, urging the Pope to use his influence to secure legalisation of their 'catacomb church.'

When Terelya finally left with his family for the West, he brought news of a fresh pilgrimage centre at Hrushiw, near Lviv, where thousands of Ukrainians had flocked after reported sightings of the Virgin Mary. Terelya's place was quickly taken by others. In December, another prison veteran, Ivan Gel, presented a fresh statement to the Supreme Soviet, co-signed by two Greek Catholic bishops. 'Stalin's tyranny drove us into the catacombs, but our Church is alive,' the statement affirmed. 'Over the past four centuries, people have tried to Polonise, Germanise and Russify us; but all such efforts have ended in utter failure.'[41]

The Pope had been invited to Lithuania again in 1987, this time for the sixth centenary of its Christian conversion. Although the idea was once more vetoed, Moscow felt obliged this time to give its reasons, which included Vatican Radio's 'anti-Soviet propaganda.' There had been speculation that the Russian Orthodox church might invite John Paul II for the 1988 Millennium. This too was apparently ruled out. But the Pope had made clear anyway he would only go to Russia if also allowed to visit Catholics in other republics.

In August 1986, more than a hundred Lithuanian priests had written to Gorbachev, asking him to ensure the Soviet constitution's provisions for religious freedom were observed in practice. They called for the release of the former *Chronicle* editor, Fr Tamkevičius, and the return of St Casimir's cathedral in Vilnius and Klaipeda's confiscated the Queen of Peace church. Lithuania's bishops had also become more assertive. In a 1985 pastoral letter, they had deplored the imposition of atheism as a 'sin against God' and called on Catholics to prepare for the conversion anniversary.[42]

The Lithuanian government had made its own preparations for the anniversary; and like its central Soviet counterpart, it had sought to devalue the role of Christianity, highlighting the Church's brutality during the late medieval northern crusades. It was pulled up sharply in an apostolic letter from the Pope in June 1987, highlighting the irony that Lithuania had 'for so long resisted the cross,' but was now covered in churches 'radiating faith and civilisation.' In every age, Lithuanians had 'stood firmly together' around the Church, John Paul II added, especially 'in times of trial' and the 'dark, sad hours' of recent history, when Christians had faced 'exile, imprisonment, deportation and death.' The cross of Lithuania's 'elect band of confessors and martyrs' had now become 'an instrument of grace and sanctification.'[43] At a Mass in St Peter's the same month, the Pope beatified Jurgis Matulaitis-Matulevičius, the Bishop of Vilnius who had guided the Lithuanian Church through the turbulent years 1918–1928, building up the Sister Servants order to which Sadūnaitė and other underground nuns belonged.

The regime's Religious Affairs Commissioner, Petras Anilionis, comprehensively upstaged, warned against any violation of religious regulations. Yet the popular pressure was becoming unstoppable. Two months after the Pope's letter, the anniversary of the infamous 1939 Molotòv-Ribbentrop Pact, in which Berlin and Moscow had connived together, was marked by demonstrations in all three Baltic republics. The rallies were illegal; but the Soviet police kept their distance. Prominent speakers included Sadūnaitė, whose temporary re-arrest the previous April had not prevented her second volume of memoirs from appearing in the West.

Fears still lingered of a possible mass crackdown in Lithuania. But Gorbachev was calling the shots now—more than the republic's own hardline regime. During the month of the demonstrations, the Soviet Central Committee adopted a new resolution on 'raising an atheist society' in Lithuania. But it instructed Lithuanian officials to find an 'operative solution' which satisfied religious needs. In early 1988, Tamkevičius's fellow-dissident, Fr Svarinskas, was freed from his Perm labour camp. Tamkevičius's turn came soon after. Despite five years in prisons and camps, the Jesuit remained unbroken and had made no compromises.

> I had been sure I'd never be set free. So when the authorities offered to release me early if I signed a confession, I'd thought about it seriously. But when they also demanded I leave the country, I refused and the plan fell through. We all understood that the authorities wanted to kill us morally, to prevent others from following our example. But they'd always faced the same problem: they could use every physical measure against us, but they couldn't convince

> people we were wrong. If we'd allowed them to, we would have destroyed the Church; and far from celebrating our freedom, we'd all have been hiding in dark corners.[44]

The regime in Vilnius had clearly lost control over the Church. In April, Lithuania's bishops visited the Vatican and were assured of the Pope's 'universal, fraternal solidarity.' The Lithuanian Church was 'confidently entering its seventh century,' John Paul II told them, as 'fresh breezes of renewal' aroused 'new strong hopes among millions.' Six years after returning to his see, Bishop Sladkevičius replaced the tired Mgr Povilonis as Bishops Conference president. Anilionis's office had not been consulted and reacted angrily. But it could do nothing; and in May, Sladkevičius was named a cardinal, Lithuania's first since the Seventeenth Century. He returned from Rome in triumph, urging hundreds of priests during a Kaunas seminary meeting to overcome their fear and minister openly. The Church would no longer be asking the government's permission, Sladkevičius added, to make appointments and recruit new ordinands.[45]

Power was slipping from the regime's grasp. In June 1988, a national reform movement, Sąjūdis, was set up under a historian, Vytautas Landsbergis. Unlike the Polish Solidarity, Sąjūdis had no obvious Catholic focus. But the Church was playing a central role in events, which were now unfolding thick and fast. In September, Bishop Steponavičius was greeted by half a million cheering people when he came back from 27 years in exile. St Casimir's cathedral was finally given back too and rededicated the following February, along with carefully preserved relics from Lithuania's patron saint. The Pope used the occasion to relaunch the Lithuanian Church's hierarchy, appointing Sladkevičius Archbishop of Kaunas and Steponavičius Archbishop of Vilnius. The dreams of two generations of Lithuanians were coming true faster than anyone could have anticipated.

The fabled *Chronicle* appeared for the last time that March. Its eightieth issue had been delayed by the re-arrest of Sadūnaitė and two other secret nuns, who had planned to take it to the Soviet capital. All three were freed a few days later, this time under orders from Moscow. At the end of the year, Lithuania became the first Soviet republic to celebrate Christmas as a state holiday.

Nationalist feeling had been running high in other republics. But the new climate of tolerance and openness was also tinged with sadness and regret. In neighbouring Belarus, where there were a hundred functioning Catholic parishes but no bishop, leading cultural personalities had written to Gorbachev in December 1986, demanding a final end to Soviet 'anti-national policies.' Just what that had meant was revealed in all its horror when a mass grave of Stalinist-era victims was found in Kuropaty Park on the outskirts of Minsk. Surviving witnesses described hearing volleys of shots overnight as they tried to sleep in nearby housing blocks, accompanied by the shrieks of mothers wailing for their children. They said the earth on the execution pits would still be 'breathing' in the morning, with blood visible on the surface.

In June 1988, the Belarus government set up a commission, which confirmed that tens of thousands of NKVD victims had been buried at Kuropaty, alongside human remains disposed of after the War.[46] An unofficial commission, Martyrology of Belarus, was also at work, collecting information about atrocities, while a Belarusan People's Front, modelled on Lithuania's Sąjūdis, defied police aggression and rallied mass protests.

Glasnost and *perestroika* had touched off a war of invective between reformists and conservatives in the rest of Eastern Europe. The old certainties had vanished, along with the familiar talk of 'geopolitical realities.' East-West tension had eased with the signing of a US-Soviet nuclear treaty at an October 1986 summit between Reagan and Gorbachev in Rejkjavík. Western government officials were in cautious touch now with some of the region's dissidents, seeing them as potential future rulers, while Western communist parties had downgraded their links with Moscow.

In *Dominum et vivificantem* (May 1986), the Pope had evoked the Holy Spirit's constant presence in history, guiding the Church and ensuring clarity of conscience in the 'monumental struggle against powers of darkness.' Atheistic ideologies had sought to 'root out religion,' as the 'father of lies' pressured man to reject God 'even to the point of hating him.' But freedom and dignity had acquired a special force in the case of persecuted Christians, for whom prayer would always have a unique power as 'the voice of those who have no voice.' Their countless acts of martyrdom had marked 'the supreme glorification of human dignity.'[47]

When the Conference on Security and Co-operation in Europe had reassembled at Vienna in November 1986 to review progress achieved under the 1975 Helsinki Agreement, the Holy See had submitted ten recommendations for strengthening religious rights, arguing that these were essential for peaceful international relations and social harmony. That same message, tinged with apocalyptic imagery, would come across clearly during the Pope's third pilgrimage to Poland, which took place in June 1987.

The pilgrimage itinerary had been discussed during General Jaruzelski's January visit to the Vatican; and as before, the regime had carefully prepared its arguments, linking the visit with church support for its reformist efforts. It could guarantee the Pope's safety, officials warned, as long as public order was maintained by the Church and the myriad of post-Solidarity groups agitating nationwide. This meant no 'impossible demands' by church leaders, no political agitation by priests, and no use of churches by people who had 'nothing in common with the Catholic religion.' 'Whatever the Pope's assumptions, both previous visits caused a widening of divisions, and contributed on balance to prolonging our socio-political crisis,' the Confessions Office told the Vatican's roving ambassador, Archbishop Colasuonno.

> We would like it if this situation did not repeat itself, and if the Pope can detach himself from 'Polish squabbles,' and as head of the Universal Church give our nation some more universal directions above and beyond current

> issues. Let us hope these directions turn out, from the viewpoint of future historical evaluations, to be more positive from the perspective of the nation which provided a pope and has a right to expect something greater from him than an entanglement in matters of less importance.[48]

The language, with its touch of pomposity, appeared to mimick that of the Pope himself, who would set SB agents scurrying by receiving the hardline President Reagan just two days before setting out for Poland. It barely concealed the loathing now felt for him by Poland's tottering communist establishment. But John Paul II was coming. It would be another damage-limitation exercise.

Poland was ahead of its neighbours in being a largely free country now. People could speak openly; small-scale entrepreneurs could contrive to buy their way through the state bureaucracy; and the official media faced stiff competition from a 'second circulation' of underground books and newspapers, appearing on an industrial scale. But it was also a tired country, worn out by endless deadlock. As in 1983, it was uncertain what John Paul II's latest homecoming would achieve. While communist power was on the wane, rumours still persisted of Church-state deals behind the scenes. Would the pilgrimage not bring comfort to Jaruzelski's regime?

Once again, events turned out differently. Welcoming the Pope at Warsaw's Royal Castle, the general spoke of his desire for peace; but peace, the Pope retorted, was linked to human rights and national dignity. On his way to the palace, John Paul II had dedicated a giant statue in Warsaw's university quarter to the late Cardinal Wyszyński, built with the grudging approval of a regime which had once excoriated his stubbornness and insubordination. A massive thunderstorn hit the city soon after—a portent of what was to come, as ten million people assembled in parks and arenas to see and hear their native prophet. At his old Catholic university in Lublin, John Paul II spoke up for academic freedom. In the southern city of Tarnów, he defended rural workers and beatified Karolina Kózka (1898–1914), a local girl who, with echoes of the Biblical Susanna, had been bayonetted and left to die in a swamp after resisting rape by a Russian soldier. In Kraków, he urged listeners to combat prejudice and untruthfulness. In coastal Szczecin and Gdynia, he championed the rights of families, young people and women.

There would be no going back, the Pope made clear. The values and ideals, hopes and aspirations of Polish society were legitimate—no social theories or acts of repression could ever invalidate or destroy them. The true meaning of Solidarity, he told a special Mass for workers outside Gdańsk, was bearing each other's burdens. What was needed now was to think in a long-term perspective, helped by the patient self-confidence supplied by Christianity.

Jaruzelski's Interior Minister, General Kiszczak, confirmed that Gdańsk, Solidarity's birthplace, had been the main focus of concern. The police had prepared the ground with a wave of detentions and house searches, while their SB partners had seized 18,000 illegal publications, 100 metres of sheeting 'with hostile slogans' and no fewer than 240 illegal printing machines. Church informers had been mobilised, including a highly placed agent, codenamed 'Szejk,' inside the Gdańsk curia, who had given blow-by-blow information about the local bishop, Tadeusz Gocłowski, and his clergy helpers. Meanwhile, Polish TV had been instructed to avoid scenes of crowds and banners. Even then, Kiszczak noted, the regime had uncovered a 'whole complex of threats.'[49]

There was more to come. Praying at Fr Popiełuszko's graveside, the Pope appeared to endorse the mission of Poland's 'radical priests.' The Church's pastors must be poor, like their flock, he told seminarians. They must safeguard the Christian roots of national culture, presenting the Christian vision with all its 'social and ethical implications.' He had special words for intellectuals, who had 'rediscovered their bond with the Church,' finding in it 'a dimension of freedom they could not find elsewhere.'

On several occasions, John Paul II welcomed pilgrims from other East European countries. In Kraków's Wawel cathedral, he appealed to Poland's popularly revered Queen Jadwiga (1374–99) to embrace their 'destinies, aspirations and struggles,' and reveal God's designs 'for Poland, Lithuania, the Russian lands.' He also challenged the assumption that change was impossible—the assumption which killed the civic spirit and the will to an active life. Work and faith, he assured listeners, would produce a better future.

Addressing the 97-strong Bishops Conference, the Pope scotched any lingering suggestions that the Vatican might be contemplating direct diplomatic ties with communist-ruled Poland. Diplomatic links would be a welcome prospect, he conceded. But this had to be a decision for local bishops. Church-state relations must always reflect state-society relations. They could never amount to an administrative relationship between two self-interested entities.

In his speech to the bishops, John Paul II assessed the lessons learned from the confrontation with communism. He spoke as if it was over—a historical challenge sent by providence 'to mobilise efforts and seek new solutions.' 'The Church has taken up this challenge,' the Pope noted confidently, 'identifying it as a providential "sign of the times." Through this "sign," it has given witness to the truth about God, Christ and Man with new depth and force.'[50] Jaruzelski's regime was mortified. It had hoped for a political boost in its efforts to cling to power. But it had drastically underestimated the Pope's authority and the Church's capacity to rally its followers. In the space of week, it had become even more isolated and discredited than before.

Could other communist establishments still hope to survive? The situation was becoming less stable by the day throughout Eastern Europe. In Czechoslovakia, the Husák regime had calculated it could withstand the reformist climate, helped by the country's relatively good living standards. At a March 1986 Party congress, Husák had duly defended the post-1968 settlement. In Czechoslovakia at least, he declared, the socialist order was immutable. There would be no question of political change. 'We shall not allow anyone to violate our laws and undermine our political system and socialist order,' Husák assured the congress, 'whatever lofty phrases he may use about freedom, democracy and the so-called struggle for human rights.' In a startling turnaround, Charter 77 accused the state media of censoring Gorbachev's speeches.[51]

Husák were pushing against the wind. The same year saw growing activism among Czechoslovakia's Christians, with a mass petition against abortion and 800,000 people, a sixth of the population, rallying for pilgrimages in Slovakia. While Cardinal Tomášek continued to speak out, Charter 77's Christian signatories featured prominently in an April 1987 letter to Gorbachev, marking his visit to Prague, which urged democratic reform and the withdrawal of Soviet troops. The visit had been delayed and shortened by disputes with the Czechoslovak regime. Once it was over, talk of change—including rehabilitation of the victims of 1968—merely intensified.

There was still no movement on key church grievances, and the arrests and jailings continued. The illegally consecrated Bishop Korec, who regularly travelled to say Mass, had his car brakes tampered with; and in October 1987, another priest, Fr Štefan Polák, was found stabbed and bleeding to death at his presbytery in Borovce, near Trnava, with his hands and feet tied to a radiator and his mouth sealed with tape. Polák had recently visited the Vatican, and was said to have been targeted for recruitment by the StB since taking over the parish in 1981. A homeless man was given 13 years for the murder in 1989, but later acquitted and found dead after apparently being pushed from a train.[52]

None of this deterred Czechoslovakia's restive Christians. In November 1987, a decade of prayer was launched by Cardinal Tomášek, with a special theme for each year, accompanied by a 16-point 'Charter of Believers.' A larger petition early the following year was signed by half a million people, making it the largest in Czechoslovakia's history. That March, a massive Christian demonstration in Bratislava's Hviezdoslav Square was brutally dispersed with police dogs and teargas. In an apparent show of contrition, the regime agreed to allow three new Catholic bishops, the first for 15 years. Even then, however, most sees still remained empty and three-quarters of Czech parishes were without priests. For all the threats and blandishments, nothing had really changed in Church-state relations.

In Hungary, a new archbishop, László Paskai, had succeeded the late Cardinal Lékai in March 1987; and by June, when four further appointments were announced, all eleven Hungarian dioceses had resident bishops. Yet here too the atmosphere was growing tense. In October 1986, thousands of young Hungarians had taken to the streets to mark the thirteeth anniversary of the 1956 uprising. Protests had continued sporadically; and when the Bishops Conference paid an *ad limina* visit to Rome in November 1987, dozens of Christians were still in prison for refusing military service.

Against this background, Paskai was not a popular choice. In an interview, he blamed the redoubtable Cardinal Mindszenty for the Church's post-War troubles and appeared to exonerate Hungary's infamous Stalinist strongman, Mátyás Rákosi. 'We could have been much more successful if fatal mistakes weren't made,' the new Catholic Primate insisted.

> If Mindszenty had not miscalculated, everything would have happened otherwise. He thought the fall of the communist regime was only a question of time, and we now know the Primate was mistaken. For this mistake, the Catholic Church had to pay a high price, losing almost all its institutions, orders and schools.[53]

Steps were taken to improve ties with approved Catholic movements and communities. At the same time, with Paskai's approval, the prefect of the Vatican's Congregation for the Doctrine of Faith, Cardinal Ratzinger, resumed attacks on the pacifist Fr Bulányi, condemning the 'false, dangerous and misleading views' set out in his typewritten book, *Order of the Church*. Ratzinger took particular issue with Bulányi's support for women priests, as well as with his notion of a priesthood open to 'anyone who leads a community.'[54] But Bulányi had become marginal to the growing web of dissent in Hungary. The situation had moved on.

Across the border in Romania, Nicolae Ceauşescu was said to be suffering from prostrate cancer as the economy nose-dived. Food queues had lengthened, prompting strikes and demonstrations, while deaths and mass arrests were reported during a worker uprising at Braşov, the country's second city, in summer 1988. A new Orthodox patriarch, Teoctist Arăpaşu, had been elected in November 1986, four months after the death of Patriarch Iustin. Like his predecessors, Teoctist was an approved choice; so nothing was expected to change, least of all in the programme of church demolitions still sweeping Romania's towns and villages.

Ceauşescu's regime denied reports that it planned to raze Bucharest's Orthodox patriarchal cathedral to make way for an underpass. Instead, it published its own figures. Since 1980, over 500 churches had been restored nationwide, including eight in Bucharest alone, where there were now 276 open places of worship, served by 400 priests. It was hard to verify such data. What was known for certain was that the *Sistematizarea* programme was continuing—to the alarm of human rights groups, as well as of neighbouring governments. There were reports that Jewish synagogues had been demolished in Moldavia, prompting complaints from the usually docile and subservient Rabbi Rosen.

The personality cult of the *conducator* was still flourishing, as propagandists competed for the finest hyperbole. Like Nero or Stalin before him, Ceauşescu was eulogised with religious imagery: 'the sacred word' and 'the Chosen One' were among images applied to him by official poets and speech-writers. Even the dictator's mother, a pious peasant from Scornicești, who had received a religious funeral, was lauded in biblical language, as the 'mother of hope' who had given birth 'to Romania's worthiest Son for the sake of the world's sorrow.'

However durable his own illusions might be at home, Ceauşescu had plainly been wrong-footed, like other hardliners, by the development of East-West relations. He had criticised the Soviet invasion of Afghanistan and the nuclear build-up. But Gorbachev himself was now doing the same.

Meanwhile, new figures had appeared on Romania's small but determined dissident scene. In the Greek Catholic Church's Cluj heartland, a French language lecturer, Doina Cornea, had become known abroad when she was denounced at a university staff meeting for recommending Western texts to her students. Cornea had been sacked in September 1983, and her home was under police guard. But she had succeeded in sending statements to the West. The ruling ideology had not only wiped out democracy and destroyed the national economy, Cornea pointed out; it had also corrupted ethics and undermined social bonds. Romanians had become a people without values, 'fed solely on slogans.'

> As a teacher, I glimpse a deeper and more general reason for this catastrophe: the cultural and spiritual devaluation of our society, caused by the imposition of a reductionist and sterilising ideology. I ask myself how we could have reached this state, and whether each one of us, small and insignificant individuals, does not bear some blame for it. If we examine ourselves thoroughly, down to the depths of our soul, will we not find we have made so many compromises, accepted and disseminated so many lies.[55]

Cornea's stress on moral and spiritual regeneration paralleled that of the Pope; and in September 1988, she wrote to John Paul II, assuring him her Church still existed, 'despite official declarations from the Romanian authorities.' By then, she had been arrested and held by the Securitate for distributing leaflets in support of the workers at Braşov. Undeterred, she wrote defiantly to Ceauşescu, denouncing the 'repression, corruption, injustice, falsehood and disinformation' characterising his rule. His 'suffocating regime' had 'suppressed individual responsibility, creativity and inventiveness,' Cornea informed the god-like *conducator*. It was becoming 'ever more difficult to bear.'

> You have razed to the ground our oldest and most beloved churches. You have dug up the graves of our past rulers. You have started to destroy the country's villages, some hundreds of years old, in order to destroy their natural life. You have crushed the inner souls of people, humiliating them in their hopes and legitimate aspirations, humbling their consciences, forcing them, through pressure and terror, to accept lies as truth and truth as lies, and thus acquiesce in their own moral crippling.[56]

By now, Romania had been attacked by the European Parliament and other bodies on charges ranging from mistreating its minorities to neglecting the old and handicapped. When the UN Human Rights Commission weighed in, Ceaușescu's Warsaw Pact allies declined to reject its report. Instead, they merely abstained, while neighbouring Hungary voted in favour. A war of words was already underway between the two communist allies, as Hungarian newspapers were banned in Romania and Hungarian Party leaders denounced for 'irredentism.' That vulnerable dissidents like Doina Cornea were also speaking out, unfazed by Securitate pressure, was a sure sign that communist power was waning.

In Yugoslavia, nationalist feeling had continued to grow, not least among the three faith groups in Bosnia-Herzegovina. The Pope had appealed for closer Catholic-Orthodox ties during the Yugoslav bishops' 1983 *ad limina* visit. There were accusations that his own focus on national identities in Eastern Europe had, in some quarters, fuelled nationalism. These were insistently rebutted by Cardinal Kuharić. The Church did not 'equate nationality and religion,' the veteran prelate told an Assumption Day Mass. To love one's nation did not mean hating other nations.

> It is our right, our truth and our act of love that we declare ourselves to be what we are. So let nobody criticise us because, on our special occasions and celebrations, we

> thank God for his gift of our beautiful homeland and sing our national anthem as part of our prayers. We resolutely reject accusations about so-called clero-nationalism. We merely live our patriotism and our consciousness, linked with the past generations and grateful for the heritage we have received... What I wish for my nation I also wish for every nation under the sun; and instructed by the Gospel, I can only wish well.[57]

Some Catholic priests had clearly stoked national passions, however, as a foil to communism. The Party daily, *Borba*, had talked of 'certain clergymen' in Subotica, 'trying to impose themselves as national protectors of Croats and Hungarians,' and of church leaders who deliberately polarised divisions between atheist and religious citizens to isolate the regime from society. There was no anti-religious campaign now, *Borba* insisted. Nor were there any 'militant atheists.'

With Yugoslavia's state debt now consuming half of all foreign earnings, however, and economic and social dislocation growing, the resurgence of national feeling was being felt in the ruling League of Communists. In Kosovo, a brutal crackdown on ethnic Albanians, masterminded by the League's new Serbian strongman, Slobodan Milošević, had provoked angry reactions from local government officials and Party members. Further south, League activists in Macedonia had urged Serbian Orthodox leaders to 'promote brotherhood and unity' by recognising a breakaway local church.[58]

By 1989, it was clear that the spirit of history, for all the confident prophecies of Marx and Lenin, had moved irrevocably against communism. In a new encyclical in December 1987, the Pope had again exposed communism's failures, pointing out how its suppression of economic initiative had led to a 'levelling down,' and to a bureaucratic apparatus which placed people in a position of 'absolute dependence' similar to that of 'the worker-proletarian in capitalism.' Communist parties had undermined the 'creative subjectivity' of their citizens by 'usurping the role of sole leader.' As for communism's claim to have overcome poverty, this was not true either. Denial of rights had impoverished the human person just as much as material deprivation.

Meanwhile, the East-West 'logic of blocs' had gravely harmed developing countries by denying them impartial aid and embroiling them in ideological conflicts. Ideology itself was one of the modern world's 'real forms of idolatry,' all of which had engendered contemporary 'structures of sin.' Each of the blocs, East and West, harboured a tendency towards imperialism and neo-colonialism; and this was why the Church was critical of both liberal capitalism and Marxist collectivism. It believed in solidarity, a determined and persevering social commitment; and it would work to ensure that 'corrupt, dictatorial and authoritarian forms of government' were replaced by 'democratic and participatory ones.' The struggle for human rights was an aspect of the 'love of the poor' to which all Christians were called.[59]

For all the fatefulness and inevitability, the endgame, when it came, was to prove bitter and protracted. In Poland, planned economic reforms were rejected in a November 1987 referendum, a clear sign that the population had lost any remaining confidence in Jaruzelski's regime. The regime responded with further concessions, allowing some unofficial publications, reviewing Poland's law on associations, and even hinting at a coalition government with non-communists. It also began talks with members of the Catholic Intelligentsia Clubs, and suggested Catholics could be brought into a new national advisory council.

The Bishops Conference rejected the gestures, seeing them as a bid to co-opt the Church without giving it any real say in decisions. Despite church offers of mediation, new strikes were violently suppressed in spring 1988. But the writing was on the wall; and in the autumn, more than eight years after the union's first appearance, the regime finally agreed to negotiate with Solidarity.

The resulting Round Table talks opened in Warsaw the following February and produced a series of agreements on power-sharing reforms. Having provided premises for the initial government-opposition meetings, the Church sent two observers, Fr Bronisław Dembowski and Fr Alojzy Orszulik, to help facilitate the Round Table. Both priests, nominated by Cardinal Glemp, were present as witnesses at crucial inner-circle talks in Warsaw's Magdalenka suburb, making the Polish Church, in effect, a third party to the final April accords.

A law was enacted by the Sejm a month later, granting the Church its long-sought legal status, clearing the way for the return of its confiscated properties and meeting its decades-old demands for pastoral freedom, access to the media and the right to form Catholic associations. The regime hoped the reforms would soften church opposition in coming June elections, in which a third of Sejm seats and the whole of a new Senate upper house would be contested by Solidarity candidates. But local priests gave vital help to Solidarity's 'civic committees,' gathering donations and allowing their churches to be used for election meetings.

Aware of its looming defeat, the regime deplored the Church's lack of 'political neutrality.' But it was too late for grievances like this; and the Polish Party was roundly humiliated as Solidarity duly won all the allotted places in a new-look 'contract parliament.' Ultimate power still remained in the Party's hands; but it was fast slipping away. When the Pope agreed to establish diplomatic relations with Poland that July, the communist government responded ecstatically, praising the Vatican's 'moral authority,' apparently without irony, and voicing the Polish nation's 'heartfelt respect' for 'the noble mission of its great Son.' A month later, the Catholic journal editor, Tadeusz Mazowiecki, who had once belonged to Piasecki's Pax, became Eastern Europe's first post-communist head of government.[60]

This time, the tide had truly turned. In Hungary, the veteran Kádár had retired in May 1988 after three decades as Party leader, further fuelling demands for reform. The government's religious affairs director, Imre Miklós, was still rejecting calls for Cardinal Mindszenty's rehabilitation and the reinstatement of religious orders. But a new law was being prepared on religious freedom, Miklós reassured his critics, while talks were also underway on a long-sought alternative to military service.

In July 1988, as large numbers of Christians returned from a Papal pilgrimage to neighbouring Austria, one bishop, Endre Gyulay of Szeged, compared the Hungarian Church to St Sebastian, the Third Century martyr who had initially survived a death sentence and offered services of 'understanding and tolerance.' A month later, as 100,000 people flocked to Budapest's St Stephen Basilica for an outdoor Mass marking 950 years since the patron's death, Cardinal Paskai announced that the government had invited the Pope to visit Hungary. Miklós travelled to the Vatican to discuss the invitation, as thousands of Hungarians also converged on Rome for a national pilgrimage.

Concessions quickly followed. Assistant bishops were appointed, and Catholic associations set up, including a Áron Márton Society, named after the revered late Transylvanian bishop. By Christmas, for the first time in 40 years, Masses were being celebrated in hospitals, while Miklós had relented and agreed to allow the religious orders back. A total of 39 announced plans to refound themselves, including the Paulines, who promptly moved back to the cave chapel on Budapest's Gellért Hill, which had once been brutally raided by the police. In April 1989, Hungary's state radio broadcast Mindszenty's 1956 appeal, while a Catholic publisher released the cardinal's *Memoirs* and the government promised to reconsider his trial. In June, the 1956 Party leader, Imre Nagy, whose execution had been ordered by Khrushchev 'as a lesson to leaders in socialist countries,' was exhumed from his unmarked grave and reburied with full state honours, in a dramatic reworking of the Hungarian folk tradition of *kegyelet*, or duty towards the dead. The Church Affairs Office, or AEH, was abolished during the same month, and an alternative introduced to military service. In October, the Bishops Conference finally dissolved the pro-regime Opus Pacis.

In Czechoslovakia, where sporadic demonstrations had continued, the Husák regime had now at last come up with some reformist gestures, offering to modify the central economic planning system and abolish 'pointless restraints and prejudices.' There had even been hints that some reform communists purged after the 1968 Prague Spring could be rehabilitated. Although the state media still trumpeted atheism, the regime had also eased certain religious restrictions, allowing an increase in seminary admissions and priestly permits. In practice, however, communist attitudes remained as rigid as ever. Dissidents sensed the Party was merely paying lip-service to *glasnost* and *perestroika*, gambling that Gorbachev would, sooner or later, be overthrown.

By 1989, this strategy was crumbling. The year began with week-long demonstrations in Prague to mark 'Palach Week,' honouring the student who had burned himself to death in 1968. It was to end with the Rome canonisation of a Thirteenth Century Czech princess, Agnes of Bohemia, and the outbreak five days later of a peaceful national uprising. Within a fortnight, the 'Velvet Revolution' had swept Czechoslovakia's communists from power.

In Romania, desperation was mounting, as food and fuel shortages amplified popular misery and senseless economic projects such as Ceaușescu's village clearances provoked outrage. The *conducator* was openly opposing Gorbachev's reforms; and in June 1987, the US Congress had duly voted to suspend Romania's favourable trade ties. Ceaușescu's megalomania appeared to be intensifying. To pay off Romania's foreign debt, he imposed daily power cuts, while women were given compulsory gynaecological tests to prevent abortions in an effort to boost the birthrate. The violent suppression of worker protests had done nothing to defuse public anger; and in March 1989, a painter, Liviu-Corneliu Babeș, burnt himself to death at a ski resort to draw international attention to his country's plight.

The regime attempted to ride out the discontent, helped by the obsequious plaudits of national figures like Patriarch Teoctist, who thanked Ceauşescu in a birthday telegram for providing a 'climate of complete religious liberty for all confessions.' The Greek Catholic Doina Cornea remained under house arrest, despite interventions by Western politicians, while banned writers such as Mircea Dinescu and Ana Blandiana were shadowed by the Securitate.

Besides uniting opinion against him in neighbouring Hungary, Ceauşescu's mistreatment of ethnic Hungarians had thrown up a leader in László Tőkés, a Reformed church pastor. In March 1989, when Tőkés refused an order to stop preaching, his compliant bishop, László Papp, attempted to evict him from his Timişoara parish. Parishioners were arrested and beaten when they came to protect him; and in November, an attack by knife-wielding assailants was fought off in the pastor's house. Six weeks later, several hundred supporters formed a human chain to block new eviction orders by a Timişoara court. Local students joined in, chanting anti-regime slogans and singing a banned patriotic song, *Deşteaptă-te, române* ('Wake up, Romanian!'). The crowd crossed the river and converged on the city-centre, where army and police units opened fire, killing at least 90.

By then, however, the protests had spread to Bucharest and other cities. After failing to rally the armed forces and Securitate, Ceauşescu fled with his wife, Elena—like the defeated Roman emperor, Maximinus II, 'stripping off the imperial insignia' and running 'this way and that, hiding in fields and villages.' Unlike Maximinus, Ceauşescu did not 'reach his own territory' and 'pay tribute to the Christians' God,' but was captured and executed at Târgovişte on 25 December by a hurriedly convened military tribunal. The man who had allowed himself to be worshipped as a 'secular god' was displayed in a pool of blood on state TV. As the Winter Revolution raged, a Catholic archbishop spoke of the 'presence of God in the streets,' of a faith which 'has lived on, through concealment and humiliation, and is now expressing itself in simple, open words and deeds.'[61]

Besides the bloodshed in Romania, the overthrow of communist rule was achieved with relative calm elsewhere in Eastern Europe. In 1848, the regimes of Louis-Philippe in France and Metternich in Austria had been unwilling to use force—even against scrappy, ill-organised acts of popular revolt. This time, the revolt was a mass one, and the will to prevail had simply evaporated. The depiction of 'the unfaithful' applied many centuries before by Christian chroniclers in Gaul—'dejected, downcast, ill-favoured and devoid of charm'—might well have been applied to regime activists now. So might the 'stiffened resistance' being shown by whole populations.

Even so, acts of martyrdom continued, as rogue regime elements used the uncertainty to settle scores and get even with the religious people they still despised. In Albania, where Enver Hoxha had died in April 1985, a few old churches had been opened to tourists and an anti-religious museum in Shkodra closed in a tentative gesture of moderation. In January 1989, however, a 66-year-old priest, Fr Pjetër Gruda, sentenced to 20 years as a Vatican spy, died in Sarandë prison just three months before a promised amnesty, thus becoming Albania's last recorded Catholic martyr.

Even in comparatively peaceful Poland, clergy remained in danger. The SB had over 114,000 employees and secret collaborators here, and was still registering new recruits in 1989. In January, its agents had made a last-ditch attempt to stall a government-opposition compromise by murdering two priests with Solidarity links. Fr Stefan Niedzielak had been an AK chaplain during the 1944 Warsaw Uprising, carrying coded messages to Cardinal Sapieha in Kraków. Narrowly escaping arrest after the War, he had become rector of St Karol Boromeo church near the capital's Powązki cemetery, and chief pastor to the Katyn Families Association, representing those left bereaved by the infamous 1940 massacre of Polish officers. Niedzielak's church had hosted Masses for the Homeland, popularised by Fr Popiełuszko, and he had been shadowed and threatened as a result. On a late January night, the priest was killed with a karate blow which broke his spine. The regime claimed he had fallen out his armchair and medical reports on the incident disappeared.

Some nights later, a 30-year-old priest from Popiełuszko's home-district of Suchowola, Fr Stanisław Suchowolec, was found dead from gas asphyxiation in his parish apartment. Suchowolec had cared for Popiełuszko's family and also celebrated Masses for the Homeland. He had received threatening calls and letters, and his car had been tampered with, while two local women claimed to have had affairs with him. Although witnesses testified that flammable liquid had been poured on the priest's floor, and a local prosecutor ruled that Fr Suchowolec had been murdered, no charges were brought.

That August, the priest who had served five years for involvement in the killing of a police officer on a Warsaw tram, Fr Zych, was found, drunken and battered to death, at the resort of Krynica Morska. The murder, which was also left unresolved, was widely believed an act of revenge by police agents.[62]

Clergy fell victim further east as well. In September 1990, a well-known Russian Orthodox priest, Fr Alexander Men, was bludgeoned to death with an axe while travelling to his church at Semkhoz, near the Orthodox centre of Zagorsk. Expelled from school for his religious beliefs, the Jewish-born Men had authored dozens of books, including a major work, *Son of Man*, introducing Christianity to Soviet citizens. Besides conducting hundreds of baptisms, he had founded an Orthodox open university and charity network, and launched a Sunday school. He had been abused for his evangelical work, however, and accused of 'crypto-Catholicism' by Orthodox bishops. The forest killing was blamed on the KGB and a shadowy right-wing group, Pamyat. Two months later, another Orthodox priest, Fr Ivan Kuz, was shot dead by unknown assailants at Bynliv in Ukraine. Police ruled out robbery as a motive for the killing of the pastor, whose body was discovered in a forest not far from his burned-out car.[63]

However shocking, these were mere incidents in the complex, fast-moving flow of events in the Soviet Union. In May 1989, the English-language *Moscow News* had published an article, 'Persecuted for their faith,' on imprisoned members of religious minorities, while in July, a bishop, Tadeusz Kondrusiewicz, had been appointed for the long-suffering Catholics of Belarus. That August, the Pope had received three metropolitans from the Moscow Patriarchate, which celebrated its fourth centenary two months later by canonising the persecuted Patriarch Tikhon. 'The present Pope is an active initiator of changes proclaimed at the Second Vatican Council,' the Soviet Party's *Komsomolskaya Pravda* confirmed in November. The turnaround was complete. 'The Vatican no longer incites crusader campaigns against communism, and we no longer define religion as opium.'[64]

Over 300,000 Ukrainians had demonstrated in Lviv that September, urging legalisation of the Greek Catholic Church, while bishops and priests had joined a rotational hunger-strike in Moscow's Arbat district. Their demands had been well received by the progressive media, as well as by reformist Soviet leaders such as Boris Yeltsin, a former Politburo member. They had also been the subject of negotiations; and it was soon disclosed that agreement had been reached with the Vatican for the Church's revival. No advance details were given; and it would take another year before an official Greek Catholic hierarchy was reconstituted. But the news unleashed an avalanche of activity. By mid-1990, over 1300 Greek Catholic churches, including Lviv's St Jura cathedral, had been taken back, sometimes forcibly, from their Orthodox occupiers.

Russian Orthodox leaders were also facing challenges from an independent Autocephallous Ukrainian Orthodox church, whose intellectual supporters villified the Russian church as a tool of Russification and KGB collaboration. The first autocephallous parish formally rejected Russian Orthodox jurisdiction in August 1989, and the first church synod was held the following June under a former Russian Orthodox bishop.

On 1 December 1989, in a move rich with poignant symbolism, Gorbachev himself, like a latter-day Constantine, visited the Pope in the Vatican. Gorbachev had acknowledged the virtues of Christianity not through battle but through failed reforms; and like the Fourth Century Roman emperor, his sincerity had long been doubted. But he assured John Paul II his Papal mission would 'leave a great footprint in history,' adding that he now shared a 'great deal of unifying thoughts and concerns' with him. 'As for religious problems, we treat them within the framework of our general understanding of universal human values. In this matter, as in others, the people are the highest authority,' the Soviet Communist Party leader conceded.

> It is important for us to establish a moral society with such eternal universal human truths as goodness, charity and mutual help. In light of the changes taking place, we believe it necessary to respect the internal world of our religious citizens.

The Pope replied that he 'knew and valued' Gorbachev's 'work for world peace.' Like the Biblical Abraham, pleading for the righteous of Sodom and Gomorrah, he counted on him to protect the rights of Catholics, as well as of Protestants, Baptists, Jews, Muslims and Orthodox Christians. He accepted an invitation to visit the Soviet Union and exchange diplomatic representatives; and he agreed with Gorbachev that 'not only structures need changing, but thinking as well.' 'Europe, as a participant in world history, should breathe with two lungs,' John Paul II told the Soviet ruler.

> For over 40 years since the end of the War, Catholics have been denied the fundamental right of religious freedom and practically placed outside the law. We hope a new law will create for them, as for all believers, the opportunity to

practice their religion openly and have their own church structures.[65]

Gorbachev was true to his word. In October 1990, the old repressive 1929 Soviet religious decree was replaced by a Law on Freedom of Conscience and Religious Organisations, which introduced wide-ranging religious liberties and guaranteed the rights of Catholics throughout the Soviet Union. By then, most republics, including Ukraine and the Baltic states, had declared themselves independent. Perhaps in penitence, or perhaps as a political gesture, the last Soviet ruler gave his parents' house at his birthplace near Stavropol to the local Orthodox parish. When he was awarded the Nobel Peace Prize, he donated part of the money to build a new church there.[66] It was indeed a time for ironies and paradoxes.

Notes

1 Raina, *Rozmowy z władzami*, p. 418.

2 Isakowicz-Zaleski, *Księża wobec bezpieki*, p. 157. Blachnicki's poisoning was confirmed by an IPN investigation; see A. Wodarczyk, *Prorok żywego Kościoła* (Katowice: Emmanuel, 2008); R. Derewenda, *Dzieło Wiary: Historia Ruchu Światło-Życie w latach 1950–1985* (Kraków: Światło-Życie, 2010). Clergy membership of Caritas increased during the early 1980s, by virtue of the pay and pensions it offered, Dudek and Gryz, *Komuniści i Kościół*, pp. 411, 421; J. Luxmoore, 'Tinker, tailor, soldier, priest,' in *The Tablet*, 12 August 2006.

3 Dudek and Gryz, *Komuniści i Kościół*, pp. 422, 426.

4 J. Luxmoore, 'The amazing afterlife of the Solidarity priest,' in *Catholic Herald*, London, 22 October 2004; on agents in Rome, Szymowski, *Agenci SB*, pp. 190–6.

5 'Analiza postaw członków PZPR wobec religii,' 18 July 1985, in *Tajne dokumenty*, pp. 430–5. Some 3000 sacral buildings were constructed in Poland during 1986 alone, according to official data; Dudek and Gryz, *Komuniści i Kościół*, pp. 424–6.

6 Raina, *Cele polityki władz PRL*, pp. 155–6; J. Luxmoore, 'Polish Catholicism under fire,' in *Ethics and International Affairs* (New York: Carnegie Council), vol. 1/no. 1 (1987), pp. 161–190.

7 Luxmoore and Babiuch, *The Vatican and the Red Flag,* p. 264.

8 Mikloško et al, *Zločiny,* pp. 326.

9 *Ibid.,* pp. 329.

10 *The Times,* 13 March 1987; *Neue Zürcher Zeitung,* 9 February 1986; J. Šimulčík, *Svetlo z podzemia: Z kroniky katolíckeho samizdatu 1969–1989* (Prešov: Vaška, 1997), p. 19; F. Dlugoš, *Dejiny Mariánskej hory v Levoči* (Levoča: Polypress, 2000), pp. 182–3.

11 Havasy, *Martyrs of the Catholic Church,* pp. 161–2; Hlinka, *Sila slabých,* pp. 271–2; Čarnogurský, *Važnili ich za vieru,* pp. 106–111.

12 *Új Ember,* 24 April 1983; figures in 'Table of major events in Hungarian church history,' Budapest, 15 May 1991, pp. 8–10; Luxmoore and Babiuch, *The Vatican and the Red Flag,* p. 265; E. András and J. Morel, *Hungarian Catholicism: A Handbook* (Vienna: Hungarian Institute, 1983), pp. 91–126.

13 Author's interview, Budapest, May 1989.

14 *Népszabadság,* Budapest, 11 May 1985.

15 Reported by many newsagencies and newspapers, including *The Wall Street Journal,* 14 June 1985; *Agence France-Presse,* 6 June 1985; *Le Monde,* 7 June 1985; *The Tablet,* 15 June 1988; *Glaube in der Zweiten Welt,* 21 June 1985. The toilet paper incident was noted by the defector, Ion Pacepa, in *Red Horizons,* pp. 280–1.

16 'Destruction of old Bucharest continues,' in *Radio Free Europe Background Report,* 15 August 1985, 10 January 1986 and 6 March 1987.

17 *Radio Free Europe Background Report,* 24 February 1986; *Neue Zürcher Zeitung,* 1 February 1986.

18 *Era Socialista,* 10 April 1984; *Radio Free Europe Background Report,* 17 July and 30 August 1985.

19 *The Independent,* London, 5 January 1988.

20 Vatican Radio, 18 February 1983; *Borba,* Belgrade, 3 August 1984. A 1984 Zagreb University survey suggested 45 percent of Croatian adults still held religious beliefs; *The Times,* 19 April 1984.

21 'Jailed Croatian priests' protest,' in *The South Slav Journal,* London, vol. 6/no. 1 (1983), pp. 94–5; other cases in *The Times,* 19 December 1983; *The Tablet,* 2 February 1985; *Katholische Nachrichten-agentur,* Bonn, 16 June 1983.

22 Cardinal Ratzinger's interview with *Jesus* magazine, November 1984; Bishop Žanić's letter to *The Tablet,* 5 January 1985.

23 Vatican Radio, 4–5 February and 9 February 1983.

24 Blažević's interview in *Polet* weekly, Zagreb, 8–15 February 1985; further discussion in *Vjesnik* and *Glas Koncila,* 17 February 1985.

25 *Politika,* Belgrade, 1 June 1982; priests' petition in *Tanjug* report, 25 May 1982; *Religion in Communist Lands,* vol. 10/no. 3 (1982), pp. 331–3.

[26] John Paul II, apostolic letter *Euntes in Mundum*, 12 June 1987, no. 5; *Slavorum Apostoli*, 2 June 1985, nos. 10–11, 27. Ivanov's idea of East-West unity was of 'two principles that mutually complement each other.'

[27] Luxmoore and Babiuch, *Rethinking Christendom*, pp. 150–1, 156; *Radio Free Europe Report*, 22 April 1985; H. Süssmuth, 'Luther 1983 in beiden deutschen Staaten: Kritische rezeption oder ideologische Vereinnahmung?' in H. Süssmuth (ed), *Das Luther-Erbe in Deutschland: Vermittlung zwischen Wissenschaft und Öffentlichkeit* (Düsseldorf: Droste, 1985), pp. 16–40; J. Olsen, 'Recasting Luther's image: The 1983 commemoration of Martin Luther in the GDR,' in T. Hochscherf et al (eds), *Divided, But Not Disconnected: German Experiences of the Cold War* (New York: Berghahn, 2010), pp. 63–76; J. Brinks, 'Luther and the German State,' in *The Heythrop Journal*, London, vol. 39/no. 1 (1998), pp. 1–17; A. Gordon, 'The Luther Quincentenary in the GDR,' in *Religion in Communist Lands*, vol. 12/no. 1 (1984), pp. 77–85.

[28] 'Document 172. To the CPSU CC,' in Corley, *Religion in the Soviet Union*, pp. 290–4.

[29] *Radio Liberty Research*, 29 June 1983 and 19 August 1986. On Ukraine and Belarus, see Dzwonkowski, *Za wschodnią granicą*, pp. 186, 281–7. In a May 1985 report, the Soviet CRA put the number of active religious groups throughout the Soviet Union at 15,202, of which around a fifth were unregistered. They were served by 17,966 'registered cult servants,' whose numbers had increased in all faiths and denominations, with the exception of Jews, Old Believers and Catholics; 'Document 173. Council for Religious Affairs, Moscow,' in Corley, *Religion in the Soviet Union*, pp. 295–9. Complaints and legal infringements had also diminished, according to the report.

[30] *Radio Liberty Research*, 14 January 1987; Przebinda, *Większa Europa*, p. 115.

[31] 'Document 192. Report on measures to strengthen work with Protestant associations in the RSFSR,' in Corley, *Religion in the Soviet Union*, 337–9.

[32] V. Astafev, in *Nash Sovremennik*, May 1986; 'Soviet writers criticised for Christian leanings,' in *Radio Liberty Research*, 5 November 1986; *Moscow News*, 16 August 1987.

[33] M. Gorbachev, *Perestroika: New Thinking for Our Country and the World* (London: Collins, 1987), pp. 162–3, 165.

[34] 'Document 177. Extract from Protocol No. 9,' in Corley, *Religion in the Soviet Union*, 314–7.

[35] *Radio Liberty Research*, 10 September 1987. An Adventist pastor, Mikhail Kulakov, also quoted St Paul: 'Forgetting what is behind and straining towards what is ahead.' Small congregations like his own were thankful

for the 'many new freedoms,' Kulakov told the conference. 'I could talk about by own past experiences,' the Adventist added, 'but I have no wish to make of a martyr of myself.'

36 Author's interview, Moscow, March 1990; K. De Wolf, *Dissident for Life: Alexander Ogorodnikov and the Struggle for Religious Freedom in Russia* (Grand Rapids: Eerdmans, 2013).

37 Przebinda, *Większa Europa*, p. 287; *The Tablet*, 8 August 1987.

38 Letter to Ukrainian Catholics, *Magnum baptisimi donum*, 14 February 1988.

39 Przebinda, *Większa Europa*, pp. 101, 197.

40 Author's interview with Filaret, Warsaw, September 1989; *The Tablet*, 20 June 1987; Luxmoore and Babiuch, *The Vatican and the Red Flag*, p. 291.

41 *National Catholic Register*, Los Angeles, 3 June 1990; author's interview with Gel, Ampleforth, August 1990; Wenger, *Rome et Moscou*, pp. 243–4. Alliluyeva (1926–2011), the only daughter of Stalin and his second wife, Nadezhda, was baptised into the Russian Orthodox church in March 1963, later turning to Greek Orthodoxy and also flirting with Hinduism. She recounted her spiritual experiences in *Twenty Letters to a Friend* (London: Hutchinson, 1967) and *Only One Year* (London: Harper, 1969).

42 *The Tablet*, 16 August 1986; Streikus, *Antykościelna polityka*, p. 222; *Radio Liberty Research*, 21 November 1986.

43 Apostolic letter *Sescentesima anniversaria*, 5 June 1986, nos. 4–7, 11.

44 Author's interviews with Tamkevičius and Sadūnaitė, Kaunas, February 1990 and September 1990; N. Sadūnaitė, *A Radiance in the Gulag* (Manassas: Trinity Communications, 1987); Streikus, *Antykościelna polityka*, p. 223.

45 Streikus, *Antykościelna polityka*, p. 226; Pope's address to the bishops of Lithuania, in *Lithuanian Information Center Bulletin*, New York, 27 April 1988.

46 The Kuropaty mass killings were revealed when the *Literatura i Mastactwa* weekly defied communist censors and published an article, 'Kuropaty—path of death,' in June 1988. J. Luxmoore, 'Life after communism,' in *The Tablet*, 22 August 1992.

47 *Dominum et vivificantem*, 18 May 1986, nos. 38, 54, 60, 65.

48 Raina, *Cele polityki władz PRL*, pp. 160–5; S. Cenckiewicz and M. Kruk (eds), *Operacja 'Zorza II': Służba Bezpieczeństwa i Komitet Wojewódzki PZPR wobec Wizyty Jana Pawła II w Trójmieście* (Warsaw: IPN, 2008), p. xi.

49 *Ibid.*, pp. xi-xxvi; J. Wąsowicz, 'O was i za was: Kulisy wizyty papieskiej w Gdańsku w czerwcu 1987 roku,' in *Kościół w godzinie próby*, pp. 229.

50 Speeches and homilies in Luxmoore and Babiuch, *The Vatican and the*

Red Flag, pp. 283–5; Dudek and Gryz, *Komuniści i Kościół*, p. 431.

51 Reported in *The Times*, 25 March 1986.

52 Report in *Hospodárske noviny*, 14 December 2007. The homeless man, Ladislav Macháč, was acquitted eight months later; see http://www.magnificat.sk/2012/10/aktualne-vyrocie-vrazdy-knaza-stefana-polaka; Dlugoš, *Dejiny Mariánskej hory*, pp. 182–3; Mikloško et al, *Zločiny*, p. 325.

53 *Wochenpresse*, Vienna, 11–13 March 1987. Paskai was cautioned by the Vatican over this interview, according to Havasy, *Martyrs of the Catholic Church*, pp. 166–7.

54 Ratzinger's letter, in *Új Ember*, 17 June 1987.

55 Text in Deletante, *Ceausescu and the Securitate*, p. 262; data for Bucharest churches in *Agerpress*, 26 January 1988, and L. Anania et al, *Bisericile osândite de Ceaușescu. București 1977–1989* (Bucharest: Anastasia, 1995); *Radio Free Europe Background Report*, 28 January and 30 December 1988.

56 Deletante, *Ceausescu and the Securitate*, pp. 266–7, 270; on the growth of dissent, Daniel and Gluza, *Słownik dysydentów*, pp. 731–722.

57 Author's interview with Kuharić, Zagreb, October 1991; *Glas Koncila*, 28 August 1983.

58 *Tanjug* report, 29 December 1983; *Borba*, 10–11 September 1983; *Radio Free Europe Background Report*, 21 February 1984.

59 *Sollicitudo rei socialis*, 30 December 1987, nos. 22, 47.

60 Raina, *Cele polityki władz PRL*, p. 180; Dudek and Gryz, *Komuniści i Kościół*, p. 439; A. Orszulik, *Czas Przełomu: Notatki z rozmów z władzami PRL w latach 1981–1989* (Warsaw: Apostolicum, 2006), pp. 516–546.

61 Author's interview with Archbishop Robu, Bucharest, January 1990; Deletante, *Ceausescu and the Securitate*, pp. 232; *Radio Free Europe Background Report*, 28 January 1988; Ceausescu's trial transcript, in '1989 in Documents,' in *Problems of Post-Communism*, September-October 2009, pp. 37–40; description of Maximinus, in Eusebius, *History of the Church*, pp. 297–8.

62 Z. Branach, *Tajemnica śmierci księdza Zycha* (Toruń: Cetera, 1999); M. Zieleniewski, *Rozkaz zabić: Tajemnicze zgony księży S. Niedzielaka, S. Suchowolca i S. Zycha* (Piła, Angraf, 1990); P. Litka, *Katyński kurier: Ks. Stefan Niedzielak* (Kraków: Wydawnictwo św. Stanisława, 2010), pp. 94–147; SB figures in Isakowicz-Zaleski, *Księża wobec bezpieki*, p. 223; reference to the Christians in Gaul, in Eusebius, *The History of the Church*, p. 144.

63 *TASS* report, 18 November 1990; *National Catholic Register*, 8 March 1982.

64 *Komsomolskaya Pravda*, 21 November 1989; Przebinda, *Większa Europa*, p. 295.

65 Text in *The Universe*, Manchester, 15 December 2009. The 3600-word

minutes, published the US National Security Archive at George Washington University, were compiled from notes by Aleksander Yakovlev (1923–2005), a Soviet Politburo member and Gorbachev adviser who attended the private Vatican meeting. It was passed on in translation from the State Archive of the Russian Federation in Moscow at the establishment of formal Russia-Vatican diplomatic relations. There were some diplomatic claims that the Pope had met Gorbachev secretly in 1987; Szymowski, *Agenci SB*, p. 140.

66 Author's interview with Gorbachev, Warsaw, March 1997. The Nobel citation noted Gorbachev's 'leading role in the peace process which today characterises important parts of the international community.'

7 MESSAGES AND MEANINGS

I saw under the altar the souls of those who had been slain for the word of God and for the witness they had borne; they cried out with a loud voice, 'O Sovereign Lord, holy and true, how long before thou wilt judge and avenge our blood on those who dwell upon the earth?' Then they were each given a white robe and told to rest a little longer, until the number of their fellow servants and their brethren should be complete, who were to be killed as they themselves had been.

Rev 6:9–11

IT WAS ALSO a time for wonder. Expert observers would debate why communist rule came to collapse so suddenly and completely in Europe. Some would trace it to a false view of mankind, and to systemic flaws and fault-lines present from the very beginning. Others would highlight economic stagnation, ideological meltdown, Western pressure and imperial over-stretch, a fractious combination of reform from above and rebellion from below, a chain of intended and unintended consequences which spiralled into a full-scale transformation.

Archive material, released in the 1990s, suggested Moscow had come to view its East European satellites as a ruinous liability, whose crushing economic cost was no longer offset by security benefits. It showed that Soviet rulers lacked the will and capacity to formulate a coherent strategy, choosing instead, when the crunch came, to let events run their course. Yet it also indicated that governments both East and West, long sceptical about far-reaching change, were caught out by the speed of events, failing to anticipate their domino-like effects. Trotsky's definition of revolution as 'the forcible entry of the masses into the realm of rulership over their own destiny' was dramatically played out in Eastern Europe, this time against the very communist vision which was supposed to have inspired them.[1]

Each nation in the region could claim to have laid the ground for this revolution. For Poles, it had been prepared by the Round Table talks and semi-democratic elections of June 1989, which took place on the day Chinese pro-democracy demonstrators were massacred in Beijing's Tienanmen Square, an outrage which hung like a menacing cloud for the rest of the year over Eastern Europe. For Hungarians, it had been the symbolic cutting of border fences with Austria that May, and the opening of the Iron Curtain to East German refugees. For Lithuanians, Latvians and Estonians, it had been the human chain of clasped hands which stretched between the three capitals that August. For Czechs, Slovaks and Romanians, it had been the popular street uprisings which erupted in November and December. For East Germans, it had been the televised breaching of the Berlin Wall, which captured the revolutionary moment in simple, graphic images.

Yet the preoccupation with the dramas of 1989 would also distort reality, by playing down the process of preparation and maturation which had occurred over the preceding period. In reality, the revolutions of 1989 had not been made not by politicians and opposition leaders, but by ordinary people who gathered in their thousands to turn ideas and initiatives into real events. It was in summoning this 'people power,' in mobilising hearts and minds, that the Church's contribution had been made.

There were echoes, in the euphoria which now swept Eastern Europe, of the rejoicing which followed the 'Great Deliverance' of the early Fourth Century, when Constantine's Edict of Toleration had ushered in a new era for the Christians of Rome. Then as now, the empire was still powerful, and Christianity was tolerated but far from dominant. But past oppression had been discredited by peaceful, persistent resistance. The rulers had lost their will to fight the faith and yielded to their own troubled consciences. The official ideology was being supplanted by loftier ideals and higher forms of morality and ethics. The historian Eusebius had written of a 'manifest visitation of divine providence,' of being 'privileged to see and celebrate such things as in truth many righteous men and martyrs of God before us desired to see on earth and did not see.' People 'released from their former miseries' were now 'acknowledging the presence of the divine,' as destruction finally overtook 'the whole brood of God's enemies.'[2]

For all the poetic licence, apocalyptic images had made a come-back in Eastern Europe. The Biblical image of the Red Sea, or sea of blood, which had closed over Pharoah's army, had a special resonance when applied to communism. So did the image in Revelation of the 'woman sitting on a scarlet beast,' with its many heads and horns, revelling drunk 'with the blood of the saints and with the blood of the martyrs of Jesus' (Rev 17:4–6). Rome with its seven hills had become Moscow; and Moscow, like Rome before it, the city with dominion 'over the kings of the earth,' had been brought to its knees by the very God it had presumed to make war upon.

Eusebius had recorded how, 17 centuries before, newly liberated citizens had 'lost all fear of their former oppressors,' and how people 'who once dared not look up greeted each other with smiling faces and shining eyes.' He had written of how, 'in less time than it takes to say it,' the names of those who had breathed 'death and threats' were forgotten, their portraits and tributes 'thrown down and smashed' and 'swept into merited oblivion.' Similar scenes of iconoclasm were now occurring in Eastern Europe. Eusebius had also described the Church's recovery in his own day, as new bishops were consecrated, Christian associations created, places of worship dedicated, and confiscated properties given back or compensated for by the state.[3] Similar acts of restitution and revival were now beginning in Eastern Europe too, as populations long starved of spiritual sustenance showed new interest in the religious life, and newly emerging democratic leaders gratefully acknowledged the role of churches in sustaining opposition to communist rule and giving the new democratic order a moral stamp of approval.

The gratitude was most evident in Poland, where the Catholic Church had supported demands for human rights when the Solidarity movement was crushed under martial law, and offered sanctuary to a myriad of opposition initiatives. But in neighbouring Czechoslovakia too, the Church's contribution in mobilising mass protest was also being acknowledged, along with the role played by Cardinal Tomášek and practising Christians in Charter 77. In Romania, where the Winter Revolution had been sparked by the arrest of the Calvinist pastor, László Tőkés, much-persecuted Greek Catholics had actively resisted for decades. Even in quiescent Hungary, Christian base communities had been a key element in the nascent civil society emerging since the 1980s. 'Our country is entering a new path,' Hungary's Catholic bishops declared, in one of many such statements by local church leaders. 'The Church will be independent of all parties and respect the state's autonomy. But it will also demand that the political authorities respect its independence and ensure appropriate conditions for its activity.'[4]

When the peaceful revolutions in Eastern Europe were followed by the collapse of Soviet rule further east, the process started again. In August 1991, a hardline 'emergency committee' made a last-ditch attempt to hang on to power, just as Constantine's rivals had done centuries before—bringing troops into the streets of Moscow and declaring Gorbachev's *glasnost* and *perestroika* at an end. The coup collapsed within 48 hours, as tens of thousands rallied to oppose it; and the Soviet Union's disintegration became inevitable. By early September, foreign governments had recognised the independence of Lithuania, Latvia and Estonia. By December, Armenians, Belarusans, Georgians and Ukrainians had regained sovereignty as well.

There was talk of miracles, as explanations were sought for the sudden turn of events, which had enabled a nuclear-armed empire, garrisoned with a million troops, to crumble in a matter of months, with barely a shot fired in anger. The Moscow coup had failed humiliatingly as a million young people flocked to Poland's Jasna Góra shrine to celebrate World Youth Day with the Pope, and as a dense summer-night fog blocked the advance of hardline tanks on the Russian parliament. Many Russians believed God had intervened, and over two-thirds now claimed to be religious.[5]

For all the euphoria, it was a time of hardship, as economic and social conditions worsened amid the confusion. For the Catholic Church, however, it was also a time of triumph. In 1900, the German writer, Adolf von Harnack, had seen the Church as 'the most inclusive and the mightiest structure, the most complicated and yet the most homogeneous,' on which 'all the forces of human intellect and soul, all mankind's elemental powers,' had been expended. The Russian Dostoevsky had portrayed the Church as a suppressor of freedom and tormentor of souls. But he too had seen it as a 'great unifying force,' which would give back faith to people who had 'long felt a loneliness without God.' The Pope would 'succeed in swaying the people by walking barefoot, naked as a beggar,' Dostoevsky had prophesied in 1873—'with an army of twenty thousand Jesuits experienced in capturing human souls. Can Karl Marx and Bakunin resist these fighters?'[6]

They could hardly have resisted when the Church stood so firmly and unequivocally on the side of the common man. In that sense at least, the tide of history had now changed. Some East Europeans saw 1989 as an answer to the 'Liberty, Equality and Fraternity' proclaimed by the French Revolution two centuries before, and as a triumph for the spirit of defiance shown by earlier national uprisings. They detected a major shift in the Church's position. Having once shunned mass social protests, the Church had now come to view them as a creative tool—natural allies in the godly cause of human rights and social justice. In contrast to bloody events in previous centuries, the Church had unequivocally welcomed the new spring tide of human liberation. But it had also tried to give the ideals of freedom and emancipation a deeper Christian interpretation beyond secular political dimensions.

Behind all of this stood the epic figure of John Paul II, who had brought millions into the streets of his native Poland. The Pope had kept the Solidarity movement united and peaceful around a clearly articulated set of objectives, and laid out the moral and spiritual parameters of a reunited Europe 'breathing with both lungs.' His ground-breaking 1979 Polish pilgrimage, with its famous soundbites ('Open the doors to Christ!'—'Renew the face of this land!') would long be remembered. Many now testified that it had marked the moment when they first glimpsed their future liberation—unmistakeable proof, if proof were needed, of the Holy Spirit's power to shape events.

In a later survey by Warsaw's Public Opinion Research Centre (CBOS), 58 percent of Poles would cite John Paul II's 1978 election as the century's 'most important event,' while three-quarters would believe his 'influence on the world's fate' had been greater than that of any other modern-day figure. For all such hyperbole, there could be no doubting the Pope's influence—a fact, well understood, ironically, by communist leaders themselves. With the struggle now over, Poland's communist strongman, General Jaruzelski, would concede that John Paul II's teachings had 'reawakened hopes and expectations of change.' Mikhail Gorbachev would speak of how the pontiff had helped his own 'understanding of communism,' duly acknowledging that the end of communist rule would have been 'impossible' without him.[7]

Another top Soviet, the ideologist Vadim Zagladin, would concede that his Party's claims had been refuted by the persistence of religious faith. The affirmation that authority comes from God provided vital protection against arbitrary power; and it was Christians themselves who had been 'precursors and champions' of the socialist ideal. 'Repression of spiritual liberty is only a step away from suppression of physical liberty,' the Soviet told his Vatican interlocutors in 1990. 'We've tried to bury religion and Christianity more than once—with what result? None at all, except for a hardening of hearts and inhumanity in personal relationships.'[8]

In April 1990, five months after Czechoslovakia's 'Velvet Revolution,' John Paul II stood before the high altar of Prague's St Vitus cathedral, where the ill-fated Archbishop Beran had once been shouted down by communist agents. It was his first visit to an East European country other than Poland, and the Vatican would soon have diplomatic relations with a dozen or more. 'Today, we stand before the ruins of one of the many towers of Babel in human history,' the Pope told the Czechs. 'You were called the Church of silence. But your silence was not the silence of sleep or death. In the spiritual order, it is in silence that the most precious values are born.'

He listed the 'immense historic tasks' the Church now faced throughout the region, as it revived seminary vocations, refounded religious orders, reorganised catechesis, renewed ecumenical ties and 'gave new life' to Catholic parishes in the spirit of Vatican II. 'The Church's solidarity with the persecuted has strengthened its moral authority,' the Pope told his congregation. 'You hold in your hands the capital of merits amassed by those who sacrificed their life and freedom. This is truly a rich inheritance. Do not squander it!'[9]

There were confident predictions that the era of ideologies had now ended, and that liberal democracy and the free market had seen off their final challenges. Young, inexperienced leaders, thrown up by dramatic events of the late 1980s, talked of a return to national unity and consensus politics in fulfilment of the legacy of Solidarity and other national movements—much as the Robespierre, Saint-Just and the youthful idealists of the French Revolution had enthused about a 'single will' and 'public conscience,' a natural tendency to choose the common good. As time went on, however, post-communist realities began to look a lot more complex.

Marxism had been mistaken—and not only in the anthropological misunderstandings so often highlighted by the Pope. It had viewed the individual as a 'molecule' with no free choice or personal autonomy, totally dependent on the 'social machine and those who control it.' This was John Paul II's deduction. Its mistaken conception of humanity had derived, furthermore, from its atheism—an atheism derived from the rationalism of the Enlightenment, which saw human and social reality mechanistically and chose class struggle as its means of action. The communist regimes had fallen because they were economically inefficient and violated the rights of working people, who had rejected an ideology 'which presumed to speak in their name.' But the 'true cause' of their collapse, the Pope concluded, had been the void brought about by atheism.[10]

Marxism had required a levelling down of the kind foreseen by Dostoevsky. 'Slaves must be equal: without despotism there has never been any freedom or equality,' the character Verkhavensky had declared in *The Devils.* 'A Cicero will have his tongue cut out; Copernicus will have his eyes gouged out; a Shakespeare will be stoned!' Yet the flaws exposed by Leszek Kołakowski and others had never been resolved. Marxism had supposed that the material base determined consciousness and the spiritual sphere. It offered the ultimate means of control—as the British writer, George Orwell, had put it via a character in his dystopian, futuristic 1949 classic, *Nineteen Eighty-Four*: 'Power is in tearing minds to pieces and putting them together again in new shapes of your own choosing.'[11] In a classless society, the alienation expressed by religion would finally be brought to an end—along with the need for God, the self-projection of alienated humanity. The superstructure would collapse once the base had shifted, bringing about a socialist paradise or 'kingdom of freedom.' But this required revolutionary force, a dictatorship of the proletariat via its Party avant-garde.

In reality, the cherished kingdom of freedom had depended on the suppression of freedom. Since there was no spiritual sphere, signs of contradiction had no logical explanation, other than as reckless acts of sabotage by a hostile class enemy who had to be mercilessly exterminated. Without any religious context, love for fellow-men became an aspiration to power, a power which, in turn, destroyed any notion of love. By contrast, the prayerful struggles which culminated in 1989 had drawn on the Church's social teaching. After a century of Marxist domination, workers had found a new guardian of freedom in Christianity—a warning to those who, in the name of political realism, wished to banish law and morality from the political arena.[12]

Attempts would be made to salvage the more positive aspects of Marxism. Even John Paul II would recall that there had been 'grains of truth' in the communist programme, as well as 'good things achieved by communism'—not least in its concern for the poor and opposition to 'unbridled, savage capitalism.'[13] As the 1990s wore on, however, other more pressing problems appeared on the horizon.

In Russia, where Gorbachev's one-time Party followers never forgave him for 'destroying the Soviet Union,' disaster loomed again in September 1993, when President Boris Yeltsin's attempt to dissolve the Congress of People's Deputies and Supreme Soviet led to clashes which left 187 dead and hundreds injured. Wars erupted in Nagorno-Karabakh, Chechnya, Georgia, Moldavia and Tajikistan, as well as in the Balkans, where at least 100,000 died in a savage four-year conflict in Bosnia-Herzegovina. Whereas Yugoslavia broke up violently, Czechoslovakia did so peacefully, leaving Czechs and Slovaks to reassert independent identities. Throughout the former Soviet Union, however, from Estonia to Ukraine, ethnic tensions and power-political rivalries were never far below the surface.

Efforts were made to rekindle public trust in the state and rid words like 'party' and 'programme' of their negative associations. But hopes quickly evaporated of some new spiritual quality in decision-making and some new consensus of values and priorities, as idealistic former dissidents from Solidarity, Charter 77 and other groups, having guided their countries through the initial transition, were outmanoeuvred and pushed aside by harder, less congenial figures.

In Poland, where at least half the population now believed General Jaruzelski had been right to impose martial law, former communists were returned to power in democratic elections just four years after 1989, with many voters preferring the sterile but secure life offered by the previous system. Similar pressures and strains were evident elsewhere in Eastern Europe, as consumerism took root, and concern for the poor and marginalised was scorned as retrograde and tainted. Visiting Poland in 1997, the Pope called on his countrymen to ensure 'elementary solidarity' prevailed over the 'unrestrained desire for profit.' Freedom needed defending against the new 'liberal ideology,' at a time when unemployment and poverty were rife, the aged faced abandonment, the sick were denied proper care, and those in jobs often suffered exploitation and inadequate pay.[14] As Poland and seven other post-communist countries prepared to join the European Union in May 2004, followed by Bulgaria and Romania in 2007, and Croatia in 2013, the process of negotiation and adaptation brought some improvement. For many, however, conditions of life remained harsh and unremitting.

In such circumstances, there was little popular appetite for dwelling on the past, or for following St Augustine's summons to emulate the 'crowns and victories' of the martyrs. The Slavic word for martyr—*mučenik* or *męczennik*—had connotations of suffering which contradicted the new spirit of the age. The crimes of communism were bitterly remembered by those who had directly suffered from them. But tales of persecution seemed, for others, out of step with the new realities, an unhelpful addition to the baggage of history. The past itself had become political anyway, with those on the right denouncing communism and those on the left sometimes defending it. Against such polarisation, the

Church might foster reconciliation. But for many, the Church itself had become part of the problem, rather than the solution.

Besides celebrating liberation, there had been hopes that hard lessons might also be learned from the era of oppression. Why had the Church encountered such hostility? Why had so many intelligent people been attracted to communism's alluring promises to neutralise inequalities and bring injustice to an end? Similar questions had been asked after the French Revolution by the Breton priest, Félicité de Lamennais, and his 'Social Catholic' confreres. They had seen the turbulence as a chance to rebuild the Church on new foundations, and for Catholic spirituality to leaven and purify the forces of popular emancipation. Their efforts had been resisted; and throughout the Nineteenth Century, the Church had found itself on the wrong side of the growing divide between paternalistic Christian ethics and rebellious secular radicalism, which had culminated in Marxism's triumph in the October Revolution.

In the Fourth Century, Eusebius had described how God had 'raised up the fallen Church, after first cleansing her and curing her sickness,' and 'clothed her with a new garment—not the old one she had had from the first.' Step by bitter step, the communist experience had transformed the Church from a bastion of reaction to a champion of freedom. Yet by the mid-1990s, the Church appeared to many to have moved back in the opposite direction—to have donned just the same garment it had worn before the communist assault. Nationalism and anti-semitism had reared their heads again, while many Catholics looked to Christianity for a new ideology and political programme. Some seized on an American model of 'democratic capitalism,' with its idealistic vision of a society combining religiousness with freedom and prosperity. Others relived the pre-War dream of a corporatist state in which the Church's privileged ascendancy was constitutionally guaranteed.

In Russia, Poland and Romania, predominant churches were accused of amassing power and wealth again, and of pressing the state to support them against rival confessions. After the 'Great Deliverance' of the early Fourth Century, Constantine had ordered all church possessions to be restored immediately without 'any argument whatever.'[15] Now too, it was only right that churches should reclaim what had been unjustly taken from them. But there was no general restitution order this time; so parishes, dioceses and religious orders had to table their property claims in the glare of negative publicity. Many believed they went too far. In Poland, Catholic priests emerged as one of the richest social groups, as ornate new churches rose out of the landscape as they had done in the Seventeenth Century baroque age, and new untried governments sought alliances with the clergy by showering them with gifts and handouts.

The Church was not against democracy: it quickly understood how it could use democracy to its own advantage. But its lack of openness posed, for many, a barrier to pluralism. For some, its high-handed insistence on religious education and the banning of abortion impeded personal freedom. The religious revival of the 1990s was avowedly anti-communist; but it was also, in many cases, anti-clerical, as bitter anti-church feeling gained sharp political edges.

The Vatican remained active in the Organisation on Security and Co-operation in Europe, renamed in 1995, and was represented, with numerous other church bodies, in the European institutions, while multilateral organisations such as the Council of Catholic Episcopates of Europe and non-Catholic Conference of European Churches sought a common East-West voice on current issues and priorities. Meanwhile, the Catholic, Protestant and Orthodox churches all backed their countries' aspirations to join the European Union. They also feared the consequences of Westernisation, however, and sought to uphold and assert moral principles and traditional bonds of identity and community as the old barriers gradually disappeared. In six pilgrimages to post-communist Poland, Pope John Paul II tried to lay the foundations of a strong and united Christian society, in which institutions shunned for decades regained legitimacy, and a stable, prosperous new order stood firmly on authentic values. He took the same message, with local variations, to neighbouring countries as well. Yet it remained debatable how far his message had been taken to heart.

The sudden collapse of communist rule had left a tangle of structural and administrative problems within the Church itself. In the former Czechoslovakia, up to 250 priests and bishops were estimated to have been ordained or consecrated under the Church's 'emergency powers' during the persecutions of the 1950s. Most had been selected by the shadowy Bishop Feliks Davídek, who had also ordained several women. Ensuring the Church's canonical and sacramental order was therefore a pressing concern. Over a hundred secretly ordained priests came forward for screening under 1992 Vatican guidelines. Of these, 57 married clergy were offered admission to a new Greek Catholic exarchate, or diocese, under Bishop Ivan Ljavinec, while 43 had their ordinations retrospectively approved by the Vatican's Congregation for Eastern Churches. For a time at least, their fate provoked controversy in Eastern Europe.

As the archives were opened, meanwhile, and once-secret documents placed in the public view, it became possible to build up a fuller picture of the cruelties inflicted by the ruling communists in their campaign against the churches. When minutes from Stalin's overnight Kremlin wartime meeting with Russia's surviving metropolitans were published in 1994, it was revealed that all three had been living in cramped Moscow apartments and bartering for food at local markets. Minutes were published in Poland of Church-state negotiations and Party discussions on how to outmanoeuvre the Polish bishops. The complexity of the Church's position was elaborated in the notes and diaries of Cardinal Wyszyński, as well as in the memoirs of Cardinal Casaroli, who defended the Vatican's 'small steps' policy without a hint of self-criticism.[16] Studies of repression were compiled by historians and researchers, while ordinary Christians were allowed to inspect the files kept on them by the secret police, now carefully stored in Poland's National Remembrance Institute. Personal testimonies were collected of persecution, imprisonment and exile, graphically recalling the sufferings endured under communist rule.

Some of the archive material was plainly misused. There were claims in the early 1990s that the Vatican had formed a 'holy alliance' with the Reagan Administration to channels funds and equipment to Solidarity in Poland, an idea widely derided by church and opposition veterans. Meanwhile, some key events still eluded the researchers. Mystery persisted over the St Peter's Square shooting of May 1981, as allegations of Soviet involvement were met by insistent Russian and Bulgarian denials. Virtually every detail of John Paul II's life and work had been scrutinised and published in his native Poland, where newspapers had reported earlier plots to kill the Pope during his 1983 and 1987 homecomings, involving rogue SB operatives, Bulgarian agents and Red Brigade terrorists from Italy. But the 1981 outrage remained unresolved. In 2009, the Vatican denied claims by a former US intelligence agent, John Koehler, that Polish priests in the Vatican had given the Soviet KGB information used to prepare the Rome attack. Although substantial documentary collections were published, detailing how communist agents had kept the future Pope under surveillance from as early as 1946, these too revealed little.[17]

Much of the material now available proved invaluable to Christian researchers. In tiny Slovenia, documents collected after an appeal by the Catholic Church's *Družina* weekly detailed the fates of 237 Catholic priests, monks and nuns killed in the years 1940–62. They were among the thousands buried anonymously at some 500 separate sites in the former Yugoslav republic.[18]

There was also a price to be paid, however, for laying bare the past. By the mid-1990s, there had been warnings that religious communities should confront their own shortcomings and recognise that they too had been infiltrated by communist informers. In the run-up to the Christian Millennium, Pope John Paul II called for a spirit of penance, urging his own Church to admit its sins and failures, as well as celebrating its heroic achievements. Some church leaders responded accordingly. In ex-Soviet Belarus, the bishops pledged to forgive Soviet-era persecutors, including those who had 'plundered and destroyed our churches, seminaries, crosses and wayside chapels,' and 'by the power of Party rulings, erased God from people's hearts and destroyed human consciences.'[19] But the Church itself was not 'free of human weaknesses,' the bishops conceded. 'We ask forgiveness that there were Catholics who collaborated with the Nazis in the Second World War and were co-responsible for the arrest and death of innocent people,' their document continued. 'We are also sorry Catholics did not always help those persecuted by the totalitarian system.'

Elsewhere, John Paul II faced resistance. Most church leaders were against admitting fault, and resented suggestions that self-criticism and *metanoia* should become Millennium themes. When it came to an accounting of consciences, the practical record looked set to vary.

In East Germany, the archive of the *Staatssicherheit*, or Stasi, filling 110 miles of shelving, were housed in a Berlin institute employing 3000 researchers under a former Protestant pastor, Joachim Gauck, who was elected German president in March 2012. At its height, the Stasi had employed 97,000 full-time agents and 173,000 informers from its Normannenstrasse headquarters and 14 regional offices. This was equivalent to one agent for every 63 East German citizens, or one in six when part-time informers were included. Comparisons were drawn between the Gauck Institute's investigations and the de-Nazification programme which had followed Germany's defeat in 1945, when the victorious Allies had banned the Nazi Party and debarred its officials from public office, arresting 100,000 on suspicion of crimes against humanity and executing 486. In the *Diktaturvergleich*, or comparison of dictatorships, the treatment of communists was a lot milder. But although parts of the Stasi archive were destroyed after the fall of the Berlin Wall, the vast amounts which remained revealed sorrows and tragedies of extraordinary proportions.

The Gauck Institute's material revealed that the twentieth directorate, or *Stasi-Hauptabteilung XX*, had maintained at least 220 agents at various levels in the country's churches, as well as an agent in the Vatican who provided 'exact details' of the 1978 conclave which elected John Paul II. Among many such examples, the directorate had kept watch in West Germany on the future Pope Benedict XVI, Fr Joseph Ratzinger, running an agent codenamed 'Birke' to monitor him from April 1974 when he visited the German Democratic Republic to lecture on 'problems of modern theology.' The extensive card file had watched how Ratzinger's influence grew in Rome, describing him after his June 1977 elevation to the cardinalate as 'the most decided opponent of communism in the Vatican.' One informer, 'IMV Georg,' had correctly forecast that he would be appointed prefect of the Congregation for the Doctrine of the Faith a full two years before the event occurred in November 1981. 'Ratzinger is currently, after the Pope and Secretary of State Casaroli, the most influential politician and leading ideologue at the Vatican,' another Stasi spy wrote in the 1980s. 'As secretary of the Faith Congregation, he can be more effective than the Pope himself in increasingly influencing the anti-communist alignment of the Catholic Church, especially in Latin America.'[20]

The Stasi's infiltration of East Germany's Evangelical *Landeskirche* had been more extensive still. Wera Wollenberger, a former Party member and daughter of a Stasi officer, had become a Christian in 1981, obtaining a theology degree and co-founding a dissident 'Church from Below.' She had two sons with her Danish-born husband, the mathematician and poet Knud Wollenberger, only to discover in 1992 that he had filed intimate reports on her as a Stasi informer throughout their marriage, containing information which could have sent his wife to prison many times.[21]

Disputes over the use of secret police archives in the screening, or 'lustration,' of clergy were destined to be acerbic throughout Eastern Europe. Some Catholic bishops had made efforts to vet their priests after the collapse of communist rule and regretted acts of collaboration in statements at the time of the Millennium. Most were aware, however, that they lacked procedures for handling accusations, and could face embarrassing exposures as the files became available to researchers.

In Lithuania, where three-quarters of all Catholic priests had signed petitions protesting Soviet human rights abuses, the Bishops Conference urged priests who had collaborated to come forward in February 2000. In Russia, however, the secretary-general of the Bishops Conference, Fr Igor Kovalevsky, insisted the collaboration issue had not been raised at all, since the Catholic Church had only 225 parishes and most of its 270 priests had come from abroad. There was no legal basis for screening priests anyway, Fr Kovalevsky pointed out; nor were there church procedures for dealing with collaboration. 'The Catholic Church lived for eight decades under a totalitarian regime, which was severely atheist and deeply hostile, so lustration and penance aren't necessary,' the priest insisted. 'A person can be against a particular government, but he must be patriotic towards his country, especially in the case of clergy.'[22]

Further west in Slovakia, several dozen priests were named on lists of former agents released by government officials in 2005, including Archbishop Ján Sokol of Trnava-Bratislava and the retired Greek Catholic bishop of Prešov, Ján Hirka, whose codenames were given as 'Svietopelk' and 'Vladimir.' Here too, the Bishops Conference asked forgiveness from those harmed by clergy collaborators, assuring them that the Church would require an 'explanation and atonement' from those involved. When it came to apportioning guilt, however, the bishops insisted the degrees of collaboration should be taken into account. Some priests had 'consciously and willingly' helped the secret police. Others had been unaware that they were being used.[23]

In the neighbouring Czech Republic, where one in ten Catholic priests were believed to have acted as informers, the Bishops Conference insisted it had vetted all clergy within two years of the Velvet Revolution and reluctantly accepted the resignation of its secretary-general, Mgr Karel Simandl, when his name appeared on an Interior Ministry list of StB collaborators. Other church leaders were subsequently named as informers by local newspapers, however, including the Bishops Conference president, Archbishop Jan Graubner of Olomouc. Appeals were made for a judicious, contextual approach to the issue, which would take account of conditions at the time, levels of police pressure and the motives for collaboration. Adamant denials were issued as well, such as by Bishop František Lobkovic of Ostrava-Opava, who rejected a report in the *Mladá Fronta Dnes* daily that he had collaborated, using the codename 'Pilzniak.'

In 2007, the Czech Bishops Conference demanded that secret police material should not be 'used to settle personal accounts.' The Church had already summoned priests and lay Catholics to penance, it objected. 'Every bishop faced persecution from the communist rulers, and several of today's church leaders paid for their faithfulness with imprisonment,' the Conference recalled in a statement. 'It is striking that society tolerates the fact that the inheritors of the persecution era are sitting in parliament right up to today as Communist Party members, without any scruple or objection from the public... No one should condemn a priest when he does not know how his name ended up in the StB material, and when the documentation shows he did not sign anything or inform on anyone.'[24]

In Hungary, the issue of clergy informers was also debated in the early 1990s by the Bishops Conference after the dissolution of the communist-backed Opus Pacis priests' peace movement. A research foundation was set up; and in 2006, church leaders asked forgiveness after a list of clergy-agents was published on the Internet. They included the Church's now-retired Primate, Cardinal Paskai, who was said by the *Élet és Irodalom* daily to have used the codename 'Tanar,' and to have risen in 1973 to the rank of 'secret agent.' Paskai was urged to confess his regime links by the veteran dissenter Fr Bulányi, who had been rehabilitated by his church superiors in 1997 after signing a 12-point profession of faith. The cardinal could help 'cleanse Hungarian public life,' Bulányi argued, by conceding that he and others had 'danced to the tune of the Party-state.'[25]

In Romania, President Traian Băsescu called for the opening of the Securitate files on clergy after demands in 2007 for the public naming of church collaborators. Here too, however, Catholic leaders saw the demands as politically motivated and stonewalled the claims of infiltration, insisting the Church would handle the matter internally by itself.[26]

In Poland, where many Department Four records had been shredded in 1989, Catholic priests had also been screened to identify those compromised by collaboration. It was in Poland, however, that the disputes were destined to be most acerbic. The end of one-party rule had been achieved by negotiation here; so there had been no clean break with the past, nor any systematic clear-out of communist-era officials. Stories quickly spread of priests who had informed for the regime even while denouncing it from their pulpits. Around one in ten Catholic clergy were estimated by the National Remembrance Institute (IPN) to have acted as SB informers. Virtually all, however, had been approached at one time or another, especially those with particular needs and vulnerabilities, with highest recruitment rates recorded during the struggle with the Solidarity movement. Church leaders were urged to pre-empt exposure by researching the archives themselves, and conducting a full-scale screening, or *lustracja*, of their clergy before the issue was seized on by journalists and academics.

Yet clergy collaboration seemed marginal when set against the Church's celebrated role in helping restore democracy. Not surprisingly, Poland's Catholic bishops resisted calls for it to be aired publicly, and for the retiring or downgrading of suspect clergy. In a 2001 newspaper letter, Poland's former Interior Minister, General Kiszczak, revealed that, when Church-state relations were normalised in 1989, he had agreed to the destruction of documents 'presenting clergy in an unfavourable light.' Historians warned that priests could still face blackmail by former SB functionaries who had kept copies of the shredded files; and that May, Cardinal Glemp conceded that some priests had indeed been 'importuned or blackmailed.'[27] Yet church leaders were still far more interested in what the archives revealed about the glory of Catholic resistance than about the shame of collaboration.

Under a 1997 law, Polish public officials were required to state whether they had 'consciously and secretly collaborated' with the SB, at the risk of being labelled 'lustration liars.' Only a few dozen of the 20,000 involved had been subsequently accused of untruthfulness. But the judicial and administrative procedures remained poorly defined. With right-wing politicians clamouring for a more complete 'de-communisation,' it was clearly easier to impugn than to exonerate those accused.

Evidence suggested the SB had added the names of dissidents to its files to discredit them, and given codenames to casual contacts who had merely been approached without agreeing to collaborate. In early 2005, however, an enterprising journalist secretly copied the IPN's database and published the names of 240,000 alleged agents on the Internet. The 'Wildstein List' appeared without supporting documentation; and for a time, names could be added or deleted at will by readers. Despite this, many of those included found themselves ostracised, with their honesty and integrity cast in doubt.

The episode highlighted the deep unfairness surrounding lustration in Poland. It also helped explain the Church's guarded reactions. Some efforts were made to confront the problem locally. In the Gdańsk archdiocese, a commission was set up after claims by a local priest that he had found the names of nine prominent clergy on a list of agents active in '*Zorza II*,' the secret police operation to disrupt the Pope's June 1987 visit. All nine denied the collaboration claims during talks with Archbishop Tadeusz Gocłowski, while the commission reported that 90 percent of Department Four files on the visit had since been destroyed, making a final analysis uncertain. It confirmed, however, that the SB had recruited some 40 secret collaborators within Gocłowski's curia alone.[28]

Such revelations fuelled media appetites; and when Pope John Paul II died in April 2005, the issue exploded into the open with a series of top-level exposures. The Dominican Fr Hejmo was forced from office by IPN accusations that he had spied on the pontiff in Rome. Meanwhile, leading Polish Catholics again urged former church agents to declare themselves, after a senior Warsaw priest, Fr Michał Czajkowski, was accused by newspapers of informing on fellow-clergy, including the ill-fated Fr Popiełuszko. Visiting Poland in May 2006, the new Pope came to the Church's defence, recalling that any *confessio peccati*, or confession of sin, should be accompanied by a *confessio laudis*, or confession of merit. 'We believe that the Church is holy, but that there are sinners among her members,' Benedict XVI reminded clergy in Warsaw's St John the Baptist cathedral. 'Yet we must guard against the arrogant claim of setting ourselves up to judge earlier generations, who lived in different times and different circumstances. Humble sincerity is needed not to deny the sins of the past, and at the same time not to indulge in facile accusations in the absence of real evidence or without regard for the different preconceptions of the time.'[29]

Shortly after the Pope's departure, however, the friend of John Paul II from his seminary years, Fr Maliński, was named by Kraków's Catholic *Tygodnik Powszechny* weekly as the shadowy 'Delta' in Cardinal Wojtyła's household. Maliński denied the claim, insisting that he had only met SB members in an effort to 'convert them;' but editors of the *Tygodnik* were adamant that they had long known of the evidence against the 83-year-old priest. The weekly was said to have had at least nine communist agents on its own staff. Its sister-publication in Warsaw, *Więź*, had also been infiltrated via the local Catholic Intelligentsia Club.

Poland's Bishops Conference warned that it would vigorously oppose any form of *lustracja* which only drew on the SB files. 'These documents were prepared by secret services hostile to the Church and movements for independence, whose agents still remain unpunished while their victims are subject to public accusation,' the bishops noted in June 2006. 'There can be no proper lustration without first uncovering the SB's structures and methods of activity.'[30]

That August, the bishops went further with a full-blown exposition. The decisive majority of priests had proved 'worthy servants of Christ,' the document insisted, in some cases paying with their lives. Those who had acted as informers would be asked to apologise and make amends, while those 'lacking the courage to admit their sins' would face canonical sanctions. But the Church would emphasise conversion and penance, rather than condemnations. 'The truth about sin should lead every Christian to a personal admission of guilt,' the bishops concluded. 'But there is no place in the Church for revenge, retribution and humiliation, even in the case of sinful people. The Church of Christ is a community of reconciliation, forgiveness and love.'[31]

Accusations of a cover-up persisted. In October 2006, Poland's Jesuit provincial banished two of his clergy to secluded monasteries after they published the codenames and positions of five top-level informers within their order. Meanwhile, a former dissident chaplain at Kraków's Nowa Huta steelworks, Fr Tadeusz Isakowicz-Zaleski, was banned from speaking to the media by his archbishop after uncovering the identities of 130 clergy agents while researching a book.

There was worse to come. In January 2007, the man appointed to succeed the retiring Cardinal Glemp as Archbishop of Warsaw, Mgr Stanisław Wielgus, was named as an informer by two separate investigating commissions. Wielgus indignantly denied the accusations, but finally admitted meeting with SB agents from the 1960s onwards and signing a collaboration pledge in 1978 during a 'moment of weakness.' He defended his actions, however, as intended 'for the good of the Church,' and finally resigned under Vatican pressure only when his consecration Mass had already begun in Warsaw's cathedral.[32]

A Central Church Commission, appointed by the Polish Bishops Conference, disclosed that up to 20 still-serving bishops had been registered as SB contacts or co-operators. But no proof had been found of 'deliberate and willing collaboration,' the Commission insisted; so their names would not be published. Most of Poland's 44 Catholic dioceses later set up their own commissions to check the SB archives. But supporters of *lustracja* urged more forthright action. The Church had already had years to verify its clergy, they complained. If it failed to be open about its past, public trust would be undermined. Had not St Peter himself denied Christ in his time of weakness, and still regained authority and honour?

Evidence from the files suggested Catholic nuns had withstood SB pressure more robustly than male clergy: throughout the 1980s, no more than 30 of Poland's 27,000 religious sisters had ever been recruited. Church historians attributed the nuns' resilience to their tighter rules and traditions of obedience. Efforts to force them to place bugs in presbyteries had usually failed, they pointed out. So had attempts to make them accuse priests of sexual harassment. When nuns had met with regime officials to obtain passports or other documents, they had reported any approach to their superiors, thus ruling themselves out as candidates for collaboration.

In the Church as a whole, however, the scandal dragged on. In January 2009, a Warsaw archdiocese commission disclosed that the Vatican's long-serving Polish nuncio, Archbishop Józef Kowalczyk, had also come into the SB's 'orbit of interest,' receiving the codename 'Cappino' while heading the Polish section of the Vatican's Secretariat of State in the 1970s. An SB report for

1984–6 had described Kowalczyk as a 'weak source,' while a Polish intelligence chief had admitted his registration as an informer was a mistake. But the SB had been interested in other Polish staffers at the Vatican as well, the report confirmed. The nuncio's own file had been destroyed two years after the collapse of communist rule, making a full record impossible.[33]

Two months after the claims against Kowalczyk, the Vatican issued a ruling of its own, noting that it had found 'no basis' for accusing any still-serving Polish bishops of 'committed and willing collaboration.' The matter was now closed, the bishops duly responded. 'Although not obliged to do so, we have faced up courageously to the communist past,' their statement declared. 'We are convinced the faithful will not succumb to attempts to undermine the moral authority of the Church and its pastors, but will pray for the Church and build it up with their loyalty.' This too was criticised by some Polish commentators, who objected that the Vatican had not been shown key documents and had based its ruling on material selected by the bishops themselves.[34] The issue of clergy collaboration was, in the end, left hanging.

Eastern Europe's Orthodox churches had also been struck by collaboration claims. Prior KGB approval was widely held to have been a precondition for all senior Russian Orthodox appointments down to that the Estonian-born Patriarch Aleksi II in 1990. In Romania, where Patriarch Teoctist was re-elected after briefly resigning in the wake of the Winter Revolution, a State Commission for Studying Securitate Archives named three Orthodox archbishops as former agents in autumn 2007. They included Archbishop Pimen Zainea of Bucovina, who had used the code-names 'Sidorovici' and 'Petru'. Six other Orthodox hierarchs were investigated at the same time. In neighbouring Bulgaria, the Orthodox church's Holy Synod requested forgiveness in January 2012 from the ageing Patriarch Maxim, when eleven of its 15 members were named as former agents by a state commission. Here too, published Communist Party documents revealed the brutality with which the regime had sought to emasculate the churches as social and cultural forces.

In January 2009, the head of Poland's minority Orthodox church, Metropolitan Sawa, admitted that he too had acted as an SB informer, while opposing Solidarity and backing the 1981 imposition of martial law. 'Our attitude to the government reflected our church's hard situation, as well as a certain fear,' the metropolitan persisted in his own defence. 'It was necessary to make compromises to save the church.' In April of the same year, a commission of Poland's small Evangelical Augsburg, or Lutheran, church confirmed 'the secret and knowing co-operation' of its presiding bishop, Janusz Jagucki. Six months later, Jagucki resigned and returned to private life.[35]

The question of how to deal with former collaborators had also perplexed the Early Church, which had been replete with its own *lapsi* and *traditores*. In his famous correspondence with the Emperor Trajan, Pliny had been warned not to rely on 'anonymously posted accusations.' But Eusebius had written of Christians 'in state employment' being dragged forward, 'white-faced and trembling,' and forced to deny their beliefs, while others had proved 'unbending, blessed pillars of the Lord.' It had been agreed, the historian noted, that those who had failed the test 'should be treated and cured with the medicine of repentance.' But Cyprian of Carthage had had trouble both with Christians who had suffered real persecution and with the many *stantes* who had kept a low profile and avoided difficult choices.[36]

For some East Europeans, however, the failure to confront the past merely proved that, beyond the surface of events, there had been no real change. The state was now officially liberal rather than communist. But it was still interfering in the lives of citizens and discriminating against true Christians. Those who had suffered imprisonment or exile could claim a degree of moral purity. Those who had not would remain, like the Catholics of

Elizabethan England, under suspicion. Apocalyptic images of good and evil were used to vilify those dissenting from church teaching, who were said to be on the same side as the former persecutors. From such a perspective, the Church had always been under attack—and always would be.

Similar claims had been made in the days of Constantine by those who also doubted the genuineness of the 'Great Deliverance,' and refused, like the Donatists, to submit to the authority of morally compromised bishops enjoying the state's favour. For such people, the age of the martyrs continued. There could be no compromise. Eusebius had lamented how 'increasing freedom transformed our character to arrogance and sloth; we began envying and abusing each other, cutting our own throats, as occasion offered, with weapons of sharp-edged words.'[37] Something not dissimilar seemed to have occurred in the Church after communism. This time, however, there was no powerful St Augustine to highlight the need for realism.

There were, in reality, plenty of new church leaders who were not compromised at all. In Lithuania, the long-exiled Bishops Sladkevičius and Steponavičius had led the Church into a new era of independence and democracy, while in neighbouring Belarus, a former Siberian deportee, Kazimierz Świątek, who had survived an NKVD death sentence and ministered secretly for more than three decades, was named head of a refounded archdiocese of Minsk-Mogilev. Former Christian dissidents assumed leadership roles in the Czech Church, where Fr Malý, the once-jailed Charter 77 signatory, became an auxiliary bishop, and Fr Duka, the secret Dominican provincial who had worked as a car plant draughtsman, rose to become Cardinal-Archbishop of Prague. In Slovakia, the Jesuit Fr Korec, secretly consecrated at just 27, also became a cardinal as Bishop of Nitra. In Romania, the Winter Revolution hero, László Tőkés, now a Calvinist bishop, became vice-president of the European Parliament.

The atmosphere of malaise in Eastern Europe nevertheless contributed to a decline in religious practices, which set in after an initial period of revival. Lithuania's Catholic bishops complained of unsympathetic government attitudes on contentious issues such as religious education and abortion, while church attendance dwindled and once-flourishing Catholic parishes ran short of priests. Throughout the former Soviet Union, dioceses and religious orders were still demanding the restitution of their properties two decades after the regime's collapse. The religious breakdowns traditionally cited for the region had born little relation to reality by 1989. Within a few years, with barely two percent of eastern Germans even baptised and church membership plummeting in the Czech Republic, the old mantra of a 'spiritual East' and 'materialist West' had clearly fallen apart.

Even in devoutly Catholic Poland, public trust and respect for the Church fluctuated sharply, as disputes intensified over its reborn wealth and influence. Poland's bishops deplored the criticisms directed at them from former Solidarity union leaders, from whom they had expected loyalty and support. Meanwhile, vocations began to fall after peaking in the stormy 1980s, dwindling to crisis proportions in the case of female orders. The Church blamed secularisation, demographic trends and a hostile social and cultural environment, although it was clear that endless disputes and controversies had played their part as well. As church attendance began to dip after the Millennium, especially among the young and better educated, attempts were made to harness the prestige of martyrs such as Fr Popiełuszko against the Church's critics, much as the confessors and witnesses of the Early Church had been used to score points in the days of Eusebius.

Pope John Paul II's hopes that shared communist-era sufferings would be a motor for closer ecumenical relations were not fulfilled either. In a May 1995 encyclical, *Ut Unum Sint*, he looked forward to a 'full communion' with Orthodox Christians and reaffirmed his belief that Europe's joint patrons, Sts Benedict, Cyril and Methodius, could stand as figureheads for inter-church dialogue.[38] But the approaches initiated by Borovoi and Kotliarov at Vatican II had yielded little. Orthodox leaders accused Catholics of proselytising in traditionally Orthodox territories, and of allowing revived Greek Catholic churches in Ukraine, Romania and elsewhere to challenge Orthodox jurisdiction. Like their Catholic counterparts, the Orthodox hierarchies accepted democracy. As the traditional closeness of throne and altar revived, however, particularly in Russia, their capacity for ties with Catholics and Protestants diminished. Nationalist groups throughout the Orthodox world looked to the church to validate their struggle, a tendency which fuelled hostility between Orthodox Serbs and Catholic Croats during the wars which followed the break-up of Yugoslavia. Meanwhile, the reborn mythology of an 'Orthodox Slavic brotherhood' restricted the independence of local church leaders, and brought Russia's Orthodox hierarchs close to endorsing the Kremlin's military campaigns in Chechnya, Georgia and Ukraine.

The Pope made some grand gestures. During his 1991 Polish pilgrimage, he became the first pontiff to pray in an Orthodox cathedral. In 1998, he became the first to visit a predominantly Orthodox country, Romania, following this up with pilgrimages to traditionally Orthodox Georgia, Ukraine, Greece and Bulgaria. His hopes of visiting Russia, however, were dashed by the Moscow Patriarchate's insistence that all significant inter-church grievances should first be settled.

In 1997, a new Freedom of Conscience Law recognised Christianity, Islam, Buddhism and Judaism as 'traditional faiths' in Russia, but restricted the freedom of Catholics and other non-Orthodox confessions. The Vatican and Moscow Patriarchate set up a working group to tackle mutual disputes, and there was talk of a meeting between the Pope and Patriarch Aleksi. In 2002, however, the war of words erupted again, when the Pope upgraded his Church's four apostolic administrations in Russia, created in 1991, to non-territorial dioceses.

Catholic-Orthodox ties were said to have improved during the 2005–2013 pontificate of the German Benedict XVI, helped by an expressed readiness to work together in defending traditional

Christian values in Europe. An international commission of theologians, at work intermittently since 1979, even drew up a 'road map' to unity in 2007, incorporating key issues such as communion, conciliarity and Papal primacy. But local disputes continued. In 2008, plans were announced by the largest of Ukraine's three rival Orthodox churches for the canonisation of Gabriel Kostelnyk, the Ukrainian Catholic priest who had switched to Orthodoxy and helped liquidate his Church at the Soviet-backed 1946 synod. Many Ukrainians saw the praise for Kostelnyk, who had been proclaimed a martyr after his murder outside Lviv's Transfiguration cathedral, as an Orthodox provocation, and deplored the implication that the notorious synod had been free and canonical.[39]

At times, relations were tense between Catholics themselves—such as over the presence of Polish priests in the former Soviet Union, competing national jurisdictions in Hungary and Slovakia, and the share-out of churches between Greek and Latin Catholics in Ukraine. Meanwhile, some communist-era phenomena continued to attract controversy. The village of Medjugorje in Bosnia-Herzegovina, where the Virgin Mary was said to have appeared to local teenagers in 1981, had attracted over 30 million visitors by the late 1990s. Promoted as a pilgrimage centre by the Franciscans, it now contained hotels and tourist centres, and had been largely untouched by the 1992–5 war. It had still not been officially recognised, however, by the Church. In 2004, its much-harassed parish priest, Fr Jozo Zovko, who had backed the visionaries from the beginning, was ordered to stop ministering; and in 2009, another Franciscan, Fr Tomislav Vlašić, was defrocked for disobedience and false teaching. Cardinal Vinko Puljić of Sarajevo urged Catholics to comply with a declaration by the then Yugoslavia's Bishops Conference that 'nothing supernatural could be confirmed' at Medjugorje, pending the findings of an investigative commission of bishops and theologians.[40]

New conditions posed a challenge to those hoping to honour the memory of communism's many martyrs. Visiting Lithuania, Latvia and Estonia in 1993, the Pope had urged the Church not to 'limit itself' to recalling past persecutions. Visiting war-torn Croatia a year later, he had called on all national groups to 'forgive and ask forgiveness,' as Poland's bishops had done with their German neighbours back in 1965. In the run-up to the Millennium, John Paul II compared the new martyrs to the 'heritage of sanctity which marked the first Christian generations,' and urged local churches to gather the relevant documentation.'[41] But Christians were also warned not to exaggerate the extent of the repressions, as their Early Church forerunners had often done, and to be conciliatory towards the new post-communist democratic states.

Communism's cost in human lives had been established with reasonable certainty, thanks to detailed studies such as the *Black Book of Communism,* published in French and other language editions in 1997. The Soviet campaign to exterminate the 'kulaks' had cost 6.5 million lives, with the 'terror famines' of the early 1930s leaving another eight million dead. Seven million more had been shot in the years after 1935, while a high proportion of the 12 million detained in 1938 had died in incarceration. Once figures were added for the rest of Eastern Europe, communism's peacetime death-toll could be conservatively estimated at 25 million. When China, Korea and other countries were included, the probable total soared to 95 million.[42]

When it came to Christian heroism and self-sacrifice, the work of documentation had been slow. In the 1990s, a Russian state commission confirmed that tens of thousands of Orthodox priests, monks and nuns had been killed in the first two decades of Soviet rule, with 45,000 Orthodox churches left in ruins, leaving 6376 clergy registered in 1939, compared to a pre-revolution total of 113,000. Most clergy had been shot or hanged; but the commission detailed how many were also beaten and tortured, drowned in ditches, even crucified on church doors by communist death squads. Tens of thousands of Muslims, Buddhists, Jews and non-Orthodox Christians had been similarly butchered.[43]

As for the fate of Catholics, no systematic study was undertaken until the late 1990s, when experts such as Roman Dzwonkowski and Irina Osipova, a researcher with Russia's Memorial organisation, revealed the extent of the repressions. Of the 1994 Catholics whose fates were known and documented, 422 priests were found to have been executed, murdered or tortured to death, with at least 120 dying in Stalin's 1937–8 Great Purge alone. A total of 962 Catholic monks, nuns and laypeople had also been killed for faith-related reasons, while all but two of the Church's 1240 places of worship had been forcibly turned into shops, warehouses, farm buildings and public toilets. Osipova's pioneering study, *In Your Wounds Hide Me,* carried interrogation and trial records from as far afield as Irkutsk, Archangel and Vorkuta.[44]

Far more attention was still being paid to the victims of Nazi occupation. During a pilgrimage to Poland in 1999, John Paul II beatified 108 Catholic wartime martyrs, including 15 priests and nuns who died at Auschwitz alongside Sts Maksymilian Kolbe and Edith Stein (1891–1942). Stein was proclaimed a new patron of Europe the same year. Another Auschwitz martyr, the Orthodox Gregory Peradze, doused in petrol and burned alive in December 1942, had been canonised by his native Georgian church, while 44 Catholic martyrs from the Dachau concentration camp, near Munich, had also been beatified. The Polish Church alone was seeking similar recognition for some 200 other Nazi victims.

Yet the work of the researchers continued. So did the task of uncovering the dead. Dozens of mass graves had been opened up in Russia, such as at Sandormoch, north of the now renamed St Petersburg, where the skeletons of 11,000 prisoners from Solovki, shot there in 1937, were strewn over a two-acre site. They included four Russian Orthodox archbishops, as well as Georgia's Byzantine Catholic exarch, Bishop Shio Batmalashvili, and the

Catholic converts, Kamilla Krushelnitskaya and Anna Brilliantova. At least 30 Catholic priests were also found at Sandormoch, all shot through the back of the head during a single autumn week. An Orthodox chapel and Catholic cross were later set up at the site.[45]

The unmarked burial places of Poland's post-War *żołnierzy wyklęte*, or doomed soldiers, had also been traced and excavated. So had Katyn Forest and other sites of the NKVD's infamous 1940 massacre of Polish officers at Miednoye in Russia, and at Kharkov and Bykivnia in Ukraine. Gorbachev had finally admitted Soviet responsibility for the atrocity in 1990, enabling President Yeltsin to visit the Katyn memorial in Warsaw's Powązki cemetery three years later. Yet Moscow had continued to impede investigations. Russia's victory in the Great Patriotic War was central to the national pride reborn under Yeltsin's successor, Vladimir Putin; so the country was in no mood to beat its breast for past misdeeds. Some of the 2000 NKVD agents involved in the Katyn killings were still alive in the 1990s, often bearing medals for past services. If the Katyn massacre were recognised as genocide, it could trigger an avalanche of compensation claims.

In 2005–6, Russia's military prosecutor, Aleksander Savenkov, duly declared the Katyn massacre a military crime, for which for the 50-year term of limitations had now expired, and ruled the dead ineligible for exoneration or rehabilitation. Several Russian newspapers, including the government's own *Rossiskaya Gazeta*, even revoked Gorbachev's admission and argued that the Nazis might have perpetrated the killings after all. Although Poland itself was home to 732 military cemeteries for Red Army soldiers, all maintained by the Polish state, it had taken till 1995 to negotiate the creation of a single military cemetery at Katyn, when a foundation stone was blessed by Pope John Paul II and laid by Solidarity's Lech Wałęsa, now Polish president. At least a million Poles could claim a link with the massacre through lost relatives; but many remained unable to visit their burial places. In 2005, when one of few massacre survivors, Mgr Zdzisław Peszkowski, petitioned the UN and Western governments to have 5 March, the day of Stalin's mass execution order, declared Katyn Day, the priest received no reply. When he asked the European Parliament to observe a minute's silence, the request was turned down.

Before visiting Poland in September 2009 for the seventieth anniversary of the start of the Second World War, Putin published a 'Letter to Poles,' setting out Russia's position on Katyn and other 'blank spots.' Poland's Catholic Church set up a joint commission with Russian Orthodox leaders to discuss reconciliation; and in July 2012, an Orthodox chapel was dedicated at Katyn by Patriarch Kirill I, along with a special Catholic altar. Some 16,000 Russian citizens had also been killed at various times in Katyn Forest, Kirill pointed out, including an Orthodox metropolitan, Serafin of Smolensk. It was just one of many 'Russian Golgothas.'[46]

By then, Katyn had become notorious all over again, when a Russian-made Tupolev TU-154 plane crashed while attempting to land at nearby Smolensk on 10 April 2010 for anniversary commemorations, killing President Lech Kaczyński and 95 Polish public figures. Russian investigators blamed the accident on errors by the Polish pilots. But many Poles remained suspicious about the disaster, which shocked and traumatised the country.

Secret burials and the destruction of the dead, a communist speciality, harked back to ancient hopes that this might prevent the resurrection of enemies—and to Sophocles' defiant heroine, Antigone, who disobeyed a royal order by burying her dead brother. Even the Romans had allowed their victims, for the most part, a fitting burial, while the early Christians had been unafraid to ask for the remains of their martyrs, just as Joseph of Arimathea had asked Pontius Pilate for the body of Christ. In his Fourth Century history, Eusebius had reflected on the 'power of martyrdom,' expressed in 'endurance and dauntless courage' and a 'nobility evident to all.' The 'greatest war' fought by the martyrs had been 'through the reality of their love,' he noted, so 'the Beast might be choked into bringing up alive those he thought he had swallowed.'[47]

In Stalin's Soviet Union, capital punishment had regained the everyday status it had enjoyed in the ancient world, when death had been imposed for the most trivial of crimes. The common people were the system's 'nuts and bolts,' so plentiful that their lives hardly mattered. But for the communities from which they came, the effect of executions was often devastating. The task now was to piece together the truth, seeing the martyrs as real people who had suffered and died in very real ways.

Over a thousand Soviet and East European Christians were included on a list of Twentieth Century martyrs compiled by a Vatican commission for Easter 2000. These were symbolic names only—the real numbers had been much higher. In Russia, a martyrology commission, launched by the Catholic Bishops Conference, gathered information on 13 candidates for beatification, including Anna Abrikosova, the Greek Catholic who died at Moscow's Butyrka prison in 1936, and Mgr Konstantin Budkievicz, the Catholic vicar-general shot in the Lubyanka at Easter 1923. The list featured two bishops, the Polish-born Antoni Malecki of Leningrad and the German Edward Profittlich of Estonia, as well as the student convert, Krushelnitskaya, whose executed remains lay somewhere at Sandormoch.

A church commission in Poland, established in November 2009, detailed the fate of over 600 witnesses to faith who had died at dozens of recorded places of execution, or at the hands of communist paramilitaries or during deportation to the east. The list featured 28 priests shot during the Soviet counter-invasion of Poland in 1945; a nun and eight laywomen murdered while resisting rape by Russian soldiers; and 24 army chaplains, including several killed in the Katyn massacre. It was later expanded to include other Christian martyrs, such as ten St Elizabeth order nuns also killed by Red Army troops while defending their chastity in the western Wrocław diocese in early 1945.

In September 2010, Germany's Bishops Conference published its own martyrology, *Zeugen für Christus* (Witnesses for Christ), with biographies of priests and bishops killed under communist rule, as well as 60 'martyrs of purity,' mostly from female religious orders. The cases of around 900 martyrs had been presented to the commission and the work had taken six years. It recalled how Catholic Church had never recognised the communist regime in the German Democratic Republic, and had routinely boycotted its institutions and rituals, leaving clergy and laity to be targeted for repression.

Romania's Interior Ministry had begun investigating the fate of priests in communist prisons and camps within months of the 1989 Winter Revolution. The information remained sketchy; and while some martyr stories could be retraced in detail, many others were already beyond reach. The names of some communist-era victims were later preserved on memorials at Romania's infamous prisons, while parishes and dioceses published material on their own local martyrs. In 2003, commissions from the country's churches drew up a 'National Christian Martyrology,' which included 150 Greek Catholics, 50 Latin Catholics, 120 Orthodox Christians and 20 Protestants. The criteria included a violent death, or death from malnutrition or torture, 'accepted in full awareness of the circumstances' through persecution resulting from 'hatred of faith and church.'[48] A governmental Institute for the Investigation of Communist Crimes, paralleling Poland's IPN, later began co-ordinating studies of the archives and collecting personal testimonies.

Such work remained difficult. Direct witnesses to early communist atrocities were fast dying out; and many martyrs had left, as Eusebius noted centuries earlier, only 'faint traces' and 'partial accounts.'[49] Few now remembered the *Holodomor*, or 'Great Famine' engineered by Stalin's regime to crush resistance to collectivisation, when Ukrainian children had starved to death in their thousands as grain mountains rotted in state warehouses. Few recalled the village purges in Russia's southern republics, when 'enemies of the people' could be denounced, tried, killed and buried in a single afternoon. Communist regimes had sought to write their perceived enemies out of history. So the documentation remained incomplete. There could be no final statistics.

Most of communism's martyrs had died in peacetime, furthermore, without the dramatic backdrop of war and occupation. The gap between formal law and practical policy had been a feature of communist rule; and many were killed for minor offences, or for no offences at all. There was often no paper chain of orders, arrest warrants and interrogation notes, nor any reliable record of personal circumstances and motivations. Few symbols of communist barbarism, meanwhile, could match Auschwitz and Dachau in the popular imagination. Unlike Nazism, which had targeted its enemies loudly and openly, communism had hidden its destructive face behind a veil of progress. Unlike Nazism, it had not been defeated. It had had time and space to evolve.

Communism still had no lack of apologists. Aspects of Stalin's rule were still being taught about positively in the schools of Russia, where the goulish remains of Lenin, the Soviet Union's founder, still lay with state honours in his Red Square mausoleum, overlooked by the fluorescent red stars still adorning the Kremlin's towers. Russia's Orthodox church, resplendent with new wealth and influence, backed demands for Lenin's reburial, along with other communist figureheads buried in the nearby Kremlin Wall, including Brezhnev, Andropov and Chernenko. In 2012, it called for his works to be banned for inciting 'hatred and extremism.' Such talk was vigorously opposed, however, by communist MPs in Russia's State Duma.[50]

After an initial period of openness, thanks to pressure from organisations like Memorial, it became harder for religious researchers to gain access to NKVD and KGB archives. Fears of exposure and prosecution played their part in the blocking of enquiries. In Ukraine, the Great Famine had been acknowledged by the ruling Communist Party only in 1990, in an act comparable to Gorbachev's recognition of the Katyn outrage. Ruled an act of genocide by a Ukrainian law of 2006, as well as by the US and two dozen other countries, it was registered as a crime against humanity by the European Parliament in 2008. Yet the vast human tragedy was still being called into question by Ukrainian government officials, some of whom still defiantly depicted it as a mere 'economic mistake.'[51]

Such attitudes critically impeded the search for justice. It was relatively easy to investigate the judicial record and rehabilitate the unjustly accused, as was done to all Catholic priests executed in the Soviet Union. Securing a reasonable sense of closure was much harder. After the 'Great Deliverance,' Eusebius had confidently quoted the prophet Isaiah: 'Lo, Our Lord dispenses justice and will dispense.' The enemies of God no longer existed, the historian enthused—'in fact they never did; for after bringing distress on other people and on themselves too, they paid to justice a penalty not to be laughed at, utterly ruining themselves, their friends and their families.'[52]

Then as now, there was a desire for revenge, of the kind promised in Deuteronomy by a God who 'takes vengeance on his adversaries' (Dt 32:43), or by Tertullian, who had imagined one-time kings 'groaning in the deepest darkness' and persecutors 'melting in the flames.'[53] Yet there was also a need for reconciliation. For some, the wisdom of Proverbs was still relevant: 'If your enemy is hungry, give him bread to eat; and if he is thirsty give him water to drink; for you will heap coals of fire on his head, and the Lord will reward you' (Pr 25:21–22). True retribution for those who had mocked the faith and victimised the faithful could be left to the Day of Judgment.

For others, however, justice had to be done in the here and now. In Poland, many former communist agents now lived on decent state pensions or had enriched themselves with lucrative businesses. A few elderly UB and SB veterans had been charged with torturing and killing; but there had been few convictions, since little could be proved. Meanwhile, not one of the Stalinist era's ill-trained hanging judges had ever been brought to court. In

March 2004, General Kiszczak received a four-year jail sentence for ordering ZOMO riot police to fire on striking miners at the Wujek and Manifest Lipcowy collieries in the first days of martial law, an outrage which left nine dead and dozens injured. It was his third trial since 1996; and the outcome was welcomed by the parish priest, Fr Bolczyk, who had ministered to grieving families. But Kiszczak's term was suspended under a subsequent amnesty, after he insisted he had acted on laws binding at the time. In June 2007, a dozen former ZOMO operatives were also given prison sentences for the massacre; and in July 2008, Kiszczak was declared 'involuntarily guilty' again. He was now in his 80s, however, and largely beyond the reach of judicial sanctions.

In October 2008, it was the turn of General Jaruzelski to go on trial, with six co-defendents, for his involvement of the Baltic port massacres of 1970 and the imposition of martial law. He was charged with 'committing a communist crime by leading a criminal organisation with military characteristics,' a reference to the Council for National Salvation which had co-ordinated the 1981 crackdown. Yet the 85-year-old general was ailing and infirm, so no sentence was passed, while many Poles wondered what purpose had been served by the spectacle. Jaruzelski had been Eastern Europe's only top communist boss to enjoy a peaceful retirement, preserving a measure of public respect, with his state and military honours intact. He had been conciliatory about the past, conceding that freedom and democracy corresponded to 'the natural needs of the human person,' and that communism had been a 'utopian idea out of step with the spirit of the times.'[54]

One episode the general could not reinterpret was the brutal murder of Fr Popiełuszko, which continued to cast long shadows over post-communist Poland. Although judicial investigations had continued, no charges had been made to stick. Two SB generals, Zenon Płatek and Władysław Ciastoń, had been acquitted of involvement in the killing in 1994; and although the acquittal was overturned two years later, Ciastoń was again cleared for lack of evidence in 2002. Poland's National Remembrance Institute later collected 90 volumes of documentation on the murder, including 66 volumes of police 'operational material' which had not been checked during the trial of Płatek and Ciastoń; and in November 2009, two other former SB agents were charged with planting weapons and leaflets in Fr Popiełuszko's Warsaw apartment. Even then, however, experts concurred that convictions would be difficult. Journalists investigating the killing had been intimidated and pressured to drop their enquiries; and in July 2008, the priest's own family disclosed that they had received anonymous warnings.[55]

Preoccupations with the judicial aspects of communist crimes suited former regime functionaries by diverting attention from the real nature of the one-party system. Communist rulers like General Jaruzelski bore responsibility for what had been done. But this would never be proved in a court of law, since it meant applying standards of legality and accountability where they had never existed. Even seeking such proof—a chain of orders and instructions—implicitly dignified the system. Polish prosecutors still hoped to bring charges against UB agents involved in the 1953 arrest of Cardinal Wyszyński, and against those responsible for harassing Catholic clergy in the 1970s and 1980s. Meanwhile, the 1989 murders of Fr Niedzielak, Fr Suchowolec and Fr Zych had been researched in detail, even identifying the SB agent suspected of delivering the fatal karate blow which killed Niedzielak. Yet hard evidence had not been secured.[56]

Similar legal problems had arisen elsewhere. Dozens of former StB agents had faced charges in the Czech Republic, thanks to evidence collected by a Parliamentary Office for Researching Communist Crimes. Here too, however, there had been few successful prosecutions. In Romania, it took till September 2013 to bring the first genocide charge, in this case against Alexandru Vişinescu, the 87-year-old former boss of Râmnicu Sărat prison, for beating and starving incarcerated intellectuals. In Lithuania, justice officials issued an arrest warrant in 2009 for Fr Juozas Bulka, a priest living in neighbouring Belarus, for helping track down and kill anti-communist partisans in the 1950s. Historians from Lithuania's official Genocide and Resistance Research Centre certified that Bulka had been recruited by the Soviet paramilitary MGB, under the codename 'Bimba,' while fighting with the *Lietuvos Laisvės Armija*, or Lithuanian Freedom Army, and been responsible for the deaths of 56 Lithuanians in eleven separate incidents. Having worked later in a Vilnius electricity factory, he had travelled to Poland's Włocławek diocese to be ordained in November 1987, and had gained renown as a priest for combating alcoholism. At his parish at Mosar, in Belarus, Bulka remained defiant, describing his victims as 'bandits' engaged in 'drunkenness, murder and debauchery.' He died in January 2010, before formal charges could be brought.[57]

Even without the consolations of justice, communism's martyrs were at least being fittingly commemorated. In March 2011, Poland's Catholic Church marked the first national Day of Doomed Soldiers, in memory of the 13,000 young people killed in gun battles or secretly executed while opposing communist rule in 1944–63. The honouring of the victims, who included dozens of Catholic priests, was combined with landscaping work at sites such as Warsaw's Powązki cemetery and Wrocław's Osobowicki Street cemetery, where dozens of young fighters had been dumped in unmarked graves after being shot or hanged in nearby prisons. A special Danuta Siedzikówna Prize was offered at schools in memory of the 17-year-old Gdańsk girl, 'Inka,' executed in August 1946 for helping anti-communist Home Army remnants.

Relics and mementos were being collected, as in centuries past, as things to see and touch which bridged the gap between the natural and the divine. Public monuments were being erected to formidable church leaders like Cardinals Wyszyński and Beran, while clergy were being awarded state honours for their courage and endurance under communism. Bishop Tokarczuk, who had defied regime pressure for three decades, received Poland's highest medal, the White Eagle, six years before his death in December 2012, sharing the honour with Cardinals Glemp and Gulbinowicz and former dissidents such as Tadeusz Mazowiecki and Jacek Kuroń.

In 2009, Poland's Polonia Restituta award was given posthumously to Fr Władysław Gurgacz, the Jesuit priest executed for his pastoral work with the *żołnierze wyklęte*, as well as to the Sister of Mercy, Zofia Łuszczkiewicz, who died of TB and cancer in 1957 after receiving three death sentences for her underground links.

In Russia, the first memorial to 'Catholics of all rites and nationalities' was installed in a mass cemetery at Levashovo, where 47,000 people had been shot by the NKVD in 1937–54. The St Petersburg authorities refused to allow exhumations and denied consent for Catholic victims to be listed by name. But this was progress at least. Orthodox churches and monasteries had been built at other massacre sites, including the melancholy Solovki islands and the Iskitim stone quarry on the River Irtysh, where a spring above the gully used for shooting prisoners was popularly said to work miracles. A church commemorating martyrs and confessors had been built at Kuropaty Park in Belarus, as well as at Moscow's Lubyanka, whose basements had once run with blood, and at the nearby killing field of Butovo, where more than 20,000 people, including hundreds of Orthodox priests and bishops, had been shot and buried between August 1937 and October 1938. Dozens of other new churches had been built in the Russian capital to replace the hundreds closed or destroyed under Soviet rule.

Not all commemorative efforts met with church approval. Plans were announced to bring tourists to the network of 130 labour camps in Vorkuta, north of the Arctic Circle, where some two million prisoners had laboured in frozen coalmines, leaving 200,000 dead, and to entertain them by 'shooting' them with coloured ink balls when they tried to escape. Similar ideas were hatched in Russia's Yakutia republic, where camp inmates had mined arsenic sulphide and built the 'Road of Bones' to Kolyma, many lying buried where they fell.[58]

Yet church leaders everywhere had also shown a readiness to forgive, as one-time communist bosses showed signs of repentance and even, in some cases, turned back to the faith. The Soviet Union's last foreign minister, Eduard Shevardnadze, had been baptised in 1992 as president of his native Georgia, while Alfonsas Brazauskas, Lithuania's last Communist Party leader, had become a practising Catholic. His one-time protector, Brezhnev, had also been baptised as a child, according to records recovered from the regional archive of his native Dniepropetrovsk. So had Brezhnev's reforming successor, Gorbachev, who had also shown a warm attitude to his one-time foe, the Pope, recounting to Italy's *La Stampa* the 'sense of the breath of the Holy Spirit' he had gained from John Paul II.

In October 2005, Gorbachev was made an archon, or noble, by the Orthodox Ecumenical Patriarchate. He denied converting to Christianity, however, and rejected media reports that he had prayed before the tomb of St Francis during a visit to Assisi. 'I was and remain an atheist,' the former communist told Russia's Interfax newsagency. 'But I think religion is important for society, and I've willingly visited churches, synagogues and mosques during my travels.'[59]

Gorbachev was not the only former Party boss to sing the Pope's praises. Poland's General Jaruzelski had paid tribute to John Paul II's 'patriotism and moral stature,' as well as to the 'great work' of the Polish Church in preserving national identity, and to the role of Poland's Catholic intellectuals in 'showing the way forward in the search for a consensus.' Although born into a devout Catholic family and educated at Marian order school, Jaruzelski had joined the communist movement and given up religion as a deportee to Siberia, even staying outside the church during his own mother's Catholic funeral. At his death in May 2014, however, he received Holy Communion from a Warsaw priest and a full Catholic funeral in the city's military cathedral, attended by Lech Wałesa and Poland's highest dignitaries.[60]

Other communist leaders had also undergone deathbed conversions. Yugoslavia's Tito had been cared for, at his own request, by Catholic nuns from Croatia, while Hungary's strongman, János Kádár, had asked to see a Catholic priest. A 2010 documentary film, 'The Last Word,' suggested Kádár had been deeply worried about the events of 1956 during his final Communist Party congress in 1989, and had come close to issuing an apology. His countrymen were less forgiving. Kádár's grave in Budapest's Kerepesi Cemetery was ransacked in May 2007 by suspected right-wing extremists. His skull was removed, along with an urn containing the ashes of his wife, Mária Tamáska. The words, 'Murderers and traitors may not rest in holy ground' were daubed on his tombstone.[61]

Despite all obstacles and impediments, the churches had remembered their own. The thousand victims of communist rule included among the Vatican's Twentieth Century martyrs were small in number compared to the many already recognised from the French and Mexican revolutions, and the thousands honoured from the Spanish Civil War. More than a dozen beatification ceremonies had been been conducted for victims of the bloody 1936–9 Spanish conflict, while the cases of hundreds more were under consideration. Republican sympathisers had accused the Church of inventing atrocity stories under Franco's dictatorship to rally popular devotions, and to suggest that the *generalissimo*'s brutal repression was divinely sanctioned. But the atrocities had been real enough. In October 2007 alone, 498 Spanish martyrs were declared blessed in Rome, mostly from religious orders such as the Dominicans, Franciscans, Salesians, Marists and Carmelites. In October 2013, another 522 were beatified, including three bishops and 82 priests.[62]

People like this had entrusted themselves to the Church's collective memory, discipline and judgement. Most had had no say when it came to the meaning and impact of their deaths, or to the narratives which took shape around them. They were at the mercy of later generations, who might or might not believe they had been chosen by God to send a message to the world. Pope John Paul II clearly believed they had been; and he had responded with a huge number of beatifications and canonisations. At the end of the second Millennium, the Pope recalled, the Church had once again 'become a church of martyrs'; and although many remained 'nameless, unknown soldiers' of 'God's great cause,' their witness should never be forgotten, since it revealed the vitality of Christian communities.[63]

This was not an argument for triumphalism. The Church should also remember 'all those times in history' when its members succumbed to intolerance and connived in 'grave forms of injustice and exclusion.'[64] New work was set in motion on dark episodes in church history, such as the Inquisition, the persecution of reformers and silence towards the Holocaust under Pius XII. In the meantime, the many martyrs of communist rule began to gain formal acknowledgement.

In November 1997, the Pope beatified Bishop Vilmos Apor, the brave Hungarian shot by a Soviet soldier at the door of his residence on Good Friday 1945, while protecting local women from rape. In March 1998, he beatified the Bulgarian Passionist, Bishop Eugen Bossilkov, executed and thrown in a Sofia prison pit in 1952 on charges of spying for the Vatican. Bossilkov was cleared posthumously of all charges in his homeland a year later, while other Catholic victims of Bulgaria's communist purges were exonerated under legal amendments in August 2010. The three Assumptionists executed with the bishop, Fr Chichkov, Fr Djidjov and Fr Vitchev, were also beatified in 2002.

In October 1998, it was the turn of Archbishop Stepinac, the wartime leader of the Croatian Church widely held to have been poisoned by Yugoslavia's communist regime after 14 years in jail and detention. Stepinac was declared blessed by John Paul II at the Catholic shrine of Marija Bistrica after a 20-year beatification process. Although cleared of crimes by the Croatian parliament in 1992, he remained controversial. A multi-media museum devoted to the cardinal, which opened in 2007 close to Zagreb cathedral, nevertheless contained testimonies from Serbian Orthodox and Jewish contemporaries who claimed to have enjoyed his protection. The anniversary of his death on 10 February 1960 was now marked nationwide as Stepinac Day. Another day, 25 August, was also set aside in Croatia as a national Day of Martyrs.

A fellow-Croatian, Fr Miroslav Bulešić (1920–1947), graduate of Rome's Gregorian University, was beatified as a martyr in September 2013, a full 66 years after being pinned to the floor of a parish presbytery at Lanisce and stabbed through the neck by communist militants. In June 2010, a lay Catholic from neighbouring Slovenia, Lojze Grozde (1923–1943), was also declared blessed for his heroic Christian loyalty under persecution. A noted poet and member of Catholic Action, Grozde was detained by communist gunmen after attending Mass at a local Cistercian monastery and accused of being a Nazi informer. The 19-year-old, from a poor peasant family, was carrying a Latin Missal and copy of Thomas à Kempis' *Imitation of Christ.* His tortured remains were found two years later in a forest near Mirna and reburied in the Catholic cemetery at Šentrupert na Dolenjskem, which rapidly became a place of pilgrimage.

Martyrs began to be honoured in Romania too. An ethnic Hungarian bishop, Bogdánffy Szilárd (1911–1953), had trained clergy secretly after the closure of Romania's Catholic seminaries, and been secretly consecrated in February 1949 by Romania's US-born nuncio, Archbishop O'Hara. Arrested by the Securitate, Szilárd was tortured in the notorious Jilava, Capul Midia and Sighetul Marmației prisons. His 12-year hard labour sentence for espionage and subversion was later overturned pending a retrial. But he died from his mistreatment and was declared blessed in November 2010 at his one-time Oradea see. The ethnic German

Bishop János Scheffler (1887–1952), from neighbouring Satu Mare, was similarly beatified in July 2011. Scheffler died after being doused in boiling water at Jilava, having smuggled a message to local Catholics, urging them to 'stay faithful unto martyrdom.' The location of his unmarked grave in the prison cemetery was recorded by an Orthodox priest and fellow-inmate.

In August 2013, it was the turn of Mgr Vladimir Ghika, the convert from Orthodoxy who had rejected advice to flee Romania after the communist seizure of power. Sentenced by a military court for high treason after refusing to break with Rome, Ghika survived more than 80 violent interrogations before dying emaciated at Jilava, where his grave was marked 'No. 807.' Because of the systematic erasing of records, long efforts had been needed to document the case of Ghika, whose body was reburied by his family in 1968 at Bucharest's Bellu Cemetery. Important testimonies had been gathered, however, from fellow-victims of persecution who were with him at Jilava in his final days. The priest's memoirs and writings were also closely examined, including a series of reflections penned in prison.

Similar labours were needed for the beatification of Bishop Anton Durcovici (1888–1951), which took place in the municipal stadium at Iași in May 2014. Born in Austria, Durcovici had gained degrees in canon law, philosophy and theology while studying in Rome, returning to Romania as a seminary teacher and parish administrator after his ordination in 1910. He too was consecrated by Archbishop O'Hara in April 1948, two years before the nuncio's expulsion, and arrested by the Securitate for refusing to erase references to Papal authority from a new regime-sponsored statute on the Church's activities. Held initially at Jilava, Durcovici was later transferred with other priests to Sighet, where he was tortured, stripped in winter weather and denied food and water. He died of malnutrition in December 1951 and was buried in an unmarked grave by prison officials, who attempted to erase all evidence of his incarceration. Witness accounts said the bishop received final absolution through his cell door from a fellow-priest, after asking other inmates to pray for him. They added that different dates had been given at the time for his death, because of his total isolation. But news of Durcovici's worsening condition had been leaked by a sympathetic warden.

The Hungarian Bishop Zoltán Meszlényi (1892–1951), who died of hunger at Kistarcsa after being locked in an isolation cell with open windows throughout the winter, was beatified in November 2009 in Budapest, 43 years after his remains were reburied in Esztergom cathedral. In October 2013, a lay Salesian, István Sándor (1914–1953), was also beatified as a martyr, half a century after being hanged for treason following a closed trial. Sándor had been briefly imprisoned by US forces after serving in Hungary's German-allied army. Rejecting the chance to flee abroad, he secretly ministered to young people after the communist takeover, working under a false name at a chemicals factory until his arrest by the AVO secret police. His executed remains were never found.[65]

Eastern Europe's many Greek Catholic martyrs were also being recognised by the Church. Visiting Ukraine in 2001, Pope John Paul II beatified 27 of them, including Fr Leonid Fedorov, the leader of Russia's small Greek Catholic Church who died in Stalin's great purge, and Archimandrite Klemens Sheptycki, who perished in Vladimir prison during an eight year hard labour term. There were nine bishops on the Pope's list, including the youthful Teodor Romzha, poisoned in hospital after his collision with a Soviet police bus in 1947, and Gregorz Khomyshyn and Jozafat Kocylovsky, who both died at a Kiev prison the same year during Ukraine's brutal post-War Soviet reoccupation.

Three Ukrainian nuns were included too: Tarsykia Matskiv, a Sister Servant of Mary Immaculate, shot by a Russian soldier when she answered her convent door in July 1944; and Laurentia Herasymiv and Olympia Bida, both Sisters of St Joseph, who died at Tomsk in Siberia. The 14 priests included the Redemptorist Fr Zenon Kovalyk, who was crucified on a wall of Lviv's Bryhidky prison, and Fr Roman Lysko, who was sealed up alive in another prison wall after going mad under torture. Fr Severan Baranyk, the Basilian monastery prior, who was found dead with cross-shaped knife slashes across his chest after being arrested by the NKVD, was also on the list, as well as a fellow-Basilian, Fr Yakym Senkivsky, holder of a theology doctorate from Austria, who was boiled to death in a prison cauldron. There was also a Greek Catholic layman, Volodymyr Pryjma, a parish choir master from Stradch, who was murdered by NKVD agents in a forest while taking Communion to a sick neighbour. Ukraine's Latin Church was seeking beatification of the eight Dominicans shot by the NKVD at their monastery in Czortkov in 1941, whose remains had been reburied in their order's vault in 1991.[66]

In neighbouring Slovakia, the ill-fated Bishop Gojdič was declared blessed in October 1991 with a martyred colleague, Fr Metod Dominik Trčka (1886–1959), who died in a Leopoldov prison isolation cell after being caught singing Christmas carols. The preservation of Gojdič's memory owed much to his friend and fellow-prisoner, Fr Marian Potaš, a one-time Basilian provincial, who secretly paid a Leopoldov worker to preserve the bishop's unmarked grave and personally arranged his exhumation and reburial in Prešov cathedral during the 1968 Prague Spring. Potaš had collected over a hundred testimonies about Gojdič, storing letters and papers in a neighbour's attic to avoid their seizure by Czechoslovakia's StB.

In January 2008, Gojdič was posthumously awarded a 'Righteous among Nations' medal by Israel for saving Jewish lives under the wartime rule of Mgr Tiso and sending information to Rome about deportations to concentration camps. 'There was no problem with his beatification—everyone agreed he was a saint, while even former communists admitted his imprisonment was a mistake. But we had to approach the work carefully, collecting and checking all the documentation,' Fr Potaš recalled later, in words which could be applied to many martyrdom cases. 'Gojdič had his weaknesses and wasn't a great philosopher. But he knew how to forgive those who harmed him, and about the need for tolerance and sensitivity to the needs of others. He also knew what would happen once communism was installed here, and took steps to advise people how they should conduct themselves. This was the main reason why he was jailed. But he had to die for a simpler reason—he was a holy person of great charisma, with a sound heart and deep social conscience.'[67]

One of the dozens of Slovak nuns jailed on treason and anti-state charges was beatified as well: the Holy Cross order's Sister Zdenka Schelingová, who died of cancer in 1955 after being tortured and denied sacraments during a 12-year sentence. Schelingová was declared blessed by the Pope in September 2003 with the Greek Catholic Bishop Vasil Hopko, another prison veteran, who died in July 1976 after living out his final years under the watchful eyes of the StB.

Romania's Greek Catholics also had numerous candidates for recognition as martyrs, headed by Cardinal Iuliu Hossu, who died under house arrest at Căldăruşani monastery. Of his six fellow-bishops, three—Valeriu Traian Frenţiu, Ioan Suciu and Tit Liviu Chinezu—also lay buried alongside Bishop Durcovici in unmarked graves outside Sighet prison. The others were Vasile Afteniu of Bucharest, shot in Bucharest's Interior Ministry basement; Alexandru Rusu of Maramureş, killed in Gherla prison; and Ioan Bălan of Lugoj, who also died confined, like Hossu, at an Orthodox monastery.

Further north in Lithuania, beatification processes were underway for Vincentas Borisevičius, the bishop shot in 1947 for his links with the Forest Brethren, as well as for Archbishop Mečislovas Reinys of Vilnius, who died at Vladimir prison in 1953, and Archbishop Teofilius Matulionis of Kaišiadorys, who spent three decades in Solovki. The cases of all three had been documented by an official Genocide and Resistance Research Centre, set up in 1997. So had that of another beatification candidate, the lay theologian Petras Paulaitis, who died after a KGB interrogation in

1986, aged 81, shortly after being released from 35 years in prison, and was buried in an unmarked grave at Kretinga.

Some communist-era figures honoured by the Church were relatively unknown. When the first martyr was beatified in Poland in June 2005, the choice fell on Fr Władysław Findysz, the parish rector arrested in November 1963 for 'inciting hatred between believers and non-believers,' who died in his presbytery after mistreatment in Krakow's notorious Montelupich Prison. While few Poles had heard of Findysz, they had certainly heard of Fr Popiełuszko, the revered Solidarity pastor, whose June 2010 beatification Mass in Warsaw's Piłsudski Square was attended by 100,000 people and relayed live on national TV. At least 80 city streets and squares had already been renamed after the priest in his homeland, along with 18,000 schools, charities and youth groups, while hundreds of statues and memorial tablets had also been unveiled in his honour. A crypt museum at St Stanisław Kostka's church, where he lay buried with a rosary sent by the Pope, included the battered cassock he wore on the night of his death in October 1984 and the string which tied his hands, and a mass of votive offerings left by 18 million pilgrims, from John Paul II down, who had since visited his grave.

When Popiełuszko had been awarded Poland's highest state honour, the White Eagle, a year earlier, the medal had been received from the Polish president by his mother, Marianna Popiełuszko. The National Bank and Postal Service issued a special coin and stamp for his beatification, while the Polish Sejm declared that his life should now be seen as 'a gift to the nation's history.' The priest's remains were reinterred in a lavish new Basilica of Divine Providence, and relics sent to churches and chapels around the country.[68]

Other Polish clergy awaited similar recognition, including pastors killed by Soviet soldiers or communist hit-squads in the 1930s and 1940s. One was Fr Michał Rapacz, the parish priest abducted and shot near Kraków in May 1946. New investigations into Rapacz's death in 1996 had identified the UB agents responsible, but had not resulted in charges. Other candidates for beatification included Fr Roman Kotlarz, whose death after a savage August 1976 police beating during the strikes at Radom had also never been fully investigated, and Fr Franciszek Blachnicki, the Light-Life founder, who died of poisoning in Germany in February 1987.

Meanwhile, processes were also underway for some of the great personalities who had guided the Church, for better or worse, through its darkest days, including the Czech Cardinal Beran and the Hungarian Cardinal Mindszenty. The remains of Mindszenty had been repatriated from Austria in 1991 and reburied in his old cathedral at Esztergom, although it took till March 2013 to obtain his full legal rehabilitation. Dozens of testimonies had been collected at formal sessions on the life of Cardinal Wyszyński, whose name now also adorned dozens of Polish streets and squares, as well as a Catholic university at his former Warsaw see. A specially established Primatial Institute at Jasna Góra housed 11,000 of Wyszyński's homilies, as well as his pastoral letters and thousands of photographs, press cuttings and casette recordings, while 40 volumes of the cardinal's collected works were in the process of being published.

Other figures on the beatification list included Áron Márton, Bishop of Alba Iulia in Romania, who was sentenced to life imprisonment in 1948 for refusing to break with Rome, and the Czech Cardinal Štěpán Trochta of Litoměřice, persecuted by the StB for similar faithfulness to the Pope. A beatification process was also launched for Trochta's tragic countryman, Fr Josef Toufar, who died from police beatings after allegedly fabricating a 'miracle' in his church in 1950. Toufar was buried under a false name in Prague's Ďáblice cemetery, where the remains of 207 other political prisoners, executed in the decade after 1948, were also discovered after the collapse of communist rule. In 1998, a former StB agent was given a five-year jail sentence for his role in Toufar's murder, although this was reduced on appeal. In the Czech Republic's Brno diocese, beatification proceedings were also underway for Fr Bula, Fr Drbola and Fr Pařil, hanged for supposed involvement in an alleged anti-communist shooting at Babice in 1951. All three priests had been exonerated of all charges by the Czech Supreme Court.

However celebrated and reverential, the 80-odd beatifications conducted by the end of 2015 represented only a tiny fraction of the huge number of communist-era Catholic martyrs. By some counts, up to 3000 other cases were also being investigated, and many were set to be honoured in the years ahead. Such gestures went some way towards acknowledging the human tragedies inflicted by communist regimes, and to providing some sense, however symbolic, of justice and reparation for their Christian victims. They also created new models and intercessors for the wider Church, enabling the experience of witness and persecution to be glimpsed and touched by later generations. 'People are still sensitive to such stories of suffering—the value of martyrdom touches all Christians, whichever confession they belong to,' one Romanian archbishop explained. 'The idea of martyrdom surpasses historical periods—it speaks of the capacity for total devotion, for the offering of life itself. These are values which can be appreciated today, despite the difficulty people may have in understanding this past epoch.'[69]

In May 2011, Pope John Paul II himself was also beatified, just six years after his death; and in April 2014, he was proclaimed a saint, in a move supported and assisted by some of his former communist opponents. The pontiff's heroic status in his native land had been highlighted when he died on 2 April 2005, when millions of Poles came together in vigils and marches, festooning their windows and balconies with candles and portraits. Some two million more made the journey to Rome for his St Peter's Square funeral, which was decked out with Polish flags and banners. Churches were now being dedicated to him, in a vivid show of recognition for his role as national liberator.

Orthodox churches had honoured their martyrs as well. In 1992, the Russian Orthodox church had 'glorified,' or canonised, Metropolitan Vladimir of Kiev, bayonetted and shot by Bolsheviks in 1918 in a field near his Pecherskaya Lavra monastery, as well as Metropolitan Venjamin of Petrograd, clad in rags and executed in 1922 after a cursory show-trial, and the Orthodox convert and charity worker, Grand Duchess Elizabeth Feodorovna, whose body had been recovered from a mineshaft in the Urals and buried in Jerusalem. Canonisation commissions were set up in each eparchy, or diocese, to collect documents and witness testimonies; and the anniversary of Vladimir's murder on 25 January was established as Russia's Day of New Martyrs.

Investigations were also launched into the fate of Nicholas II and his family, already canonised with their murdered servants in 1981 by the US-based Russian Orthodox Church Abroad. The remains of the Tsar, his wife Alexandra, their daughters, Olga, Tatyana and Anastasia, and four others were identified after the excavation of a grave near Yekaterinburg in 1991 and reinterred seven years later in St Petersburg's St Peter and Paul cathedral. A church council duly declared the family 'passion-bearers,' or saints deemed to have suffered while following Christ's will. It canonised 1765 martyrs and confessors by name, as well as others whose identities were not known, in the greatest saint-making ceremony in Russian church history.

Such mass actions provoked misgivings. There were natural uncertainties about individual acts of martyrdom and over the motives of the persecutors. Many had been killed on trumped-up charges as spies, saboteurs and class enemies, while many had also died *in odium fidei* (in hatred of the faith). But were these people all genuine martyrs? Had some not died *in odium caritatis* (in hatred of love), rather than for the faith itself? Such questions were far from new. They had troubled Christians in the Early Church, who knew the mantle of martyrdom could not be claimed, only conferred by the Christian community. Clement of Alexandria had excluded some Christians who did not 'preserve the character of faithful witnesses,' arguing that they had suffered 'a futile death' by failing 'to know the real God.' Meanwhile, St Augustine had maintained that it was the cause, rather than the manner, of a death which defined it as martyrdom—*non poena sed causa*.[70] Reckless self-sacrifice, suicidal masochism and ostentatious defiance clearly compromised a claim to martyrdom. In the post-communist world, these issues inevitably arose again.

There were other misgivings too. The testimony of martyrs was a source of gratitude and pride for the Church. But it also made the Church uneasy. It unnerved those with troubled consciences; and it upstaged the authority of the Church's leaders. This had also been a problem in the Early Church. The martyrs formed part of the 'cloud of witnesses' spoken of by St Paul (Heb 12:1), who remained with the Church, supporting and inspiring it. But their eternal presence was a summons to vigilance and struggle against the attractions of comfort and security. If one church member suffered, St Paul had insisted, all suffered together (1 Co 12:26). But not everyone in the Church had suffered; and the Church's powerless were now challenging its powerful—or at least those who had co-operated with the powerful.

In St John the Divine's vision, the souls of those 'slain for the word of God' were restless. 'They cried out with a loud voice: O Sovereign Lord, holy and true, how long before thou wilt judge and avenge our blood on those who dwell upon the earth?' (Rev 6:9–10) That was a difficult summons for those who had never themselves faced arrest, interrogation, imprisonment or exile. Some, not surprisingly, were reluctant to acknowledge the martyrs' heroism.

Poland's Cardinal Glemp was one example. By his retirement in December 2006, after a quarter-century as Archbishop of Warsaw, Glemp had ordained 1202 priests, created 118 parishes and consecrated 59 new churches, as well as hosting eleven Papal visits and presiding over an unprecedented expansion of Catholic movements. But his troubled relationship with the martyred Fr Popiełuszko had continued to haunt him. Although the Polish

Church had completed a beatification process for Popiełuszko in 2001, this had been suspended for undisclosed reasons, only resuming when his 1200-page dossier was eventually passed to Rome. Even then, it had taken a pleading letter to the Pope to rescue the process from an envisaged ten-year delay.

Church leaders were uneasy about the forcefulness of Popiełuszko's testimony, set against their own diplomatic accommodations. Published discussion minutes and correspondence between church and communist negotiators suggested the Warsaw archdiocese had resisted regime demands for Fr Popiełuszko to be reined in, and had recognised his martyr status immediately after his death. But Glemp had admitted giving Popiełuszko 'paternal reprimands' under government pressure; and in a May 2000 homily, he had apologised for 'failing to save Fr Popiełuszko's life.' Yet the apology was disingenuous: the real accusation against the cardinal was that he had made Popiełuszko more vulnerable by distancing the Church from him. The priest's posthumously published diary had clearly demonstrated this. Glemp had since tried to put a positive spin on his own role—even playing himself, with died hair and makeup, in a film about Fr Popiełuszko in Polish cinemas. Interviewed during his final months as Primate by the Polish Church's information agency, KAI, he denied trying to block the priest's beatification, but conceded that he had urged the saintly Popiełuszko to avoid 'creating such a froth around himself.'[71]

The reservations of church leaders like this were mild when compared to the calumnies heaped on those judged false martyrs in the Early Church. Eusebius had written contemptuously of those who 'slip into the Church like a pestilential and scabby disease, and do the utmost damage to all whom they succeed in smearing with the horrible, deadly poison concealed on them.'[72] Although the influence of local bishops had varied dramatically in Eastern Europe, as between those of the Eastern and Western Roman Empire, there had been no such sharp swings in the Church between tolerance and persecution.

The debate on personal and collective guilt for the crimes of communism had been taken up a gear by the lustration controversy. It was now acknowledged that the communist programme had enjoyed considerable support, especially among naive intellectuals, after the Second World War. The admission was painful, just as it had been for Germans after the Holocaust; and even then, former Party members sought to avoid being implicated themselves by blaming excesses on abusive officials, like the 'uncontrollables' of the Spanish Civil War. George Orwell had observed in Spain how people instinctively discounted atrocity stories from their own side, but readily believed those told about their opponents. In the Fourth Century, Eusebius had recalled seeing 'places of worship thrown down from top to bottom,' and church pastors 'hiding disgracefully in one place or another, while others suffered the indignity of being held up to ridicule by their enemies.'[73]

The worst acts of Roman cruelty had been just a distant memory by Eusebius's lifetime, just as the anti-Christian savagery of the early Bolshevik years had been long past for those living in the 1970s and 1980s. Yet many deep questions remained. Had communist institutions claimed governmental legitimacy, or had the whole system been no more than a criminal interlude, a seizure of power by a gang of thieves? Was everyone who lived under communism implicated as an accessory, or were some truly blameless?

Whichever answers were offered, there would still be a need for vigilance. Direct harassment and persecution might have ended, but religious freedom had to be defended. Complaints about the infringement of religious rights were still being heard regularly in Russia and other countries, where tolerance could still depend on political expediency, as well as on legal and moral norms. They were still being publicised by monitoring organisations such as Britain's Keston Institute, set up in the 1960s by an Anglican priest, Michael Bourdeaux, who had been shocked as an exchange student to find just 41 Orthodox churches still open in Moscow out of the 1600 before the revolution.

But religious freedom was no longer an East-West issue. It was being challenged in Western Europe too, as popular distrust and elite contempt for faith groups grew after the Islamist attacks of September 2001. Some discerned a new and intolerant secular individualism, which sought to debar religion more completely than ever from public life. Others saw a deliberate assault on Christian values from a profit-led consumer establishment, backed by a cynical media and indifferent mass culture, which viewed churches and faith groups as an obstacle to their cultural and social hegemony. This was not the secularism which Vatican II's pastoral constitution, *Gaudium et Spes,* had recognised and accepted, when Church and state were separate but nevertheless co-operated for the common good of society. It was a secularism which ridiculed and excluded, and which seemed poised, in the words of Pope Benedict XVI, to become 'an ideology enforced through politics,' presenting itself as 'the only voice of rationality.'[74]

John Paul II had made Europe's reunification a central theme of his pontificate. Yet he too had detected a 'new culture,' which risked reducing 'prestigious symbols of the Christian presence' to 'a mere vestige of the past.' The result, he feared, had been a silent apostasy by people now living 'as if God did not exist.' Church leaders were aggrieved that the European Union had shown little interest in the continent's Christian heritage or the cause of religious freedom. In December 2000, a Charter of Fundamental Rights had reaffirmed the rights to 'freedom of thought, conscience and religion,' and barred discrimination on grounds of faith and belief. Yet there was new disappointment when, in December 2007, the EU's constitutional Lisbon Treaty made no reference, in hundreds of pages of provisions, protocols and declarations, to God or Christianity, opting instead for a vaguer invocation of Europe's 'cultural, religious and humanist inheritance.' There was much to be relieved about—not least the Treaty's Article 16C, which guaranteed 'the status of churches in member-states' and committed the EU to maintain an 'open, transparent and regular dialogue' with them as full and permanent partners in public debate. But Poland's Catholic bishops deplored what they saw as a 'falsification of historical truth and deliberate marginalisation of Christianity.' Church communities everywhere felt themselves to be on the defensive.[75]

In a 1993 encyclical, *Veritatis Splendor*, the Pope had warned of the creeping abandonment of any sense of right and wrong, quoting Isaiah 5:20: 'Woe to those who call evil good and good evil, who put darkness for light and light for darkness.' Many currents of modern thought, he argued, were losing touch with the transcendent and becoming 'explicitly atheist,' thus fostering 'an alliance between democracy and moral relativism.' Some people had convinced themselves that binding moral norms led to authoritarianism and intolerance, and that it was Christianity, and the Catholic Church in particular, which had inflicted the greatest evils and injustices in history—not the anti-Christian totalitarian regimes which had slaughtered millions in living memory. The fate of martyrs offered the best possible antidote for such delusions. They had shown 'the absoluteness of the moral good...a single testimony to that truth which, already present in the creation, shines forth in its fullness on the face of Christ.' Those who failed to understand martyrdom would cease to understand the Gospel itself. Those who viewed martyrs as misguided fanatics would become complicit in their deaths.[76]

In the new era of secularism and atheism, however, it was only to be expected that stories of martyrdom would be treated critically, and sometimes drily dissected by psychologists and psychiatrists. Some would find elements of paranoia and psychopathic self-will in martyr narratives which plainly contradicted prevailing norms. Others would argue that they violated healthy ties of loyalty and self-interest, and infringed any realistic sense of justice, honour and duty. Martyrs could not be heroes, since they defied the social order. Their challenge was counter-cultural and counter-intuitive, since it saw greater value in death than in life. Some would insist that martyrs had died for nothing, since all religious belief was an illusion anyway.

None of this was new. The Acts of the Apostles had detailed the scorn and derision heaped on the Christian faith during St Paul's beleaguered travels, lamenting how 'everywhere it is spoken against' (Ac 28:22). Then as now, anti-Christian propagandists like Porphyry had pushed ironically for a literal interpretation of Scripture, accusing moderate Christians who spoke allegorically of spreading 'diabolical confusion.' St Augustine had debunked Porphyry's claim to be 'a lover of virtue and wisdom' and to speak 'in the pride of vain science.' St Jerome had accused him of 'making points which many times the men of the Church have answered,' and exploiting the credulity 'of the naive among our followers, and the poorly informed among his own.' But Porphyry had persisted, charicaturing the faith, sneering at talk of miracles, and sarcastically pondering why the Christian God allowed suffering in the world.[77]

Similar mockery had been directed against Christianity at the time of the French Revolution. Were its priests and pastors not fuelling fanaticism, defying science, indoctrinating the young and dividing society? The encyclopaedist, Denis Diderot, had voiced contempt for clergy who peddled 'a tissue of absurdities.' The *philosophes* 'do not promise or threaten hell,' Diderot had insisted. Nor had they ever killed priests—although 'the priest has killed many *philosophes*.'[78] Similar claims were being made in the new post-communist Europe, prompting calls once again for a stepped-up secularising agenda in the interests of freedom and stability.

In traditionally Catholic countries such as Spain and France, where the Church still enjoyed wealth and influence, anti-clericalism and anti-religiousness could claim a historic justification. Right or wrong, it was at least a coherent political option. In other countries, however, it was merely the caprice of intellectuals and educators, many nursing anachronistic misconceptions about the power of churches. People like this would have concurred with

Feuerbach in the Nineteenth Century on the dangers posed by 'minds perverted and crippled by a superhuman, ie. anti-human, anti-rational religion and speculation.' Today too, they would agree that 'to place anything in God, or to derive anything from God, is nothing more than to withdraw it from the test of reason… Hence self-delusion, if not wicked, insidious design, is at the root of all efforts to establish morality, or right on theology.'[79] Feuerbach had based his critique, however, like Celsus and Porphyry long before him, on a deep study of the Bible and Christian writings. He had also given his anti-religious crusade a political and social purpose. By contrast, the new atheists often showed a hazy knowledge of religion, and seemed more interested in scoring points than arriving at any objective evaluation. Many seemed driven by personal resentments; and some allowed these to turn to hatred—just as in the Roman Empire, when the very name 'Christian' signified non-conformism and was enough to bring the harshest condemnation.

The new atheism also stoked a revisionist debate about communist attitudes to religion. For if atheists were naturally enlightened and tolerant, how could they have inflicted discrimination and persecution? The communist regimes had indeed gone after Christians. But they had done so not out of hostility to religion, but because churches were, in Lenin's words, 'organs of bourgeois reaction,' and because religious people were judged to have sided with the class enemy.

Debates not dissimilar had occurred in the Roman Empire, whose rulers were said to have nothing against forms of religious worship, only against treason and subversion. In reality, then as now, politics and ideology were one and the same. The rulers had hounded Christians as a threat to the political order. But they had also despised their beliefs—the Romans as a source of corruption and immorality, the communists because, as Lenin had decreed, 'every religious idea, every idea of God, even flirting with the idea of God, is unutterable vileness.'[80]

There was still, nevertheless, confusion over the meaning of martyrdom, and over the role of Christian witnesses in the struggle for freedom and justice. In the wake of September 2001, martyrdom had a bad image. Modern society remained conscious of the power of sacrificial blood, and could be awestruck by those who, after Christ, had given their lives for some great cause. But it was distrustful of invocations to higher absolute goals, scornful of melodrama and exhibitionism, and likely to be repelled rather than impressed by the Old Testament story of Abraham's pious readiness to sacrifice his son Isaac. In the predominant humanist canon, human nature was supreme; and its prime motivation was shunning death and seeking happiness. How, by such reasoning, could St Paul make sense in professing himself unable to choose between death and life (Ph 1:21–22)?

In history, where Christians had seen witnesses, the Romans had more often seen criminals; where the two Thomases, Becket and More, had been revered as martyrs, the secular power had branded them traitors; and where Fr Popiełuszko had been lauded for his stand, Poland's communist rulers had accused him of spreading a 'politics of hatred.' Against regimes which governed immorally and unjustly, Christians had always faced much the same dilemma. As the German Dietrich Bonhoeffer had acutely foreseen, Christians under totalitarian rule faced 'the terrible alternative of either willing the defeat of their nation in order that Christian civilisation may survive, or willing the victory of their nation and thereby destroying civilisation.' Bonhoeffer had known which alternative to choose. But he had done so with a fearful heart, knowing he had a 'responsibility towards history,' and that true responsibility meant having the courage to sacrifice everything for God.[81]

The state had also become adept, however, when it came to dealing with would-be martyrs. Gone were the public spectacles which had surrounded Polycarp and Perpetua or the martyrs of Tudor England. Tertullian had noted how martyrs gained power when they were 'before the eyes of men.' Origen had spoken in his famous *Exhortation to Martyrdom* of a 'great theatre,' filled with 'spectators to watch your contests and your summons to martyrdom.'[82] No such publicity had been available to modern-day martyrs. The communist and Nazi regimes had relegated them to the cold statistics of labour and concentration camps, making sure they disappeared and posed no public affront to the ruling ideology.

Governing establishments were even more skilled now. They could blur distinctions, confuse definitions, deny identities and individualities, and depict those who dissented as pathologically self-centred and psychologically unstable. Totalitarian regimes had portrayed their enemies as reactionaries and *untermenschen.* Modern liberal humanists were more likely to present them as idiots and morons, who abused public tolerance and good taste, and should not be given the oxygen of publicity. It was possible to argue that ultimate freedom lay in the right to choose between life and death, as St Paul had done, and in the capacity to determine one's manner of death. But many would also argue with Nietzsche that martyrdom ultimately expressed arrogance and self-exaltation, and reflected a will to power. Nietzsche had rejected the notion that life should be preserved at all costs. But if something was worth dying for, then was it not also worth killing for? In the early Third Century, Perpetua's own father had scolded her pride as she was arraigned by the Roman prosecutor. The historian of Rome, Edward Gibbon, had observed that Christians themselves had inflicted far greater severity on each other 'than they ever experienced at the hands of the infidels.'[83]

These were some of the ideas and interpretations gaining currency as communist rule receded into history among Europeans. They helped explain why the task of commemorating communism's many martyrs would prove difficult—and why stories of heroic Christian resistance and noble suffering were likely to be quietly ignored, or even written out of the record completely. When the 25th anniversary of the collapse of communist rule was celebrated in late 2014, the role of the Church and

Pope in Eastern Europe's liberation was largely passed over. Only brief references were made to them in the many books published for the occasion, which coloured their accounts heavily with current Western prejudices and preoccupations. There was universal agreement on the historic dimensions of 1989, and on the great expansion of freedom and democracy which the year had heralded. Yet the voice of the martyrs in securing Europe's freedom was barely audible.

Notes

1 L. Trotsky, *The History of the Russian Revolution* (London: Pluto Press, 1977), p.17. See also G. Lawson, *Negotiated Revolutions: The Czech Republic, South Africa and Chile* (Ashgate, 2005), p. 72; J. Luxmoore, 'From Solidarity to Freedom,' in A. Hertzke, *The Future of Religious Freedom: Global Challenges* (London: Oxford University Press, 2013), pp. 181–4.

2 Eusebius, *History of the Church*, pp. 278, 303–4.

3 *Ibid.*, pp. 305, 332.

4 Text in Luxmoore, *After the Fall: Church and State Rebuild 1990–1999* (Baltimore: Catholic International, 2000), p. 228.

5 *Moscow News* survey, in Luxmoore and Babiuch, *Rethinking Christendom*, p. 157.

6 From Dostoevsky's article in *Citizen* no. 41 (1873); quoted in M. Mihajlov, *Underground Notes* (London: Routledge, 1977), pp. 52–3; from Harnack's *What is Christianity?* in Luxmoore and Babiuch, *Rethinking Christendom*, pp. 203–4.

7 Author's interview with Jaruzelski, Warsaw, 8 February 1991; Gorbachev's column in *La Stampa*, 3 March 1992, and author's interview, Warsaw, 19 March 1997; CBOS survey, in J. Luxmoore and J. Babiuch, 'Popierają, ale czy rozumieją,' in *Rzeczpospolita*, 11 June 1996.

8 V. Zagladin, 'Perestroika: A new way of thinking,' in *Catholic International*, vol. 2/no. 18 (October 1991), p. 866.

9 'Speech to clergy, religious and committed laity,' Holy See Press Office, 21 April 1990; Luxmoore and Babiuch, *The Vatican and the Red Flag*, pp. 297, 303.

10 John Paul II, *Centesimus Annus*, 1 May 1991, no. 35.

11 O'Brien's explanation of the Party's aims, in G. Orwell, *1984: A Novel* (Harmondsworth: Penguin, 1989), pp. 273, 280–2; F. Dostoevsky, *The Devils* (Penguin Classics, 1953), p. 418.

12 John Paul II, *Centesimus Annus*, nos. 23, 25; Luxmoore and Babiuch, *The Vatican and the Red Flag*, pp. 307–309.

13 From the Pope's *La Stampa* interview, 2 November 1993.

14 'Homily at Legnica Airport,' Holy See Press Office, 2 June 1997.

15 Eusebius, *History of the Church*, pp. 314, 323; on Polish Church property claims, 'Nieruchomości Kościoła katolickiego w Polsce w latach 1918–2012,' in *Katolicka Agencja Informacyjna*, 2 July 2013.

16 S. Wyszyński, *Pro Memoria: Zapiski z lat 1948–1949 i 1952–1953* (Warsaw: Soli Deo/Apostolicum, 2007), and later volumes; A. Casaroli, *Il martirio della pazienza* (Turin: Einaudi, 2000).

17 *The Tablet*, 10 October 2009; *Ecumenical News International*, 22 February 2009 and 27 September 2009; C. Bernstein and M. Politi, *His Holiness: John Paul II and the Hidden History of Our Time* (New York: Doubleday, 1996), pp. 235–45; and 'The Holy Alliance,' in *Time Magazine*, 24 February 1992.

18 *The Tablet*, 31 August 2013; A. Pust, Z. Reven, B. Slapšak (eds), *Palme mučeništva: Ubiti in pomorjeni slovenski duhovniki, redovniki in bogoslovci in nekateri verni laiki* (Celje: Mohorjeva Družba, 1995).

19 'Akt dziękczynienia, przeproszenia i przebaczenia Kościoła na Białorusi,' in *Katolicka Agencja Informacyjna*, 5 December 2000; J. Luxmoore, 'The cardinal who triumphed over Stalin,' in *The Catholic Herald*, 5 October 2011.

20 *Der Spiegel*, 22 November 2011; *Catholic News Service*, 5 October 2005; *Deutsche Welle*, 3 October 2005. A spokeswoman for the Federal Stasi Commission confirmed that only two of at least eight spies assigned to Cardinal Ratzinger had been identified, including a Benedictine priest, Fr Eugen Brammertz, codenamed 'Lichtblick,' who died in 1987. However, she added that the Stasi had collected information 'superbly well'; H. Moll (ed), *Zeugen für Christus: Das deutsche Martyrologium des 20. Jahrhunderts* (Augsburg: Dominus-Verlag, 2010). See also the nine-volume Enquete-Kommission, *Anfarbeitung der Geschichte und der Folgen der SED Diktatur in Deutschland* (Frankfurt: Suhrkamp Verlag, 1995).

21 *New York Times*, 12 April 1992. Wollenberger became a Bundestag member with the Greens and later CDU; V. Wollenberger, *Virus der Heuchler: Innenansicht aus Stasiakten* (Berlin: Espresso/Elef Press, 1992; *Mein Weg zur Freiheit: Von nun an ging's bergauf* (Berlin: Langen Müller, 2002); *Ich wollte frei sein. Die Mauer, die Stasi, die Revolution* (Munich: Herbig Verlag, 2011).

22 Author's interview, *Catholic News Service*, 29 January 2007.

23 'Stanovisko KBS k zvrejňovaniu zväzkov bývalej ŠtB,' 23 February 2005, document on the Katolícka Cirkev na Slovensku website, Bratislava.

24 *Mlada Fronta Dnes*, 8 February and 19 May 2007; 'Prohlášení ČBK k případům spolupráce se Státní bezpečností,' 26 January 2007, and 'Kardinál Vlk navštívil archivy Státní bezpečnosti,' 1 February 2007; http://tisk.cirkev.cz.

25 *The Universe*, 17 October 2010; *Élet és Irodalom*, Budapest, 24 February 2006; *Népszava*, 7 September 20143. Bulányi published documentation in his case in *Nagypénteki levél* (Good Friday Letter), Budapest, 1993; A. Máté-Tóth, *Bulányi und die Bokor-Bewegung* (Vienna: UKI, 1996).

26 Author's interview, *Catholic News Service*, 29 January 2007.

27 Jasna Góra homily, 3 May 2011; on Kiszczak, *Rzeczpospolita*, 13 December 2001; *Gazeta Wyborcza* interview, 3 February 2001; *Polityka*, 6 November 2013.

28 *The Universe*, 11 September 2008; Cenckiewicz and Kruk, *Operacja 'Zorza II'*, pp. 31–76.

29 'Meeting with Clergy,' Warsaw Cathedral, Holy See Press Office, 25 May 2006.

30 'Komunikat biskupów po spotkaniu w Poznaniu i Gnieźnie (dokumentacja),' in *Katolicka Agencja Informacyjna*, 25 June 2006; *The Tablet*, 12 August 2006; 'Oświadczenie redakcji Tygodnika Powszechnego,' in *Tygodnik Powszechny*, 30 May 2006, and 'Historia wywiadu z księdzem Malińskim,' 23 October 2007; Malinski's book, *Ale miałem ciekawe życie* (Kraków: WAM, 2007).

31 'Memoriał Episkopatu Polski w sprawie współpracy niektórych duchownych z organami bezpieczeństwa w Polsce w latach 1944–1989,' in *Katolicka Agencja Informacyjna*, 28 August 2006.

32 *KAI* despatches, 7 January 2007; *The Tablet*, 13 January 2007.

33 'Kościelna Komisja Historyczna: kilkunastu biskupów zostało zarejestrowanych jako TW,' in *Katolicka Agencja Informacyjna*, 27 June 2006; Jan Żaryn and other historians in *Gazeta Wyborcza*, 20–22 February 2007; *The Universe*, 25 February 2007; 'Ks. Józef Kowalczyk był inwigilowany przez SB i został potraktowany jako "kontakt informacyjny",' *KAI* despatch, 6 January 2009; *Rzeczpospolita*, 29 January 2009.

34 'Oświadczenie Konferencji Episkopatu Polski (dokumentacja),' in *Katolicka Agencja Informacyjna*, 11 March 2009.

35 Luteranie.pl website report, and *Rzeczpospolita*, 18 April 2009; *Gazeta Wyborcza*, 17 April 2009; Romanian CNAS report in *The Tablet*, 20 October 2007.

36 C. Moss, *The Myth of Persecution* (New York: Harper One, 2013), p. 148.

Anonymous accusations were judged 'out of keeping with the spirit of our age' even by Trajan; Middleton, *Martyrdom*, pp. 39–40; Eusebius, *History of the Church*, pp. 212, 215.

37 *Ibid.*, p. 257; opposition to compromised bishops, in Salisbury, *The Blood of Martyrs*, pp. 157, 161–2, 200.

38 John Paul II, *Ut Unum Sint*, 25 May 1996, nos. 52–4, 60–1.

39 *Catholic News Service*, 1 October 2008.

40 *The Tablet*, 30 June 2007, 13 September 2008, 25 February 2012; K. Šego, *Međugorje: Razgovori s vidiocima (Zagreb:* Glas Koncila, 2011); 'Međunarodni Susret Međugorskih Voditelja,' in *Katolička Tiskovna Agencija*, Sarajevo, 10 March 2005.

41 Apostolic Letter, *Tertio Millennio Adveniente*, 10 November 1994, no. 37.

42 Figures from various sources, in Luxmoore and Babiuch, *The Vatican and the Red Flag*, pp. 321.

43 J. Luxmoore, 'The Iron Curtain's secrets,' in *The Tablet*, 23 January 1999.

44 I. Osipova, *Hide Me Within Thy Wounds: The persecution of the Catholic Church in the USSR* (Fargo: Germans from Russia Heritage Collection, 2003); R. Dzwonkowski, *Skazani jako szpiedzy Watykanu* (Warsaw: Apostolicum, 1998), and *Losy duchowieństwa katolickiego w ZSRR 1917–1939: Martyrologium* (Lublin: Towarzystwo Naukowe, 1998); B. Czaplicki and I. Osipova, *Kniga Pamjati: Martirolog katoličeskoj cerkvi v SSSR* (Moscow: Serebranniye Niti, 2000); new figures in *The Universe*, 10 November 2010.

45 Zugger, *The Forgotten*, pp. 224–6. The identity of Bishop Batmalashvili and other executed 'anti-Soviet elements' was confirmed by the Helsinki Human Rights Union.

46 'Kontakty Kościoła katolickiego w Polsce z Rosyjskim Kościołem Prawosławnym,' in *Katolicka Agencja Informacyjna*, 9 July 2012; reports 15 July and 4 November 2012; *Catholic News Service*, 2 September 2008.

47 Eusebius, *History of the Church*, p. 149.

48 J. Luxmoore, 'Romanian Christian churches prepare list of communist-era martyrs,' in *Catholic News Service*, 11 April 2003; also CNS reports, 19 March 2008 and 28 October 2010.

49 Eusebius, *History of the Church*, p. 2.

50 *The Tablet*, 17 November 2012; *Interfax* report, Moscow, 8 November 2012.

51 Some Ukrainian church leaders have called for denying the famine genocide to be ruled a crime; *The Tablet*, 15 December 2012.

52 Eusebius, *History of the Church*, pp. 312–3.

53 From Tertullian's *On Spectacles*; in Moss, *The Myth of Persecution*, p. 206.

54 Author's interview with Jaruzelski, Warsaw, 8 February 1991.

55 *Rzeczpospolita*, 15 July 2008; J. Luxmoore, 'The amazing afterlife of the Solidarity priest,' in *The Catholic Herald*, 22 October 2004; 'Unfinished legacy of a martyr,' in *The Tablet*, 29 May 2010.

56 *The Universe*, 27 September 2008; J. Żaryn, 'Zabić księdza' in *Rzeczpospolita*, 20 January 2009; P. Litka, *Katyński kurier: Ks. Stefan Niedzielak* (Kraków: Wydawnictwo Św. Stanisława, 2010), pp. 36–8, 93–147.

57 *Gazeta Wyborcza*, 15 March 2009; 'MGB–KGB smogikų nusikaltimai laukia įvertinimo' (Genocide and Resistance Research Centre of Lithuania, 24 March 2004); http://genocid.lt/Aktual/mgb.htm; *Ecumenical News International*, 18 March 2009.

58 *Gazeta Wyborcza*, 16 June 2005; *AsiaNews.it*, Rome, 28 March 2014.

59 *The Universe*, 6 June 2009; *Interfax* reports, 11 December 2006 and 21 March 2008.

60 *Catholic News Service*, 26 May 2014; 'Kanclerz Kurii Polowej WP potwierdza fakt udzielenia sakramentów gen. W. Jaruzelskiemu,' in *Katolicka Agencja Informacyjna*, 30 May 2014.

61 *The Tablet*, 11 December 2010.

62 P. Preston, *The Spanish Holocaust: Inquisition and Extermination in Twentieth-Century Spain* (London: Harper, 2012), pp. 221–302, 471–518; B. Bunk, *Ghosts of Passion: Martyrdom, Gender and the Origins of the Spanish Civil War* (London: Duke University Press, 2007), pp. 34–49, 61–87.

63 *Tertio Millennio Adveniente*, no. 37.

64 *Ibid.*, nos. 33–6.

65 *Catholic News Service* reports, 5 November 2009, 29 August 2013, 22 October 2013 and 15 May 2014; on Ghika, M. Vasiliu, *Une lumière dans les ténèbres: Mgr Vladimir Ghika* (Paris: Cerf, 2011), and A. Boariu (ed), *Lettres a mon frère en exil* (Paris: Galaxia Gutenberg, 2008).

66 *Catholic News Service*, 21 November 2006.

67 Author's interview with Potaš, Prešov, September 1999; J. Luxmoore, 'The quiet saints of the gulag,' in *The Tablet*, 27 May 2000; M. Potaš, *Dar Lásky: Spomienky na Biskupa Pavla Gojdiča* (Prešov: Rád sv. Bazila, 1999), pp. 240–294.

68 'Ks. Jerzy Popiełuszko—nowym błogosławionym,' in *Katolicka Agencja Informacyjna*, 6 June 2010; *Catholic News Service* report, 7 June 2010.

69 Author's interview, Bucharest, 27 June 2011; *Katolicka Agencja Informacyjna*, 21 August 1998; Bodó et al, *Márton Áron*, pp. 89–104.

70 From Clement's *Stromaties*, and Augustine's Sermon on Martyrdom, in Middleton, *Martyrdom*, pp. 7, 82–6.

71 'Prymas Polski wyznaje winy Kościoła,' in *Katolicka Agencja Informacyjna*, 20 May 2000; 'Prymas Glemp: Nigdy nie byłem przeciwny procesowi beatyfikacyjnemu ks. Popiełuszki,' 4 March 2009.

72 Eusebius, *History of the Church*, p. 37.

73 *Ibid.*, p. 258; G. Orwell, 'Looking back on the Spanish Civil War,' in *A Collection of Essays* (New York: Doubleday, 1954), p. 197.

74 Homily in St Peter's Basilica, 18 April 2005; in Luxmoore and Babiuch, *Rethinking Christendom*, pp. 211–2; *La Repubblica* interview, Rome, 19 November 2004.

75 'Oświadczenie Prezydium Konferencji Episkopatu Polski,' in *Katolicka Agencja Informacyjna*, 21 June 2004.

76 John Paul II, *Veritatis Splendor*, 6 August 1993, nos. 94, 101. These points are well argued in J. Salij, 'Chronić pamięć naszych męczenników,' in *Pastores*, Warsaw, vol. 2/no. 27 (2005), pp. 159–163.

77 R. Bercham, *Porphyry against the Christians* (Leiden: Brill, 2005), pp. 142–3, 165–8; De Soucey, 'Memory and Sacrifice,' pp. 99–121.

78 J. Mason and R. Wokler, *Denis Diderot: Political Writings* (Cambridge University Press, 1992), pp. 82–5.

79 Feuerbach, *The Essence of Christianity*, pp. viii, 274.

80 V.I. Lenin, 'The attitude of the Workers Party to religion,' in *Collected Works*, vol. 15 (Moscow, 1972), pp. 405–10.

81 D. Bonhoeffer, *Letters and Papers from Prison* (London: SCM, 1953), pp. 13–24; E. Bethge, *Dietrich Bonhoeffer: Eine Biographie* (Gütersloher Verlagshaus, 2004), p. 736; Baldwin-Smith, *Fools, Martyrs, Traitors*, pp. 327–8.

82 *Ibid.*, pp. 96–7.

83 Quoted in M. Budde and K. Scott (eds), *Witness of the Body: The Past, Present and Future of Christian Martyrdom* (Grand Rapids: Eerdmans, 2011), p. 4.

EPILOGUE

Beyond Europe, communism was far from over. Communist regimes remained defiantly entrenched in China and Southeast Asia; and while these had come some way from the severity of their early years, the Chinese government was still highlighting the Catholic Church's links with 'colonialists and imperialists,' and smarting over Pius XII's 'breathing of hatred' for Mao's 1949 revolution. Rigid Stalinism was still the order of the day, meanwhile, in North Korea, where all Christian clergy had been killed or deported after the 1950–2 war. North Korea is still formally home to Catholic dioceses at Hamhung and Pyongyang; but regular services were permitted at just one officially approved Catholic church in the capital, a city of 2.7 million, as well as at two nearby Protestant churches and an Orthodox church.

That still left Cuba, the only communist state the Vatican had always maintained ties with. In November 1996, to ease the isolation imposed by US sanctions, Fidel Castro had arrived in Rome and handed John Paul II an invitation. The Pope had arrived, after protracted negotiations, in January 1998, urging Castro to remember that modern states should shun 'all extremes of fanaticism or secularism,' and never again attempt to harness either atheism or religion for their own purposes.[1]

With the exception of North Korea, communist rule had clearly evolved; and so had the criteria and requirements of Christian witness. Yet the communist-era martyrs were now also part of Christian history. They could be seen as worthy modern-day successors to the martyrs of the Early Church. In the Sixteenth Century, the English Protestant John Foxe had attempted to apply the paradigms of early Christian witness to his own day, seeing similarities between the personalities and motivations of persecution victims from both eras, as well as in the circumstances of their deaths. Parallels might also be drawn for the martyrs of Eastern Europe and the Soviet Union. The political and ideological context had been different, the methods of repression less ostentatious. But communist rule had also produced its Polycarps and Perpetuas, its Cyprians and Tertullians. Whereas earlier accounts of martyrdom had been heavily embellished, furthermore, with elements borrowed and idealised from prior Jewish and Greek narratives, the communist-era martyrs had been absolutely real. They had witnessed and suffered in living memory. Their stories could be retraced and documented with rigour and objectivity.

Once communist rule had ended, that was something of a priority. 'Ah most valiant and blessed martyrs!' the author of one passion story had proclaimed in the Third Century. 'Truly you are called and chosen for the glory of Christ Jesus our Lord! Any man who exalts, honours and worships his glory should read for the consolation of the Church these new deeds of heroism.' No one in post-communist Europe was likely to engage in such hyperbole. But many would have agreed with Eusebius that the martyrs' fates deserved a 'most careful record' and could teach lessons about endurance and fortitude 'for the enlightenment of future generations.'[2] Then as now, the martyrs had little if any certainty as to where they might belong in the wider struggle for the Christian faith, and little if any say over how they might be used as reference points towards some final destiny. It was for those who came after them to judge; and this meant carefully checking and recording names, dates and accounts, and reflecting thoroughly on what these dramatic and tragic testimonies portended for the present day.

The Slovak Cardinal Korec, who had been in jail with the now-Blessed Bishop Pavol Gojdič and Zdenka Schelingová, as well as with other beatification candidates such as Bishop Ján Vojtaššák, had no doubt the *potestas tenebrarum*, or power of evil, spoken of by St Paul had surfaced again in his lifetime. Christians had been called to make great sacrifices. 'People seeking to live as believers under such barbaric conditions had to call on the power of the Holy Spirit—yet there always were believers, and their numbers constantly increased,' the Jesuit cardinal explained. 'The communists' devastation of the Church revealed the baseness human beings are capable of when they discard their consciences. Yet it was against this backdrop of communist crimes that the greatness of those who suffered but never surrendered shone forth.'[3]

Korec's Belarusan counterpart, Cardinal Kazimierz Świątek, had written a modest account of his 'long winter in Stalin's Gulag,' recalling the 'endless enclosures of barbed wire where thousands of prisoners died' and his own isolation in the Siberian arctic, where he had used a ceramic cup as a chalice and hidden consecrated hosts in a matchbox for dispensing to fellow-prisoners. He remembered the camp commandant's surprise that a man on whom 'there was no need to waste a bullet' had survived the fatigue and hardship. With communist rule now over, however, Świątek also saw the need for forgiveness. 'For most Catholics, it came as a surprise that this forgiveness could be offered by someone who still bore the marks of persecution on his own body,' the veteran church leader conceded.

> Yet never, even when various sentences were passed against me, did I feel any desire for revenge. As people, we must forgive, remembering Christ's words: "Judge not, that you may not be judged." Over its 2000-year history, the Church has faced good years and bad, from the first centuries when they threw Christians to the lions, to the persecutions of the French Revolution and Stalinism. But it has endured and will endure.[4]

Not everyone had seen the challenge to Christians in such stark eschatological terms. Poland's Cardinal Wyszyński had believed the cause of Christ could be served through 'apostolic work,' as well as through bloodshed and suffering. Compromises and concessions were sometimes necessary; and Wyszyński would have insisted with Tertullian that 'a Christian is an enemy to none'—neither the Roman Empire nor the Soviet Bloc. He had been ready to support the post-War communist programme, believing the mines and heavy industry of his native Poland should be state-owned under trade union control. But he had also seen that Marxism would seek ineluctably to destroy religion, and had understood the crucial value of martyrdom—the 'eighth sacrament.' Blood must always flow somewhere—'not only in the chalices at Mass, but also in the living chalices of human souls'—so the Church could remain 'in good health, filled with vigour and strength.' No one could fully know God's plan of salvation and where current sufferings fitted into it. What mattered in the meantime, as St Paul had noted, was to avoid shame and humiliation by serving Christ 'with full courage'—whether through 'fruitful labour' in life, or through the heroism of death (Ph 1:20–22). 'Something would have been wrong if I had not experienced imprisonment—what was happening to me was very appropriate,' Wyszyński had duly concluded after his arrest in 1953. It was a time when two types of people were in jail: 'either criminals or people with principles.' 'I saw more and more clearly that the most appropriate place for me, given the current status of the Church, was in prison.'[5]

The cause had existed for 2000 years, and people were still being seized and killed for it. The guards had changed, the locks had rusted, the prisons had fallen into ruin; yet the cause remained 'alive, fresh, young, full of allure' because Christians still had the courage to stand up for their faith. This was not the same as self-indulgent defiance or ostentatious devotion. Christ had warned of 'whitewashed tombs,' which appeared outwardly beautiful but were really 'full of dead men's bones and all uncleanliness' (Mt 23:27–80). Wyszyński preferred the analogy of 'a warehouse of empty boxes.' But the meaning was the same. 'Anyone who remains silent before his enemies emboldens them,' the Polish cardinal had concluded from his cell.

> The terror that is practised by all dictatorships draws its effectiveness from the timidity of the apostles. The first

> goal is to force people into silence through fear. Silence has its apostolic significance only when I do not shrink from my oppressors. This is what the silent Christ did. And by this sign he revealed his courage. Christ did not allow himself to be terrorised. When he went forth to meet the rabble, he said openly, 'It is I'.[6]

That need for courage and integrity under pressure was a lesson to be learned from the communist repression. But there were other lessons as well. One was that the Church must always be independent of the state. This did not mean aggressive or negative separation: the two should co-operate where possible, as Poland's 1997 constitution acknowledged, 'for the individual and the common good.'[7] But the Church should maintain its autonomy; and it should also stay united. Since the French Revolution, repeated attempts had been made to create an alternative Catholic church, independent of Rome. They had failed; and this helped explain why so many regimes had reacted with harassment and persecution. Yet these, however fearsome, were less dangerous to the faith than accommodation and indifference. The Church had always survived regime brutality. But it might not survive internal division, public apathy, the compromising of its values and the corruption of its canonical order.

For all the determined openness of men like Wyszyński, the Church was wary of revolution. It accepted armed resistance against prolonged and obvious tyrannies. But violence, as the Church's 1993 Catechism made clear, could only be justified under particular conditions: '(1) There is certain, grave and prolonged violation of human rights; (2) all other means of redress have been exhausted; (3) such resistance will not provoke worse disorders; (4) there is well-founded hope of success; and (5) it is impossible to foresee any better solution.'[8] Some of these conditions had indeed applied under communist rule, at least in its savage early stages. But peaceful resistance, the weapons of conviction rather than destruction, offered very real possibilities as well. They had played their part in bringing down the pagan

Roman Empire, an outcome which would have appeared as unimaginable in the Third Century as the overthrow of communism had appeared for most of the Twentieth. They had worked more recently in the hands of Mahatma Gandhi and Martin Luther King. 'Security and justice lie not in completely overthrowing the old order but in well planned progress,' had been the verdict of Pope Pius XII in the 1940s.

> Uncontrolled passionate zeal always destroys everything and builds nothing. It inflames cupidity, never cools it. Since it does nothing but sow hate and ruin, far from leading to reconciliation, it drives men and political parties to the laborious undertaking of building anew, on ruins left by discord, the edifice which they started.[9]

In principle, the Church respected the social, economic and political systems which mankind, in its restless creativeness, had devised. It was ready to co-operate with them—if they upheld basic ethical values, respected human dignity and protected essential rights, including the fundamental right to religious freedom. It also believed it was possible for Christians to live in any system, provided they were allowed to retain their free will, core beliefs and essential principles. In the end, however, no system could be relied on to offer conditions for a full Christian life. 'There is no permanence for man: it is a condition which is at once natural to mankind, yet most contrary to his inclinations,' the Catholic Pascal had warned in the Seventeenth Century. 'We burn with the desire of finding a secure abode, an ultimate firm base on which to build a tower which might rise to infinity; but our very foundation crumbles completely, and earth opens up before us unto the very abyss.'[10]

Nor could any system, whether authoritarian or democratic, be relied on to ensure justice and satisfaction for the victims of earlier misrule. 'The fire you threaten me with cannot go on burning for very long; after a while it goes out,' Polycarp had warned his persecutors. 'But what you are unaware of are the flames of future judgement and everlasting torment which are in store for the ungodly.'[11] Yet for most communist-era villains, judgment and retribution, at least in the temporal world, never came. Many enjoyed a comfortable retirement, unrepentant and undisturbed, while their murdered victims lay unaccounted for in their shallow graves, or where they had collapsed, emaciated and exhausted, in the ice and silt of Siberia. Perhaps this had been a price worth paying for communism's mostly peaceful overthrow. But it also sowed deep frustrations and fuelled misgivings that ethical truths and moral values had been left fatally corrupted.

There were other lessons to be learned as well from the Church's communist-era experiences. One was that it should never again leave itself vulnerable to attack by siding with the vested interests of power and privilege. This had been the charge levelled against the Church by all revolutionary movements—that it had placed itself on the wrong side of history by standing against the forces of equality and emancipation. It now had to reposition itself, find its rightful place in a democratic environment, and play a constructive role as a modernising social and cultural force. However enlightened and reasonable, the Church would always have its enemies, who would find reasons to attack it, as they had done since the days of ancient Rome. So the Church had to be adept and judicious in how it handled them. As communist rule had demonstrated, some would continue fighting the Church—whether it opted for resistance or for appeasement. So its leaders needed to take the long view, as Cardinal Wyszyński had done, patiently reassuring their critics and rebutting their opponents, while safeguarding the Church's mission and legacy for the future. They had to find the right balance between testimony and diplomacy, confrontation and collaboration, and avoid compromising the Church's spiritual and moral independence for the sake of institutional protection and material advantage. They also had to avoid being pushed into outright opposition, or provoked into over-reacting with rhetorical refusals and condemnations.

Repression and persecution might, under certain circumstances, strengthen the faith and rejuvenate the faithful. But they had also come perilously close to destroying the Church in countries like Albania. They would always be a scourge; and everything should be done to avoid them. Without tolerance, people were condemned to live, as the English Jesuit, Robert Persons, had observed, 'in perpetual torment of hatred, suspicion, jealousies, aversions, detestations and deadly hostilities the one with the other—a state more fit for hell than for any peaceable Christian commonwealth.'[12]

Martyrdom itself was a complex phenomenon. The deaths of martyrs enhanced the redemptive meaning of Christ's own passion and death, by giving order and meaning to the chaos of a violent world. 'Sublime and illustrious as martyrdom is,' Cyprian of Carthage had noted centuries ago, 'it is the more needful now, when the world itself is turned upside down, and while the globe is partially shattered, and failing nature gives evidence of the tokens of its final destruction.'[13] Perhaps the same need for martyrdom had arisen under communist rule. But being ready for martyrdom, for imitating Christ's self-sacrifice, required an effort of will, courage and clear-sightedness which not everyone was capable of. In the Sixteenth Century, Thomas More, now the Church's patron saint of politicians, had cautioned his own children on this point. For those brought up well in a good community, More observed, it was 'no mastery' to get to heaven. It was harder by far when no 'good counsel' was available, in a society which rewarded vice and punished virtue. In such adverse conditions, preparedness was needed. So were endurance, character and hope, the qualities inherited from Christ and identified by St Paul (Rm 5:3–5), and shown as much by the modern-day martyrs as by the likes of Perpetua, Polycarp and Ignatius.

The struggle for the faith had cosmic dimensions; and the aim of the persecutors, often astute and well-educated, was not to inflict physical death but to induce spiritual surrender. Resisting them meant thinking out one's moves in advance and having one's answers ready, as Christ had warned his followers (Lk 21:14). Even then, the struggle would be harsh. Every death with honour would be a victory, every ignominious retraction a defeat. But for every hero of the faith, there would be many who failed the test, and many more who, like Cyprian of Carthage's *stantes*, avoided the test entirely by simply lying low and escaping detection.[14]

Like the Romans before them, communist interrogators had attempted to terrorise the faithful into abandoning their faith; and sometimes the threat of torture could work better than torture itself. Physical pain, once inflicted, could take the sufferers away from reality, giving them inner strength and focusing their concentration on higher purposes. It could weaken loyalty to the state, instead of enforcing it. The Christians of ancient Rome had been aware of this. 'It is another flesh that suffers when the soul is in heaven,' Cyprian had apparently concluded. 'The body does not feel this at all when the mind is entirely absorbed in God.'[15] The victims of communist rule were aware of it too. But torture could have the opposite effect. For those in pain, everything important—truths, principles, loyalties, secrets—could cease to matter as the world receded and the power of the persecutor grew. The communist-era persecutions had shown once again the heights of greatness the human spirit might attain, but also the perils and failures it might be exposed to. Courage and endurance could not be communicated or taught; and no one could be sure how they would conduct themselves. Some might proudly repeat the boast of the early Christians—insisting not only *Christianus sum* ('I am a Christian'), but also 'I have always been and always will be a Christian.' Others would easily find some convenient formulary for saving themselves and avoiding pain. A hero could suddenly become a coward, an ordinary individual a bastion of valour.

That so many had ridden out the storm under communist rule merited deeper reflection. After the wartime Shoah, it was said that the Jews had created a Holocaust narrative, identifying victims and assembling their stories into a collective, comprehensive martyrology. The Nazi regime had sought to strip its victims of their identity and destroy their very humanity, convincing itself that those dying in vast numbers were sub-human, unworthy of further consideration. Such barbarity had shattered any belief in progress or in a rationally organised society. It also struck at the concept of a loving, caring God, whose ultimate purpose was benign.

Courageous figures like Fr Jerzy Popiełuszko might insist that good would overcome evil. But this necessitated a powerful faith. What could be done in the meantime was to turn to those who, in their separate ways, had achieved such a faith, and derive comfort and inspiration from their example. The virtues required of martyrs were, in the end, much the same as those required of any committed Christian. But only a few Christians would be called to martyrdom, and there was no way of knowing whom they might be. Some, in the tradition of the English Becket, had seemed very far from saintly, while many had not served as moral exemplars or lived particularly pious lives. But the mission of martyrs, however clumsy and imperfect, was to keep the Church awake, to remind it of what Christian witness ultimately entailed, and to prove by their own sufferings that fallible Christians were still capable, *in extremis*, of true integrity and devotion. The German Protestant Dietrich Bonhoeffer, who was read underground in Eastern Europe, was one of many who had studied earlier martyrs before becoming martyrs themselves. He spoke with some knowledge when he noted how Christ assumed 'visible form in his Church' through Christians 'exposed to public insult' who suffered and died for his sake. 'Here we see the divine image created anew,' Bonhoeffer noted.[16]

The Church was duty-bound to preserve the memory of those who had recreated the divine image in this way. Their stories and narratives helped bind Christian communities to Christ, as well as to each other through shared experiences. If the purpose of Christ's own life had become clear through his death, the same was true of those who followed him. Christ's own trial before Pilate had established a paradigm for others. Like the later martyrs, he had denied acting against the secular power, insisting 'My kingship is not of this world' (Jn 18:36). He had also forgiven his persecutors, maintaining a dignified silence in the face of their accusations, begging God to spare him if possible, but also being ready for death. 'I lay down my life, that I may take it again,' Jesus explained to his disciples. 'No one takes it from me, but I lay it down of my own accord. I have power to lay it down, and I have power to take it again' (Jn 10:17–18).

That faithful readiness for all eventualities had been emulated by martyrs through the ages. True Christians never actively sought martyrdom. In the early Third Century, Clement of Alexandria had warned those who allowed themselves to be taken 'out of daring' and did not 'avoid persecution.' They would make themselves accomplices 'in the crime of the persecutors,' Clement cautioned them. Twelve centuries later, Thomas More had also warned against the sin of pride. Those who showed too much enthusiasm for death would deny God's gift of life. But Christians should nevertheless be ready to imitate Christ if called. Accepting suffering, affliction and degradation did not mean masochism. Nor could martyrs expect to be other-worldly mystics who felt no pain. The pain would be real enough; and they would see it as an opportunity to express their love for God. That love had to be unconditional, since there would be dark times and low points when God himself would seem absent.[17]

Some would insist, all the same, that martyrdom was only made possible by the grace and love of God. How else could fallible human beings, with all their flaws and weaknesses, endure such torments? Some martyr stories had contained rhetorical flourishes about how faith and devotion could ease physical agonies and mental terrors. But the agonies and terrors were inescapable. Surviving them had to mean obtaining help from a higher force. 'If human endurance is considered in this passion, it begins to be incredible,' St Augustine had duly noted in his famous Sermon on Martyrs. 'If divine power is acknowledged, it ceases to be amazing.'[18] The bodies of the martyrs, Augustine was confident, would be restored at the resurrection, bearing their scars and wounds as prized adornments. Their communion with God was obvious, since God had judged them worthy of martyrs' crowns. Some, like Polycarp and Ignatius, had followed Socrates and Christ in concluding that they could do more good by dying than by living—or at least by accepting rejection from the corrupt contemporary order around them. In a world of extremes, Christians were needed to offer examples of reason, moderation and propriety—to show that goodness lived on, at least in the sphere of consciences. 'Criminals are eager to conceal themselves, avoid appearing in public; they are in trepidation when they are caught; they deny their guilt when they are accused,' Tertullian explained.

> But what is there like this in the Christian's case? The only shame or regret he feels is at not having been a Christian earlier. If he is pointed out, he glories in it; if he is accused, he offers no defence; interrogated, he makes voluntary confession; condemned, he renders thanks. What sort of evil thing is this, which lacks all the ordinary peculiarities of evil—fear, shame, subterfuge, penitence, lamenting?[19]

That was something of a high benchmark. But the point, then as now, was a valid one. Like the Romans before them, communist persecutors had done everything to brand Christians guilty according to the prevailing secular laws, and to prevent them from gaining prestige or respect for their stance. St Paul had enthused about the power of faith, recording how the Biblical martyrs and prophets had 'conquered kingdoms, enforced justice... won strength out of weakness' because of it (Heb 11:32–34). But the power of faith was, in the end, also an expression of human dignity. Martyrs through the ages had died for their religious beliefs. But they had also died for themselves, with the courage, integrity and self-control which signified a triumph of the human will and brought the promise of a better world.

Under communism too, Christian martyrs and witnesses had reprieved society by upholding the faith and saving the Church. Lenin's system of rule had made it hard to live honestly, and even harder to achieve goodness or aspire to sanctity. That many did, by conscious choice and effort of will, was an important mark of redemption. The heroism and self-sacrifice of the few had compensated for the timidity and indolence of the many, atoning for sins and failures, and contributing to the liberation and salvation of whole communities. The ancient Book of Maccabees had paid tribute to the 'noble bravery' of Eleazar and other martyrs, who had died 'for nobility and goodness,' thus demonstrating how reason could control emotions. 'All people, even their torturers, marvelled at their courage and endurance, and they became the cause of the downfall of tyranny over their nation,' the chronicler recorded. 'By their endurance they conquered the tyrant, and thus their native land was purified through them' (4 M 1: 8–11).

Similar claims could be made for the martyrs of communism. They had purified a corrupt order by showing that human beings were indeed capable of heroic goodness and sanctity. All of this had come at a heavy price. The cries of pain of torture victims were still audible in the consciousness of Christians, along with the groans of forced labourers and the gasps of execution victims—like the choking of Perpetua in the amphitheatre or the screams of Agathonike leaping into the Pergamon fire. So, from the wildernesses of Siberia or the darkness of Albanian dungeons, was the cry of Christ from Psalm 22 on the Cross: 'My God, my God, why hast thou forsaken me?' (Mk 15:34)

Like Christ, the carpenter's son, most martyrs had come from obscure origins. It would have seemed inconceivable that their isolated acts of witness, hushed up by manipulatory disinformation, might one day help shake the immutable power and invincible might of the ruling Party. That they did, aided by faithful fellow-Christians and wise church leaders, suggested power and might had to be understood differently.

'They will lay their hands on you and persecute you,' Christ had warned his followers. 'You will be delivered up even by parents and brothers and kinsmen and friends, and some of you they will put to death; you will be hated by all for my name's sake' (Lk 21:12; 16–17). That had certainly been true for much of communist rule, as Bolshevik death squads went on killing sprees, Stalin's infamous *troika* tribunals quietly despatched their victims, and Party-appointed judges pronounced their treason and espionage sentences in the post-War years. Yet the challenge facing Christians would ultimately be the same whether in war or peace, repression or freedom. 'I have heard from our fathers,' St John Chrysostom was said to have written, 'that there were indeed real Christians once upon a time, during the persecutions.'[20] While persecution and martyrdom might prove inspirational, however, they were not necessary for a truly Christian life. Christ's words at the Last Supper, 'This is my blood which is shed for you,' had always offered the reassurance that the need for blood sacrifices had been satisfied. The Church needed its martyrs; but it also needed steadfast hearts and willing minds. As St Augustine had pointed out, when the first great era of martyrs came to an end, trials and tribulations would always be there, even for those living in peace and freedom.

In the aftermath of the French Revolution, when the first attempts of the modern era had been made to eradicate the Church and the faith, de Tocqueville had observed how the destruction of religion paralysed the powers of the intellect. 'Such a condition cannot but enervate the soul,' the French commentator concluded, 'relax the springs of the will and prepare a people for servitude.' Under communist rule, people at all levels of society had reached the same conclusion. 'If there is no God—i.e. a force which has power over the laws of nature—then there is no freedom,' noted the Croatian dissident, Mihajlo Mihajlov. 'If man is not part of the divine being, then he is the slave of the so-called objective world and its laws... God is the rejection of all law, God is absolute freedom, and man is free insofar as he is the son of God.'[21]

Preaching at Jasna Góra in 1991, as East Europeans celebrated their new freedoms, Pope John Paul II recalled the unending struggle of good and evil captured in St John's Revelation. Its first portent was Mary, 'clothed with the sun, with the moon under her feet, and on her head a crown of twelve stars,' crying in the pain of childbirth. Its second was the Evil One, the red dragon with 'seven heads and ten horns,' who waited to devour the Child who would 'rule all the nations with a rod of iron' (Rev 12:1–5). With or without communism, the Pope warned his youthful audience, the cosmic struggle would continue. The two nights of Bethlehem and Golgotha would remain embedded in the Christian consciousness. So would the need for vigilance and courage. In the modern world, there would be martyrs, as there always had been; and for those who were known, recognised and honoured, there would be many more who died alone and forsaken, their names and testimonies preserved only in the unwritten annals of eternity. What mattered was that the repressers and persecutors would never have the last word. Suffering and death might be unavoidable. Yet the story would not end with them.

Notes

1 'Homily in Havana,' Holy See Press Office, 24 January 1998, in Luxmoore and Babiuch, *The Vatican and the Red Flag*, pp. 318–9.

2 Eusebius, *History of the Church*, p. xxvi; quote on martyrs from the 'Passion of Perpetua and Felicitas,' in H. Musurillo (ed), *Acts of the Christian Martyrs* (Oxford: Clarendon, 1972), p. 131.

3 Author's interview with Korec, Nitra, 10 September 1999.

4 Author's interview with Świątek, Warsaw, 15 April 1996. At his death, aged 96, in July 2011, Świątek was praised by Belarus's Orthodox metropolitan, Filaret, for 'following the divine call of faithfulness to Christ, even unto death,' as well as for his later 'calls for patience, sorrow and love for enemies.'

5 Wyszyński, *Pro Memoria*, pp. 412, 585; *A Freedom Within*, pp. 7, 25, 267.

6 *Ibid.*, pp. 79, 95.

7 Constitution of the Republic of Poland, 2 April 1997, Article 25: 3.

8 *Catechism of the Catholic Church* (London: Chapman, 1995), no. 2243, p. 484.

9 Pius XII, Address, 13 June 1943, in R. Gill, *A Textbook of Christian Ethics* (London: Bloomsbury, 2014), p. 219; J. Eppstein, *The Cult of Revolution*

in the Church (London: Arlington House, 1974), p. 43.

10 From Pascal's *Pensées*, section 2, no. 72, in R. Mulvaney, *Classic Philosophical Questions* (New York: Pearson, 2012), pp. 62–3.

11 'The Martyrdom of Polycarp,' in *Early Christian Writings*, p. 128.

12 R. Persons, 'A Treatise Tending to Mitigation,' in R. Sell and A. Johnson (eds), *Writing and Religion in England 1558–1689: Studies in Community-Making and Cultural Memory* (Farnham: Ashgate, 2009), p. 59.

13 Cyprian, 'On the glory of martyrdom,' no. 11, in A. Roberts, J. Donaldson and A. Coxe (eds), *The Ante-Nicene Fathers, Vol. 5—Fathers of the Third Century* (New York: Cosimo, 2007), p. 582.

14 W. Roper, *The Life of Sir Thomas More* (London: Burns, 1905), pp. 27–28; A. Silva, *The Last Letters of Thomas More* (Grand Rapids: Eerdmans, 2001), pp. 72–89. See also B. Gregory, *Salvation at Stake: Christian Martyrdom in Early Modern Europe* (Cambridge: Harvard University Press, 1999), pp. 342–3; and N. Kellog, 'Philosophy as Training for Death: Reading the ancient Christian martyrs' acts as spiritual exercises,' in *Church History* vol. 75/no. 4 (2006), p. 740–5.

15 Musurillo, *Acts of the Christian Martyrs*, p. 235.

16 D. Bonhoeffer, *The Cost of Discipleship* (London: Macmillan, 1966), p. 342.

17 From Clement's 'Miscellanies,' in Baldwin-Smith, *Fools, Martyrs, Traitors*, pp. 172. These points are well argued in S. Weil, *Gravity and Grace* (London: Art, 1987), pp. 79–82, and *Waiting for God* (London: Routledge, 1951), pp. 66–9; C. Moss, *The Other Christs: Imitating Jesus in Ancient Christian Genealogies of Martyrdom* (Oxford University Press, 2010); N. Verbin, 'Martyrdom: a Philosophical Perspective,' in *Philosophical Investigations*, vol. 35/no. 1 (2011), pp. 68–87.

18 St Augustine, 'Sermon 76,' in Salisbury, *The Blood of Martyrs*, p. 179.

19 From Tertullian's 'Apologia,' in Middleton, *Martyrdom*, p. 61; St Augustine, *City of God* (Harmondsworth: Penguin, 1972), p. 1062.

20 St John Chrysostom, A Commentary on the Acts of the Apostles (http://www.orthodoxebooks.org), p. 282.

21 Mihajlov, *Underground Notes*, p. 146; from de Tocqueville's *Democracy in America*, chapter 5, in Luxmoore and Babiuch, *Rethinking Christendom*, p. 205.

INDEX OF NAMES

INDEX OF PLACES

Lightning Source UK Ltd.
Milton Keynes UK
UKOW04f0611250216

269071UK00003B/7/P

9 780852 445846